Business and Security

Public–Private Sector Relationships in a New Security Environment

sipri

Stockholm International Peace Research Institute
Signalistgatan 9, SE-169 70 Solna, Sweden
Telephone: 46 8/655 97 00
Telefax: 46 8/655 97 33
Email: sipri@sipri.org
Internet URL: http://www.sipri.org

Business and Security
Public–Private Sector Relationships in a New Security Environment

Edited by

Alyson J. K. Bailes and Isabel Frommelt

sipri

OXFORD UNIVERSITY PRESS
2004

OXFORD

UNIVERSITY PRESS

Great Clarendon Street, Oxford OX2 6DP
Oxford University Press is a department of the University of Oxford.
It furthers the University's objective of excellence in research, scholarship,
and education by publishing worldwide in

Oxford New York

Auckland Bangkok Buenos Aires Cape Town Chennai
Dar es Salaam Delhi Hong Kong Istanbul Karachi Kolkata
Kuala Lumpur Madrid Melbourne Mexico City Mumbai
Nairobi São Paulo Shanghai Taipei Tokyo Toronto

Oxford is a registered trade mark of Oxford University Press
in the UK and certain other countries

Published in the United States
by Oxford University Press Inc., New York

© SIPRI 2004

British Library Cataloguing in Publication Data
Data available

Library of Congress Cataloguing in Publication Data
Data available

ISBN 0-19-927450-9

Typeset and originated by Stockholm International Peace Research Institute
Printed in Great Britain on acid-free paper by
Biddles Ltd., King's Lynn, Norfolk

Contents

Preface   *xi*

Acronyms   *xiii*

Introduction   1
Business and security: public–private sector interface and
interdependence at the turn of the 21st century
Alyson J. K. Bailes
    I.   Introduction: interdependence old and new   1
   II.   11 September 2001 as catalyst   5
  III.   Two years on: new agenda items, second thoughts?   8
  IV.   Other players, other interests   18
   V.   This book   23

Part I. The general framework: goals and norms

Editors' remarks

1. Security and the responsibilities of the public and private sectors   27
István Gyarmati
    I.   Introduction   27
   II.   New threats, new thinking   28
  III.   The new role of the private sector   30
  IV.   Conclusions   31

2. Public–private sector cooperation   33
Erik Belfrage
    I.   Introduction: the development of modern terrorism   33
   II.   The role of private corporations in the provision of security   34

3. What price values?   37
Daniel Tarschys
    I.   The ambivalence of value and the obscurity of price   37
   II.   Values in public policy and in the European institutions   38
  III.   Envoi   44

Part II. Cutting off resources for terrorism and crime: the global and European dimensions

Editors' remarks
4. An international response to terrorism   47
Claes Norgren
    I.   Introduction   47
   II.   Terrorism: a threat to the international community   48

III.	Countering terrorism	51
IV.	Measures to counter terrorist financing	52
V.	Success or failure?	54
VI.	The way forward	56
VII.	Conclusions	58

5. Counter-terrorism measures undertaken under UN Security Council auspices — 59

Thomas J. Biersteker

I.	Introduction	59
II.	The role of the UN Security Council in efforts to counter terrorist financing after 11 September 2001	60
III.	An assessment of the effectiveness of UN Security Council measures	63
IV.	Legal issues, problems and challenges	67
V.	Conclusions	73

6. Strategic export controls and the private sector — 76

Evan R. Berlack

I.	Introduction	76
II.	The US approach	76
III.	The evolution of international approaches to export controls after 1945	78
IV.	Characteristics and limitations of existing regimes	79
V.	The impact of new priorities: non-proliferation and terrorism	81
VI.	Conclusions	82

7. The European Union: new threats and the problem of coherence — 84

Niall Burgess and David Spence

I.	Introduction	84
II.	The EU's policy responses to the September 2001 attacks	87
III.	Remaining challenges for the EU	95
IV.	Conclusions	100

8. Banking in an international and European framework: the case of Liechtenstein — 102

Georges S. Baur

I.	Introduction	102
II.	International initiatives	103
III.	New developments in international law	103
IV.	Liechtenstein as an example	104
V.	The private sector	107
VI.	Future developments	109

9. The resources and tactics of terrorism: a view from Russia — 111

Vadim Volkov

I.	Introduction	111
II.	The dual role of states	112

III.   Asymmetric warfare   113
    IV.   The social resources of terrorism   115
     V.   Conclusions   118

Part III. Business and conflict

Editors' remarks

10. Business investment, humanitarian problems and conflict   121
John J. Maresca
      I.   Introduction   121
     II.   Conflict as the multiplier of humanitarian problems   122
    III.   Differentiating legitimate business from criminal activity   122
     IV.   Why invest in conflict-torn areas?   123
      V.   The business–humanitarian relationship   123
     VI.   The special role of resource companies   124
    VII.   Meeting security requirements   125
   VIII.   Respect for human rights   125
     IX.   The role of sanctions   127
      X.   The need for business–humanitarian dialogue and   128
           cooperation

**11. Conflict diamonds: the De Beers Group and the Kimberley   129
Process**
Andrew Bone
      I.   Introduction   129
     II.   The Kimberley Process   133
    III.   An example well set?   135

Annex 11A. The Kimberley Process Certification Scheme   140

12. Oil and conflict: Lundin Petroleum's experience in Sudan   148
Christine Batruch
      I.   Introduction   148
     II.   Sudan's war   148
    III.   Lundin in Sudan   150
     IV.   Lessons learned   160

**13. The role of humanitarian organizations: the case of the   161
International Committee of the Red Cross**
Gilles Carbonnier
      I.   Introduction   161
     II.   Business and the economy in conflict prevention   162
    III.   Challenges for business in conflict areas   164
     IV.   Dialogue between companies and the ICRC   166
      V.   Conclusions   169

Part IV. Preserving the legitimate economy and critical infrastructure

Editors' remarks

14. The security of business: a view from the security industry   173
Crispin Black
    I.   Introduction   173
    II. The services available   174
    III. Survival planning: never a state monopoly?   175
    IV. Terrorism and intelligence   177
    V.   Conclusions   181

15. Survival planning for business: a view from Nokia   183
Urho Ilmonen
    I.   Current threat assessment   183
    II. What has changed after 11 September 2001?   183
    III. Why is security needed and what is the focus?   184
    IV. Vulnerabilities and attacks increase   184
    V.   Emergency response and business planning   185
    VI. Partnership with the authorities?   185
    VII. Conclusions   186

16. Defending against cyber terrorism: preserving the legitimate economy   187
Olivia Bosch
    I.   Introduction   187
    II. Cyber terrorism   187
    III. Attribution and business continuity planning   191
    IV. Globalization and the role of business in cyber security   193
    V.   Conclusions   195

17. The concept of critical infrastructure protection   197
Jan Metzger
    I.   Introduction   197
    II. CIP from an operational perspective   197
    III. CIP from a conceptual perspective   200
    IV. Criticality   201
    V.   Conclusions and recommendations   207

18. Critical energy system infrastructure protection in Europe and the legitimate economy   210
Kevin Rosner
    I.   Introduction   210
    II. Implications of the new European security framework   211
    III. Developing CESI protection models and strategies   214
    IV. Conclusions   216

Part V. The economic consequences of terrorism: can we afford to be safe?

Editors' remarks

19. The economic consequences of terrorism 219
Patrick Lenain
    I.   Introduction: the shock of the new 219
    II. A less safe world 220
    III. Is the private sector spending more on security? 222
    IV. The insurance problem 223
    V. Tighter border controls and their costs 225
    VI. The impact of growing security and military spending: has 227
        the 'peace dividend' been reversed?
    VII. Conclusions 230
Box 19.1 New cargo-inspection procedures 226
Table 19.1. US Government spending on national defence, fiscal years 228
        2000–2003

Part VI. The security–economy linkage in a global perspective

Editors' remarks

20. A view from the League of Arab States 235
Saad Alfarargi
    I.   Introduction 235
    II. Obstacles to a just system of collective global security and 236
       governance
    III. Rich men's and poor men's agendas 237
    IV. The way to a common agenda? 239

21. A view from Africa 242
Said Adejumobi
    I.   Introduction 242
    II. Terrorism: the political and economic dimensions 243
    III. 'Business as terror' in Africa 245
    IV. Prioritizing security in Africa 250
    V. Conclusions 252

Annex. A comment on immigration controls and education in the 255
United States
Phyllis O. Bonanno

Appendices
Isabel Frommelt

1. Institutions in the field of security, active or interested in the   261
public–private sector interface: government and international
institutions, academic and research bodies, and non-governmental
organizations

2. Private-sector organizations and institutions, active or interested   296
in the field of security

3. Select bibliography   310

About the authors   315
Index   320

Preface

The threats to security in today's world respect neither national nor sectoral boundaries. As the horrific events of 11 September 2001 showed, neither the world's largest nor its smallest states can guarantee absolute safety for their citizens. Transnational terrorist and criminal groups, or even fanaticized individuals, can exploit the openness and interconnectedness of modern societies to inflict shocking casualties in the most unexpected places. The cost must be reckoned not only in human lives and suffering, but also in direct and indirect economic damage and the often widespread disruption of peaceful productive activity. In today's globalized conditions, the seismic waves of such disturbance pass literally around the world and not even the most tranquil corners can escape their effects.

To tackle both the causes of such violence and its effects, the first requirement now as ever is an equitable, effective and enforceable international legal order. The world's smaller states have special reason to understand this; but they can also see especially clearly the limitations of traditional, state-led defence as a solution. When whole societies and their economies become targets, not only the assets needing protection, but also the means of protecting them are increasingly to be found not in governmental but in private-sector hands. Private business itself has become a security actor with great responsibility and potential: in conflict prevention and reconstruction, in drying up the flow of finance and dangerous materials to men of violence, and in making its own operations and society's essential infrastructures more 'surviveable'—to mention only the most obvious examples.

To be effective, national and international responses to the new security agenda must find the right ways to engage private business as an ally and a partner. To be viable, these solutions must be capable of protecting economies without draining them dry or stifling them in the name of security. To be legitimate, they must set both business and government activity in the framework of fair and transparent norms, while also respecting the fundamental rights of the citizen. To succeed in the long term, they must take account of the interests of all the world's constituencies and avoid the trap of becoming a 'rich man's agenda'.

These complex challenges were the subject of an international conference on Business and Security held at Vaduz in September 2003, supported by the Liechtenstein Government in the framework of its programme on peace research and conflict prevention adopted in December 2002. The proceedings of the conference, and the present volume based upon them, were the fruit of a close collaboration between the Stockholm International Peace Research Institute (SIPRI) and the Liechtenstein-Institut. The conference itself was a success in promoting understanding and the exchange of good ideas between experts from business and governmental, academic and institutional back-grounds. We hope that this modest volume, without claiming to offer complete coverage or complete answers, will further widen the span of debate and will stimulate the search for good public–private sector partnerships, in all frameworks and at all levels of security where they may apply.

Our special thanks are due to all who attended, organized and provided support for the conference; to Ambassador Dr Josef Wolf, Professor Daniel Tarschys and Isabel Frommelt for various indispensable personal contributions; to all the authors represented in this volume; to Nenne Bodell, head of the SIPRI Library, for her invaluable research assistance; and to Senior Editor Connie Wall, assisted by editors Teslin Seale and Angelina Sanderson, for editing all the contributions in this volume.

Otmar Hasler   Alyson J.K. Bailes
Prime Minister of Liechtenstein   Director, SIPRI

February 2004

Acronyms

AGT	Azerbaijan–Georgia–Turkey
AIDS	Acquired immune deficiency syndrome
AML	Anti-money laundering
AU	African Union
BCP	Business continuity plan
BEET	Business Executive Enforcement Team
BIS	Bureau of Industry and Security
BW	Biological weapon
C-TPAT	Custom–Trade Partnership Against Terrorism
CBP	Customs and Border Protection
CDHAP	Community Development and Humanitarian Assistance Programme
CEPMA	Central Europe Pipeline Management Agency
CEPS	Central Europe Pipeline System
CERT	Computer Emergency Response Team
CERT/CC	Computer Emergency Response Team Coordination Center
CESI	Critical energy system infrastructure
CI	Critical infrastructure
CIIP	Critical information infrastructure protection
CIP	Critical infrastructure protection
CIS	Commonwealth of Independent States
CLO	Civil Liberties Organisation
COARM	Conventional Arms Exports (Working Group)
COCOM	Coordinating Committee on Multilateral Export Controls
CPS	Continuous Planning System
CSI	Container Security Initiative
CSR	Corporate social responsibility
CTAG	Counter-Terrorism Action Group
CTC	Counter-Terrorism Committee
DDTC	Directorate of Defense Trade Controls
DDU	Due Diligence Unit
DERF	Defense emergency reserve fund
DHS	Department of Homeland Security
DRC	Democratic Republic of the Congo
DSL	Defence Systems Limited
EAR	Export Administration Regulations
EC	European Community

ECRI	European Commission against Racism and Intolerance
EEA	European Economic Area
EITI	Extractive Industries Transparency Initiative
EO	Executive Outcome
EPSA	Exploration and Production-Sharing Agreement
ERP	Emergency Response Plan
ESDP	European Security and Defence Policy
ETA	Euskadi Ta Askatasuna (Basque Fatherland and Liberty)
EU	European Union
EWOK	Einsatzgruppe zur Bekämpfung der Wirtschaftskriminalität und organisierte Kriminalität
FATF	Financial Action Task Force on Money Laundering
FBI	Federal Bureau of Investigation
FEMA	Federal Emergency Management Agency
FFTR	Federal funds target rate
FIU	Financial Intelligence Unit
FSF	Financial Stability Forum
FTO	Foreign terrorist organization
FY	Fiscal year
G7/G8	Group of Seven/Eight industrialized nations
GC	Global Compact
GDP	Gross domestic product
GIN	Global issues network
GNPOC	Greater Nile Petroleum Operating Company
GRECO	Group of States Against Corruption
GRI	Global Reporting Initiative
GUUAM	Georgia–Ukraine–Uzbekistan–Azerbaijan–Moldova
HIV	Human immune deficiency virus
IAEA	International Atomic Energy Agency
ICC	International Chamber of Commerce
ICC	International Criminal Court
ICRC	International Committee of the Red Cross
IMF	International Monetary Fund
IRA	Irish Republican Army
ISO	International Standards Organization
IT	Information technology
ITAR	International Traffic in Arms Regulation
JIC	Joint Intelligence Committee
MFA	Ministry of Foreign Affairs
MNC	Multinational corporation
MONEYVAL	Select Committee of Experts on the Evaluation of Anti-Money Laundering Measures

MPRI	Military Professional Resources Incorporated
MTCR	Missile Technology Control Regime
NATO	North Atlantic Treaty Organization
NBC	Nuclear, biological and chemical (weapons)
NCCT	Non-Cooperative Countries and Territories
NEPAD	New Partnership for Africa's Development
NGO	Non-governmental organization
NPO	National partner organization
NSG	Nuclear Suppliers Group
OAU	Organization of African Unity
OECD	Organisation for Economic Co-operation and Development
OFAC	Office of Foreign Asset Control
OLS	Operation Lifeline Sudan
OPEC	Organization of the Petroleum Exporting Countries
OSCE	Organization for Security and Co-operation in Europe
PAC	Partnership Africa Canada
PCCIP	President's Commission on Critical Infrastructure Protection
PEP	Politically exposed person
PMC	Private military company
PPP	Public–private partnership
PSC	Private security company
PSI	Proliferation Security Initiative
RAF	Red Army Fraction
RUF	Revolutionary United Front
SARS	Severe acute respiratory syndrome
SCO	Shanghai Cooperation Organization
SDGT	Specially designated global terrorist
SDN	Specially designated national
SDNT	Specially designated narcotics trafficker
SDT	Specially designated terrorist
SPLM/A	Sudan People's Liberation Movement/Army
TEL	Terrorist exclusion list
TRIA	Terrorism Risk Insurance Act
UAE	United Arab Emirates
UN	United Nations
UNDP	United Nations Development Programme
UNGA	United Nations General Assembly
UNITA	União Nacional para a Independência Total de Angola (National Union for the Total Independence of Angola)
UNODC	United Nations Office on Drugs and Crime
VWP	Visa Waiver Program
WDC	World Diamond Council

WHO	World Health Organization
WMD	Weapons of mass destruction
WTC	World Trade Center
WTO	Warsaw Treaty Organization
WTO	World Trade Organization

Introduction

Business and security: public–private sector interface and interdependence at the turn of the 21st century

Alyson J. K. Bailes

I. Introduction: interdependence old and new

On 11 September 2001, when terrorists struck at the United States, 1000 employees of the investment bank Cantor Fitzgerald Securities were working in one of the towers of the New York World Trade Center. Nearly 700 of them perished in the attack, a greater loss than that suffered by any other single employer, and the firm's headquarters was physically wiped out. Many other companies and their employees also suffered. This attack was one of the plainest and most painful demonstrations of the shared vulnerability of the state, society and the business community, even on the territory of the world's sole superpower. Logically enough, in the weeks and months that followed, these events were to prompt a whole new debate on the several and joint roles of the public and private sectors in tackling their common security challenges.

Interdependence and interaction between these two spheres of human activity are of course nothing new. Since the first organized societies came into being, the guarantee of physical security has been a condition for productive economic activity, and the economy has needed to produce surplus resources to feed and equip its defenders. Should the relationship between the public and private sectors malfunction or get out of balance, everyone would suffer. The inadequate provision of defence for a prosperous community tempts aggressors and undermines confidence and stability. Spending too much on defence, on the other hand, can quickly drain the economic resources which such policies are designed to protect—even if the spending brings great profit for a while to one part of the business sector.

There are other complexities in the basic relationship between defence and business, involving elements of both parallelism and complementarity. Economic strength is in itself a source of influence which helps states to steer security perceptions and processes in directions that are profitable to themselves. To a certain degree it may also be a deterrent: a rich society can not only afford good defences but also recover faster and retaliate harder against anyone who harms it. Defence-related production is a branch of the economy, often an extremely profitable one, which can make major contributions to full employment and produce shared and spun-off technologies that are also useful for the civil sector. Where defence exports are possible, they may earn money, influence and respect all at the same time. Economic 'sticks and carrots'—sanctions on the one hand, and aid payments or trading privileges on the other—can play an explicit and effective part in the pursuit of security-policy goals.

In modern conditions, these interactions have increasingly been played out not only at the national level but also in the framework of regional and global multilateral institutions concerned with defence and security, or economic cooperation, or both. The experience of the 20th century raised governmental and popular awareness of certain aspects of the business–security linkage, especially during World War II and thereafter. Access to raw materials and protection of trade routes were important aims and conditions of Allied victory in that war. During the cold war which followed, the West's economic and technological superiority was a consciously wielded and perhaps ultimately decisive weapon in its strategic competition with the Communist bloc. Western strategic export controls were developed, not for the first time in history but at the international level and far more systematically than before, to prevent the leakage of such valuable assets to the East. At the same time, the Communist experience showed that attempting to integrate security and business in the simplest and apparently strongest way, by state control of the whole economy in peace as well as in war, did not foster prosperity or even produce an effective defence machine. The Western values that were seen as triumphing and conquering new ground with the collapse of the Soviet Union and the Warsaw Treaty Organization (WTO, or the Warsaw Pact) included the concepts of the market economy and free enterprise.

The principal Western defence alliance, the North Atlantic Treaty Organization (NATO), had developed its own systems to commandeer and mobilize private-sector assets in the event of a crisis, but these systems were based on a philosophy of minimal and latest-possible interference with economic processes. In peacetime, defence and economic goals could not simply be conflated because Western prosperity depended heavily on factors—and could be hit by dangers—existing outside the sphere of the East–West military confrontation. The clearest example was the oil supply, which was endangered by conflicts and political changes (notably in the Arab world) that were only marginally related to any kind of Communist action. The West did not organize its response to and defences against the oil crises of 1973–74 and 1979–80[1] through NATO. The methods which major Western powers used to protect their worldwide economic supplies and markets (and to influence their trade partner countries) did, to be sure, often include defence instruments—aid, training and defence sales, as well as force deployments. Until the 1990s, however, these instruments were typically used under national responsibility and with at best ad hoc coordination. The gradual shift towards a presumption

---

[1] See, e.g., Heinebäck, B., SIPRI, *Oil and Security* (Almqvist & Wiksell: Stockholm, 1974).

of multilateral security action even when dealing with shared interests outside the scope of NATO commitments might be traced back to the coordinated Western naval patrols and de-mining operations to protect international shipping in the Persian Gulf during the 1980–88 Iraq–Iran War. It came very clearly into focus with the 1991 Gulf War.

In some respects—and not just because of the obsolescence of much of the cold war-related planning or the expansion of free markets—the 1990s could be seen as a time when traditional notions of the defence–business linkage, and people's attitudes towards it, began to shift and diversify. This in turn reflected both the flow of events and a certain fragmentation of different countries' and constituencies' view of the security agenda. At the end of the cold war many predicted that the global policy focus would shift from military security to 'human' or 'soft' security issues such as development and the fight against poverty, disease, environmental threats and so forth.[2] One effect would have been to highlight the role of the private sector as the deliverer, and often initiator, of the processes and services involved in this dimension. In the early 1990s, however, the work of Western security institutions came to be dominated by crisis-management tasks (within and outside Europe) requiring the use of military forces. The need for civilian inputs—from non-governmental organizations (NGOs) and business as well as from government—for successful crisis containment and resolution and post-conflict reconstruction was increasingly appreciated as the decade progressed. The main policy push, however, was still towards rebuilding Western *military* capabilities which had been eroded in the rush to enjoy a 'peace dividend'.

Many governments remained keenly interested in balancing such defence efforts with continuing or increased contributions in other realms of human security. The trouble here was that the Western community could not agree either on the issues to be given priority or on how to handle them. For example, West European and many other states saw the threat of human-provoked or -aggravated climate change as so severe that it justified accepting strong international discipline and possibly economic sacrifices. The USA did not agree on either the characterization of the threat or the responses. Population growth and control was another area of policy hit by conceptual divisions. As a result, the role which private business was exhorted or expected to play in helping to tackle such challenges was quite different, depending on whether it was listening to the US, or a European, or another government—a particular complication for multinational enterprises.

This is not to say that the role of business in the security process and discourse was reduced. On the contrary, it may be argued that in the last decade of the 20th century the independence, the variety and the salience of private-

---

[2] See Hagelin, B. and Sköns, E., 'The military sector in a changing context', *SIPRI Yearbook 2003: Armaments, Disarmament and International Security* (Oxford University Press: Oxford, 2003), pp. 281–300.

sector roles in global security all increased.[3] When supporting crisis operations, business acted as a voluntary partner in a way that could not have applied during mobilization for traditional national defence: meaning *inter alia* that it could expect reward at market rates. In some circumstances, companies were accused of having been motivated by profit to connive at or even foment violent conflict in territories where the results were expected to strengthen their commercial position.[4] Precisely because of earlier defence cutbacks, governments found themselves needing to use private services on contract for functions previously carried out by uniformed personnel (e.g., for transport and supply, laundry and catering, and even medical support). New crises created new openings and a demand for mercenary troops, private armies or at least private security guards.[5] The defence industry faced an overall drop in demand and sales, sharpest in the European region, but to the extent that it could still find customers it could engage with them more freely across a worldwide variety of markets without regard to previous cold war 'camps'. A number of non-ideological but insufficiently disciplined military transfers—for instance, from the former Warsaw Pact states saddled with poor-quality surplus equipment to cash-strapped developing states, including those in crisis regions—were thought to have had tangible effect in fuelling new conflicts or prolonging existing ones.[6] These phenomena contributed to a general concern and debate among policy analysts: both about the way in which the control of security processes was slipping out of the grip of states to sub-state, trans-state and non-state actors, and about the lack of any evident framework of international regulation or institutional competence for dealing with these new levels of action.[7]

During the 1990s, significant progress was made in defining the impacts of the private sector on security and in bringing them within the scope of public and institutional policy formation, in such specific fields as business behaviour in conflict zones and help in combating organized crime.[8] The most dramatic

---

[3] See, e.g., Wenger, A. and Möckli, D., *Conflict Prevention: The Untapped Potential of the Business Sector* (Lynne Rienner: Boulder, Colo., 2003); and Nelson, J., *The Business of Peace: The Private Sector as a Partner in Conflict Prevention and Resolution* (International Alert, Prince of Wales International Business Leaders Forum and Council on Economic Priorities: London, 2000).

[4] See also chapters 11 and 21 in this volume.

[5] There is increasing interest in the notion of 'private peacekeeping' and there have already been occasions on which non-governmental actors have completed substantial mediating and monitoring tasks. See Fidler, S., 'Proposal for private soldiers in peacekeeping gathers steam', *Financial Times*, 6 Nov. 2003; and for details of a new private-sector initiative, the Global Peace and Security Partnership (GPSP), see URL <http://www.gpsp.co.uk>. On mercenaries and private military and security companies see also chapters 13, 14 and 21 in this volume.

[6] Bailes, A. J. K., Melnyk, O. and Anthony, I., *Relics of Cold War: Europe's Challenge, Ukraine's Experience*, SIPRI Policy Paper no. 6 (SIPRI: Solna, Sweden, Nov. 2003), available at URL <http://editors.sipri.se/recpubs.html>.

[7] Guéhenno, J.-.M., *The End of the Nation-State* (University of Minnesota Press: Minneapolis, Minn., 2000); Cooper, R., *The Post-Modern State and the World Order*, 2nd edn (Demos: London, 2000); and British House of Commons, *Private Military Companies: Options for Regulation*, HC 577 (Stationery Office: London, 2002), available at URL <http://www.fco.gov.uk/Files/kfile/mercenaries,0.pdf>.

[8] See chapters 10 and 12 in this volume on these 2 issues.

security-related controversy surrounding the role of the private sector arose, however, in a different and much broader context.

The last years of the 20th century were the heyday of a general anti-globalization agitation which inherited much of the role, as well as the activists, of earlier peace movements.[9] Constituencies in developing states and their Western sympathizers painted 'big business' in this context almost in the role of a traditional bloc adversary—as a force threatening to crush the identity and independence of its suppliers and consumers, not just to deny them their fair share of prosperity. Correspondingly violent methods were used by the extreme wing of protesters against private-sector targets (e.g., branches of the McDonald's restaurant chain) or governmental targets (e.g., summit meetings). Similar patterns of behaviour were seen in the 'eco-terrorist' movement (attacking targets seen as particularly guilty in the desecration of the environment, such as whaling vessels and logging companies) and the animal rights movement (attacking laboratories, privately as well as publicly owned).[10] More peaceful methods of product boycott and image spoiling were used by the anti-fur lobby and by groups concerned about the exploitation of labour in the developing countries, especially child labour, by companies in the sportswear industry. It was the economic results of these actions that made the corporate world take notice. Apart from any direct costs of hostile action, sales in all parts of the world were vulnerable to the shift of opinions and priorities among the segments of better-off consumers whose loyalty these companies needed to hold. The growth, to a great extent voluntary, of the private sector's corporate responsibility movement—with its various strands ranging from philanthropy in the local community to codes of conduct for subsidiaries in conflict regions[11]—can be seen in large part as an act of self-defence.

II. 11 September 2001 as catalyst

While far from comprehensive, this historical sketch shows that the issue of public–private sector interactions in security was undergoing flux and complex development even before the fatal events of September 2001. Beyond a doubt, however, the terrorist attacks and the reactions to them of the USA and other states gave the 'new security agenda' a massive boost, supplying perhaps the strongest motive felt since the cold war to bring business relationships back to the core of security policy. The attacks highlighted existing and new

---

[9] In terms of substance and popularization techniques, it also built on previous 'consumer rights' agitation.

[10] Coker, C., International Institute for Strategic Studies (IISS), *Globalisation and Insecurity in the Twenty-first Century: NATO and the Management of Risk*, Adelphi Paper no. 345 (Oxford University Press: Oxford, 2002).

[11] For institutional guidelines developed in these fields see United Nations, 'The Global Compact', URL <http://www.unglobalcompact.org>; and European Commission, Employment and Social Affairs, *Promoting a European Framework for Corporate Social Responsibility*, Green Paper (European Commission: Brussels, 2001), URL <http://europa.eu.int/comm/employment_social/soc-dial/csr/greenpaper_en.pdf>. See also chapter 12 in this volume; and the Internet site of the Business Humanitarian Forum, URL <http://www.bhforum.ch>.

elements of shared vulnerability; ways in which the state might seek more help from business to tackle threats; ways in which business might need more help from the state; and the need for more systematic frameworks of process and regulation to make all these interactions effective. At the same time, the events of September 2001 split the international security consensus—most dramatically within the 'wider West'—on the true nature of the most serious threats and the preferred approaches for dealing with them. Business found itself facing not so much a unitary 'new agenda' as a situation in which rival hypotheses were pursued on a trial-and-error basis, with the potential to bring sudden gains and also sudden new dangers to private-sector players, among others.

In the most simple and direct way, the attacks showed that government, business and society alike could find themselves being targeted by trans-national terrorist movements, without compunction or discrimination and on a massively destructive scale. The damage suffered by the private sector extended far beyond the numbers of offices and documents destroyed or even the individuals lost—indeed, many of the worst-hit companies showed remarkable effectiveness and resilience in maintaining or rebuilding their operations.[12] The greatest sums were lost in the insurance, travel (especially airlines) and tourism sectors. Many other industries were affected by the damage to confidence and change in consumer habits.[13] Government did not find its own revenues hit to anything like the same extent, but it had to bear the executive burden of identifying and punishing the culprits and working out how to prevent further attacks. The US Government's response was to push to the top of its security agenda not only the 'war on terrorism' per se but also efforts to control the proliferation of weapons of mass destruction (WMD—or nuclear, biological, chemical, NBC, weapons) which could pose similar or greater 'asymmetric' threats to the world's population.

As 2001 moved into 2002, the fact that the al-Qaeda terrorist network had its main base in Afghanistan brought the problem of chaotic and irresponsible 'failed states' into the same perceived threat complex, to be joined soon by Iraq as a 'rogue state' suspected of both WMD proliferation and terrorist support.[14] Even where the private sector was not directly invoked as a partner or vehicle for carrying out this set of policies, it came to be affected in numerous practical ways: by spending under the new US 'Homeland Security' programme (see section III); by stricter aviation security norms; by other security rules and practices introduced to prevent the import of undesirable persons and objects; by the supplies and services purchased for the wars in Afghanistan and Iraq; by the contracts available or expected to be available for reconstruction in these countries; and by independent consumer decisions, such as the

---

[12] 'Devastated firms begin their fight for survival', *Financial Times,* 12 Sep. 2001; and 'Assault on America: aftermath', *Financial Times,* 13 Sep. 2001.

[13] Figures are provided in chapters 2 and 19 in this volume.

[14] Anthony, I. *et al.,* 'The Euro-Atlantic system and global security', *SIPRI Yearbook 2003* (note 2), pp. 47–78.

rush to buy gas masks and other protective items (fuelled also by the anthrax scare in the USA in late 2001).[15] To the extent that the crisis was a crisis also for the USA's allies and neighbours, and that most of the corrective measures required some form of contribution by other powers, private companies outside the United States were affected not just by the knock-on effects of US transactions but by parallel developments in their own countries and regions.

There were some respects in which the crisis refocused attention much more specifically on the role of business as a partner for government. One of the first initiatives, developed among United Nations (UN) member states and embodied in the UN Counter-Terrorism Committee (CTC), was to block private-sector financial transfers to known terrorists and to freeze their assets.[16] This added to pressures which had already been developing (in the context of corporate governance as well as anti-crime endeavours) to eliminate or at least clean up the activities of international channels which could be used for money laundering.[17] In the post-September 2001 climate it was easier to get consensus for doing so even at the expense of some inroads into banking privacy. Another existing policy topic that was strongly boosted by the new threat priorities was the control of exports of strategically sensitive goods and technologies, especially those connected with NBC weapons; delivery vehicles such as missiles; and associated 'intangibles' such as scientific knowledge and research results.[18] Clearly, these measures could not be enforced without the compliance, willing or enforced, of private-sector producers in all relevant countries. Last but not least, the aftermath of the war in Iraq (to a much greater extent than after the war in Afghanistan) highlighted the importance of private-sector support for post-conflict reconstruction in the form of both technical assistance and investment. It also showed how hard it could be to secure private-sector support and to ensure that it would be provided on terms regarded as fair by all.[19]

The converse process—of business seeking additional help from governments—was limited, at least in the short term, essentially to the problem of

[15] On the anthrax episode see Hart, J., Kuhlau, F. and Simon, J., 'Chemical and biological weapon developments and arms control', p. 675, and Zanders, J. P., 'Weapons of mass disruption?', *SIPRI Yearbook 2003* (note 2), pp. 683–90.

[16] The CTC was established by UN Security Council Resolution 1373, 28 Sep. 2001, and is mandated to monitor the implementation of the resolution by all states and to increase the capability of states to fight terrorism. On the CTC see URL <http://www.un.org/Docs/sc/committees/1373/>; and chapter 5 in this volume.

[17] See chapters 4 and 8 in this volume.

[18] Anthony, I., 'Supply-side measures', pp. 727–48, and Ahlström, C., 'Non-proliferation of ballistic missiles: the 2002 Code of Conduct', pp. 749–59, *SIPRI Yearbook 2003* (note 2).

[19] The difficulties experienced in Iraq included the physically insecure environment for repair and construction work, which both contributed to and was aggravated by the delay in re-establishing basic infrastructure; problems over establishing a trustworthy legal framework for the handling, e.g., of Iraqi debts and contracts old and new; accusations of favouritism and anti-competitive behaviour by the occupying powers in according contracts to their own companies; and suspicions of inflated pricing and inadequate performance by the latter. See Gregory, M., 'Rebuilding Iraq's oil installations', BBC News World Edition, 23 June 2003, URL <http://news.bbc.co.uk/2/hi/business/3013168.stm>; Gregory, M., 'Management challenges Iraq style', BBC News World Edition, 2 July 2003, URL <http://news.bbc.co.uk/1/hi/business/3038864.stm>; and Nordland, R. and Hirsh, M., 'The $87 billion money pit', *Newsweek*, 3 Nov. 2003, pp. 22–29.

insurance.[20] Insurers sought to cover themselves by dramatically increased premiums for air transport firms, which in turn claimed that they could not continue to conduct their business (in the face of an existing drop in profits) unless government provided support. The USA and the European Union (EU) agreed to do so, but only for limited periods at a time, aware of the risk of providing disguised anti-competitive subsidies which had long been a sore issue in this industry. More room for manoeuvre was perhaps seen at the level of reinsurance capacity. The US Congress moved to propose a federal reinsurance plan (covering 90 per cent of claims over the first $10 billion) on lines already familiar from European practice.

In general, however, it was noteworthy how self-reliant the business sector proved—or chose to remain—in finding ways to accommodate its losses and in making its own judgements on how to create or improve corporate survival plans. More time will need to pass before it can be judged whether these reactions reflected general and permanent characteristics of resilience in the globalized business system, or whether they were affected by special circumstances that might not apply in the case of repeated attacks. There could also be other, less visible or obvious expressions of the trauma suffered. One wonders, for example, whether reduced profit projections, an increased consciousness of risk and a strong instinct to protect one's own may have played some part in the faltering of world free trade endeavours in 2001–2003 and the failure of the 2003 World Trade Organization Cancún summit meeting.[21] (It is easier to identify the part played in worsening the atmosphere by the animosities between different world constituencies created by, in particular, US military countermeasures.)

III. Two years on: new agenda items, second thoughts?

As the world passed the second anniversary of 11 September 2001, the relatively simple lines of reaction and policy development sketched above had come to seem more inadequate than ever for capturing how the international security agenda actually has been, or should be, evolving. The threat analysis drawn up after the al-Qaeda attacks has come under stronger question (and from more directions) over time, as have the correctness and ultimate utility of the countermeasures chosen. Other challenges shared by the public and private sectors which are only indirectly linked with the original 'asymmetric threats' complex have risen to the forefront of policy and analytical attention. The creation of new rules and frameworks for public–private sector interaction, other than in very specifically targeted cases, remains an entirely open field.

From the first, the language of the United States in calling for participation in a global 'war on terrorism'—with its image of a single, uniformly hostile

---

[20] See chapter 19 in this volume.
[21] World Trade Organization, 5th Ministerial Conference, Cancún, Mexico, 'The Ministerial Statement', 14 Sep. 2003, URL <http://www.wto.org/english/thewto_e/minist_e/min03_e/min03_14sept_e. htm>.

opponent—had been challenged by those who saw terrorism as an older, more diverse and diversely motivated phenomenon. Many doubted that simple connections could be drawn between terrorists, NBC weapon proliferators and 'rogue states';[22] others questioned whether this group of 'new threats' really deserved to be elevated so far above other (military and non-military) dangers to the West. It was possible to support new efforts against international terrorism and yet to argue that its causes could most effectively be addressed by legal, political, developmental and cultural measures—while forceful action might risk merely creating new terrorists.[23] It is interesting to note that, with the possible exception of those standing to profit from higher defence expenditure and spending on homeland security, business leaders did not on the whole join the militant or the scare-mongering tendency. As shown by the chapters in this volume,[24] their calculations of the seriousness of the terrorist challenge were made with the methods of risk assessment rather than defence-style analysis, and led to correspondingly nuanced conclusions. For a company operating globally, the physical and commercial risks arising from old-fashioned conflict and internal violence, crime, corruption and hostile or misplaced government action still come objectively further up the scale of concern than all but the most apocalyptic forms of terrorist action.[25] A survey of 331 large companies in July 2003 found that their expenditure on corporate security had gone up on average by just 4 per cent since 2001, much of which could be ascribed to higher insurance premiums.[26] The new US Homeland Security budget for 2002 represented a much larger and more sudden proportional hike in spending.[27]

The prominence given to WMD in the initial threat picture has been to an extent undermined by the inability of the occupying powers to find clear evidence of active programmes in Iraq after the fall of President Saddam Hussein. The reliability of related Western intelligence and the way it was used in the policy-making process have come under attack, *inter alia* through a formal enquiry process in the UK.[28] Over the same period, provocative and irresponsible behaviour by North Korea and suspicion over Iran's intentions have made clear that the nuclear proliferation danger is real and demands attention

---

[22] Delpech, T., *International Terrorism and Europe*, Chaillot Papers no. 56 (EU Institute for Security Studies: Paris, 2002), available at URL <www.iss-eu.org/chaillot/chai56e.pdf>.

[23] Simpson, G., 'Terrorism and the law: past and present international approaches', *SIPRI Yearbook 2003* (note 2), pp. 23–31; and Stepanova, E., *Anti-terrorism and Peace-building During and After Conflict*, SIPRI Policy Paper no. 2 (SIPRI: Solna, Sweden, June 2003), available at URL <http://editors.sipri.se/recpubs.html>.

[24] See especially chapters 15 and 19 in this volume.

[25] For a discussion of the range of risks and also the difficulties in evaluating them see Briggs, R., *Doing Business in a Dangerous World: Corporate Personnel Security in Emerging Markets* (Foreign Policy Centre: London, 2003).

[26] See chapters 15 and 19 in this volume.

[27] This is not meant to imply that government spending exceeded corporate spending in gross cash terms—given the scale of company budgets overall, the balance is probably very much the other way. It has been estimated that the US private sector alone had spent more than $150 billion on its own 'homeland security' measures since 21 Sep. 2001. Bernasek, A., 'The friction economy', *Fortune*, 18 Feb. 2002, pp. 103–12.

[28] On the Hutton Inquiry see URL <http://www.the-hutton-inquiry.org.uk>.

almost irrespective of the ultimate findings on Iraq: but the USA itself has chosen to address these cases by non-military methods. All that said, it is important to note that the *international/multilateral* measures taken under the impact of the September 2001 attacks in fields related to terrorism and WMD are not easily reversible and that no one is, in fact, proposing to reverse them. The EU has independently committed itself to an Action Plan to combat WMD proliferation which implies pushing even further for improvements in export controls (including investigation of the control of 'intangibles'), monitoring and inspection, and the destruction of surplus capacities among other things.[29] All these are fields where action will affect the environment for business and would best be pursued with the help of business. The same can be said of one major new initiative which has united the USA, leading European states and Australia, among others—the Proliferation Security Initiative (PSI), providing for searches of ships suspected of carrying WMD in international waters.[30]

Meanwhile, the consequences of the March 2003 attack on Iraq by the USA, the UK and their partners have taken on dimensions quite different from what the US Administration expected and have created a correspondingly wide range of issues for business. Dogs which have not barked yet include any new major slump in travel and consumer confidence or any significant change on the oil market—partly because it has turned out to be so difficult to restart Iraq's own oil exports even at the previous levels. The still difficult and in some ways deteriorating security environment in Iraq has delayed the start of major reconstruction, deterred the private-sector investments that this would require, and made it difficult for private contractors to help even in urgent tasks like restoring electricity supply.[31] The handling of Iraqi debt has become a sensitive issue, and one of those highlighting how hard it is to find practical (let alone widely accepted) solutions for Iraq except under the aegis of the UN.[32] Most dramatic from an economic viewpoint have perhaps been the escalating costs of the US operation, running at \$3.9 billion per month in 2003,[33]

[29] Council of the European Union, 'Action Plan for the Implementation of the Basic Principles for an EU Strategy against Proliferation of Weapons of Mass Destruction', Brussels, 13 June 2003, URL <http://ue.eu.int/pressdata/EN/reports/76328.pdf>.

[30] Boese, W., 'U.S. pushes initiative to block shipments of WMD, missiles', *Arms Control Today*, vol. 33, no. 6 (July/Aug. 2003), p. 26, available at URL <http://www.armscontrol.org/act/2003_07-08/securityinitiative_julaug03.asp>; and Weiner, R., Center for Nonproliferation, Monterey Institute of International Studies, 'Proliferation Security Initiative to stem flow of WMD matériel', 16 July 2003, URL <http://cns.miis.edu/pubs/week/030716.htm>. The PSI was established as a global initiative by the United States on 31 May 2003; the Statement of Interdiction Principles was released on 4 Sep. 2003 by 11 state participants (Australia, Canada, France, Germany, Italy, Japan, the Netherlands, Poland, Portugal, Spain and the USA). See 'Proliferation Security Initiative', URL <http://www.globalsecurity.org/military/ops/psi.htm>.

[31] On the other hand, the post-conflict environment has provided new ground for experiment with the provision of private security services by Western companies. See Catán, T. and Fidler, S., 'The military can't provide security. It had to be outsourced to the private sector and that was our opportunity', *Financial Times*, 30 Sep. 2003, p. 13.

[32] Monderer, M. and Mulford, D., 'Iraqi debt, like war, divides the West', *Financial Times*, 23 June 2003, p. 13.

[33] See United Press International, 'Rumsfeld doubles Iraq cost estimate', *Washington Times*, 10 July 2003.

with further costs in 2004–13 estimated to reach \$85 billion to \$200 billion, depending on the assumptions made about force levels.[34] On 25 March 2003 the US Administration asked Congress for a supplementary budget of \$74.7 billion and in October for a further \$87.9 billion for costs connected with Iraq. Together with the large sums still being spent on homeland security and the estimated further increase of 6.1 per cent in the main US defence budget in 2003, these expenses pushed the federal budget overall into a record end-year deficit. At the same time, the US external trade budget was expected to post a deficit of some \$401 billion in 2003 (equivalent to 3.7 per cent of gross domestic product), rising to \$480 billion in 2004.[35] Opinions differ on how dangerous these trends are. The US Administration continues to maintain that high spending and tax concessions can actually boost recovery. What seems clear is that the financial and economic price of military action in Iraq is influencing the business environment both in the USA and abroad, for good or ill, much more than any *direct* costs of the terrorist action of 11 September 2001 could have done.

As time has passed, some in the USA have also begun to question the effectiveness and proportionate costs of specific measures taken in the context of homeland security. Tougher entry visa rules for a range of Islamic and developing countries have obstructed customers' and clients' entry to the USA as well as handicapping, for example, educational exchanges.[36] It is feared that the USA's proposals under the Visa Waiver Program (VWP)[37] to enforce new standards of machine-readable passports incorporating bio-data for hitherto visa-free entrants—still under discussion with other countries—may involve both large conversion costs and, at least during a transitional period, processing delays. New security measures in the field of aviation have to a great extent been accepted as necessary by air passengers but have undoubtedly extended overall travel times, while some of them have entailed significant material costs for the operators. The US Administration's Container Security Initiative (CSI) and Custom–Trade Partnership Against Terrorism (C-TPAT), which have attracted comment from foreign firms and governments because of their substantial extraterritorial effects, have been more contentious.[38] In the

---

[34] See Holtz-Eakin, D., 'Letter to the Honorable John M. Spratt, Jr. regarding the estimated costs for the occupation of Iraq', US Congressional Budget Office, URL <http://www.cbo.gov/showdoc. cfm?index=46838sequence=0>.

[35] See US Congressional Budget Office, 'CBO's current budget projections', URL <http://www. cbo.gov/showdoc.cfm?index=1944&sequence=0>.

[36] See the annex to Part VI, on the education issue in the United States. The revelation on 23 Oct. 2003 that 125 000 special screenings of visa applications since 11 Sep. 2001 had not yielded a single case of refusal on security grounds set off a new wave of protest from Congress and business representatives. Alden, E., 'Security screening "hurts US interests"', *Financial Times*, 24 Oct. 2003, p. 6. For further criticisms see Alden, E., 'US companies say visa restrictions hamper business', *Financial Times*, 4 Nov. 2003, p. 4.

[37] For details of the countries to which the requirements will apply, the deadlines and developments in the VWP see US Department of State, 'Visa Waiver Program', URL <http://travel.state.gov/vwp. html>.

[38] For a critical account of the C-TPAT see chapter 15 in this volume, and for full details of the CSI and the C-TPAT see chapter 19. A good journalist's review is Murray, S., 'Importers pay the price of heavy security', *Financial Times*, 13 Jan. 2004, p. 8.

United States, particular criticism has been directed against choices made in the area of biological weapon (BW) defence: a massive planned programme of smallpox vaccination faltered against the resistance of many personnel in the health sector and because of legal complications, and has been criticized for diverting resources from *inter alia* research and development of defensive measures against anthrax.[39]

As pointed out above, there are of course winners as well as losers in the business world under almost any imaginable contingency. One of the most dramatic changes in US security behaviour since September 2001 was the increase of 11.4 per cent in real terms in the national defence budget for 2002, followed by a further 6.1 per cent in 2003 and a planned 2.4 per cent increase in 2004. The resources are designed to be spent mainly on new-technology items where US manufacturers have a lead, while existing procurement programmes will continue to run with only slight readjustments or compensating cuts.[40] Coincidentally (although basically reflecting a similar concern to protect the US heartland), spending on the US ballistic missile defence programme was estimated at $6.71 billion in 2003 and to be about $7.73 billion in 2004.[41] For the US defence industry there is little downside to these facts, but—aside from the question of possible macroeconomic damage—they do create issues for the US Administration's defence modernization policy and for relations with foreign governments and suppliers. Defense Secretary Donald Rumsfeld has shown a general preference for 'lean' US forces stripped of surplus roles and costs, and the Department of Defense has been concerned for some time about the results of industrial mergers which have put certain private-sector suppliers in a near-monopoly position, risking non-competitive pricing.[42] The experiences of 11 September 2001 and the wars in Afghanistan and Iraq have, however, provided new impetus for the US forces to invest in advanced technologies for which few if any non-US suppliers are available, while the political backwash prompted some Republicans in Congress to draft clauses for the US fiscal year 2003/2004 defence appropriations bill which would virtually outlaw purchase from non-US sources.[43] The impact of all this on the already troubled US–European defence insutrial relationship will need

---

[39] On the obstacles to the smallpox programme (but from a point of view committed to its continuance) see Bicknell, W. J. and Bloem, K. D., *Smallpox and Bioterrorism: Why the Plan to Protect the Nation is Stalled and What to Do*, Cato Institute Briefing Paper no. 85 (Cato Institute: Washington, DC, 5 Sep. 2003), available at URL <http://www.cato.org/pubs/briefs/bp-085es.html>. For a more critical report see MacKenzie, D., 'US "too busy" to spot a smallpox outbreak', *New Scientist*, vol. 177, no. 2384 (1 Mar. 2003), p. 10.

[40] Sköns, E. *et al.*, 'Military expenditure', *SIPRI Yearbook 2003* (note 2), pp. 307–12.

[41] US Missile Defense Agency estimates for FYs 2003 and 2004, URL <http://www.acq.osd.mil/bmdo/bmdolink/pdf/fy03aft.pdf> and URL <http://www.acq.osd.mil/bmdo/bmdolink/pdf/budget04.pdf>, respectively.

[42] Sköns, E. and Baumann, H., 'Arms production', *SIPRI Yearbook 2003* (note 2), pp. 373–403.

[43] See Brun-Rovety, M., 'US Senate set to approve $400bn defence spending bill', *Financial Times*, 13 Nov. 2003, p. 4. On the embarrassment caused to the US Defense Department by this development see Spiegel, P. and Alden, E., '"Buy American" stance toned down', p. 1, and 'Rumsfeld blinked after "Buy America" veto call', p. 3, *Financial Times*, 27/28 Sep. 2003. The administration finally succeeded in watering down the offending clause to one with purely advisory effect. It is fair to add that the protectionist aspects of the proposals have been opposed by both US and European trade associations.

to be monitored, but it can safely be predicted that it will, among other things, feed the tendencies both for more self-assertive European approaches to the US defence market and for closer intra-European collaboration.[44]

While these consequences of the original post-September 2001 agenda are still working themselves out, there has been time for further and newer themes to emerge within the spectrum of security issues concerning both business and government. The one flowing most directly from new analyses of the terrorist risk is the preoccupation with critical infrastructure protection (CIP)—the question of how to maintain energy delivery and distribution, telecommunications, and critical transport links within and between nations in the face of either terrorist sabotage or more natural and accidental risks. Heightened concern about this is logical, given the constantly increasing dependence of government itself (and official defence mechanisms) on computerized systems and long-range energy supply; the steady trend towards privatization and internationalization of all such supplies and services; the instant and massive disruption which a breakdown in any part of the system may cause to society (as shown by a string of electricity blackouts in the USA and Canada, the UK, Italy, and Denmark and Sweden in August–September 2003);[45] and the relative vulnerability of these networks to physical and more insidious attacks (*vide* computer viruses and hacking). Studies of this problem—supported by both governments and industry—are increasingly taking on an international character, and CIP is now firmly on the agenda of the EU, NATO and the NATO Partnership for Peace among others. It may be linked with, or seen as a specialized aspect of, civil emergency planning, which is undergoing a similar revival of interest after something of a lull since the end of the cold war.[46]

In actuality, the issues arising outside the terrorism–WMD complex which have had the greatest impact on business conditions in the two years since September 2001 have come from quite a different realm: that of human and animal health. The epidemic of foot-and-mouth disease in early 2001 caused the death of millions of animals in Europe, mainly through compulsory slaughter, and a protracted stoppage of the affected countries' meat trade. Concern about human immunodeficiency virus (HIV) infection and acquired immune deficiency syndrome (AIDS) peaked again in 2003 with the announcement of a new US policy initiative,[47] a UN report about the lack of funding for anti-AIDS work in Africa[48] and alarming new statistics on the advance of the disease[49]—all of which underlined that this has become a front-

---

[44] This issue is also discussed in Sköns and Baumann (note 42).

[45] See chapter 18 in this volume.

[46] See chapters 16 and 17 in this volume.

[47] 'The president's Emergency Plan for AIDS Relief', Fact sheet (White House, Office of the Press Secretary: Washington, DC, 28 Jan. 2003), available at URL <http://www.whitehouse.gov/news/releases/2003/01/20030129-1.html>.

[48] Joint United Nations Programme on HIV/AIDS (UNAIDS), *Accelerating Action against AIDS in Africa* (UNAIDS: Geneva, 21 Sep. 2003), available at URL <http://www.unaids.org/html/pub/UNA-docs/ICASA_Report_2003_en_pdf.pdf>.

[49] UNAIDS and the World Health Organization (WHO) estimated that 34–46 million people were living with HIV/AIDS worldwide and that total deaths had reached 2.5–3.5 million by late 2003. Joint

rank *security* issue for many countries in Africa and elsewhere. It is an increasing challenge for business, too, as illustrated by a headline in *The Financial Times*—'Outsourcing the business of life and death'[50]—where the 'business' is procuring AIDS protection for workers in South African companies. Dwarfing these concerns in the short term, however, was the spring 2003 epidemic of human severe acute respiratory syndrome (SARS) in East Asia and Canada. The epidemic caused an estimated \$9 billion in economic losses in North-East Asia and a further \$1 billion in South-East Asia, through factory shutdowns, slumps in travel and tourism, and the cost of counter-measures.[51] While security experts have sought lessons in the episode for the nature of and best responses to possible deliberate BW attacks,[52] it is more to the point to note that SARS itself has not been eliminated nor foolproof techniques agreed upon for preventing or controlling any future outbreak. Meanwhile, in an instance where human action (albeit with non-hostile intent) has developed into a security scare of comparable scale and economic impact, the USA continues to argue both with developing-world aid recipients and with European customers about the safety of its food exports produced from genetically modified crops. This last issue is a reminder that, even with the best of intentions, developments in commercial science and technology may not only be a source of solutions for new security challenges, but can also produce phenomena which are at least perceived by the general public as threats in themselves.

Last but not least, the crisis of confidence faced by several Western governments over the credibility of the information underpinning their security-policy decisions and—in some cases—also about the ethical quality of their tactics has found an echo in the continuing heart-searching over the quality of 'governance' in the private economic sector.[53] Without overstretching the

---

United Nations Programme on HIV/AIDS (UNAIDS), *AIDS Epidemic Update, December 2003,* UNAIDS/03.39E (UNAIDS: Geneva, Dec. 2003), available at URL <http://www.unaids.org/EN/resources/publications/corporate+publications/aids+epidemic+update+-+december+2003.asp>.

[50] Reed, J., 'Outsourcing the business of life and death', *Financial Times,* 18 Sep. 2003, p. 10.

[51] Asian Development Bank (ADB), 'Assessing the impact and cost of SARS in developing Asia', *Asian Development Outlook 2003 Update* (ADB: Manila, Oct. 2003), pp. 75–92, available at URL <http://www.adb.org/Documents/Books/ADO/2003/Update/sars.pdf>. The Canadian Tourism Research Institute of the Conference Board of Canada suggested that up to that date Canada had similarly lost some C\$1.5 billion, equivalent to 0.15% of Canada's annual real gross domestic product. Darby, P., 'The economic impact of SARS', Special Briefing, May 2003, URL <http://www.dfait-maeci.gc.ca/mexico-city/economic/may/sarsbriefMay03.pdf>. As for air travel, in May 2003 SARS brought a 21% drop in flight bookings over the previous year, and bookings did not start to rise again above the 2002 level until Sep. 2003. International Air Transport Association figures, quoted in 'Passengers return to international flights', *Financial Times,* 4 Nov. 2003, p. 8.

[52] Prescott, E. M., 'SARS: a warning', *Survival,* vol. 45, no. 3 (2003), pp. 207–26.

[53] The aspects of this which are already being tackled most systematically at the international level are the financial operations associated with organized crime and the problem of corruption. The United Nations Convention Against Transnational Organized Crime, adopted by the UN General Assembly and opened for signature in Dec. 2000—covering i.a. money laundering and human trafficking—entered into force on 29 Sep. 2003, albeit without the adherence of the USA or of most EU member states. For the text of the convention see URL <http://www.unodc.org/unodc/en/crime_cicp_convention.html>. On 1 Oct. 2003, negotiations were completed on the United Nations Convention Against Corruption, opened for signature at Mérida, Mexico, on 9–11 Dec. 2003. See the Internet site of the United Nations Office

parallel, it may be noted that such recent business scandals as those involving the Enron Corporation and WorldCom Incorporated in the USA, and Vivendi Universal and others in Europe, have also involved issues about the quality of information made available to the public and about conspiratorial behaviour leading to the subversion of normal control mechanisms.[54] In both contexts, leaders have been blamed for building high-risk patterns of behaviour on shaky or non-existent foundations of fact. The sternness with which the US Administration, in particular, has striven to punish and control Enron-type excesses has in turn become a new source of transatlantic tension: European companies and governments have raised concerns about the extraterritorial application of new US boardroom disciplines to their own US-linked or US-registered operations.

For all this multiple evidence of the interplay and interdependence of public- and private-sector security concerns, it cannot be said that 2002 and 2003 have witnessed any breakthrough in the way in which these two constituencies talk and work together. To take the example of terrorism, the irritation felt by many businesses over the impact of perhaps insufficiently thought-through countermeasures on their operations has been compounded by frustration that government seems uninterested in benefiting from their expertise, notably in risk assessment and management, or the huge amount of information on international processes and individuals that they gather in their own operations.[55] (Of course, any new system which might be developed for exploiting such expertise would run into delicate problems of data privacy and 'end-use', just as has happened in the case of disclosures relevant to money laundering and to travel safety.) On the other hand, the insurance industry is still calling for more serious governmental attention to be given to the problem of its vulnerability should even one further terrorist incident with large loss of life occur in the near future.[56]

Part of the problem is the continuing lack of any single clear institutional framework or process where the two sectors could review the whole security agenda together. The problem is far from being one of a total vacuum. Numerous initiatives have been taken, especially since the 1990s, to set up: (*a*) groupings or networks of business people to address security issues in individual countries; (*b*) international private-sector initiatives in association with the United Nations, such as the Global Compact;[57] (*c*) consultation mechanisms between governments and their national business communities on

on Drugs and Crime (UNODC) at URL <http://www.unodc.org/unodc/en/crime_convention_corruption. html>.

[54] On Enron see URL <http://www.enron.com>, on WorldCom (now MCI) URL <http://www.mci. com>, and on Vivendi URL <http://www.vivendiuniversal.com>.

[55] In Aug. 2003 the US Defense Advanced Projects Research Agency (DARPA) had to abandon, amid widespread derision, a planned scheme for a 'terrorism futures' market where companies' inside information could be reflected in collective 'betting' on likely future attacks. As pointed out at the time, however, the premise of harvesting companies' know-how was far less foolish than the particular method proposed. Harford, T., 'All bets are off at the Pentagon', *Financial Times*, 2 Sep. 2003, p. 8.

[56] See chapter 19 in this volume.

[57] See note 11.

specific issues of policy framing and implementation;[58] and (*d*) some corresponding international mechanisms, between a specific intergovernmental community or agency and private sector representatives from the countries involved. The difficulty is that all these approaches—except (*d*) in a very few cases—are voluntary, not formalized, and have thus resulted in an extremely varied (and not necessarily well-prioritized) pattern of coverage.

Very broadly speaking, business has tended to organize itself most systematically in the field of conflict prevention/management/reconstruction and 'conflict commodities';[59] to some extent on issues of critical infrastructure protection; vis-à-vis the security issues related to 'globalization', such as the environment; and for national coordination purposes in countries with a high consciousness of threat (and/or of international security responsibility).[60] Governments have most often sought dialogue with business on matters where their dependence on the private sector for policy execution is most obvious: export control and technology transfer issues,[61] infrastructure protection, national emergency planning in general, and of course their own requirements for private-sector services in the defence operational as well as equipment field. The control of WMD-relevant and other strategically sensitive exports is an area of rather well-developed consultation mechanisms and it needs to be, given the complexity of the balances that need to be struck and the need for constant adaptation to new possibilities of both equipment and technology 'leakage'.[62] The fact remains that there is no truly comprehensive process allowing *all* relevant businesses to consult regularly with *all* relevant governments on the spectrum of currently urgent issues, even within the narrower

[58] As an example, the US National Strategy for Homeland Security of 2002 calls for government to work with business on developing protection strategies for 14 critical sectors. See URL <http://www.whitehouse.gov/homeland/book/>.

[59] For a definition of these commodities and discussion of policy options see Pauwels, N., *Conflict Commodities: Addressing the Role of Natural Resources in Conflict*, ISIS Briefing Paper no. 27 (International Security Information Service, ISIS Europe: Brussels, Mar. 2003), URL <http://www.isis-europe.org/isiseu/brieflist/No.27_Conflict_Commodities.pdf>.

[60] *Vide* the Business Executives for National Security (BENS) network in the USA; see URL <http://www.bens.org>.

[61] See chapter 6 in this volume.

[62] Concerns about dangerous transfers have to be matched in this field against legitimate commercial and technology-development objectives, especially given that many of the commodities in question are of dual (military and civilian) use. The increasing interest in controlling intangible 'knowledge assets' relevant to proliferation, as well as hardware and software, will pose quandaries given the international character of many modern private-sector research teams. The way ahead may lie in more targeted controls, focusing on blocking leakage to the most dangerous destinations (state and non-state) rather than using generic export and transfer bans. As regards consultation mechanisms, in 1991 the USA established the Business Executive Enforcement Team (BEET) in the form of a secure electronic network linking over 3000 individuals in dual-use exporting firms with the Office of Export Enforcement in the Bureau of Industry and Security of the US Department of Commerce. See URL <http://www.bxa.doc.gov/enforcement/beets.htm>. The network is used both to inform business people of, and to let them pass comment on, official concerns and developments. In an alternative model, in 1994 the Swedish Chamber of Commerce established the Swedish Export Control Society (ECS; in Swedish, Sveriges Exportkontrollförening) to inform companies' export licensing specialists of developments in Swedish, EU and US policies and to coordinate the expression of these constituents' views back to the government. See URL <http://www.chamber.se/exportcontrol> (in Swedish). The ECS holds an annual meeting with all its members, can summon ad hoc meetings, issues a newsletter and operates otherwise through a secure electronic network.

sphere of military security—let alone the whole variety of security challenges reviewed above.

To some extent the gap is filled—and the worst kind of policy incoherence avoided—by discussions and personal networking between public and private sector leaders in wholly unofficial contexts such as the annual meetings of the World Economic Forum, which apart from anything else have a valuable educational effect (allowing each side at least to hear what the other is thinking and doing).[63] Any attempts to improve intra-sectoral dialogue would need to take the benefits of such non-constrained intercourse into account, and perhaps start from the premise that 'good' and 'comprehensive' in this context does not necessarily equate to 'formal' or 'obligatory'. The expressions of need voiced from the business side are strikingly often couched in terms of *information* and *early warning*—in essence: 'tell us what you're planning in good time and we might be able to help you with it more than you think, as well as adjusting better to the consequences for ourselves'. Voluntary information exchange and consultation mechanisms could meet quite a lot of these requirements, while leaving flexibility for subsequent operational cooperation to take the form most appropriate for the case in hand.

There are, in fact, at least two pitfalls to be avoided in any more formal attempt at reinforced dialogue and collaboration. Across the field as a whole, at both the national and international level, the latest evolution of the security agenda offers a clear temptation to 're-nationalize' (or the equivalent): that is, to resume executive and/or juridical control of functions essential for security which have passed into private-sector hands in the course of free-market developments (or perhaps have always lain there). The lesson cited above of the Warsaw Pact command economies should signal some of the dangers along this path. The more recent evidence of hastily conceived security measures damaging the 'good' economy more than the 'bad guys' underlines the danger even of indirect regulatory approaches when they are divorced from economic reality. This is not to say that everything can and should be left to voluntary actions from the private-sector side. Many of the issues at stake are ones where consistent universal coverage and a 'level playing field' are the very essence of an appropriate security solution. The free play of voluntarism and market forces not only cannot guarantee these requisites but also may lead to distortions (e.g., solutions disproportionately favouring the larger northern hemisphere companies which take most of the initiatives, or *excessive* philanthropy leading to clientage and aid dependence) which in the long run make things worse. This leads on to the second consideration: the all-too-real risk— illustrated by the airline insurance issue—that actions apparently constituting rational steps in mutual support between government and business may have (intended or accidental) anti-competitive effects, damaging both to the overall health of the economy and the environment for international cooperation. At

---

[63] On the World Economic Forum see URL <http://www.weforum.org>.

present, the world's strongest defence and security institutions are not those most sensitive to such risks or best seasoned in avoiding them.

All this suggests that it will be very important, when building any more systematic new framework for public/private interaction on the new agenda, (*a*) to maintain a bias towards the 'lightest' possible means of control for solving any given problem (e.g., regulation rather than executive action, contracting rather than requisitioning), and (*b*) to use or at least involve international forums whose primary competence lies in the economic sphere. The roles played by the World Bank, the World Trade Organization, the Organisation for Economic Co-operation and Development (OECD), and relevant parts of the UN machinery have been entirely appropriate from this point of view. The time could now be ripe for more activism in this field by the EU (and through EU–US dialogue), as well as in the framework of the Group of Eight (G8) major industrialized nations.

IV. Other players, other interests

With all the complexities that increased public/private sector interaction on the new security agenda may imply, it is still too simplistic a model because there is—in reality—a very important third side to the triangle. The *individual citizen* enters into the equation as well, and in a number of guises. First and foremost, he or she may be thought of as the actual and potential *victim* of every kind of security malfunction so far mentioned: the target for terrorism and crime as well as armed warfare, the sufferer from collapse of services or disease or a disintegrating environment. His or her degree of objective vulnerability, in prosperous as well as developing societies, is arguably greater than ever in history before because his/her simplest needs (food, warmth, movement) depend on the operation of complex technical systems far beyond the individual's ability to control—or in many cases, even understand. It is not unreasonable that citizens should look increasingly to their governments to ensure, nationally or collectively, that these support systems of modern society are protected as a high priority and that 'normal service is restored' as fast as possible after any breakdown. As soon as things go wrong, as they did in the spate of urban power breakdowns in the autumn of 2003, it becomes clear that these expectations are among the strongest ones invested by the ordinary people of many nations in their ruling structures and in the international groupings they belong to. For different reasons in different parts of the world, as noted above, citizens are also increasingly aware of the impact of the private sector's activities on many of these issues and are prepared to use their own purchasing strength and consumer choice to signify their judgement on its performance.

When governments and/or companies make less than optimal choices in pursuit of their 'duty to protect', however, citizens can be hurt in other ways than through simple lack of protection. They will ultimately receive the bill for any material measures taken, whether by the state (through paying taxes) or by the private sector (through higher prices). Their political and human rights, access to information and education, freedom of economic activity and freedom to travel could be hit by many different types of 'corrective' measures tending to tighten central controls and disciplines. The atmosphere and efficiency of the multi-ethnic, multi-sectarian societies in which an increasing proportion of the world's citizens live will be damaged if the effect of security measures is to stigmatize and discriminate between elements with different ethnic and religious backgrounds. A safe society does demand individual alertness, but it may tip into paranoia and probably become more prone to violence if the culture of 'snooping' and denunciation of fellow citizens gets out of hand. The economic conditions for ordinary people's activity may be skewed in more subtle ways if government and industry organize their collaboration in the style of a mutually beneficial 'cartel' while leaving the impact on individuals out of account. All this is just one dimension of a much more general and permanent quandary for security policy (referred to in section I): the risk of crushing by inappropriate protection the very assets and values that the policy sets out to protect.

The citizen is not only the object of security solutions, but may also be a *part of the problem*. Individuals cause or aggravate emergencies through initial error and negligence (including neglect of preventative measures), failure to respond appropriately to the strings of abnormal events which lie behind so many large emergencies, failure to follow security instructions after the alarm is given, and so forth. It is striking to note how many security experts in the business world identify their own employees, in this sense, as their primary security risk.[64] Moreover, in a free-market environment where much security equipment and advice is for sale at a price, individuals can make the rational handling of emergencies more difficult by inappropriate preparation (e.g., purchasing the wrong equipment, panic buying and hoarding) as well as by inappropriate responses. It is very difficult to blame people for this given the general lack of control and understanding of complex new security processes, which makes it often virtually impossible for them to work out independently what would be the 'right' thing to do in the face of a given threat or emergency. The key point which emerges is that many solutions for countering the new-style threats to society will lie as much in the *behavioural* field—requiring change in the role of citizens themselves—as in the regulatory sphere proper to government, or the technical sphere where business is supreme.

The right approach to developing such multi-faceted answers cannot be to marginalize and disenfranchise the ordinary person even further. Ignorance, passivity, and the 'dumbing down' of security judgement in individuals can only lessen the resources available both to the state and business for their mutual support, and reduce the resilience and adaptability of society as a whole. Rather, the emphasis should be on finding ways to increase the general

---

[64] See chapter 15 in this volume.

public level of understanding, confidence, preparedness, self-reliance (within reason), and—not least—the consciousness of responsibility to help even weaker and more vulnerable members of the community. It should go without saying that simply lecturing people on the nature and seriousness of the challenges is not enough, and can merely make things worse when it amounts to frightening them without offering clear remedy. Panic is a deliberate weapon of all kinds of 'bad guys', and is the enemy of good security policy both short- and long-term.[65] Conversely, it is a bad mistake for government to belittle and simplify actual threats or to claim that it can provide a simple executive solution, when this is not only untrue but liable to be exposed as such sooner rather than later. The question of how to build more genuine and lasting forms of partnership between government, business and the citizen—whether through education, information, consultations, media actions,[66] exercises, new forms of citizen's service,[67] and/or the mobilization of civil society's own groups and structures—would provide material for another major publication in itself.

Practically all the analysis in this chapter suffers another major limitation in that it reflects an essentially Western-inspired and West-centric agenda, leaving the interests of *other regions of the world* out of account. It is important here not to fall into simplistic assumptions about opposing 'Northern' and 'Southern' agendas. The threats of terrorism, proliferation and rogue-state behaviour hurt even more people and often hurt them more directly in the developing countries than they have done (at least so far) in the world's richer societies. Globalization has made the security challenges for different regions more comparable overall and has increased inter-regional dependence in a way that should banish any 'zero-sum' notion of Northern and Southern security. All players' interests are best served by freedom to trade and communicate in peaceful, predictable surroundings, so all have a prima facie interest in working together to eliminate the various saboteurs and parasites of the global security system. These are not only idealistic statements but may be shown to have some reflection in reality, if one considers (for instance) the role of oil-producing countries in bringing the world through the period after September

---

[65] Zanders (note 15).

[66] Since the massacres in Rwanda and the conflicts of the 1990s in South-Eastern Europe in particular, awareness has grown that the media have a dynamic effect not just in reporting conflicts to the outside world but in influencing opinion and action within the conflict area. There is a growing consensus that the international community's task in such cases should include providing its own sources of unbiased (especially radio) broadcasting, and if possible, suppressing any local media which by projecting a 'hate' message de facto become parties to the conflict. During the 2003 conflict in Iraq, major innovations were made in techniques of outwards-directed reporting ('embedded' journalists, etc.), but the actual and potential *local* role of democratic media is an aspect that has hitherto been somewhat under-discussed.

[67] Since the end of the cold war the clear trend among countries in the wider European area has been to move away from national defence systems based on conscription towards the greater use of professional forces, often linked with changes in the role of reservists. Even in countries still making extensive use of conscription (e.g., states in Northern Europe), the proportion of young men in each generation called up for service is dropping because of overall force cuts. In countries which are reluctant to lose the notion of citizens' service altogether (e.g., because of its perceived bonding and democratizing effect), one solution would be to devise new forms of non-military service devoted to internal and functional security needs, as well as to social and humanitarian ones.

2001 without a major price shock, or the very wide range of countries who have cooperated with the UN Counter-Terrorism Committee.

Nevertheless, there are both in theory and actuality several ways in which the pursuit of Western public–private sector security agendas since 11 September 2001 could create difficulties vis-à-vis other world regions, generally with greatest cost to the interests of the latter. The first problem is that Western analysts may not consider carefully enough the need for extending their corrective policies to other regions, and/or may underestimate the help the latter could provide. Several regional organizations outside Europe have in fact discussed their own anti-terrorism, anti-proliferation measures since September 2001,[68] but these developments have tended to be under-reported and the EU, for example, still needs to do much more to achieve practical synergy with such groups (inspired as they often are by the EU's own model). The critical infrastructure and energy supply issue is one for which, patently, solutions will only be as good as the weakest link in the chain. Attention should be given as a priority to the standards of protection in both neighbouring and more distant supplier countries. Again, the new understanding of the terrorism/proliferation nexus and the importance of emerging security dimensions such as infrastructure, migration control or disease control will need to be factored far more carefully than they are at present into developed-world policies for crisis prevention, management and post-crisis reconstruction in other parts of the globe. Events in Iraq up to the present have provided an almost perfect negative model of what happens when these aspects are not properly understood or planned for at the time of intervention and when the right capacities are lacking for addressing them afterwards.

Iraq also illustrates the next set of problems: those which arise when the remedies chosen by the West for its own perceived security problems are based on mistaken or inadequate theories about the rest of the world's role in creating them; or when methods are used which are counterproductive when applied in the real extra-European environment; or when there is a tendency more generally to discriminate against non-Westerners both in practice and in terms of perception. The biggest debate that has already taken place under this heading is the familiar one about the need to tackle the causes of terrorism, not just its manifestations. The wrong kind of forceful action against the latter, and the use of wrong methods to coerce or buy developing countries' support, may

---

[68] E.g., the members of the Asia–Pacific Economic Cooperation (APEC) forum agreed in Oct. 2003 on a number of joint measures to tackle aspects of the 'new security agenda' such as the dismantling of terrorist organizations, imposition of controls on shoulder-launched anti-aircraft missiles, enhancement of security at seaports, cutting off of terrorist finance, and measures against WMD proliferation. See 'Bangkok Declaration on Partnership for the Future', 21 Oct. 2003, URL <http://www.apecsec.org. sg/content/apec/leaders_declarations/2003.html>. Similar measures had previously been discussed by the Association of South-East Asian Nations (ASEAN) (see 'ASEAN efforts to counter terrorism', URL <http://www.aseansec.org/14396.htm>) and the African Union (see 'Decision on terrorism in Africa', Assembly/AU/Dec.15(II) 2003, URL <http://www.africa-union.org/Official_documents/Decisions_ Declarations/Assembly%20AU%20Dec%2015%20II.pdf>). These issues were also raised at the Special Conference on Security of the Organization of American States (OAS), meeting at Mexico City on 27–28 Oct. 2003. See OAS, 'Declaration on security in the Americas', URL <http://www.oas.org/ csh/ces/en>.

carry a wide range of costs. They may create new enemies for the West (and new terrorists, criminals, mercenaries, arms traffickers, etc.); worsen regional divisions and antagonisms; create new local arms races and actual incentives to proliferate WMD (if the proven possession of WMD is perceived as a defence against superpower attack); and blur the messages which the West wishes to project about the need for reform, democracy and legality world-wide.[69] They may also cause concrete damage to the security and stability of individual non-European states. The element of discrimination or differential damage to the interests of developing countries may arise from new security-related obstacles to travel and trade, the creation of new operating costs which only more prosperous operators can bear, the disproportionate burden placed by new international norms on smaller states,[70] and so on. On top of all this comes the risk that non-Westerners in general and their religions and political–social–economic practices will be stamped in general terms as 'the enemy' or at least become a source of mistrust and apprehension. It should go without saying that the interests of Western business and the conditions for its mutu-ally beneficial operation in non-Western areas can only suffer from the com-pound effect of all such mistakes, even if—inevitably—some niches are cre-ated in the process for wrongful and disproportionate gains.

The third type of problem arises when Western-led policies leave out of account the other important challenges affecting the rest of the world, both in the traditional security sphere and more widely, or exalt the currently fashion-able 'rich man's agenda' over these other issues to an unjustified extent. The whole point about 'asymmetrical' threats is that they buck the trend: most security processes in the world still favour the stronger over the weaker play-ers and the richer over the poorer. As the UN Secretary-General pointed out in his report in 2003 on progress under the UN's Millennium Declaration,[71] the bulk of mankind is still struggling with security challenges as basic as finding food, water and fuel, keeping their children alive, and avoiding death at the hands of fellow citizens or abusive rulers. Climate change is yet another factor which will hit the developing world harder than the developed: a recent World Health Organization (WHO) report suggests that the bulk of the 300 000 pro-jected deaths per annum from climate-related disease and natural disasters in 2030 will affect the poorest countries.[72] The majority of armed conflicts are

[69] The United Nations Development Programme argued that US and other Western policies since 11 Sep. 2001 had made it easier for less-than-democratic regimes in the Arab world to restrict citizens' freedoms further and to resist reform, as well as hampering human contacts between these countries and the West itself. See United Nations Development Programme (UNDP), *Arab Human Development Report 2003: Building a Knowledge Society* (UNDP: New York, Oct. 2003), summary available at URL <http://www.undp.org/rbas/ahdr/englishpresskit2003.html>.

[70] Leahy, J., 'South Pacific islands hit by wave of regulation after terrorist attacks', *Financial Times*, 8 Jan. 2003, p. 3.

[71] United Nations, Implementation of the United Nations Millennium Declaration: Report of the Secretary-General, UN document A/58/323, 2 Sep. 2003, available at URL <http://www.un.org/millenniumgoals/>.

[72] McMichael, A. J. *et al.*, World Health Organization (WHO), *Climate Change and Human Health: Risks and Responses* (WHO: Geneva, 2003); for a summary of the report see URL <http://www.who.int/globalchange/publications/cchhsummary/en>.

internal to developing states and have only limited connections to terrorism, let alone any inherent anti-Western agenda.[73] If new-style Western security policies neglect and shift resources away from such issues, the West's own security is bound to suffer—and probably first of all, through the effects of such regional disorder and decay on interdependent economic processes including raw material supply and migration flows. When issues like the threat to the global environment or the new trends in epidemic disease are considered, the interlocking of 'rich men's' and 'poor men's' security destiny is all the plainer

It is probably safe to guess that major companies and private-sector groupings are less likely than governments to let themselves be distracted from this last agenda, just as they are less likely to get the 'asymmetrical threats' out of proportion. Their jet-setting executives and expatriate operators are among the most genuine 'citizens of the world', more so than many national officials and certainly more so than national politicians. One of the benefits of a closer and more comprehensive public–private sector dialogue on security priorities and remedies would be to enlist these broader business perspectives and to hear business's (often very perceptive) view on the dynamics and needs of other regions. It could not, however, offer a complete remedy for the risks of West-centricity until and unless some way can be found to draw in the representatives of the private sector from all non-Western regions as well.

V. This book

This book is based on the proceedings of the international conference on Business and Security: Protecting the Legitimate and Blocking the Illegitimate, which was held at Vaduz, Liechtenstein, on 5–6 September 2003 by SIPRI and the Liechtenstein-Institut in the framework of the Liechtenstein Government's programme on peace research and conflict prevention. The chapters which follow consist, by and large, of more developed versions of the talks which were delivered at that conference, taking into account also the points made in subsequent discussion. They are grouped in thematic parts, each with a further short introduction by the editors of this volume.

The aim of the SIPRI–Liechtenstein-Institut Conference, aside from the interest of the subject matter, was to bring together an unprecedented mix of private-sector leaders, researchers, NGOs and other independent activists, and public-sector representatives from governments, parliaments and international institutions. UN agencies, NATO, the EU, the OECD, and the Organization for Security and Co-operation in Europe (OSCE) were all represented. The agenda was drawn up with a view to illustrating the broad span of issues relevant to the private–public sector security dialogue and cooperation since

[73] Wiharta, S. and Anthony, I., 'Major armed conflicts', pp. 87–108, and Eriksson, M., Sollenberg, M. and Wallensteen, P., 'Patterns of major armed conflicts 1990–2002', pp. 109–21, *SIPRI Yearbook 2003* (note 2).

11 September 2001, and to examining these challenges from a variety of angles—including the cogent questions of 'Can we afford to be safe?' and 'Is this just a rich man's agenda?'.

The mix of perspectives achieved at the conference is also reflected in this book, in the different styles as well as the substance of the chapters. Individual contributions are not necessarily 'balanced', although their ensemble is designed to be so. It should thus be emphasized that, as always in such cases, the views expressed by the various authors are their own and should not be taken to reflect the views either of SIPRI or of the Liechtenstein Government.

Given the limited time available for the conference at Vaduz, some issues of considerable importance for both government and business had to be left to one side. This volume is, correspondingly, far from being able to offer truly comprehensive coverage. An obvious omission is any discussion of the defence industrial sector itself. At the functional level, much more could have been said, for example, on the corporate ethics agenda (including the security relevance of corruption); the theme of aviation security; the reliability of energy sources (as distinct from energy distribution); and the issue of security of supply in general. It is possible that some of these matters may be addressed in the course of further activities under the Liechtenstein Government's programme.

The book does, however, aim to fulfil a wider function of reference and to provide a platform for further research and activism through its appendices, prepared by Isabel Frommelt. They gather together information not hitherto available in a single place on security institutions (official, academic or non-governmental) and business organizations, respectively, that are active in or interested in the public–private sector interface in this field. These listings, too, inevitably reflect the limits of SIPRI's own knowledge and access to information. If readers are aware of any omissions under the defined categories, and can supply the appropriate references, they are invited to draw them to the editors' attention.[74]

[74] Email address: director@sipri.org.

Part I

The general framework: goals and norms

Editors' remarks

The three chapters in the opening part of this volume are based on 'keynote' speeches delivered at the conference on Business and Security. Their dual role is to outline the novelty, urgency and mould-breaking character of the latest security threats—in other words, to show *why* a new look at public–private sector cooperation is needed—and to suggest some first guidelines for *how* this cooperation might be approached.

Writing on the basis of long experience in national and international public-sector work, and in private business, respectively, István Gyarmati and Erik Belfrage both stress the universal and *intrusive* character of today's terrorist and criminal threats. The ordinary citizen is personally and permanently exposed in a way that is quite different from the nuclear stalemate of the cold war. Every branch of business may be damaged physically and economically, and driven to change its working habits. Globalization of the economy creates universal interdependence, while globalization of information flows has the potential to universalize terror. The traditional state apparatus neither wields the means nor can raise the resources to protect against these challenges completely. Those functions which are traditionally reserved for states, such as a deterrent posture and military retaliation, have far less impact on the new adversaries. Companies' and citizens' help to detect the wrong-doers, to starve them of resources and to 'harden' all vulnerable social targets against them is not just vital but of larger proportional weight in the security balance than even before.

Gyarmati and Belfrage both discuss the best means of bringing government and business together to work on these challenges. They both advise sensitivity to the private sector's own needs, its limitations and its principles (e.g., on controlling the end-use of any information handed over to state organs). The new partnerships should not be a matter of subordinating business in any crude and narrow way to the police functions of the state. The broader the interface can be between all fields of governance and all the private sector's representative groupings, the better. The more the methods of coordination can approximate to industry's own natural networking practices, the more effective they are likely to be.

Both authors also touch on the importance of a fair and transparent legislative framework. The chapter by Daniel Tarschys takes up this normative aspect of the challenge in much greater detail. He recalls that the world is not only driven, and civilized societies do not only measure themselves, by the kind of 'values' that can be quantified in financial terms or by the indices of military strength. The closer one looks at these latter types of statistics, in any case, the more ambiguous they become. The story of Europe since World War II has been one of steady (if painful and incomplete) progress towards defining other 'values' of a political, legal and moral kind, which should guide policy making at both the national and the international level. The current juncture, when violent threats are moving closer to the individual grass roots of society and at the same time becoming more truly universal, is no moment to throw away the hard-won achievements of our era in protecting both individual and universal rights. The almost biblical question inherent in Tarschys' analysis—what profit would there be in saving the world's riches but losing its soul?—hangs as an open challenge over the rest of this volume.

1. Security and the responsibilities of the public and private sectors

István Gyarmati

I. Introduction

The 21st century began with an event in the United States that signalled the end of an historic era. The aircraft that destroyed the New York World Trade Center and a part of the Pentagon demonstrated that the cold war era, and even the post-cold war era, has come to an end; that old concepts of security no longer apply; that new threats have emerged which are much more realistic and no less devastating than those of the cold war; and that defence against them has proved to be extremely difficult.

The cold war era was characterized by threats that threatened to destroy much of humankind, if not all life on earth. However, those threats were relatively remote. There were one or two moments in history when the threats became imminent and tangible for a few days, but rationality always prevailed: states have never resorted to violence that threatens their very existence. Deterrence based on mutual assured destruction worked because retaliation was both credible and unacceptable.[1]

The post-cold war era did not last long. For little more than a decade, the world lived in a self-invented illusion. People believed that a new age had emerged—one in which violence and wars would become less and less probable and less and less frequent. They believed that negotiations would become the major, if not the only, way to prevent—or manage and resolve—armed conflicts. The fact that devastating wars were fought in the 1990s, even in Europe, did not disturb this illusion. People did not want to let it be disturbed. Rather, they insisted that those conflicts were the exception: that the rule would become the absence of violence and wars, and that the reign of international law and 'universal values' would be accepted by all and rule the world forever.

The signs which signalled that this 'wonderful, wonderful world' might be an illusion or, in the best case, a temporary situation were ignored. Although the general trend in the number of conflicts was one of decline[2] and most of the conflicts in Europe were no longer violent, there was also evidence point-

---

[1] The nuclear stalemate in US–Soviet relations in the 1960s led to the adoption of the doctrine of mutual assured destruction (MAD), according to which no country would attack another if it knew that the attacked side had the capability to inflict unacceptable damage on the attacker.

[2] For data on major armed conflicts see Eriksson, M., Sollenberg, M. and Wallensteen, 'Patterns of major armed conflicts, 1990–2002', *SIPRI Yearbook 2003: Armaments, Disarmament and International Security* (Oxford University Press: Oxford, 2003), pp. 109–21. These data show a decline in the number of conflicts over the period except for the 3 years 1991, 1993 and 1998.

ing the other way. None of the post-cold war conflicts in the wider European area has yet been completely resolved, and several of them have been merely 'frozen', with the risk of revival at any time if a solution is not found. There has also been an increase in organized crime, failed states and terrorist activities, especially in preparations for or actual large-scale attacks. In 1999 the North Atlantic Treaty Organization (NATO) Washington Summit stated that terrorism would be one of the most serious threats in the future,[3] but NATO and others still failed to take this seriously into account. Significant steps were not taken to prepare for the eventuality of terrorist attacks, let alone to prevent them. A few indecisive steps were taken, such as the US attacks ordered in 1998 by President Bill Clinton against the network of radical groups affiliated with and funded by Osama bin Laden in Afghanistan and Sudan.[4] However, not even the United States took the challenge seriously then, and the European states did not devote real thought to steps to prevent possible terrorist attacks against their territory.

II. New threats, new thinking

On 11 September 2001 the unthinkable happened. Not only was a large-scale terrorist attack carried out, not only did the terrorists use very unconventional means to inflict large-scale damage and kill a large number of civilians, but the attack was launched in the 'sacred land' of the United States, which for a long time had seemed and had viewed itself as invulnerable. This changed the nature of thinking, especially in the USA. The United States now feels and behaves like a country at war. It has a mission—one which has replaced its decades-long fight against communism—and it has a new enemy. Europe has reluctantly joined (in principle) the 'war on terrorism' and taken some steps, especially in the non-military area; but the European states have never really believed that terrorism was seriously threatening them, nor that terrorism would be an overwhelming, clear and present danger, *the* most important threat to security.

US and European thinking has now evolved towards a general recognition that some kind of a threat from terrorists and organized crime does exist, as well as of the possibility that such groups may acquire weapons of mass destruction (WMD). This view has gained ground in spite of the differences between the USA and Europe as regards how imminent and how dangerous this threat really is. Accordingly, there has been some, in many cases very serious and effective, cooperation in areas other than the military between the USA and Europe, especially between the police and in the area of financial

[3] 'Terrorism constitutes a serious threat to peace, security and stability that can threaten the territorial integrity of States. We reiterate our condemnation of terrorism and reaffirm our determination to combat it in accordance with our international commitments and national legislaton.' NATO, Washington Summit Communiqué, 'An Alliance for the 21st Century', Press Release NAC-S(99)64, 24 Apr. 1999, para. 42, URL <http://www.nato.int/docu/pr/1999/p99-064e.htm>.

[4] For the text of the Clinton statement on the threat and the rationale for the military strikes see BBC News Online, URL <http://news.bbc.co.uk/2/hi/americas/155412.stm>.

and transportation services. This type of collaboration has made headway, despite the fact that the US leadership is reluctant to accept assistance in any form other than for the direct satisfaction of the United States'—real or perceived—needs, and the implementation of their (often unilateral) decisions.

The new threats have created new needs to protect countries, property and lives. These threats are totally new in nature. Before 11 September 2001 governments believed that they knew what the potential threats were and where they were coming from. It was almost impossible to launch a surprise attack. Only a missile attack was considered a realistic threat to homelands because there would be no warning time, but such an attack by states was highly improbable. The new threat is very different. The enemies that would carry out such an attack are totally without any restrictions, either moral or pragmatic, other than the limits of the destructive capability available to them. When states plan for attacks they have to keep in mind the possible damage to their own territory and property as well as casualties among their soldiers and citizens. States want to protect these as much as possible and, even in conflicts where attempts to limit damage have proved futile, the intention was there. This is why states are vulnerable to retaliation and terrorists are not. They have no state, no territory, no property, no soldiers and no citizens to protect. They are not afraid of death—on the contrary, they welcome death when it makes them martyrs. According to the beliefs of some, this is the highest honour they can achieve.

This statement presupposes that terrorists adhere to a religion, in most cases to Islam. This appears to be a fact of life: recent prominent and successful terrorists, those involved in the 11 September attacks and other incidents, happened to belong to the Islamic religion. This is a highly sensitive subject. Political correctness in most cases prevents open discussion of the issue, but it must be faced and analysed. While this subject is outside the scope of this chapter, it must be noted that this religion provides the necessary ideology to encourage martyrdom and this reinforces the fact that these terrorists cannot be deterred by the prospect of retaliation or death.

In addition, the danger that terrorists could take possession of WMD, and that they would not hesitate to use them, strengthens the vital need to prevent terrorist attacks. Prevention is, of course, a very wide concept. It generally requires good intelligence and police work, the cutting off of the resources that finance terrorists, and so on. However, in many cases these measures alone will not be sufficient. Pre-emption is frequently the only means of prevention. This means that states will need military and police forces that can carry out such pre-emptive strikes: and this in turn raises many questions, including the legitimation of pre-emptive strikes and the role of international law and international institutions. Again, deeper analysis of these problems would go well beyond the limits of this chapter. Physical protection of people and property, however, is an issue that cannot be left aside: if we acknowledge that not all terrorist attacks can be prevented, we need to ensure that all necessary means are at our disposal for protection against such attacks.

Organized crime is another present and actual threat that must be taken into account. Criminals have always existed and the need for protection against criminal activities is nothing new. Organized international crime, however, has reached new dimensions: the destructive power of organized crime groups has become greater than ever before, and criminal groups have embedded themselves in state structures in a large number of states, even within Europe. This has led to an extremely dangerous threat and an extremely difficult, but crucial, task of prevention. Prevention is all the more problematic because of the increasing difficulties faced by states in providing the necessary financial and other means for their traditional functions, including the provision of security for their citizens and their property. This is not likely to change in the foreseeable future. The increasing demands for security and, consequently, for resources to finance security measures, and the simultaneous decrease of funds available for this purpose, make the situation extremely dangerous and difficult to manage.

III. The new role of the private sector

On the positive side, private groups are starting to recognize that security can no longer be provided by the state alone. Countless companies now specialize in security, from personal bodyguards and doormen in large apartment blocks, and private transportation services, to small private armies protecting property, aircraft, hotels and other vulnerable potential targets.

All this makes it clear that the security of citizens and property can no longer be viewed as the responsibility solely of the state. Citizens and companies can no longer claim that they have paid their dues to the state and that all they need to do is simply wait and see what the state does to protect them. These new threats have generated a process that is gradually 'privatizing security' in many countries,[5] but it is not a totally new phenomenon. In several countries, such as Israel, the United States and several Latin American countries, private security companies have long been part of everyday life. The process has, however, accelerated significantly over the past decade. It began as a response to increased and significantly more violent crime, especially in the developing world, but also in many 'new democracies'. Russia, Ukraine, South-Eastern Europe and the Central Asian former Soviet republics lead the list, but from time to time violence has become more prominent even in the leading transition countries, such as Hungary, Poland or Slovakia.

The increased importance of some regions in the world economy as a result of globalization has also contributed to this process. Many crucial raw materials can be found in areas subject to violence of various kinds. The need for secure transport of these materials as well as other products also raises serious security concerns.

---

[5] On private military or security companies see also chapters 13, 14 and 21 in this volume.

Private companies and individuals have recognized these dangers and have started to respond by creating their own security services. Many large companies are creating complex security services, albeit with different emphasis. Insurance companies concentrate on intelligence and analysis, since they need information about risks in order to be able to generate appropriate insurance rates, but they are much less concerned about the physical security of assets on the ground. The concern of transportation companies, on the other hand, has to do with the physical security of assets and persons. Accordingly, they focus more on creating the necessary circumstances for physical security.

Since 11 September 2001, terrorism has also figured as a concern for individuals and private companies. The general view still is that this is a job for governments, but this is bound to change soon, or has already started to change. Several industries are particularly concerned about security—primarily the aviation industry, which has been exposed to terrorism more than any other. Other industries will follow. Transportation, the food industry, chemical and medical facilities, water reservoirs, distribution and transportation systems, computer networks and many other branches are exposed to terrorist abuse and attacks and will have to concern themselves more with their own physical security than they have done in the past.

All this will require significant resources. Airlines have already started adding special surcharges for security. This has largely been accepted by customers, because the danger is so obvious and personalized. No one travelling by air can pretend to feel immune to terrorist hijackings or other attacks. Accordingly, people have been willing to pay a modest extra charge in the belief that this will increase their flight security, as it appears to have done. This is an example that will be much more difficult to follow in other industries, where the threat is more indirect, less obvious and less personalized. These sectors and their customers will demand that the state play a greater role, and private contributions will be more difficult to secure.

Nonetheless, it is obvious that neither states and governments nor private persons and companies alone will be able to cope with these new threats. Both organized crime and global terrorism will be with us for a long while, and defence against them, including the defence of persons and physical assets, will become increasingly more difficult and expensive.

IV. Conclusions

Bold and innovative steps must be taken to make cooperation between the public and private sectors in the field of security more efficient. First, there is a need for dialogue between the sectors in order to demonstrate that the days have ended when security was the concern of only governments and when private persons and companies contributed only by paying their taxes (and by voting for governments on the basis of criteria that included the perception of which candidate would be more effective in protecting 'law and order').

Close, permanent cooperation is now necessary to ensure an acceptable level of security in private lives and businesses.

This dialogue must be structured and purpose-oriented. Appropriate institutions will be needed to conduct it. The initiative would best come from private business, since not only are governments more reluctant to share their power, but government initiatives are also viewed by private business with a high degree of suspicion—and rightly so. Governments, in turn, must be ready and forthcoming, recognizing that private business will not only invest in its own interests but may also take over some functions of government and spend money for goals which so far have been financed only by governments.

Such dialogue frameworks could concentrate on chambers of commerce, industry and agriculture, and could also include trade unions—provided that unions can adapt and take on new tasks other than the perhaps outdated task of protecting individual employees. On the side of government, the task should not be delegated to any one ministry. Instinctively, governments will assign this job to ministries of the interior, but it would be a mistake to reduce the task to a police job. As mentioned above, protection against organized crime and global terrorism requires a high level of coordination between almost all government agencies, including ministries of the interior, defence, finance, tourism, armed forces, border guards, police, secret services, and so on. Consequently, they must all participate in dialogue and cooperation with private business. The cooperation process must be run overall by the chief executive's office, the prime minister or the president, and must also involve the legislative branch.

The role of the legislative branch is very important, since the involvement of private business in the issues of security—the 'privatization of security'—requires the adaptation of laws and other legal instruments. On the one hand, legislation is necessary to legalize private security companies, to secure the rights they need in order to be able to perform their tasks legally. On the other hand, it is important that these rights remain limited to the tasks in hand and do not make such agents part of the government's security apparatus. This is not an easy balance to strike, especially in those countries where private security companies are part of the criminal network.

The new approach to security requires new laws, new institutions and a lot of new resources. First and foremost, however, it requires new thinking on the part of the major players. Governments must recognize that they will not be able to guarantee their citizens and businesses the level of security that they legitimately expect and need. Private companies must realize that they need to invest in their own security and beyond, and that such investments can only be effective if they cooperate with the governments concerned.

2. Public–private sector cooperation

Erik Belfrage

I. Introduction: the development of modern terrorism

Security has been an important policy area for private corporations since World War II, although the industries engaged in defence production have had a traditional interest in security issues. The areas of particular interest at that time were industrial espionage, banks and other companies involved in keeping and transporting valuables, and corporations in socially unsafe and turbulent countries or regions.

Corporations in the industrialized world have relied largely on the host state for the provision of security. However, the advent of modern international terrorism in the 1960s and 1970s, and most dramatically the tragic events of 11 September 2001, have radically changed this situation. The newer types of threat are posed by guerrilla movements that have sprung up in Latin America since the 1958 Cuban revolution; organized Palestinian terrorist organizations; violent groups in Northern Ireland, the Basque country and Corsica; as well as leftist movements that pursued their objectives by spreading fear and violence, such as those which were active in Germany and Italy in the 1970s and 1980s.

Modern technology, including technological developments that brought the worldwide establishment of television as the primary information medium, has also radically changed the situation. Terrorism now has a wide theatre stage from which to publicize its goals and spread fear.

Until September 2001, there seemed to be some form of restraint on terrorist activities. Terrorist organizations appeared to be conscious that achieving their goals would imply one day sitting down at the negotiating table to obtain something in return for the cessation of terrorist actions: and there is truth in the saying that 'kidnappers rarely kill their victims'.

Private corporations started to become targets of terrorist acts because they were seen as symbols. They also came to be seen as a source of money to be extorted through kidnappings, a crime which started on a larger scale in Latin America and later spread to Europe.

By the 1980s one could detect a new pattern in terrorist acts, reflecting more ideological, but also more ethnic and religious, motives of a fanatical character. There was a tendency for terrorist incidents to have less of a purely symbolic character, while lethality increased dramatically. The emergence of the al-Qaeda network has further reinforced this trend. It is difficult to identify a concrete or measurable goal that this movement could one day hope to achieve, whether through negotiations or otherwise. The attacks of 11 September 2001 represented a quantum leap in many respects. Only in terms of cost, this single attack event has been estimated to have incurred in direct costs, $40 billion; increased US federal expenditures, $100 billion; tourism losses, $16 billion; airline losses, $15 billion; financial services losses, $77 billion; and other losses $41 billion—a total of $289 billion.[1]

At the corporate level, there have been ripple effects: corporations have begun to move from landmark buildings and city centres, which has resulted in a drop in real estate value. Corporations have further increased their reserve stocks of critical components. The movement of people and goods has become more complicated and more time-consuming, and there has been a shift in investment patterns away from the more 'difficult' parts of the world, thus hitting the less developed regions.

In parallel with these developments in terrorism activity, the accelerating globalization process has dramatically increased the speed of financial exchanges. This has in turn created new opportunities for large-scale fraud and money laundering: hundreds of billions of dollars in 'illegal' money flow annually through the financial system. In 1989 states reacted by creating the Financial Action Task Force on Money Laundering (FATF)—a new type of international cooperation.[2]

At the same time, corporations depend increasingly on intellectual property rights as the fruit of their major investments in research and development. These intellectual property rights must thus also be protected.

The situation today, compared to just a few decades ago, is radically different. States can obviously no longer provide adequate protection in all fields, and corporations have limited resources and ability to reduce this vulnerability. They need to reassess the risks when deciding on investments and future developments. A clear trend can also be seen for corporations to place greater focus on crisis management as a gauge of their increased preparedness in the event of a crisis.

II. The role of private corporations in the provision of security

What is the proper role for corporations in the field of national security and enhanced protection against terrorist attacks? In general, corporations are prepared to help and spend resources in order to prevent those threats that are likely to jeopardize the company in question, but they are also likely to maintain a rather narrow focus on their own firms and disregard general threats against society as a whole. In other words, corporations will continue to monitor a rather narrow perimeter, while leaving responsibility for society and critical infrastructure to government authorities. At the same time, there is cer-

[1] International Chamber of Commerce (ICC) Commercial Crime Services' annual lecture, by Brian Jenkins, 18 June 2003; see 'Don't let the terrorist threat strangle the economy', 19 June 2003, URL <http://www.iccwbo.org/home/news_archives/2003/stories/terrorist.asp>.

[2] The FATF is an intergovernmental body whose purpose is to develop and promote national and international policies to combat money laundering and terrorist financing. It was established in 1989 at the the Paris Summit of the Group of Seven industrialized nations (the G7). For more on the FATF see URL <http://www1.oecd.org/fatf/>; and chapter 4 in this volume.

tainly a greater preparedness on the part of corporations to participate in the fight against terrorism, for instance, by providing information and technical solutions. Corporate actors in the financial industry have the potential and the willingness to improve their cooperation with official bodies on the general problem of money laundering and on the more specific problem of preventing financial resources from falling into the hands of terrorist organizations.

The battle against modern terrorism resembles in many respects the fight started many decades ago against Mafia organizations in the United States and Europe, where the key to success has undoubtedly been *infiltration* as a working method. Corporations and their individual officers could be helpful in this respect as well. A third way forward would be the worldwide implementation of a new system of secure individual identity cards. While many may regard this measure as an infringement of personal integrity, in the long run it could provide an efficient method for denying individuals who lack proper identification access to airlines, official and private buildings, and so forth. Such a measure would, of course, require a significant element of cooperation with the private corporate world.

In general, corporations and their trade associations have access to an enormous amount of information through their customer base. They see and hear a lot that could be useful for the public sector in the battle against terrorism. Modern information technology now facilitates both the compilation of and access to such data in a cost-efficient manner. The private sector might be prepared to share that information with governments—but only, of course, if it receives absolute guarantees against political and other misuse of the data. Associated with private corporations are several services, such as those of auditors, lawyers, real-estate agents and even art dealers, which should also be called upon in the battle against modern terrorism.

An important initiative was taken with the establishment of the Computer Emergency Response Team (CERT) system[3]—a network of national and regional teams throughout the world for the collection and dissemination of information on computer-security threats, vulnerabilities, incidents and incident response. The CERT system functions fairly well and has led to the prevention of serious threats against computer and electronic information systems. Another important initiative would be to create a 'TERT'—a Terrorism Emergency Response Team—for the instant reporting, analysis and monitoring of incidents throughout the world that affect corporate security in a broader sense. Such a system is widely felt to be needed and could also lead to further private–public sector cooperation in the counter-terrorism effort.

---

[3] CERT teams have been established in, e.g., Australia, Canada, Denmark, Japan, Switzerland and the Asia–Pacific (the US Department of Defense also operates a CERT facility). The first team—the CERT Coordination Center (CERT/CC)—is operated by the Software Engineering Institute (SEI) of Carnegie Mellon University, Pittsburgh, Pennsylvania. CERT/CC was formed within the SEI by the Defense Advanced Research Projects Agency (DARPA) in 1988, and in 2003 announced a partnership with the US Department of Homeland Security for the creation of a new US-CERT coordination point. For more on CERT/CC see URL <http://www.cert.org/>. See also chapter 15 in this volume.

Modern terrorism has shown a distinct ability to be 'creative' in the way in which it perpetrates its acts. This creativity must be matched in the fight against terrorism. There need to be new thinking and acting 'out of the box'. In a fundamental sense, the modern economically developed world is growing increasingly vulnerable, and its enemies are well aware of this. Societies have to match their ability to disrupt critical systems by being even more creative and unpredictable in the ways in which they protect and defend these systems.

3. What price values?

Daniel Tarschys

I. The ambivalence of value and the obscurity of price

The title suggested for this chapter, 'What price values?', brings to mind the words of Oscar Wilde, who defined a cynic as 'a man who knows the price of everything and the value of nothing'. A writer in *The Financial Times* recently applied this profound insight to economists rather than to cynics,[1] but that might rather exaggerate the knowledge of prices among economists—who at least seem to quarrel on the topic.

The concept of value or values is in fact a tricky one. It is one of those *faux amis*, or false friends, that mean different things in different languages, in this case the languages of different professions. When a banker hears the word values he does not necessarily think about the same thing as, say, a bishop. Material values exist but so do values in a different sphere—the moral values of ethics and political philosophy.

This is essentially the old philosophical dichotomy of matter and mind. The best guide to that distinction is Bertrand Russell, who answered the question 'what is matter?' by the words 'never mind' and the question 'what is mind?' by 'no matter'.

The issue may be addressed first from the banker's perspective. Bankers are surrounded by values that are difficult to assess—many kinds of assets that are in enterprises or real estate and used as collateral security for credits that the banker hopes to see again some day. Banking is supposed to be easy to evaluate, because there are only two possible outcomes: either the money comes back, or it does not. Even in this context, however, appearances can be deceiving, and many values are not what they appear to be. Bankers could give long lectures on gold that glitters, gold that does not glitter and glitter that is not gold. Such distinctions are apparently important for success in that particular profession.

Today, assets of uncertain value are not a monopoly of the private sector. Soon after the Enron scandal of 2001–2002, one of the world's leading experts on budgeting, Professor Allen Schick, drew comparisons between the accounting standards of Enron and those of various governments. They showed that there was not a single technique in the bookkeeping practices of this corporation that had not been skilfully mastered by public bookkeepers as well.[2]

---

[1] Kay, J., *Financial Times,* 28 Aug. 2003, available at URL <http://www.johnkay.com/in_action/297>.
[2] See Schick, A., 'Fiscal risks and fiscal rules', 21 May 2002, available at URL <http://www1.worldbank.org/publicsector/pe/peamcourse/Schick.pdf>.

SIPRI also knows something about this problem, because it has long been concerned with a type of public assets that are particularly difficult to assess—those traded in arms transfers. An annual figure for the global turnover is given in SIPRI's Yearbook,[3] but it is not an easy figure to arrive at. SIPRI experts know all too well the problems connected with the effects of offset arrangements, deceptive prices and other ways of camouflaging expenditure on cannon just as well as the cannon themselves.

The values changing hands in these transactions do at least have a price, but once they have ended up in a military arsenal somewhere it is very doubtful whether they have a price at all. Counting arms flows is difficult enough, but counting stocks is even more forbidding. What price can be put on a hangarful of jet fighters? What is an army battalion worth these days? What about the cost and value of research and development? What is the value of a half-finished project that may become a success, or a fiasco?

There are several obvious ways of imputing values to military assets, by the cost invested in them or by some intelligent estimate of expected returns, but it is not easy to arrive at meaningful figures. It is becoming no easier with the current tendency, in public finance circles, to move from accounting in cash terms to 'accrual' accounting, which attempts—beyond immediate outlays—to capture the long-term costs and benefits of all possible types of object.

Accrual accounting is not yet practised so much in budgeting, but about a dozen member states of the Organisation for Economic Co-operation and Development (OECD) have started to use it in their financial reporting.[4] This method raises many questions that never required an answer before. What is the Eiffel Tower worth in more precise terms, or the National Archives, or the Houses of Parliament? Who should be charged for using them? Nor does accrual accounting become much easier when it is extended to the military field. Some general-purpose assets can be capitalized and depreciated, but that is tricky with tanks and missiles. What about surplus assets and decommissioned facilities that still cost money to guard although their use value is down to zero, or perhaps even negative? There is still abundant work to be done by future economists in trying to dispel the mysteries surrounding military values and prices—and plenty of work for SIPRI.

II. Values in public policy and in the European institutions

Turning from more material interpretations to the lodestars and lofty ideals known as our common values, it is encouraging to note how this topic is coming increasingly to the forefront and that increasing attention is being paid to moral and political principles in many different settings.

---

[3] Stockholm International Peace Research Institute, *SIPRI Yearbook: Armaments, Disarmament and International Security* (Oxford University Press: Oxford, annual), chapters on international arms transfers.

[4] Blöndal, J. R., 'Accrual accounting and budgeting: key issues and recent developments', *OECD Journal on Budgeting*, vol. 3, no. 1 (2003), pp. 43–60.

In academic circles, there is now much more discussion about the ethical implications of various studies and experiments than there was a few years ago. Many such issues are raised by recent advances in the medical sciences and through their implementation in health care. As an example, the Swedish Government's National Council on Medical Ethics deals with a number of the very tough choices facing policy makers, practitioners and patients.[5] Many similar bodies are wrestling with the same dilemmas, throughout Europe and throughout European national health care systems.

A mounting interest in values can also be seen in the national politics of many countries. In 1998 the Norwegian Government appointed a special Commission on Human Values to contribute to a broad mobilization of Norwegian society for human values.[6] Dutch politics in recent years has not only revolved around the politics of Pim Fortuyn and populism[7] but also around values. The same tendency is to be found in many other countries.

What is perhaps especially interesting for observers in Europe is the increasing attention being paid to the concept of 'common European values'. This may be noted in several settings: in the Council of Europe, in the Organization for Security and Co-operation in Europe (OSCE) and recently in the European Union (EU). The place of values in these three organizations is worth addressing here in greater detail.

The Council of Europe

The Council of Europe is certainly the oldest body dedicated to defending and preaching European values. Its mission included the latter from the very start. The Council of Europe was established in 1949 to help heal the wounds of World War II and re-establish peaceful relations between the nations of the continent. At the top of its initial agenda was the task of restoring and deepening the respect for human rights which had so recently been trampled under foot by the war machines and the totalitarian regimes.

This led first of all to the adoption of the 1950 European Convention for the Protection of Human Rights and Fundamental Freedoms[8] and to the construction of the control machinery today embodied in the European Court of Human Rights, seated in Strasbourg.[9] Important additional protocols were later adopted, such as the Protocol on the Death Penalty, and supplementary conventions such as the 1987 Convention for the Prevention of Torture and Inhuman or Degrading Treatment or Punishment, and the 1997 Convention for

---

[5] See the Internet site of the Swedish National Council on Medical Ethics at URL <http://www.smer.gov.se>.

[6] See the Internet site of the Commission on Human Values at URL <http://www.verdikommisjonen.no/english.htm>.

[7] Fortuyn was the leader of the populist Lijst Pim Fortuyn party, espousing the right-wing radical agenda in the Netherlands. He was assassinated on 6 May 2002, after a strong performance by his party in the run-up to the national elections. See, e.g., BBC News Online, 'Obituary: Pim Fortuyn', URL <http://news.bbc.co.uk/2/hi/europe/1971462.stm>.

[8] The convention is reproduced at URL <http://www.echr.coe.int/Convention/webConvenENG.pdf>.

[9] On the court see URL <http://www.echr.coe.int>.

the Protection of Human Rights and Dignity of the Human Being with regard to the Application of Biology and Medicine (the Bioethics Convention).[10]

The Council of Europe has created many instruments to safeguard human rights and the rule of law, such as the European Commission against Racism and Intolerance (ECRI), which advises governments on their strategies against xenophobia, and the European Committee for the Prevention of Torture and Inhuman or Degrading Treatment or Punishment, which performs on-the-spot inspections in prisons, police stations, psychiatric wards and other places of forcible detention. A third body worth mentioning is the Venice Commission, which supports the constitutional development of countries in transition to democracy.[11]

Pluralist democracy was also a key value promoted from the very outset. The Council of Europe took a clear position against all forms of dictatorship, which earned it extreme resentment from totalitarian and authoritarian regimes but made it attractive to the resistance and dissident movements emerging in Portugal and Spain as well as in countries behind the Iron Curtain. When these countries made their transition to democratic governance there were immediate contacts with the Council of Europe, and in 1989 a special guest status in the Parliamentary Assembly of the Council of Europe was invented to accelerate the prospective reunification of the continent.[12]

A gradual enlargement of the Council of Europe followed in the 1990s, as membership was granted to countries that had taken their first steps towards pluralist democracy and started building or rebuilding their legal systems and judiciary institutions. A long and heated discussion ensued, however, on the question of which countries should qualify, focusing on the concept of European values. It was not easy to agree on how these ideals could best be served: by accepting applicant states which expressed a belief in these ideas and a strong determination to adapt their systems accordingly, or by taking a tougher line which acknowledged their commitment but pointed out that they still had a long way to go and told them to come back when they had really accomplished something. Two alternative strategies for enlargement were at stake: cautious trust, or tough conditionality and uncompromising demands.

The answer came to be somewhere in between. No country was admitted just in return for glib promises, nor was the barrier set so high that they could not get over it. Many countries complained about double standards, and certainly double standards existed. In effect, a variety of thresholds were constructed so as to allow for serious efforts to be rewarded and for progress to be duly recognized. Some negotiations for entry lasted one year, others as long as four years, and during this period an intense dialogue was maintained on European standards in different fields as well as a concrete advice and consul-

---

[10] See URL <http://conventions.coe.int/Treaty/en/Treaties/Html/126.htm>; and URL <http://conventions.coe.int/treaty/en/treaties/html/164.htm>, respectively.

[11] On the ECRI see URL <http://www.coe.int/t/E/human_rights/ecri>; on the European Committee URL <http://www.cpt.coe.int/en>; and on the Venice Commission URL <http://www.venice.coe.int>.

[12] On the Parliamentary Assembly see URL <http://www.radaeuropy.sk/english/documents_coe/parliamentary_assem/assembly.html>.

tations to promote desirable reforms. A Swiss representative in the Council of Europe Parliamentary Assembly coined the description of this strategy as a two-handed formula ('der Herrgott hat uns zwei Hände gegeben'[13]): one to bang on the table or to wave as a clenched fist in protest against unacceptable violations, and the other to welcome and reach out to help.

Within the old member states, there were those who were apprehensive that the soul of the Council of Europe would be lost through this rapid enlargement process. However, a solid majority came to be convinced that European values could be efficiently promoted through a combination of intense cooperation and continued vigilance. On this basis, inclusion could be considered better than exclusion.

Second thoughts may be justified regarding some details of the schedule of accessions, but it would not be right to conclude that European values suffered in this process—quite the opposite. If the history of the Council of Europe is examined and its five completed decades compared, it would be hard to claim that any of them devoted so much attention to the core values of human rights, democracy and the rule of law as did the period after 1989.

The rule of law is a broad notion, but one of its central components is the building of reliable judiciary institutions and adequate responses to insecur-ity—which is in the broader sense the topic of this volume. One of the key tasks undertaken in the process of enlargement of the Council of Europe has been to support the efforts of the new member states to upgrade their capacity in this field and to strengthen their defences against crime in various forms. Some 20 conventions and over 100 recommendations of the Council of Europe are related to this objective, including extradition rules and measures against corruption and money laundering.

In the course of these developments the very concept of European values revealed itself as something of a conundrum. What values?, people asked. Had not some of the worst crimes in world history been committed by Europeans? What about the gulags, the Holocaust and the colonial massacres? The answer is of course that the notion of values is normative, not descriptive. The issue is not the actual behaviour of Europeans in the past, but rather the principles and standards that enlightened Europeans have agreed upon to constitute their guidelines for the future. Even today there are serious violations of these prin-ciples, with European governments among the sinners. The various supervi-sion mechanisms within the Council of Europe exist to deal with such prob-lems, sometimes supplemented by targeted forms of assistance to governments that are trying to tackle them on the home front.

A second question often raised in the past decade referred to the geographi-cal component in the concept. Are there really 'European' values as distinct from US values or Asian values? The answer needs to be divided into two parts. One the one hand, the normative core of mankind's common values cor-responds to a set of universal principles laid down in the 1948 United Nations

---

[13] Literally, 'The Lord God has given us two hands'.

Universal Declaration of Human Rights and UN Covenants.[14] Human rights are essentially universal, even though Europeans have added some accents of their own. On the other hand, an empirical attempt could be made to try to learn what people in different continents really believe in. This would in fact find some differences. According to the European Values Survey, 86 per cent of Europeans say that they prefer a democratic political system. The corresponding figure for Africa, Asia and South America is much lower, mostly under 50 per cent.[15] What can also be found in Europe is strong support for the welfare state (almost 70 per cent) and relatively strong support for the market economy (56 per cent in the current EU member states and 61 per cent in Eastern Europe). A certain shift can also be seen 'from traditional values (law and order, material security, rigid social norms) to post-material values (self expression, quality of life, tolerance and openness'.[16]

So far as the Council of Europe is concerned, the point to note is that values could be kept centre-stage in its work because most of the economic problems were being handled somewhere else. Many of the instruments invented by the Council exist to defend and promote core European values, and that is why the commitment to such values was always an important condition for membership.

The Organization for Security and Co-operation in Europe

The OSCE has hardly any value-related accession criteria since this body embraces all the states in the wider Europe, plus Canada and the United States. Nevertheless, there is a proud history of value promotion in this organization as well. In the Helsinki Final Act of 1975,[17] the recognition of human rights was given a prominent place. Even if the regimes of the Soviet bloc had no intention at the time of honouring these solemn commitments, but accepted them mainly for other purposes—not least the recognition of established borders—they were soon reminded of them by dissident movements in their own societies. Helsinki Watch (now part of Human Rights Watch), the Helsinki Human Rights Committee and Charta 77 were all built on the idea of confronting tyrants with their own pledges.[18] It was a daring enterprise but eventually quite fruitful, in that the pledges survived the tyrants.

---

[14] See URL <http://www.un.org/Overview/rights.html>.

[15] European Commission, 'Evolution of values and deep-seated attitudes in Europe', Background paper for the Athens meeting, 18 Apr. 2003, Round Table on A Sustainable Project for Europe, URL <http://europa.eu.int/comm/dgs/policy_advisers/experts_groups/gsk_docs/background_paper_athens_en. pdf>.

[16] European Commission (note 15), p. 2.

[17] See URL <http://www.osce.org/docs/english/1990-1999/summits/helfa75e.htm>.

[18] On Helsinki Watch see URL <http://www.hrw.org>; on Charta 77 URL <http://www.bariery. cz/en/nadace>; and on the Helsinki Human Rights Committee URL <http://www.geocities.com/ CapitolHill/Senate/1447/RIGHTS9.HTM>.

The European Communities and the European Union

The third and largest of these European bodies was for a long time the least value-oriented of them all. For much of their early decades, the European Communities (EC) concentrated almost exclusively on trade, customs, investments, competition and monetary matters, with very little time for such issues as human rights or the expansion of democracy. These matters did, however, arise in the external relations of the EC, as objectives for development cooperation or as conditions for trade concessions, but for a long time they played no significant role in the EC's internal affairs. They appeared in the 'Copenhagen criteria' for the enlargement of the EU to include Central European applicants[19] and in the 'third pillar' of justice and home affairs cooperation added through the 1992 Maastricht Treaty,[20] but it is really only in the past few years that any real breakthrough has been made towards a strong value orientation in the EU.

The situation in 2003 is quite different. An obvious example is the EU Charter of Fundamental Rights, which will most likely become the second part of the new constitution.[21] At the first European Convention, where this Charter was worked out, many interventions called for a shift in emphasis in the Union from purely economic concerns towards moral standards and political principles. 'Die Union ist nicht nur Wirtschaft und Währung, sondern auch Werte'[22]—that was how this idea was expressed in German, with better alliteration than any other language could offer. This conviction was widely embraced by the participants in the first convention.

Now that the second (constitutional) European Convention has concluded its work, it is evident that this reorientation is supported broadly. There seems to be a growing consensus that mutual economic benefits are not enough to keep the Union together, and that it also needs some sort of spiritual dimension. Spiritual does not have to mean religious—that is another discussion—but it should convey at least an attachment to moral and political principles, to a set of common ideals embodied in the European socio-economic model: perhaps best summed up as freedom combined with social justice.

This may prove to be only the beginning of a new departure for the EU. This body—a difficult one to describe because it is already more than an international organization but still less than a state (an 'unidentified political object', in the words of Jacques Delors)—is on the verge of the fourth stage of

---

[19] The accession criteria for new EU members were adopted by the Copenhagen European Council in 1993; they are available at URL <http://europa.eu.int/comm/enlargement/intro/criteria.htm>.

[20] The text of the Treaty on European Union (Maastricht Treaty) is available at URL <http://europa. en.int/abc/obj/treaties/en/entoc01.htm>.

[21] The text of the Charter of Fundamental Rights of the European Union is available in *Official Journal of the European Communities,* C 364/19 (18 Dec. 2000), also available at URL <http://www. europarl.eu.int/charter/pdf/text_en.pdf>. The European Convention, created to discuss the future of the EU in 2002–2003, recommended the incorporation of the Charter in the draft Treaty establishing a Constitution for Europe which it produced in July 2003; see URL <http://european-convention.eu.int/docs/Treaty/cv00850.en03.pdf>.

[22] 'The Union is not just about economy and currency, but also about values.'

its historic development. The Common Market, the Internal Market and the Monetary Union have more or less been completed, but the next project—the Citizens' Europe—is still only on the drawing board. For those who want European integration to continue, it is precisely in the sphere of values that there is much more work to be done.

Something called 'cohesion policy' does exist in Europe, but that has so far been a specific undertaking mainly emphasizing the economic development of more backward areas. That is all very well, but if Europeans are serious about cohesion there are many other things to do in such important fields as culture, education, mass communication and the preservation of our heritage. Should the EU embark now on a serious policy for European cohesion, it would need not just to borrow part of the agenda of the Council of Europe but to implement it on a much wider scale—which would require a major reshuffle of its resources.[23]

III. Envoi

This brings the argument back to its starting point. What price values? What kind of sacrifices should Europeans (and others) be prepared to make in order to promote common ideals and to strengthen the rule of law, the respect for human rights and the consolidation of democracy, in Europe and around the globe? These objectives should surely be placed high on the policy agenda, whether from the standpoint of economic considerations, security considerations or simply the desire to live in a better world. Mind and matter point in the same direction: whether from materialistic motives or idealistic conviction, we arrive ultimately at the same end station. Prices need to be known and correctly calculated, otherwise economies would grind to a halt. Principles and convictions need to be taken just as seriously. If the world wants to keep its communities, countries and continents together, there is no alternative to basing them on a set of common values.

---

[23] See Tarschys, D., *Reinventing Cohesion: The Future of European Structural Policy*, Report no. 17 (Swedish Institute for European Policy Studies: Stockholm, 2003), available at URL <http://www.sieps.su.se/_pdf/Publikationer/200317.pdf>.

Part II

Cutting off resources for terrorism and crime:
the global and European dimensions

Editors' remarks

The chapters in this part of the volume focus on phenomena and policy challenges which, if not wholly new, have been more sharply illuminated and pushed up the priority scale by the events of 11 September 2001. Transnational terrorism has become a purveyor of mass death and destruction, and the common enemy of states, private enterprises and whole societies. Writing from a mixture of official, private-sector and analytical perspectives, the authors here group their reflections around two main questions. Do we know what terrorism is and what is the right way to fight it? Have we gone far enough, or perhaps too far, in enlisting private financial institutions and other branches of business as allies in the campaign?

The difficulty of the first question lies partly in the fact that modern-day terrorism takes many forms, while 'terror tactics' may be resorted to by an even wider range of actors. The means needed to detect and defeat a network-based, multi-target organization such as al-Qaeda are not the same as for the more familiar, territorially based and 'single-issue' breed of terrorists that the world has known for centuries. As Vadim Volkov points out, 'When states try to define this [trans-national] type of enemy in terms that reflect their own image, they are likely to fail or waste resources'. Private-sector organizations may come closer to the systemic models adopted by terrorists, and so have a better chance of understanding them: but their own long communication lines and multinational patterns of interdependence unfortunately only make them more vulnerable to attack. A second problem is that there is no single accepted international definition of terrorism or single list of terrorist organizations and persons which lends itself to all the different purposes of anti-terrorist activity. This is coming to matter more, the more the international community develops its responses in the shape of formal, often legally binding, regulations demanding the compliance of public- and private-sector entities alike.

The help of the private sector is needed precisely because modern terrorists, and the traffickers in mass destruction materials and technologies who might supply them, operate in a sub-state underworld together with drug peddlers, money launderers and criminals of other kinds. State and interstate action alone, including the coercive use of military power, has great difficulty in hitting or at least in destroying such targets. Hence the new wave of national and international measures taken since 2001 to regulate private-sector financial transfers, and tighten strategic export controls, in the hope of blocking the supply of money and materials to terrorist recipients. The logic of such approaches—to manipulate globalized processes against those who would abuse the freedoms of globalization—is impeccable, and they have already borne some fruit: although there is still some way to go (as the chapter on the European Union shows) to coordinate all relevant intra-institutional resources and extra-institutional relationships. For business, however, the consequential burdens are heavy in both material and psychological terms. As Georges Baur puts it, 'More security for the financial centre leads to more insecurity for the individual financial intermediary'. The authors stress the difficulties created when states and institutions define prohibited materials and destinations in unclear, out-of-date or inconsistent terms. They also point out the unfairness of blaming business for contributing to 'new threats' before the official world has even defined them as threats. Their plea that business should be used less as a tool, and more as an adviser and true partner, is echoed in other parts of this book.

4. An international response to terrorism

Claes Norgren

I. Introduction

Terrorism has for a long time plagued countries throughout the world. In Europe, for example, the Euskadi ta Askatasuna (ETA, Basque Fatherland and Liberty) Basque separatists, the Irish Republican Army (IRA) and the Red Army Fraction (RAF) operated and spread fear in the late 20th century. The attacks on the United States on 11 September 2001, however, clearly changed perspectives on terrorism. These events represented a new and important development, not only politically but in a number of other dimensions as well.

The United States' reaction to the attacks was clear and strong. In his address to Congress on 20 September 2001, President George W. Bush declared that 'enemies of freedom committed an act of war against our country'. Outlining his prescription for the US response, the president stated: 'Our war on terror begins with al Qaeda, but it does not end there.... Our response involves far more than instant retaliation and isolated strikes.... We will starve terrorists of funding, turn them one against another, drive them from place to place, until there is no refuge or no rest'.[1] The international community was also quick to respond to the attacks. The United Nations, the North Atlantic Treaty Organization (NATO) and other international organizations soon engaged themselves in an enhanced effort to combat terrorism.

The threats of terrorism must be seen in a broad context, and it is important to have a multilateral approach to dealing with them. A strategic part of such an effort is the countering of terrorist financing. The Financial Action Task Force on Money Laundering (FATF) has an important role to play in this area.[2]

---

[1] See White House, 'Address to a joint session of Congress and the American people', URL <http://www.whitehouse.gov/news/releases/2001/09/20010920-8.html>.

[2] The FATF (see URL <http://www.fatf-gafi.org/>) is an ad hoc group comprised of the member states of the Organisation for Economic Co-operation and Development (OECD; see URL <http://www.oecd.org/>) and several other major countries. Its secretariat is at the OECD in Paris. The FATF has developed international standards for combating money laundering and terrorist financing. The member countries, territories and organizations of the FATF are: Argentina, Australia, Austria, Belgium, Brazil, Canada, Denmark, Finland, France, Germany, Greece, Hong Kong, China, Iceland, Ireland, Italy, Japan, Luxembourg, Mexico, the Netherlands, New Zealand, Norway, Portugal, Russia, Singapore, South Africa, Spain, Sweden, Switzerland, Turkey, the UK and the USA, as well as the European Commission and the Gulf Co-operation Council. A number of international bodies and organizations have observer status in the FATF. See also chapters 5, 7 and 8 in this volume.

II. Terrorism: a threat to the international community

Terrorism old and new

The September 2001 events have placed the problems of terrorism high on the political agenda. The US declaration of a war against terrorism triggered a wave of national and international reactions. It is clearly wrong to see terrorism, as such, as a new phenomenon. It has, however, become an important problem for the international community because of the way in which modern societies function.

Some would question whether today's terrorist threats constitute a 'new' type of terrorism, pointing to the facts that such conflicts have existed in many regions and that several features of modern terrorism are not different from the historical terrorism motivated by religion and sects.[3] Others take the view that the current form of terrorism, typified by al-Qaeda, is new because it does not pursue clearly defined political goals, but rather aims at the destruction of society and the elimination of large segments of the population. Another extreme example is the Aum Shinrikyo (Supreme Truth) cult in Japan.[4]

In any event, terrorism has spread geographically and has entered a period of increased violence and bloodshed. The conflicts in the Middle East have increased in violence at the same time as there have been new types of violence, such as the bombing of the New York World Trade Center in 1993, the gas attack with sarin in the Tokyo underground system and the bombing of the Murrah Federal Building in Oklahoma City in 1995, and, finally, the attacks of 11 September 2001.

Terrorism in a new environment

Today's terrorism poses a significant threat to the open, globalized international community. This threat is different from previous terrorist threats, just as the world itself has changed dramatically.

Technology has enabled new means of communication, transport and interaction, which terrorists can also use and exploit. Globalization has been propelled not only by these developments but also by the opening up of transnational business and the reduction of inhibiting controls. It is in the wake of globalization that terrorism has developed new channels and new means. Even terrorism has become globalized.

Furthermore, the threats are different because the harm that can be caused is more severe. Technology has developed new military capabilities, such as nuclear, biological and chemical (NBC) weapons, which are available not only

---

[3] Norell, M., 'Den "nya" terrorismen', eds M. Norell and K. Ströberg, *Tankar om Terrorism: Två Studier Kring ett Modernt Fenomen* [Thoughts on terrorism: two studies of a modern phenomenon], FOI-R-0494-SE (Totalförsvarets forskningsinstitut (FOI, Swedish Defence Research Agency): Stockholm, 2002), (in Swedish).

[4] Henderson, H., *Terrorism* (Facts on File: New York, 2001).

to governments but also to terrorists. These new 'mass destruction' capabilities are a growing reality. While there is room for argument over how realistic and serious these threats are, the need to reckon with the possibility that terrorists may inflict major damage has already changed the environment in which they operate. Similarly, the communication networks which modern military technology offers for governments can also be disrupted by terrorist groups. The term 'cyber terrorism' represents a new and growing concern.[5]

The economic and financial environment in which terrorism operates today has also changed. Modern financial markets, with free movement of capital, react swiftly to changed perceptions of risk. Terrorist threats are thus an important new reality with greater potential economic impact than before. The risks of terrorist attacks are now continuously assessed in financial markets, and the perception of a sudden increased threat can make stock prices and exchange rates fall. The implication of this is that the threat today takes on wider dimensions, with correspondingly grave economic consequences.

Globalization thus provides a new environment in which the role of terrorism must be reviewed. It has led to positive effects in many ways but markets are not, on their own, capable of meeting collective needs. In economic terms, the risk or threat of terrorism is such a collective need. If these risks are not dealt with, the economic and financial effects could be serious. Moreover, the costs associated with such risks are not evenly distributed between countries. George Soros has published an interesting analysis:

Contrary to the tenets of market fundamentalism, financial markets do not tend toward equilibrium; they are crisis-prone. Since 1980, there have been a number of devastating financial crises, but whenever the center is threatened, the authorities take decisive action in order to protect the system. As a consequence, the devastation is confined to the periphery. This has made countries at the center not only wealthier but also more stable.[6]

State-sponsored terrorism is another component of the new environment. The end of the cold war led to the emergence of new states and new political realities. Some governments use terrorists as cost-effective instruments. A so-called 'guns for hire terrorism' has raised concern. The US Department of State has listed seven countries as sponsors of terrorism: Cuba, Iran, Iraq, Libya, North Korea, Sudan and Syria.[7]

The end of the cold war created new and fragile governments in a number of countries where the relationships between organized crime and organized political groups are among the causes of concern. Some countries rely heavily on the production and sale of drugs at the same time as they need arms to con-

---

[5] Alexander, Y. and Swetnam, M. S., *Usama bin Laden's al-Qaida: Profile of a Terrorist Network* (Transnational: Ardsley, N.Y., 2001). See also chapter 16 in this volume.

[6] Soros, G., *The Bubble of American Supremacy: Correcting the Misuse of American Power* (PublicAffairs: New York, 2003).

[7] US Department of State, Office of the Coordinator for Counterterrorism, 'Patterns of global terrorism: overview of state-sponsored terrorism', 30 Apr. 2003, URL <http://www.state.gov/s/ct/rls/pgtrpt/2002/html/19988.htm>; see also Hoffman, B., *Inside Terrorism* (Gollancz: London, 1998).

trol their territory. This close link creates a dangerous element. Problems related to the illegal trade in weapons and drugs and the use of the financial system for money laundering are another component of this new environment.

These new threats expose societies to what could be called a double asymmetric dilemma. First, societies are exposed to asymmetric warfare because of the threat of massive, high-impact surprise attacks on societies by non-state, transnational groups. Second, terrorists who live in the logic of war confront societies that live in peace and are confined to peacetime instruments. This creates a dilemma, since non-democratic means cannot be used to take action, but this risks making the efforts to counter the threats less efficient.

Today terrorism poses new and more serious threats not only to countries but also to the international community as a whole. At the same time as these new and more dangerous forms of terrorism have emerged, the more local and territorially defined terrorist problems continue to be a threat. Terrorism constitutes a more complex and broad range of threats than ever before. There is thus a clear case for the international community to react to these new conditions. In doing so, it must first examine the new nature of the threat and design adequate measures to counter it. This calls for enhanced international support and cooperation.

The need for a new definition of terrorism

In order to be able to respond to the new challenges, it is important to have a common view on how to define the problem. Since the magnitude of the problem has grown and the threats are more collective in nature, the international community would benefit from a common approach to taking appropriate measures. If there is not a consensus, it will be difficult to mobilize the international community for any serious action.

There are a number of different views on the definition and interpretation of the problems.

The US Central Intelligence Agency adopted a broad definition of terrorism which has been accepted by the US State Department: 'The threat or use of violence for political purposes by individuals or groups, whether acting for or in opposition to establish governmental authority, when such actions are intended to shock, stun, or intimidate a target group wider than the immediate victims'.[8]

Another definition has been offered by James Adams: 'A terrorist is an individual or member of a group that wishes to achieve political ends using violent means, often at the cost of casualties to innocent civilians and with the support of only a minority of the people they claim to represent'.[9]

---

[8] For a list of such definitions of international terrorism see ASEAN Mass Communication Studies and Research Center (AMS@R), 'A selection of recent academic and governmental definitions', URL <http://www.utcc.ac.th/amsar/about/document7.html>.

[9] Adams, J., *The Financing of Terror* (New English Library: Sevenoaks, Kent, 1986).

Bruce Hoffman distinguishes terrorists from other criminals by viewing terrorism as political in its aims and motives, violent, designed to have far-reaching psychological repercussions beyond the immediate target, conducted by an organization with an identifiable chain of command or conspiratorial cell structure, and perpetrated by a sub-national group or non-state entity.[10]

The UN General Assembly adopted Resolution 54/109 against the financing of terrorism in 1999.[11] This resolution used a generic definition of terrorists. The resolution provided that any person commits an offence 'if the person . . . provides or collects funds with the intention that they should be used or in the knowledge that they are to be used . . . in order to carry out . . . an act which constitutes an offence within the scope of and as defined in one of the treaties in the annex of the resolution'.

To some, these different definitions and views on how to define terrorism are a major shortcoming. Clearly, the generic UN definition offers room for different views on its nature, but it can be argued that it is necessary to have such a definition to mobilize significant support. Individual countries might have different views on definitions: India, for example, views the conflicts in Kashmir as manifestations of terrorism, and Russia regards the Chechens as terrorists. Other countries might view certain organizations as terrorists. As long as the common denominator carries a sufficient critical mass of consensus, however, this does not matter.

The UN definition is generic in nature and has the advantage, or drawback, of being dependent on a sufficient level of consensus of what terrorism is. This further increases the importance of a multilateral approach to terrorism. What is needed is perhaps not a new definition but a consensus on the problem.

III. Countering terrorism

There are several, not mutually exclusive, ways in which terrorism can be countered. The first and perhaps the most immediate reaction by governments is to use the agencies of law enforcement and military capabilities. This can be seen as a targeted instrumental and reactive response to the problems, involving measures to eliminate the activities of the people and organizations that carry out terrorism. The detection and prevention of terrorist acts certainly call for this type of enforcement, but it is seldom sufficient.

A second measure is to proactively take political action in order to affect the environment in which terrorists operate. This can involve cooperation with other governments and the international community. It can also involve a long-term effort to proactively eliminate the social problems that can give rise to terrorism.

---

[10] Hoffman (note 7).

[11] UN General Assembly Resolution 54/109, 9 Dec. 1999, available at URL <http://www.un.org/law/cod/finterr.htm>; in this resolution the UN adopted the International Convention for the Suppression of the Financing of Terrorism.

A third type of measure is to apply general controls and restrict certain freedoms in order to take action against those who misuse this freedom. The control of borders and air transport has recently increased. Such limitations are, however, clearly problematic in today's globalized world. Reducing the freedom to travel and the integrity and privacy of the individual entails great risks. The political and economic costs associated with such action are clearly high.

A fourth type of measure is to counter terrorists via the funds they need to finance their operations. This type of measure has been successfully used in the campaign against drugs; and after the events of 11 September 2001, it has been an increasingly important part of the effort to combat terrorism.

IV. Measures to counter terrorist financing

The USA acted quickly after the September 2001 attacks. On 24 September President Bush released Executive Order 13224 on Terrorist Financing, in which he declared that the events constituted an unusual and extraordinary threat to the United States' national security, foreign policy and economy.[12] He therefore declared a national emergency. Furthermore, he ordered that all the property of listed suspected terrorists should be blocked in the United States.

It was immediately clear that these events were not only relevant for the USA. They caused severe problems and disruptions in financial markets throughout the world. The international community was alerted to this new and major threat and took action. Countering terrorist financing was declared a priority.

At an extraordinary plenary meeting on 29–30 October 2001, the FATF expanded its mandate beyond anti-money laundering and decided to develop standards for the countering of terrorism financing through the adoption of the Eight Special Recommendations on Terrorist Financing.[13] This new direction of work for the FATF fell within the logic of the approach it had developed in the area of money laundering. The techniques used to launder money are essentially the same as those used to conceal the sources of, and uses for, terrorist financing. Although funds used to support terrorism may originate from legitimate sources, criminal activities, or both, the problems and the remedies were similar.

The FATF Eight Special Recommendations

As with the 1999 UN General Assembly resolution, the FATF does not define the term 'financing of terrorism' in detail in the Eight Special Recommenda-

---

[12] White House, Office of the Press Secretary, 'Executive Order on Terrorist Financing: blocking property and prohibiting transactions with persons who commit, threaten to commit, or support terrorism', 24 Sep. 2001, URL <http://www.whitehouse.gov/news/releases/2001/09/20010924-1.html>.

[13] For the Eight Special Recommendations see URL <http://www.fatf-gafi.org/>.

tions. Rather, it urges countries to ratify and implement the 1999 International Convention for the Suppression of the Financing of Terrorism.[14]

The FATF Special Recommendations include the criminalization of terrorist financing; measures to freeze and seize terrorist assets; international cooperation in criminal investigations, including the sharing of information; increased control of alternative remittance systems; and adequate information on wire transfers. More specifically, the Recommendations stipulate the following.

1. Each country should implement measures to freeze the funds or other assets of terrorists and terrorist organizations in accordance with UN resolutions on the prevention and suppression of the financing of terrorist acts.

2. Each country should take action to ensure that individuals and legal entities that provide for the transmission of value, including transmission through an informal money value transfer system or network, are licensed or registered and subject to the same standards as apply to banks and non-bank financial institutions.

3. Each country should take measures to require financial institutions, including money remitters, to provide accurate and meaningful originator information. The information should remain with the transfer throughout the payment chain in order to assist in investigations. Such financial institutions should conduct enhanced scrutiny and monitoring of suspicious transactions.

4. Each country should review the adequacy of its laws and regulations regarding non-profit organizations in order to determine whether they can be used for terrorist financing purposes. The goal is to avoid the misuse of non-profit organizations by terrorists.

The FATF members have made a clear political commitment to implement the Eight Special Recommendations. Since the Special Recommendations are general in nature, the FATF has issued Interpretative Notes and Best Practice Guidelines. The Eight Special Recommendations, together with the Forty Recommendations on Money Laundering as revised in 2003,[15] now provide a comprehensive and consistent framework for enforcement. On a number of fronts, the international community has responded quickly and taken action: Legislation has been put in place; awareness has been raised; and illegal funds have been detected, frozen and confiscated.

Cooperation between the FATF and international financial institutions

In order to enhance the assessment of countries' compliance with the FATF Recommendations, a programme for cooperation between the FATF and the International Monetary Fund (IMF) and the World Bank was developed in

---

[14] See note 11.

[15] For the 20 June 2003 Forty Recommendations on Money Laundering and the Interpretative Notes see URL <http://www.fatf-gafi.org/>.

2002. The programme included a common assessment methodology and cooperation at the practical level.

In this programme the FATF, with the IMF and the World Bank, managed to broaden their outreach and develop the assessment methodology. Although the programme touched upon sensitivities within the IMF and the World Bank, it proved possible to implement it as intended, and the resulting cooperation—now being evaluated—will most likely be made permanent.

Assessment of technical assistance needs

In order to better direct technical assistance to countries with underdeveloped structures, the FATF has responded to requests from the international donor community under the Counter-Terrorism Action Group (CTAG) of the Group of Eight (G8) industrialized nations.[16] The FATF is carrying out assessments, in the area of terrorist financing and, with certain countries, of their need for technical assistance.

The use of technical assistance is a productive means for reducing collective risks and strengthening the resilience of financial markets and law enforcement. This has been a successful priority for the IMF and the World Bank in their work.[17]

V. Success or failure?

More than two years after the September 2001 attacks, it is important to assess the results of the efforts to combat terrorism and terrorist financing. No overall assessment has been carried out yet, but it is interesting to look at the evidence thus far.

The US Federal Bureau of Investigation (FBI) describes the results and the progress that have been achieved in the following way: 'Since September 11, 2001, more than 3,000 Al-Qa'ida leaders and foot soldiers have been taken into custody around the globe; nearly 200 suspected terrorist associates have been charged with crimes in the U.S.; and as many as a hundred terrorist attacks or plots have been broken up worldwide'.[18]

Other observers point to the weaknesses in the implementation of international standards; differences between countries in the attitudes and approaches to terrorism; and the problems associated with chasing small-scale transfers by terrorists, which can be like finding a needle in a haystack.

In accordance with UN Security Council Resolution 1455, the UN Monitoring Group released a report on the implementation of measures in December

---

[16] On the CTAG see also chapter 5 in this volume.

[17] It was also a feature built into the work of the new UN Counter-Terrorism Committee: see chapter 5 in this volume.

[18] See Federal Bureau of Investigation (FBI), 'FBI counterterrorism', URL <http://www.fbi.gov/terrorinfo/counterterrorism/waronterrorhome.htm>.

2003.[19] The focus was on measures related to al-Qaeda, the Taliban, and related individuals and entities. The main conclusions were that progress is being made worldwide, by law enforcement agencies and military and security forces, in dealing with al-Qaeda. Progress has also been made in cutting off al-Qaeda financing: a large part of its funds have been located and frozen, although many sources have not been identified and al-Qaeda continues to receive funding. Extensive use is being made of alternative remittance systems: al-Qaeda has shifted much of its financial activity to areas in Africa, the Middle East and South-East Asia. This report notes that controlling charities so that they cannot be misused by terrorists has proved to be extremely difficult.

The report also notes that 'shell companies' and offshore trusts are being used to conceal the identity of individuals engaged in the financing of terrorism. This is further complicated by a reluctance on the part of states to freeze tangible assets, such as business and property. In general, critical views have been expressed in many countries about the risk that measures will be too intrusive and infringe individual rights.

To make an overall assessment of the effectiveness of policies, it is crucial to define the objectives. Clearly, the overall objective in this case is to minimize the risk of terrorist attacks. As a means to achieve that overall objective, the FATF has established standards, monitors implementation and contributes to technical assistance. Other international organizations and national governments have other means to achieve the overall objective.

When assessing policy impact, a number of further points must be kept in mind. First, international standards need to be promptly implemented. Implementation of core legislation has generally been prompt and swift. However, it is clear that the implementation of more precise and thorough regulations is taking time and that it suffers from important differences in legal approach. Second, the reporting of suspicious transactions related to terrorist financing is an important input for national authorities. This reporting is not currently compiled on a global basis, and the reporting systems function unevenly from one country to another. Some countries have a much lower volume of reporting than could reasonably be expected. Third, the quality and quantity of international cooperation seem to have improved through the efforts of the FATF and other organizations.

In terms of frozen or seized assets, the amounts reported hitherto are not impressive when they are compared with the normal volume of financial business. However, the assets needed to finance terrorism are often rather small. The amounts frozen in the USA are far greater than in the European Union

---

[19] United Nations, 'Letter from the Chairman of the Security Council Committee established pursuant to Resolution 1267 (1999) concerning Al-Qaida and the Taliban and associated individuals to the President of the Security Council', UN document S/2003/1070, 2 Dec. 2003, available at URL <http://www.un.org/Docs/sc/committees/1267/1267SelectedEng.htm>. UN Security Council Resolution 1455, 17 Jan. 2003, is available at URL <http://www.un.org/documents/scres.htm>.

(EU), partly because some EU countries lack efficient regimes for freezing assets.

It is too early to judge how cases that have been dealt with or sanctions that have been implemented by national authorities will evolve. It seems clear, however, that terrorists are adjusting their behaviour and have started to diversify the risk of being detected by changing their channels of money transfer. Such behaviour is to be expected and has already been demonstrated in the case of money laundering. Reports also note that al-Qaeda now operates in a more decentralized way and needs less money to operate.

The level of terrorist activity is also difficult to assess. Some argue that al-Qaeda continues to receive ample funding not only to carry out its own activities but also to finance affiliated terrorist groups and to acquire new weapons. In any event, the level of terrorist activity has been deemed sufficiently high to warrant the US authorities' raising of the level of threat in December 2003 from 'code yellow' (elevated risk of terrorist attacks) to 'code orange' (high risk of attack).[20]

VI. The way forward

Measures have been put in place to counter terrorist financing, but much more remains to be done. A clear indication of a will to do more was expressed by the finance ministers of the Group of Seven (G7) industrialized nations and the heads of central banks at their September 2003 meeting in Dubai.[21] Together with representatives from the Islamic world, they met to discuss problems related to the use of informal payment systems for the financing of terrorism. The meeting concluded that further work is needed and that the G7 should focus on the problems associated with these new informal channels of money transfer to terrorists.

Another indication of will is presented in a December 2003 UN report which points to the need to strengthen both the measures and their application.[22] The suggestion put forward was to draft a tougher and more comprehensive UN resolution.

In addition, the FATF is continuing to assess its policies. In this context, the efforts to improve the efficiency of measures to combat terrorist financing should be guided by the following three principles.

1. The international community should be united in its objectives and understandings in the fight against terrorist financing.

---

[20] See US Department of Homeland Security, 'Threats & protection: Homeland Security Advisory System', URL <http://www.dhs.gov/dhspublic/display?theme=29>.

[21] See 'Statement of G7 finance ministers and central bank governors', Dubai, 20 Sep. 2003, URL <http://www.g7.utoronto.ca/finance/fm030920.htm>.

[22] See United Nations (note 19), Enclosure, 'Second Report of the Monitoring Group established pursuant to Security Council Resolution 1363 (2001) and extended by resolutions 1390 (2002) and 1455 (2003), on sanctions against Al-Qaida, the Taliban and individuals and entities associated with them'.

2. Terrorist financing should be seen as a central issue in the fight against terrorism.

3. There should be no safe hiding place for terrorist funds.

In order to improve the international system, governments need to improve their own systems. At the international level the FATF needs to continue its efforts in the area of developing standards and assessing implementation. Another important but difficult issue is how to take measures against national systems that do not comply with the standards.

Improved implementation of standards

The current system for sharing information on terrorists via the UN lists has a number of weaknesses.[23] Although these lists are important, those individuals who feature on the lists are not likely to be active terrorists after they have been identified. The most important task is therefore to facilitate smooth cooperation and information exchange between law enforcement authorities.

This raises the question of how to take action when there is a lack of implementation of and compliance with standards. The solution thus far has been peer pressure and technical assistance. More formal measures, such as a 'naming and shaming' exercise, have not been on the international agenda. If the implementation of current measures does not improve further, discussion along those lines might develop in a longer perspective.

Enhanced efforts to address informal transfers of funds

The transfer of funds through informal systems, organizations and by other means continues to pose an obstacle to the efficient countering of terrorist financing. Alternative remittance systems, non-profit organizations and cash couriers are the prime concern.

The FATF has set standards for alternative remittance systems in the Eight Special Recommendations. The objective is to stop the misuse of systems such as hawalas for informal transfer of terrorist funds.[24] However, the standards allow for very different applications and the question is whether these standards properly address the current challenges. In many countries the hawala system is important for illiterate workers, and it is a major channel where normal banks do not operate.

Attitudes towards the regulation of these systems differ in many respects. In some countries hawalas are licensed and supervised, while regulation is poor or non-existing in other jurisdictions. For the international community there is a delicate balance to strike in this area. If over-strong measures are imposed

---

[23] For more on the UN lists of suspected terrorists see chapter 5 in this volume.

[24] On the hawala system see also chapter 5 in this volume.

against informal channels, there is a risk that they will go underground. If measures are not strong enough, terrorists will exploit the loopholes.

Non-profit organizations may be misused as a cover for illegal activities, such as terrorist financing. However, in many countries they are an integral part of the social welfare system, providing a safety net for the poor. A number of both social and religious aspects must be taken into account in attempts to stop any illegal activities with which they may be associated. Also in this area, the FATF has set up international standards. While implementation of the standards thus far seems to have been less effective, the 2003 G7 Dubai high-level meeting discussed these problems together with possible remedies. It was argued that there should be strong surveillance of charities on the basis of the requirements for good corporate governance. Applying such measures is important and should be a cooperative effort.

The issue of cash couriers has also been raised as a pressing problem. This is clearly not a new phenomenon but, in the light of the problems that terrorism poses, it needs to be seen from a new perspective. There are reports that some countries in the Arab world, for example, have problems related to the cross-border transfer of cash. It is clear that there is a strong link between terrorism and drugs, in turn linked to smuggling. In considering remedies, it should be noted that several types of government agency might need to be involved. The customs authorities could play a role here in an intensified effort against terrorist financing.

VII. Conclusions

The terrorism of today must be addressed differently from before. Technology and globalization have made the risks and effects not only greater but also more collective in nature. This calls for an international, multilateral response.

Terrorist financing is a strategic area for the international community to address when fighting terrorism. The FATF has taken measures, but more needs to be done.

An important factor in countering the financing of terrorism is the breadth of participation in and commitment to the process. Membership of the FATF is important: from being an ad hoc organization open primarily to member states of the Organisation for Economic Co-operation and Development (OECD), it has embarked on a process of broadening its outreach by including other countries. Russia and South Africa became members in June 2003. India, which has important contributions to make and has been affected by terrorist acts, is the next country to join. There are significant risks associated with addressing the new terrorist threats, but action must be taken to protect both individuals and the interests of the international community.

5. Counter-terrorism measures undertaken under UN Security Council auspices

*Thomas J. Biersteker**

I. Introduction

An intensive debate has been carried out since 11 September 2001, within the academic community and in policy-making circles across the globe, about both the depth and the permanence of the changes in national and international policy that have taken place since the attacks. Although much uncertainty surrounds the consequences and future of practices of preventive intervention, and the acceptance of compromises of civil liberties in the pursuit of national security, one area where change has been significant is financial re-regulation. The leading and innovative role which the United Nations has played in the process is often underestimated.

This chapter describes and assesses the implications of the multilateral effort to block the financing of terrorist operations that has been undertaken under the auspices of the UN Security Council and its committees, particularly the Counter-Terrorism Committee (CTC) and the '1267 Sanctions Committee'.[1] First, the chapter considers the UN's general response to the terrorist attacks and the innovative aspects of the CTC process, as well as the division of labour between the CTC and the 1267 Committee. Second, it presents a preliminary assessment of the effectiveness of these UN efforts to combat the financing of global terrorism. Third, it suggests some of the principal issues, problems and challenges that have emerged (or are likely to emerge in the near future) from efforts to regulate terrorist financing—including individual

---

[1] Both committees are made up of all 15 members of the UN Security Council. The CTC was established by UN Security Council Resolution 1373, 28 Sep. 2001, and is mandated to monitor the implementation of the resolution by all states and to increase the capability of states to fight terrorism. On the CTC see URL <http://www.un.org/Docs/sc/committees/1373/>; and on its guidelines URL <http://www.un.org/Docs/sc/committees/1373/guidelines.htm>. See also chapter 5 in this volume. The '1267 Sanctions Committee' was established by UN Security Council Resolution 1267, 15 Oct. 1999, and was given an extended mandate in 2000 in Resolution 1333 (see section IV below). See United Nations, 'Security Council committee established pursuant to Resolution 1267 (1999) concerning Al-Qaida and the Taliban and associated individuals and entities', URL <http://www.un.org/Docs/sc/committees/1267Template.htm>; and for its guidelines see 'Guidelines of the Committee for the Conduct of its Work', adopted on 7 Nov. 2002 and amended on 10 Apr. 2003, URL <http://www.un.org/Docs/sc/committees/1267/1267_guidelines.pdf>.

* This chapter is based mainly on: Biersteker, T., with Romaniuk, P., 'The return of the state? financial re-regulation in the pursuit of national security after September 11', ed. J. Tirman, *Maze of Fear: Security and Migration after September 11th* (Social Science Research Council and New Press: New York, forthcoming 2004). The research support of the Watson Institute's Targeting Terrorist Finances Project (Sue Eckert, Elizabeth Goodfriend, Aaron Halegua and Peter Romaniuk) and the research assistance of Jesse Finkelstein and Daniel Widome are gratefully acknowledged.

human rights issues associated with the UN's process of listing terrorist individuals and organizations, the costs to business of compliance with new regulations, and questions about the changing nature of terrorist financing in response to the re-regulation of formal channels of financial transfer.

II. The role of the UN Security Council in efforts to counter terrorist financing after 11 September 2001

Before the attacks of 11 September 2001, there was no coordinated, global, multilateral effort to suppress or constrain the financing of acts of terrorism, and 'the existing prescriptions were woefully inadequate in dealing with the multi-dimensional nature of the challenge'.[2] There were efforts under way within the UN system to strengthen the 1999 International Convention for the Suppression of the Financing of Terrorism,[3] but they came in the wake of 25 years of financial market liberalization and financial deregulation across the globe and lacked a broad base of political support.

Immediately after the attacks, the UN Security Council acted decisively. On 12 September 2001 it adopted Resolution 1368,[4] establishing a legal basis for further action against global terrorism. The resolution invoked Article 51 of the UN Charter, recognizing the inherent right of self-defence and essentially legitimating subsequent US military action in Afghanistan against the perpetrators of the 11 September attacks. With the passage of UN Security Council Resolutions 1373 and 1377,[5] the Security Council expressed its clear intention to act to block terrorists' access to financial support. As Jamaican Ambassador Curtis Ward wrote, '[T]here was no lack of political will among Security Council members, and the council achieved unanimity on its chosen course of action'.[6]

Resolution 1373 deals mainly with blocking or suppressing the financing of terrorist groups. It calls for criminalizing active or passive support for terrorists, for the expeditious freezing of funds, for the sharing of operational information by UN member states, and for the provision of technical assistance to enhance multilateral cooperation in this area. This resolution also established an innovative process to implement the terms of the resolutions under the guidance of the CTC. Chairs of UN Security Council committees can be decisive in determining the effectiveness of the committees, and the appointment of UK Permanent Representative to the UN Sir Jeremy Greenstock to head the

---

[2] Ward, C. A., 'Building capacity to combat international terrorism: the role of the United Nations Security Council', *Journal of Conflict & Security Law*, vol. 8, no. 2 (2003), p. 291.

[3] The convention was adopted by the UN General Assembly in Resolution 54/109 on 9 Dec. 1999; for the full text see URL <http://www.un.org/Depts/dhl/resguide/r54.htm>.

[4] For UN Security Council Resolution 1373, 28 Sep. 2001, see URL <http://www.un.org/Docs/scres/2001/sc2001.htm>.

[5] For UN Security Council Resolution 1377, 12 Nov. 2001, see URL <http://www.un.org/Docs/scres/2001/sc2001.htm>.

[6] Ward (note 2), p. 293.

CTC, combined with genuine political will to act against terrorist financing, contributed greatly to the success of institutional innovation in this area.

Among the most innovative aspects of Resolution 1373 is its reporting process. Paragraph 6 calls upon states to file written reports on the actions they have taken to implement the resolution, following a common set of questions and guidelines established by the CTC. Following review of these reports, UN Permanent Representatives can be called before the committee to clarify key points in their reports, which are addressed in the next instalment of the reporting process. Every country report submitted to the CTC is made publicly available on the UN's Internet site,[7] but not everything in the reports is made available: member states may prevent the disclosure of sensitive information by submitting a confidential annex to their reports.

The CTC process recognizes that many states may require technical and financial assistance in implementing the resolution. Resolution 1377 invites states to seek assistance with implementation when necessary. It calls on member states to assist each other to implement the resolution fully and invites the CTC to explore further ways in which states can be assisted by international, regional and sub-regional organizations. The CTC facilitates the provision of financial support to states lacking administrative capacity by making information available to potential assistance providers about global assistance needs through the Internet-based CTC Directory of Counter-Terrorism Information and Sources of Assistance,[8] through offers of bilateral assistance from member states which are willing to provide help, and through the provision of support to the multilateral donor community.

In June 2003 the Group of Eight industrialized nations (G8) adopted the Action Plan on Capacity Building to support the activities of the CTC and created the Counter-Terrorism Action Group (CTAG).[9] The coordination of multinational support, however, remains a CTC activity.

Finally, Resolutions 1373 and 1377 recommend that states be encouraged to appoint a central contact point on implementation in their capital cities. The Counter-Terrorism Committee has published the CTC Directory of Contact Points, updates it at regular intervals, and encourages all states to make use of the directory for contacts on matters related to implementation of resolutions on terrorist financing (recognizing that the process has costs and the related personnel requirements can often be an inhibiting factor).[10] Thus, with regard to its reporting and monitoring system, offers of assistance, identification of contact points and insistence on transparency, the CTC has provided a model

---

[7] See the CTC site at URL <http://www.un.org/Docs/sc/committees/1373/submitted_reports.html>.

[8] For CTC Directory of Counter-Terrorism Information and Sources of Assistance see URL <http://www.un.org/Docs/sc/committees/1373/ctc_da/index.html>.

[9] See 'Chair's summary', Evian, France, 3 June 2003, URL <http://www.mofa.go.jp/policy/economy/summit/2003/c_summary.pdf>.

[10] For the CTC Directory of Contact Points see 'Letter dated 22 July 2003 from the Chairman of the Security Council Committee established pursuant to resolution 1373 (2001) concerning counter-terrorism addressed to the President of the Security Council', UN Security Council document S/2003/786, 31 July 2003, available at URL <http://www.un.org/Docs/sc/committees/1373/contact_points.html>.

of institutional innovation for dealing with terrorist financing that is likely to be drawn upon in future UN targeted sanctions efforts. The final report of the Stockholm Process on Implementing Targeted Sanctions suggests that 'important precedents have been established that could be drawn upon in future UN Security Council resolutions targeting sanctions'.[11]

The CTC has focused primarily on the long-term, strategic aspects of the problem of combating the financing of terrorism, dividing its work into three phases. Phase A is directed at legislative action and changes in the legal environment to criminalize financial support for terrorist activities in member states. Phase B is directed towards improvements in administrative capacity, while Phase C will be directed towards improved coordination within states, particularly between the public and private sectors.[12] For the management of the day-to-day operational details—the actual listing of terrorist organizations and individuals who support them—the UN has relied on the 1267 Committee. This committee was originally created to implement the provisions of targeted sanctions directed first against the Taliban regime, and later also against members of the al-Qaeda network who closely supported the Taliban.[13] The 1267 Committee is charged with responsibility for listing, de-listing and providing detailed identifying information about those charged with terrorist activities.

Like the CTC, the 1267 Committee has also developed important new institutional innovations. In response to growing concerns expressed by human rights advocates, it has developed guidelines for both the listing and de-listing of names of terrorist organizations and individuals. The committee requires that proposed additions to the list include, 'to the extent possible, a narrative description of the information that forms the basis or justification for taking action', as well as 'relevant and specific information to facilitate the identification of the persons listed by competent authorities'. For the listing of individuals, this entails the provision of 'name, date of birth, place of birth, nationality, aliases, residence, passport or travel document number'.[14] Like the CTC Committee, the 1267 Committee requires states to submit reports on their progress related to the resolution and posts these reports on its Internet site.[15]

The UN Security Council has not been alone in the effort to develop a global multilateral framework to combat the financing of terrorism. The Financial

[11] Wallensteen, P., Staibano, C. and Eriksson, M. (eds), *Making Targeted Sanctions Effective: Guidelines for the Implementation of UN Policy Options,* Stockholm Process on Implementing Targeted Sanctions, Final Report (Uppsala University, Department of Peace and Conflict Research: Uppsala, 2003), para. 127, pp. 57–58, available at URL <http://www.smartsanctions.se/reports/Final%20report%20complete.pdf>.

[12] For a detailed elaboration of these phases see Eckert, S., 'Application of Resolution 1373 and the Counter-Terrorism Committee to halting illicit resource flows', ed. K. Ballentine, *Peaceful Profits: Approaches to Managing the Resource Dimensions of Armed Conflict* (International Peace Academy: New York, forthcoming 2004).

[13] See UN Security Council Resolutions 1333, 19 Dec. 2000, and 1390, 16 Jan. 2002, available at URL <http://www.un.org/documents/scres.htm>.

[14] 'Guidelines of the Committee for the Conduct of its Work' (note 1), pp. 2–3.

[15] See the Internet site of the 1267 Committee at URL <http://www.un.org/Docs/sc/committees/1267/1267AnnComm.htm>.

Action Task Force (FATF)—an intergovernmental body established in 1989 under the auspices of the Organisation for Economic Co-operation and Development (OECD) to develop national and international policies to combat money laundering and terrorist financing—has proposed Eight Special Recommendations on terrorist financing as a supplement to its Forty Recommendations on Money Laundering.[16] The World Bank and the International Monetary Fund (IMF) have jointly begun to explore how best to design global standards for anti-money laundering (AML) efforts and for combating the financing of terrorism;[17] and the Wolfsberg Group of leading international banks has issued a statement and guidelines for its members on the suppression of the financing of terrorism.[18]

III. An assessment of the effectiveness of UN Security Council measures

It is too early to say definitively how effective the UN Security Council's measures directed against the financing of global terrorism have been. However, a research team at the Watson Institute for International Studies of Brown University, Providence, Rhode Island, has been investigating the extent to which countries across the globe are implementing the new sweeping counter-terrorist measures. Its Targeting Terrorist Finances Project[19] is examining the reports of different countries along with other sources of country-specific information; evaluating countries according to the degree of implementation, using markers ranging from 'the policy is under review or consideration' to 'new legislation criminalizing the financing of terrorism has been promulgated', 'assistance with implementation has been requested', 'administrative infrastructure to implement counter-terrorism measures has been identified, established, and given new resources to regulate this area', to 'there is substantial evidence of compliance' (i.e., banks and institutions involved in financial transactions have received notice, have established or modified internal procedures, have begun to use name-recognition software, or terrorist assets have been identified) and 'there is evidence of enforcement' (i.e., assets have been frozen and/or prosecutions pursued and penalties have been imposed for non-compliance).

Based on a preliminary assessment of the available data (primarily from examination of the reports received from countries in Europe, North America,

---

[16] For the revised (2003) FATF Forty Recommendations see URL <http://www.oecd.org/fatf>, and for the Eight Special Recommendations of 31 Oct. 2001 see URL <http://www1.oecd.org/fatf/pdf/SRecTF_en.pdf>. See also chapter 4 in this volume.

[17] Development Committee (Joint Ministerial Committee of the Boards of Governors of the Bank and the Fund on the Transfer of Real Resources to Developing Countries), 'Intensified Work on Anti-Money Laundering and Combating Financing of Terrorism (AML/CFT)', 25 Sep. 2002, available on the IMF Internet site at URL <http://www.imf.org/external/np/mae/aml/2002/eng/041702.htm>.

[18] For the Wolfsberg Principles and Statement see URL <http://www.wolfsberg-principles.com/>.

[19] On the Watson Institute project see URL <http://www.WatsonInstitute.org/project_detail.cfm?ID=51>.

the Middle East and East Asia), there is strong evidence to suggest that the UN process has made significant progress in criminalizing terrorist financing and improving financial administrative capacity in member states. With regard to reporting, all the 191 UN member states have filed reports with the CTC on compliance with counter-terrorist resolutions.[20] This, in itself, is an extraordinary achievement: both Iraq and North Korea submitted reports in 2001 and 2002, and North Korea submitted a report in 2003. Most states have filed more than one report, and the majority of the reports follow the detailed structure laid out by the CTC. In a briefing prepared to evaluate the CTC process, Walter Gehr, a member of the group of experts convened by the UN, observed that 'the overwhelming majority of the reports follow the structure of Resolution 1373'.[21] Similarly, Ambassador Curtis Ward, the CTC's Advisor on Technical Assistance, has concluded that every state has had to adopt new legislation in order to meet all the requirements of Resolution 1373.[22]

There is also evidence that both the quality of reporting and progress on criminalizing terrorist finance have improved over time. In the first round of reports submitted to the CTC, in late 2001 and early 2002, many states claimed that they already had sufficient legal instruments to criminalize the funding of terrorist activity, stating that they were using AML legislation to meet their legal obligations to criminalize terrorist financing. More recently, during the dialogue between states and the CTC prior to the second round of reports, members of the CTC used their meetings and correspondence to bring to member states' attention the critical difference between AML legislation and legislation on terrorist financing. As Gehr argues, 'The difference between money laundering and the financing of terrorism is that moneys used to fund terrorist activities are not necessarily illegal. Assets and profits acquired by legitimate means and even declared to tax authorities can be used to finance terrorist acts, too'.[23] Aninat, Hardy and Johnston have elaborated on this point:

[T]errorist financing differs from money laundering in several ways that affect public policy. It may be much more difficult to detect than money laundering because it is directed mainly at future activity: it is possible that the only offense that has been committed when the financing takes place is conspiracy to commit a terrorist act. Also, the amounts of money needed to finance terrorism are widely believed to be relatively small. The September 11 attacks on the World Trade Center and the Pentagon were believed to have required less than $1 million—compared to either normal commercial transactions or typical volumes of money being laundered by, say, large drug trafficking operations, which might total several hundred billion dollars a year.[24]

---

[20] For the reports as made public on the CTC Internet site see URL <http://www.un.org/Docs/sc/committees/1373/submitted_reports.html>.

[21] Gehr, W., 'Recurrent Issues (briefing for member states on 4 April 2002)', URL <http://www.un.org/Docs/sc/committees/1373/rc.htm>.

[22] Ward (note 2), p. 299.

[23] Gehr (note 21), p. 2.

[24] Aninat, E., Hardy, D. and Johnston, R. B., 'Combating money laundering and the financing of terrorism', *Finance and Development*, vol. 39, no. 3 (2002).

Reviews of second-round reports to the CTC (completed on 31 December 2002) suggest that, as the dialogue between member states and the CTC proceeds, states are beginning to move beyond reliance on AML legislation and to promulgate new laws specifically on terrorist financing.

As described above, UN Security Council Resolution 1377 invites states to seek assistance with implementation and calls on member states to assist each other to implement the resolution fully. Ambassador Curtis Ward, Advisor on Technical Assistance to the CTC, wrote that 'over fifty States indicated in their first reports that they needed assistance to implement the resolution'.[25] This number has grown to 91, as more states reach a clearer understanding of what is expected of them. According to Ward, the greatest needs for assistance appear to be in drafting anti-terrorism law and in developing banking and financial legislation and regulations.

Most countries have shown progress either on criminalizing the wilful collection of funds for terrorism and/or on providing a legal basis for the freezing of the funds of terrorist groups and individuals. New legislation has either been adopted or is formally under review in most countries. AML rules have been tightened in Europe and the Middle East (although not to the same extent in Asia) and, as indicated above, additional countries are beginning to recognize—in part owing to the CTC policy dialogues—that AML regulations may not be sufficient to suppress terrorist financing.

Most countries have signed the international conventions on terrorism. A comparison of their first and second reports to the CTC shows that progress has been made in nearly all countries. Many have signed additional international and/or regional conventions on related matters in the two years since the attacks of 11 September 2001. In that month, fewer than a dozen states had signed all 12 international conventions and protocols related to the prevention and suppression of international terrorism.[26] By July 2003, the number had grown to more than 40.

Only the USA and the European Union (EU) have developed their own lists of groups and individuals legally identified as terrorists; most countries rely on the lists provided by the UN.[27]

In its effort to support the establishment of an administrative infrastructure to implement counter-terrorism measures, the CTC has appointed an assistance team to dispatch information about common standards and best practices, and it has published a Directory of Counter-Terrorism Information and Sources of Assistance on its Internet site.[28] It is not clear how many states have utilized this resource to date, but Ward reports that CTC assistance teams, in bilateral consultations with states, evaluate the gaps in administrative capacity

[25] Ward (note 2), p. 302.

[26] For the UN conventions see URL <http://untreaty.un.org/English/Terrorism.asp>.

[27] On the US lists see section IV; and for the EU lists of Persons and Groups and Entities see Council Common Position 2003/651/CFSP, 12 Sep. 2003, Annex, in *Official Journal of the European Union*, L 229, vol. 46 (13 Sep. 2003), pp. 42–45.

[28] For this directory see the CTC Internet site at URL <http://www.un.org/Docs/sc/committees/1373/ctc_da/index.html>.

and facilitate assistance from willing donors.[29] Most countries have identified an implementing agency or intra-governmental mechanism for administering controls on terrorist financing, and nearly all have identified central contact points for the CTC.

Compliance is a critical indicator, and there is evidence that private-sector banks and financial institutions have been notified about new regulations in most countries, although this trend is less evident in some of the major countries in Asia. Most countries have also imposed new reporting requirements on financial institutions, although formal audits have been used less frequently. EU member states tend to be the most prone to conduct audits and investigations into charitable organizations, and to apply special measures for high-risk centres under their jurisdiction. Until 2002, virtually no nation, with the exception of the United Arab Emirates (UAE), had any measures in place for the regulation of informal money transfer systems, or hawalas.[30] Saudi Arabia claimed that hawalas did not operate in the country and that all its financial institutions were under the administrative mandate of the Saudi Monetary Authority. By October 2003, however, the US Government had registered well over 16 000 money service businesses of this kind which were operating on US territory. Australian officials have pursued similar measures, and Hong Kong has been described by Australian regulators as 'setting the standard' in this area.[31] Pakistan and the UAE have also introduced new legislation on the operations of hawalas.

Finally, with regard to enforcement, there is not much evidence that additional funds have been frozen—beyond the total of $112.2 million frozen in the first few months after September 2001. Even this figure may be inflated, since it appears to include funds frozen under UN Security Council Resolution 1267 (November 1999). Some states mention investigations being pursued or under way, but few can present new evidence of concrete success. Many still assert that their financial system is not susceptible to misuse by terrorists, while others still maintain that they are complying with Resolution 1373 by virtue of existing AML legislation.

Of the $134 million in assets of terrorist organizations blocked as of October 2003, $36 million was frozen by the United States and $98 million by other countries (including approximately $24 million by Switzerland, $11.9 million by the UK, $5.5 million by Saudi Arabia, and an undisclosed amount by the UAE). Prosecutions have been pursued, especially in the USA, Germany and Indonesia, but few have so far resulted in the freezing of additional funds. The

---

[29] Ward (note 2), p. 303.

[30] On the hawala system of unregulated international financing see *Terrorist Financing*, Report of an Independent Task Force sponsored by the Council on Foreign Relations, Maurice Greenberg, Chair, William F. Wechsler and Lee S. Wolosky, Project Co-Directors, Oct. 2002, available at URL <http://www.cfr.org/pdf/Terrorist_Financing_TF.pdf>.

[31] Interview with senior Australian government official by members of the Watson Institute Targeting Terrorist Finances Project, Aug. 2003.

USA has applied the USA Patriot Act of 2001[32] outside the country (actions against correspondent accounts in Belize, India, Israel, Oman and Taiwan) which has allegedly resulted in the seizure of an additional $2 million, but federal judges have sealed the records of these cases. There is virtually no evidence of the suspension of any banking licences, but there have been convictions in the United States for 'material support'.

In its parallel multilateral effort to monitor implementation, the FATF reported that as of September 2003, 132 countries had participated in its self-assessment exercise to compare their current practices against the FATF standards embodied in its Eight Special Recommendations.[33] It uses these self-assessments to identify countries for priority technical assistance from the World Bank, the IMF and the UN.

In summary, important policy changes have been introduced throughout the world, from Europe and Russia to offshore financial centres such as Bahrain and Hong Kong. There have been important expressions of a global willingness to do something about terrorist financing, even if material progress to date has been relatively modest.

IV. Legal issues, problems and challenges

How sustainable are these efforts? Is there a growing acceptance of financial re-regulation by state actors across the globe? There are two principal sets of issues, problems and/or challenges that have emerged from the multilateral effort to freeze terrorist finances: (*a*) issues surrounding the listing of individuals and organizations accused of supporting terrorists financially; and (*b*) legal problems and challenges stemming from the lack of parallel implementation of policy in different legal jurisdictions.

Listing

Who is listed?

One of the central challenges associated with freezing terrorist finances is deciding whom to list. It is usually possible to identify the core leaders of terrorist organizations but more difficult to find information about their aliases, key financiers, critical support personnel and front organizations. Coordination of intelligence gathering from different national agencies is often difficult, as is agreement on evidentiary standards across different national jurisdictions. Furthermore, commonly used names and the different methods of translitera-

---

[32] The Uniting and Strengthening America by Providing Appropriate Tools Required to Intercept and Obstruct Terrorism Act of 2001 (the USA Patriot Act of 24 Oct. 2001) is available at URL <http://www.epic.org/privacy/terrorism/hr3162.pdf>. See also the annex to Part VI in this volume.

[33] FATF, 'Annual Report 2001–2002', 21 June 2002, URL <http://www1.oecd.org/fatf/pdf/AR2002_en.pdf>, especially Part B, 'The self-assessment of FATR members vis-à-vis the Eight Special Recommendations'. For the status of responses as of 16 Sep. 2003 see URL <http://www1.oecd.org/fatf/pdf/SATFResponse_en.pdf>. On the FATF see also chapter 4.

tion used by different intelligence agencies can lead to errors involving the listing of innocent individuals. It is important for the domestic agencies engaged in international efforts to combat global terrorism to provide as much identifying information as possible about the targets of UN Security Council resolutions and domestic enabling legislation.

The Office of Foreign Assets Control (OFAC) of the US Department of the Treasury maintains a list of specially designated nationals (SDNs), specially designated narcotics traffickers (SDNTs), and specially designated terrorists (SDTs).[34] The November 2003 list of specially designated global terrorists (SDGTs) and foreign terrorist organizations (FTOs) is more detailed and comprehensive, but it still lacks adequate detail about many of the names on the list. Without this level of information, it is difficult for financial institutions to know precisely which accounts and transactions should be investigated.

Providing more identifying information about potential targets requires enhanced multilateral cooperation, including the sharing and coordination of sensitive intelligence information. However, intelligence agencies are reluctant to provide information on all potential targets. For example, the US authorities considered Ali Qaed Sunian al-Harithi[35] (also known as Abu Ali) important enough to assassinate him on 3 November 2002, even though he was not included on any of the official lists of suspected terrorists. The lists are designed to identify who does banking for the terrorist networks. The goal is often to remove a node in the financial network rather than to penalize directly those who commit terrorist acts. The listing process can be used as a preventive mechanism. In some cases the goal is to block potential movements of funds that could support a terrorist act. In other cases, a name may be omitted from the list deliberately in order to be able to follow the movement of funds in and out of a monitored account for subsequent intelligence purposes.

Whose list is authoritative?

In addition to the difficulty of determining which names should be listed, there is the challenge of determining which list is the most authoritative. In the case of UN Security Council resolutions on financial sanctions, the USA has provided most of the intelligence for the UN list. The USA has collected information from its intelligence services, and the OFAC has disseminated its list to US financial institutions. The list was also given to European states, which could choose to delete or add names to it. However, because of the difference in intelligence capacities between the USA and Europe, the listing process is another example of US operational hegemony.

During the later stages of the UN's targeted sanctions against the regime of Slobodan Milosevic in the former Yugoslavia, and especially in the aftermath of targeted financial sanctions against the Taliban and al-Qaeda, the EU

---

[34] For the OFAC list of specially designated nationals and blocked persons of 10 Nov. 2003 see URL <http://www.ustreas.gov/offices/eotffc/ofac/sdn/t11sdn.pdf>.
[35] This name is listed with various spelling, such as Qaed Senyan al-Harthi.

invested more effort in developing its own lists. Nevertheless, the US list continues to be far more extensive and detailed than the EU lists. US domestic legislation permits the United States to maintain a long, consolidated list of terrorists and terrorist organizations to facilitate implementation of measures. This approach differs from that of the EU, which regularly updates its regulations to reflect the numerous additions and deletions of names by different UN committees but did not create a counter-terrorism list of its own until December 2001.

The lists maintained by the UN lie somewhere between the US and EU lists, in both length and level of detail, although recent changes in the listing procedures announced by the 1267 Committee have brought the UN lists closer to those of the USA in terms of level of detail.[36] For most states, the lists maintained by the UN sanctions committees have the most legitimacy, but the fact that there may be only a partial consensus on the list of individuals or organizations across different jurisdictions (US, EU and UN) creates potential enforcement problems.

In the specific case of al-Qaeda, the first targeting of the network was focused on the Taliban regime and was imposed by UN Security Council Resolution 1267. Although there was a delay in developing a list of individuals after the resolution was adopted, the Sanctions Committee eventually issued a list in November 2001.[37] With the adoption of UN Security Council Resolution 1333,[38] the mandate of the 1267 Sanctions Committee was extended beyond the Taliban to include 'Usama bin Laden and individuals or entities associated with him as designated by the Committee, including those in the Al-Qaida organisation'. From that point onward, until 11 September 2001, the work of the 1267 Committee focused on the selection and preparation of a team of monitors to be stationed on Afghanistan's borders, with the aim of improving the effectiveness of the sanctions. That initiative was called off, however, following the attacks. With the adoption of UN Security Council Resolution 1390,[39] the scope of the 1267 Sanctions Committee was broadened once more to include 'Usama bin Laden, members of the Al-Qaida organisation and the Taliban and other individuals, groups, undertakings and entities associated with them'.

Wrongly listed individuals or organizations

Since individuals can be listed erroneously, it is important that procedures be established to enable them to petition for the removal of their names from the

---

[36] See UN Security Council document S/2003/669/Corr.1, 17 July 2003, for the improvements in the UN consolidated list.

[37] See UN Security Council document S/2002/65, 15 Jan. 2002, para. 35. An addendum to the 26 Nov. list was issued on 26 Dec. 2001.

[38] UN Security Council Resolution 1333, 19 Dec. 2000, para. 8(c), URL <http://www.un.org/Docs/scres/2000/sc2000.htm>.

[39] UN Security Council Resolution 1390, 28 Jan. 2002, para. 2, URL <http://www.un.org/Docs/scres/2002/sc2002.htm>.

list. This issue was first taken up in the reports of the Interlaken Process on the targeting of UN financial sanctions[40] and in the Bonn–Berlin Working Group on Travel and Aviation-Related Bans.[41] Following the passage of Resolution 1390, the 1267 Committee established a procedure—the first of its kind—for those wrongly listed to petition for removal of their names from the list. The procedure allows petitioners (individuals or groups) to petition the government of their country of citizenship or residence to request a review of their case. It is incumbent upon petitioners to provide justification for their request. The petitioned government is asked to review the information. It may approach the government or governments that originally requested the listing to seek information and hold consultations bilaterally on the case so that member states can resolve the matter between them. Where this is not possible, the 1267 Committee may decide whether to de-list the individual or group, by consensus, in effect operating with a unit veto system. The details of the de-listing procedures are set out in the guidelines of the 1267 Committee.[42]

This issue has important human rights implications, as evidenced by the legal suit filed in the European Court of Justice by Swedish citizens of Somali origin over the listing by the USA and the EU of the Al-Barakat Group of companies.[43] Indeed, the de-listing procedures developed by the 1267 Committee were intended to address this kind of issue. Establishing procedures for appeal and potential removal of the names of individuals and groups wrongly designated as being associated with the financing of terrorism is important for sustaining momentum on the regulation of terrorist financing. As the Council on Foreign Relations Task Force on Terrorist Financing recommended,

Legitimate disquiet in some quarters concerning the potential for due process violations associated with the inaccurate listing of targeted individuals can retard progress in global efforts. Since the full sharing of sensitive intelligence information is unlikely, the establishment of such procedures will take such concerns 'off of the agenda' and prevent them from being used as an excuse for ineffective implementation.[44]

---

[40] Seminars have been held in Interlaken, Switzerland, on targeting UN financial sanctions since Mar. 1998, in cooperation with the Swiss Federal Office for Foreign Economic Affairs. See URL <http://www.smartsanctions.ch/start.html>.

[41] See especially Swiss Confederation, in cooperation with the United Nations Secretariat and the Watson Institute for International Studies of Brown University, *Targeted Financial Sanctions: A Manual for Design and Implementation—Contributions from the Interlaken Process* (Thomas J. Watson Institute for International Studies: Providence, R.I., 2001), pp. 28–29; and Brozska, M., Bonn International Center for Conversion (BICC), 'Design and implementation of arms embargoes and travel and aviation related sanctions: results of the "Bonn–Berlin Process"', 2001, comment 16, pp. 56–58, URL <http://www.bicc.de/events/unsanc/2000/pdf/booklet/booklet_sanctions.pdf>.

[42] 'Guidelines of the Committee for the Conduct of its Work' (note 1), pp. 2–3.

[43] This group is variously listed also as the Al-Barakaat network of financial groups.

[44] *Terrorist Financing* (note 30), p. 32.

Challenges of parallel implementation

Legal frameworks

Because private-sector financial institutions operate on the front lines of efforts to block terrorist finances, they need to be protected in domestic law from potential claims arising from their compliance with UN Security Council resolutions and other enabling legislation. If they are not provided with this legal protection, the freezing of funds could cause a financial institution to be in violation of its fundamental obligations to its clients and customers. This concern can be addressed by the inclusion of a 'non-liability' provision in enabling resolutions or legislation, calling on states to implement the intent of the resolution, 'notwithstanding the existence of any rights or obligations conferred or imposed by any other international agreement or contract, license, or permit granted before the date of adoption [the coming into effect of the measures contained in] this resolution'.[45]

Ironically, only about 20 states (including the UK and the USA) have legislation in place that automatically enables them to apply national measures to give effect to decisions called for in UN Security Council resolutions. Extending this practice more widely has been a priority of international efforts to coordinate policies on targeted sanctions, both financial sanctions and arms embargoes, as reflected most recently in the final report from the Stockholm Process on Implementing Targeted Sanctions.[46] If some kind of legal protection is absent in legal jurisdictions, harmonized, global implementation will break down and there will be significant loopholes in the system.

Different definitions

Given that terrorism is a global problem and that responses to it require multilateral cooperation, clarity and consistency of definition and interpretation across different state legal jurisdictions are vital. Different definitions of what is an 'asset', and efforts to block 'funds' only rather than transactions involving 'income bearing assets', have led to inconsistent implementation of financial sanctions between Europe and the USA in the past. This created loopholes for potential sanctions violators (potential 'sanctions havens') and would provide the same for terrorist organizations. The clarity of the language used in UN Security Council resolutions and in national enabling legislation became a principal focus of two Interlaken conferences, in 1998 and 1999. They produced consensual definitions of terms such as 'funds and other financial resources', 'owned and controlled directly or indirectly', 'to freeze', 'financial services' and 'assets'.[47] These definitions can be utilized in contemporary

---

[45] Swiss Confederation in cooperation with the United Nations Secretariat and the Watson Institute for International Studies (note 41), p. 41.

[46] *Making Targeted Sanctions Effective* (note 11), especially paras 223–43, pp. 81–86.

[47] Swiss Conferation in cooperation with the United Nations Secretariat and the Watson Institute for International Studies (note 41), pp. 62–70.

efforts to combat global terrorism. The 1999 International Convention for the Suppression of the Financing of Terrorism defines only three terms: 'funds', 'state or governmental facility' and 'proceeds'.[48]

Capacity of regulatory institutions

While broad-based multilateral cooperation is necessary for an effective global effort to combat terrorism, the experience with financial sanctions suggests that most countries lack an adequate administrative capacity to implement UN Security Council resolutions effectively. The international effort to pursue sanctions reform has tried to identify 'best practices' at the national level for both financial sanctions and arms embargoes. Efforts are also under way to utilize sanctions assistance missions, technical assistance at the regional level, financial support for those most directly affected by compliance with sanctions resolutions, mutual evaluations, 'naming and shaming', trans-governmental cooperation, and private-sector initiatives to ensure that there is broad multilateral participation in sanctions efforts. Given the urgency of the threat posed by global terrorist organizations, there is a pressing need for the dissemination of 'best practices' to financial centres and to the countries most likely to be transit points for terrorist funds. Inconsistent (or non-existent) administrative implementation creates potential havens for illicit funds.

Capacity of private financial institutions

The same computer technology that enables terrorist networks to exploit the globalization of financial markets and move funds instantaneously across the globe can also be employed against them. Financial institutions throughout the world can be encouraged to utilize one of the numerous 'name recognition' computer programs widely available on the market. This software could help them to determine—electronically and instantaneously—whether they are holding the accounts of any individuals or organizations identified as terrorists. It is very difficult to search accounts and identify names and aliases without some kind of computer software assistance. Until recently, however, only the largest US-based banks routinely used name-recognition software to identify the targets of UN resolutions. Neither smaller US banks nor most major financial institutions in Europe and Japan have made use of this technology. The first European exceptions have been Deutsche Bank and, more recently, Lloyds Bank of London.

Beyond its utility in identifying transactions involving listed individuals, a new generation of technology could be deployed to identify patterns of suspect transactions that deviate from common norms in the frequency, size or destination of transactions. Indeed, it was an observation of this kind of deviation from normal patterns of transactions that led a Boston-based bank employee to raise questions about suspicious transactions involving the al-Barakat organi-

---

[48] International Convention for the Suppression of the Financing of Terrorism (note 3), Article 1.

zation in 1999.[49] The use of computerized surveillance technology raises important, and legitimate, concerns about the potential violation of fundamental civil liberties from this new form of electronic intrusion, and new norms will need to be developed to establish limits on the invasion of privacy.

Retroactive reporting

The processes of targeting terrorist finances and financial sanctions are essentially similar. Both efforts entail the identification of names and corporate (or institutional) entities, both require extensive multilateral coordination, and both rely on the cooperation and participation of private-sector financial institutions for effective implementation. Experience with efforts to target financial sanctions suggest that UN Security Council resolutions or national enabling legislation to block or freeze the assets of terrorist organizations should also authorize financial institutions to trace funds retroactively.

Requiring states to report on the movement of funds within their jurisdiction in a parallel manner for a specified period prior to efforts to freeze or block the movement of terrorist funds could generate valuable information about the location and movement of financial assets about to leave a jurisdiction. Thus, even if the funds cannot be blocked, they can be traced and their movement back into the global financial system can be monitored. This could prove vital for intelligence-gathering purposes. The identification of funds in this manner would also facilitate the process of 'naming and shaming' havens for the assets of global terrorist organizations, as the FATF has done with regard to havens for money laundering.[50] Financial institutions across different national jurisdictions need to have parallel authority to report retroactively.

V. Conclusions

The attacks of 11 September 2001 prompted a virtual sea change in the tolerance of financial re-regulation across the globe. The UN's Counter-Terrorism Committee and 1267 Committee have played a critical role in harmonizing state regulatory policies to advance the global effort to suppress and freeze terrorist finances. While terrorist groups' access to finance can never be halted entirely, it can be disrupted, forced into other channels, and more generally degraded in important respects. The multilateral effort to restrict the sources and to trace the financial flows of funds to terrorist groups can also assist with other forms of intelligence-gathering operations and help illuminate details of the operations of global terrorist networks.

---

[49] Willman, J., 'Trail of terrorist dollars that spans the world', *Financial Times*, Special Report, 29 Nov. 2001, available at FT.com, URL <http://specials.ft.com/attackonterrorism/FT3RNR3XMUC.html>.

[50] See Financial Action Task Force on Money Laundering (FATF), *Annual Review of Non-Cooperative Countries or Territories*, 20 June 2003, URL <http://www1.oecd.org/fatf/pdf/NCCT2003_en.pdf>.

It remains to be seen, however, whether this change can be sustained. As suggested above, it is likely to face continuing legal challenges related to the process of listing terrorist individuals and groups and is also likely to be hampered by sovereign claims for exception that inevitably produce inconsistency in implementation across different jurisdictions. A certain degree of difference across national jurisdictions can be healthy, because it provides a basis for policy experimentation and innovation. Too much variation, however, can undercut the creation of a coordinated global response to the kind of global network that al-Qaeda has benefited from in the past and the threat that it continues to pose. Finally, the costs of compliance for states and for private-sector financial institutions are increasingly beginning to raise questions about the utility of regulatory policies in this area.

The report of the Council on Foreign Relations Task Force on Terrorist Financing concluded in October 2002 that 'US efforts to curtail the financing of terrorism are impeded . . . by a lack of political will among US allies'.[51] This contributed to a vigorous debate about the extent to which key US allies such as Saudi Arabia had complied with efforts to freeze and suppress terrorist financing, particularly after it was discovered in November 2002 that charitable donations from members of the royal family in the Saudi Arabian Embassy at Washington had ended up in the bank accounts of some of the terrorists who committed the attacks of 11 September 2001. This controversy flared up again in the summer of 2003, when the White House classified pages relating to Saudi Arabia from a Joint Congressional Intelligence Committee report.

The global effort to target terrorist finances is part of a larger effort on the part of the George W. Bush Administration to strengthen the capacity of the state to provide a bulwark against the threat from global terrorism. Some analysts have suggested that they have detected a surge of interest on the part of both US and foreign organizations that want to be up to the US standard—from typical banking channels to insurance companies and brokerage firms.[52]

In the final analysis, will the re-regulation of finance to suppress the financing of global terrorism work, and is it worth all the effort? Are the benefits worth the growing costs of compliance? There is strong evidence to suggest that al-Qaeda learned that the formal banking system was unreliable for its purposes, after its financial assets were frozen following the bombings of the US embassies in Nairobi and Dar-es-Salaam in 1998.[53] Accordingly, global terrorists may have moved into informal financial transfer systems, begun to store value in 'conflict diamonds',[54] and relied increasingly on traditional

[51] *Terrorist Financing* (note 30), p. 8.

[52] See, e.g., Silverman, G., 'War on terror helps clean up money-laundering', *Financial Times*, 8 Apr. 2003.

[53] Farah, D., 'The role of conflict diamonds in al Qaeda's financial structure', Paper presented at the Social Science Research Council (SSRC) Conference on International Law, International Relations, and Terrorism, Washington, DC, 14–15 Nov. 2002, available at URL <http://www.ssrc.org/programs/gsc/gsc_activities/farah.page>.

[54] On conflict diamonds see chapter 11 in this volume.

forms of currency and commodity smuggling. Nevertheless, it is important to continue to monitor and regulate routine financial transactions. There is significant intelligence value in monitoring formal financial movements. The existence of legal prohibitions and the enforcement of new laws criminalizing the wilful contribution to terrorist organizations may prove to be a powerful deterrent to those tempted to support them.

While increased controls potentially pose threats to the free movement of capital and to some civil liberties, they have the potential for creating positive synergies and long-term benefits in related issue areas, from drug trafficking to tax evasion. In August 2003, US Government officials invoked provisions of the USA Patriot Act to investigate and freeze the accounts of Latin American leaders accused of corruption in their home countries.[55] If these trends continue, they could provide the basis for a nascent form of global governance in this critically important arena. In 10 years' time, we may look back on this period as the beginning of a major change in the institutions, operations and procedures of the entire global financial system.

[55] Lichtblau, E., 'US cautiously begins to seize millions in foreign banks', *New York Times*, 30 May 2003.

6. Strategic export controls and the private sector

Evan R. Berlack

I. Introduction

Since 11 September 2001 there has been a fresh surge of interest in international mechanisms for cutting off at the source supplies of weapon-related items and finances to dangerous actors. Strategic export controls, and the groups of states which enforce them, are among the relatively few instruments which in principle could serve a policy of denial aimed at both non-state actors, such as terrorists, and states. What exactly do such controls entail? First, they include controls on the export of all items designed for military use, including not only lethal weapons but also items with potential military use, such as electronics, avionics, metals and telecommunications. Second, the controls may regulate the export of dual-use items which generally have been designed for commercial use but are also viewed as having applicability for military use, such as computer software. Third, controls may regulate the export of any other item if it is known to be for use either in a nuclear, biological or chemical (NBC) weapon programme or in a programme to develop or produce missile delivery systems for such weapons.

II. The US approach

In the United States, separate laws and regulations and government agencies control the export of dual-use items and of military-use items, respectively. The Bureau of Industry and Security (BIS) of the US Department of Commerce administers the Export Administration Regulations (EAR), including the Commerce Control List of Dual-Use Items.[1] The US Department of State's Directorate of Defense Trade Controls (DDTC) administers the International Traffic in Arms Regulation (ITAR), which incorporates the United States Munitions List.[2]

This US bifurcation of administrative and legal controls over dual-use and military-use items is not typical for other developed countries. The British Government, for example, through the Department of Trade and Industry,

---

[1] On the EAR and the Commerce Control List of Dual-Use Items, see 'Introduction to Commerce Department export controls', URL <http://www.bxa.doc.gov/licensing/exportingbasics.htm>. The EAR database is available at URL <http://w3.access.gpo.gov/bis/ear/ear_data.html>.

[2] On the DDTC see URL <http://pmdtc.org> and on the United States Munitions List URL <http://pmdtc.org/docs/ITAR/22cfr121_Part121.pdf>, Part 121.

maintains similar controls over both dual-use and military items.[3] This approach is the one followed by most North Atlantic Treaty Organization (NATO) member governments as well as by Australia, Japan and other states. The bifurcated US system imposes a higher threshold—including higher costs—on the US private sector inasmuch as the policies and detailed procedures, not to mention the nuances, for administration of the controls can have significant differences as between the two systems.

Moreover, the extent of controls over strategic items is in certain respects more extensive under the US system than in other developed countries. US controls on the export of dual-use and military items are extraterritorial: the United States asserts a right to control not only the export but also the re-export of such items anywhere in the world, whether or not US citizens are involved in the transactions. No other developed country's export controls system adopts this posture, which can result in US enforcement actions being taken against non-US citizens and companies: they may be placed on a US denial list which prohibits any further trade with these entities. US controls on technology transfers create additional challenges for multinational companies, although these controls are not necessarily exclusive to the USA.

Other countries are adding such controls to their national control regimes. For example, British national export controls and the European Union (EU) Council Regulation 1334/2000[4] extend control to 'intangible' transfers of technology and know-how.[5] Within the EU, the Conventional Arms Exports (COARM) Working Group, which brings together national officials from member states, has endorsed the importance of considering effective legal controls on electronic transfers of the software and technology associated with items on the EU Common List of Military Equipment covered by the 1998 EU Code of Conduct on Arms Exports.[6] US controls on technology transfers to foreign nationals within the USA, however—so-called deemed exports—are unique and particularly troubling for the allocation of technical expertise within multinational companies, especially when the personnel are of Chinese or, to a lesser extent, Indian nationality.

---

[3] On the Department of Trade and Industry see URL <http://www.dti.gov.uk/>.

[4] For Council Regulation (EC) no. 1334/2000 on setting up a Community regime for the control of exports of dual-use items and technology, of 22 June 2000, see *Official Journal of the European Communities*, L 159/1 (30 June 2000), available at URL <http://europa.eu.int/comm/trade/issues/sectoral/industry/dualuse/docs/dualuse_1334.pdf>.

[5] For more on 'intangible' transfers see Anthony, I., 'Multilateral weapon and technology export controls', *SIPRI Yearbook 2001: Armaments, Disarmament and International Security* (Oxford University Press: Oxford, 2001), pp. 631–35.

[6] For the Code of Conduct on Arms Exports see URL <http://projects.sipri.se/expcon/eucode.htm>. For the Common List of Military Equipment see *Official Journal of the European Communities*, C 191/2 (8 July 2000), available at URL <http://www.nisat.org/EU/EU%20Common%20list%20of%20military%20equipment/Common%20list%20of%20military%20equipment.pdf>.

III. The evolution of international approaches to export controls after 1945

The cold war directly influenced the thrust of strategic controls for many years. The then NATO member states (except Iceland) as well as Australia and Japan participated in the Coordinating Committee on Multilateral Export Controls (COCOM), an informal but effective multilateral arrangement directed at the Soviet bloc and China in 1950–94.[7] COCOM maintained three comprehensive lists of strategic dual-use and military items to be controlled, and a list of proscribed recipient countries, although these lists were not made public until after the end of the cold war. Proposed exports of the more sensitive items by any member state required prior notification within COCOM, and proposed exports of the most sensitive items were subject to veto by any member.

Since the end of the cold war, the primary motivation for strategic export controls has been the non-proliferation of weapons of mass destruction (WMD) and conventional weapons. The objective has changed from protection against broad military attack by a known adversary to that of denying WMD to any end-user and denying conventional weapons to irresponsible governments and to terrorists. However, the targets of denial have not necessarily shifted radically, and only a limited number of states (led by the former Warsaw Pact members now entering NATO) have moved from the position of targets to that of participants in the control regimes. In the United States, China remains a concern, particularly within the Department of Defense, as does Russia, in a more muted vein, reflecting the perpetuation of cold war concerns and fixations.

In general, the international focus of the strategic export controls serving a non-proliferation objective rests with a number of self-constituted multinational regimes based on political commitments.[8]

1. The Wassenaar Arrangement on Export Controls for Conventional Arms and Dual-Use Goods and Technologies was formed in the years following the demise of COCOM and inherited COCOM's lists of dual-use and military items intended for use in conventional weapons. Its membership was meant to be broader than that of COCOM and has included Russia from its establishment, in 1996. However, unlike COCOM, it has not embodied the 'veto' mechanism and is not targeted on any named country or group of countries.

---

[7] On COCOM see Adler-Karlsson, G., *Western Economic Warfare 1947–1967: A Case Study in Foreign Economic Policy* (Almqvist & Wiksell: Stockholm, 1968), pp. 50–56; Anthony, I., SIPRI, *Arms Export Regulations* (Oxford University Press: Oxford, 1991), pp. 207–11; and Davis, I., SIPRI, *The Regulation of Arms and Dual-Use Exports: Germany, Sweden and the UK* (Oxford University Press: Oxford, 2002), pp. 32–36.

[8] For more on these export control regimes and their membership see Anthony, I., 'Supply-side measures', *SIPRI Yearbook 2003: Armaments, Disarmament and International Security* (Oxford University Press: Oxford, 2003), pp. 727–48; and the SIPRI Internet site at URL <http://projects.sipri.se/expcon/expcon.htm>.

While participating states have made a political commitment not to export any item on the control lists without prior assessment, unlike the other multilateral groupings the Wassenaar Arrangement does not have any agreed guidelines to be applied in making those assessments.[9]

2. The Nuclear Suppliers Group (NSG), the Missile Technology Control Regime (MTCR) and the Australia Group, which focuses on chemical and biological weapons, are all regimes which originated in the cold war era because of particular non-cold war-related events. The trigger was India's acquisition of a nuclear capability in 1974 in the case of the NSG, which included the Soviet Union as an original member. Certain missile proliferation events gave the motive to create the MTCR in 1987, and the use of chemical weapons in the 1980–88 Iraq–Iran War gave rise to the Australia Group, formed in 1985. All these groups have developed comprehensive lists of items which should be controlled by member governments. The Wassenaar Arrangement started with the COCOM lists.

IV. Characteristics and limitations of existing regimes

The four multilateral export control regimes suffer from several problems. First, the participation in the regimes is limited and widely overlapping—composed largely of NATO member states and candidate members, plus Argentina, Australia, Brazil, Japan and South Korea. Russia participates in all except the Australia Group, but many key players relevant to the regimes' effectiveness have not joined. China and India do not participate in any of the regimes.[10] Nor are any of the smaller developing countries with rapidly emerging high-technology sectors such as Indonesia, Jordan, Singapore, Taiwan and Thailand; nor active distributing and trans-shipment points, such as the United Arab Emirates. These critical gaps in participation in the multilateral regimes do not serve non-proliferation objectives. Since the private sectors in participating states are placed at a serious disadvantage by the disciplines and restrictions involved, there is almost an incentive for some dual-use industries, especially those in the information-technology and telecommunications sectors, to relocate to attractive non-member economies, such as India.

Second, the multilateral export control regimes are voluntary in nature and have no enforcement mechanisms, relying instead on 'peer pressure'. None of them has adopted COCOM's veto mechanism, which itself was only workable because the COCOM lists were not made public and depended on the shared perception by members of a common threat. Most but not all of the regimes do have a nominal rule against 'undercutting': the avoidance of granting a licence

---

[9] However, the participating states have agreed on a list of elements that states may wish to take into account on a voluntary basis when making assessments.

[10] China is an adherent to the MTCR and is expected to join both the MTCR and the NSG in 2004.

by one government where it is known that another government has denied a similar licence. However, this important rule depends for its effect not only on governments abiding by it but also on their being ready to exchange adequate information on licence requests and denials in the first place. In general, the voluntary basis means that the export control regimes of participant countries can vary widely in their scope and effectiveness, particularly in terms of legal enforcement. National judgements are also liable to differ. Should a licence be issued for an item to be used by the Indian Space Research Organisation to help launch commercial satellites? Many MTCR participants say 'certainly', but the USA says 'not yet': such a transfer might give a boost to the Indian missile programme.

Third, the geographic coverage of the multilateral regimes is subject to different application by participant governments. There is no rule in any of the regimes as to which countries are to be targeted except in the case of the NSG, where it is clear that exports to non-states parties to the 1968 Treaty on the Non-proliferation of Nuclear Weapons (Non-Proliferation Treaty, NPT) as well as to non-members of the International Atomic Energy Agency (IAEA) and to nuclear facilities which are not subject to IAEA inspection, should all be controlled by member states.[11] The MTCR and the Australia Group publish general guidelines on their Internet sites.[12] When private-sector companies— especially multinational companies—formulate their long-range marketing plans, ideally, they would like to have specificity, certainty and uniformity in order to be compliant with strategic export controls. However, at present, they must deal with national export control authorities in the countries from which they operate.

There is a serious and inevitable time-lag problem in adjusting all the multi-lateral lists to the emergence and strategic significance of new technologies. To compensate for the time taken in updating agreed control lists, a growing number of states have introduced 'catch-all' or end-use controls which apply to any items known to be for use in NBC weapon programmes or for the missile delivery systems for such weapons. These controls are discussed fur-ther below. The updating of control lists and the issue of how catch-all con-trols can be implemented are two respects in which more active private-sector participation could be particularly beneficial. Last but not least, there are seri-ous timing problems resulting from administrative dysfunction in national governments, especially in the USA, which delays the implementation of new versions of the lists. The lists may take months to agree on, and they have no effect on the private sector until they are published.

[11] For the Non-Proliferation Treaty see URL <http://www.un.org/Depts/dda/WMD/treaty/>, and for the IAEA member states see URL <http://www.iaea.or.at/About/Policy/MemberStates/>.

[12] For the MTCR see URL <http://www.mtcr.info/english/index.html>, and for the Australia Group see URL <http://www.australiagroup.net/index_en.htm>.

V. The impact of new priorities: non-proliferation and terrorism

With the advent of non-proliferation as the chief objective of export controls, the picture has become much more ambiguous and uncertain for the private sector. The focus is now on individual 'rogue states', which may be found in any of several regions, rather than on long-standing 'blocs' of relatively familiar adversaries. There is no international consensus as to which countries are the 'rogues' or on whether there should be controls on a broad range of items. Indeed, Iraq was a rare example of a country which had attracted such a consensus through successive United Nations resolutions. Moreover, the non-proliferation objective has meant that exports to certain dangerous activities carried out both in countries of concern and by dangerous individuals or groups that are not among the normal subjects of international regulation should be controlled. This has placed a much higher burden of responsibility on the private sector. Export control compliance has become much more complicated and demanding.

This latter development has been highlighted by the adoption by most leading developed countries of the 'catch-all' concept in their export control regulations. The concept was adopted in the USA in 1990 and has been reflected, for example, in the EU dual-use regulation and in a number of national export control regimes.[13] The catch-all concept imposes an obligation on the private sector to bring to the attention of its export control authorities any situation in which an end-user is thought to be using an item for the design, development or manufacture of a weapon of mass destruction, *whether or not* the item is contained in an applicable control list. In many export control systems, this obligation applies only if the exporter is certain about WMD end-use. In the USA, however, the obligation attaches if the exporter either knows, or *has reason to suspect*, the presence of WMD end-use.

Two ideas lie behind the catch-all concept. The first is that new information may require controls to be introduced more quickly than control lists can be updated. The second is that the private sector may in some instances have better access to information about the activities of end-users than the national intelligence authorities do. In effect, the concept makes the private sector a partner with governmental authorities—a role which is not generally welcomed by private-sector companies.

In the United States, the government has reacted to private-sector concerns by publishing a so-called Entity List: the entities on the current list, which are subject to licence requirements for the export or re-export of specified items, are located in China, India, Israel, Pakistan and Russia.[14] In general, any item

---

[13] On the EU dual-use regulation and on the catch-all clause, see Davis (note 8), chapter 3.

[14] See US Department of Commerce, Bureau of Industry and Security, 'The Entity List: entities of proliferation concern listed in supplement no. 4 to part 744 of the Export Administration Regulations', URL <http://www.bxa.doc.gov/Entities/Default.htm>.

destined for an Entity List end-user requires a licence, whether or not it is identified on the list. While the Entity List concept helps to reduce the uncertainty of the catch-all concept, the obligation of US exporters and re-exporters to report possible WMD end-users continues, whether or not an end-user is on the Entity List.

The focus of strategic export controls in the post-cold war period has been mainly on denial of sensitive items to other states, but increasing attention has been paid to denial to terrorist groups and individuals. The emphasis on terrorist end-use was dramatically intensified after 11 September 2001. The Australia Group was the first regime to respond by broadening its list with terrorist groups in mind.[15]

Precisely because the subject of denial to terrorist end-users is now so important, there is a need for a much greater clarification and rationalization of the role to be played by the private sector in this respect. UN sanctions create a requirement for national controls that can deny any material or technical assistance to any designated terrorist group or individual as well as any group or individual planning to carry out a terrorist act. End-use-based export controls can play a part in implementing this commitment. At present, the counter-terrorism objective is clouded by a proliferation of lists of potential terrorists issued by governments and multilateral bodies—for example, the EU, Interpol, the UN and the USA.[16] The duplications and differences among the lists create uncertainty as to private-sector responsibilities. Added to this is the absence of guidelines from governments as to how to use these lists—for example, how to match names of end-users against the names on the list.

VI. Conclusions

Strategic export controls are meaningless without the full participation of the private sector. Where governments have organized themselves to implement and enforce export controls, there has generally been no lack of will on the part of the private sector to comply and assist. However, the number of governments which have made the effort to reach out to those involved in and affected by enforcement is still relatively small, even among the states participating in the multilateral regimes. The more governments do so, and the more the multilateral regimes are expanded to fill the gaps in participation, the greater the potential will be for the private sector to make a significant contribution, especially as the counter-terrorism effort expands.

---

[15] As explained in chapters 4 and 5 in this volume, much activity has also centred on stemming the financing of terrorist groups: e.g., through the UN Counter-Terrorism Committee, and the Financial Action Task Force on Money Laundering (FATF) of the Organisation for Economic Co-operation and Development (OECD). On the FATF see URL <http://www1.oecd.org/fatf>.

[16] On these lists see chapters 5 and 8 in this volume.

At present, the framework of the multilateral export control regimes provides a valuable forum for the exchange of information and ideas among the governments represented at the periodic meetings of these regimes. International solidarity would be even more complete, the evolution of export control endeavours better informed, and their implementation more fully and uniformly effective if the private sector could also be represented at these meetings.

7. The European Union: new threats and the problem of coherence

Niall Burgess and David Spence

I. Introduction

The events of 11 September 2001, and the policy challenges posed by the United States' reactions to them, had an impact on a European Union (EU) already in the midst of historic change. The successful introduction of the single European currency and the first steps towards a European Security and Defence Policy (ESDP) had created new momentum in the monetary and security fields. Today, the admission of 10 new Central European and Mediterranean members to the EU in the spring of 2004, and two additional members in 2006, are set to bring 100 million new citizens into the Union, creating new borders, new neighbours and new priorities.

Even before the attacks of September 2001 made the world seem a more threatening and demanding place, EU leaders were grappling with the longer-term implications of enlargement, and with the question of how the EU could live up to its new potential and meet its new responsibilities. Concern about the effectiveness of EU governance and decision making prompted the decision to hold an independent European Convention in 2002–2003 to debate the future of the Union, and to follow it up with an Intergovernmental Conference (IGC), *inter alia* to consider a new Constitution for Europe. It was hoped that the constitution would be adopted by 2004.[1]

There was also a more specific debate within the EU about its ability to ensure European and world security and of the instruments it can wield directly towards that end. The original 'big idea' of European integration had been to work for peace and to build security indirectly, through the inextricable economic and social integration of former enemy states in Europe. Yet for decades the EU and its precursor organizations had focused on essentially domestic goals. Efforts to establish the EU as an international actor had begun by the 1970s and accelerated particularly after the end of the cold war. Much was achieved regarding the reach, salience, instruments and procedures of Europe's international policy,[2] but critics argued that there were still basic flaws of both a political and an institutional nature. EU member states

---

[1] On the European Convention and for the Draft Treaty establishing a Constitution for Europe, presented to the European Council on 18 July 2003, see the Convention Internet site at URL <http://european-convention.eu.int/bienvenue.asp?lang=EN>.
[2] For a description and critique of these developments see Cameron, F., *The Foreign and Security Policy of the European Union: Past, Present and Future* (Sheffield Academic Press: Sheffield, 1999); and Everts, S., *Shaping a Credible EU Foreign Policy* (Centre for European Reform: London, 2002).

regarded the sensitive areas of foreign, security and defence policy as central to their notion of national sovereignty. They resisted the same kind of pooling of sovereignty that had long been seen within the economic and other internal fields, or in foreign trade. They were particularly allergic to placing any control of the resources devoted to security, or of specific operational decisions, in collective European hands. Another problem was the significant differences in foreign policy culture, experiences and expectations within member states as well as between them and the European Commission.[3]

At the institutional level, a succession of treaty changes during the 1990s left the EU with a Byzantine system of differentiated decision making. Neither a state nor an international organization, it has defied simple definition, although the characterization of the Union by Jacques Delors, former President of the European Commission, as 'an unidentified political object' captures the continuously open-ended nature of the European project.[4] As a result, some matters directly relevant to the security of the EU's common territory and assets (such as intelligence collection and sharing, and the running of police forces, military and civil defence and disaster response, not to mention armed forces) have remained a purely national responsibility, while those matters which come within a collective EU framework can be handled in at least three significantly different procedural contexts.[5]

The historic European Community (EC)—the 'first pillar'—covers those areas where member states have ceded sovereignty to the Union. In relation to security threats and peace building, the most important areas are those relating to trade, external economic and financial programmes and assistance.

In the Common Foreign and Security Policy (CFSP)—the 'second pillar'—member states coordinate policies but retain national sovereignty over decision making in most areas. This is the area of activity which has developed rapidly in recent years, especially in the security field through the development and deployment of new police and military crisis-management instruments following the institution of the ESDP in 1999.[6] Most of this new activity has been in the Western Balkans, although the deployment in June 2003 of Operation Artemis in the Democratic Republic of the Congo (DRC) is an indication of the EU's more global ambition.[7]

---

[3] For a description of foreign policy cultures and the role of national foreign ministries in EU affairs see Hocking, B. and Spence, D. (eds), *Foreign Ministries in the European Union: Integrating Diplomats* (Macmillan: Basingstoke, 2002).

[4] Delors, J., 'Where is the European Union heading?', Presentation in the United States on 20 Mar. 2001, available at URL <http://www.notre-europe.asso.fr/fichiers/DiscoursIV01-en.pdf>.

[5] For a detailed analysis of the 3-pillar system see Demaret, P., 'The treaty framework', eds D. O'Keeffe and P. Twomey, *Legal Issues of the Maastricht Treaty* (Chancery Law: London, 1994), p. 3.

[6] Helsinki European Council, Presidency Conclusions, 10–11 Dec. 1999, Annex IV: 'Presidency reports to the Helsinki European Council on "strengthening the common European policy on security and defence" and on "non-military crisis management of the European Union"', available at URL <http://ue.eu.int/en/Info/eurocouncil/index.htm>.

[7] Operation Artemis (also known as the Interim Emergency Multinational Force, IEMF) was deployed in Bunia, capital of Ituri Province, DRC, on 12 June 2003 for a period of 3 months, later extended to 15 Sep. 2003. See 'EU launches the Artemis military operation in the DRC', 12 June 2003, URL

Justice and Home Affairs (JHA) activity—the 'third pillar'—provides a framework for cooperation between Ministries of Justice and the Interior and police forces. It has a front-line role in combating organized crime and terrorism within the European Union, but it is also the most complex area of cooperation, partly because of the reluctance of governments to agree to policies which risk undermining national legal systems and procedures, potentially placing their overall security at stake.

During the 2002–2003 European Convention, a lively debate developed over how each of these instruments should be sharpened to tackle the relevant aspects of security, and over whether and how they could be wielded by some kind of single decision-making centre in the EU and under stronger and more consistent leadership. The repercussions of the September 2001 terrorist attacks brought urgency to this debate and linked it to the larger question of the EU's mission in the world. The attacks were a reminder that external enemies could strike from within, that even the richest and most peaceful 'homelands' were not immune, and that defence could not be achieved with the classic, state-level tools of security alone. The USA's forcible reactions put pressure on the EU to demonstrate its own seriousness and efficiency in tackling the new mass-impact terrorism—the transnational character of which made Europe a key theatre for corrective action—and forced European states to confront possible differences of analysis, priorities and even values between themselves and the USA over the exact nature of the threat and how to handle it. By 2003, the USA's decision to launch military action against Iraq without a United Nations mandate and only a limited coalition of partners had exposed the EU to its most painful political split for many years. The question thus became not only what Europe should do to tackle terrorism and related challenges in its own and its future members' interests, but also where it should take its stand in relation to the USA and other potential partners. Europeans of several different schools of opinion came to believe that the only way forward was to be a great deal clearer about Europe's own security philosophy and policy, as well as a great deal more effective in pursuing it.

The EU Security Strategy, prepared by the High Representative for the CFSP Javier Solana and adopted by the European Council in December 2003,[8] was one of the first fruits of this realization. The strategy document identified terrorism as a key threat facing the European Union and as one of the first fields for follow-up action. It also linked terrorism to other key threats, including state failure, regional conflicts, proliferation and organized crime.

<http://europa-eu-un.org/article.asp?id=2428>; and Dwan, R. and Wiharta, S., 'Multilateral peace missions', *SIPRI Yearbook 2004: Armaments, Disarmament and International Security* (Oxford University Press: Oxford, forthcoming 2004).

[8] European Council, Solana, J., 'A Secure Europe in a Better World: European Security Strategy', Brussels, 12 Dec. 2003, URL <http://ue.eu.int/solana/docs/031208ESSIIEN.pdf>. The initial report was presented by Solana to the European Council at Thessaloniki, Greece, on 20 June 2003; see URL <http://ue.eu.int/pressdata/EN/reports/76255.pdf>.

Terrorism puts lives at risk; it imposes large costs; it seeks to undermine the openness and tolerance of our societies and it poses a growing strategic threat to the whole of Europe. Increasingly, terrorist movements are well resourced, connected by electronic networks and are willing to use unlimited resources to cause massive casualties.

The most recent wave of terrorism is global in its scope and is linked to violent religious extremism. It arises out of complex causes. These include the pressures of modernisation, cultural, social and political crises, and the alienation of young people living in foreign societies. This phenomenon is also a part of our own society.

Europe is both a target and a base for such terrorism: European countries are targets and have been attacked. Logistical bases for al Qaeda cells have been uncovered in the UK, Italy, Germany, Spain and Belgium. Concerted European action is indispensable.[9]

II. The EU's policy responses to the September 2001 attacks

The immediate response of the European Union to the September 2001 attacks was one of strong political support for the United States. Through a succession of meetings, the EU lobbied other governments to ratify a number of United Nations conventions, to implement UN Security Council Resolution 1373,[10] and to support a comprehensive convention against terrorism. There was also strong support for the military operations in Afghanistan which began on 7 October 2001, based on Security Council Resolution 1368.[11] Individually, EU member states contributed to the US effort to combat the al-Qaeda network and to end the Taliban regime in Afghanistan.[12]

This political response broadly reflected public opinion across Europe. Ever since 1996, surveys have shown a slow but steady increase in feelings of insecurity across the EU. For most Europeans, maintaining peace and security, combating terrorism, and fighting organized crime and drug trafficking are priorities which come close in order of importance to tackling unemployment and poverty.[13] A survey of EU and US opinion in the autumn of 2002 showed little difference between British, French, German, Italian and US respondents when it came to their concern about the possibility of terrorist attacks in their countries.[14]

---

[9] 'A Secure Europe in a Better World' (note 8).

[10] UN Security Council Resolution 1373, on threats to international peace and security caused by terrorist acts, 28 Sep. 2001, available at URL <http://www.un.org/Docs/scres/2001/sc2001.htm> . See also chapter 5 in this volume.

[11] UN Security Council Resolution 1368, on threats to international peace and security caused by terrorist acts, 12 Sep. 2001, available at URL <http://www.un.org/Docs/scres/2001/sc2001.htm>.

[12] On the war in Afghanistan see Cottey, A., 'Afghanistan and the new dynamics of intervention: counter-terrorism and nation building', *SIPRI Yearbook 2003: Armaments, Disarmament and International Security* (Oxford University Press: Oxford, 2003), pp. 167–94.

[13] See European Commission, *Eurobarometer: Public Opinion in the European Union*, Report no. 58 Mar. 2003; and *Eurobarometer 59*, July 2003, both available at URL <http://europa.eu.int/comm/public_opinion>.

[14] See Pew Research Center for the People and the Press, 'Americans and Europeans differ widely on foreign policy issues: Bush's ratings improve but he's still seen as unilateralist', Washington, DC, 17 Apr. 2002, 'URL <http://people-press.org/reports/print/php3?ReportID=153>.

In preparing a policy response, the EU faced the challenge of bringing together a wide array of possible instruments from its various pillars against what was then clearly seen as a strategic threat. In the aftermath of 11 September, EU activities were reviewed in each of these fields in a succession of council meetings involving foreign, interior, finance, transport and telecommunications ministers.

The resulting EU and national action to combat terrorism, both internationally and within the European Union, extended across a very broad spectrum and underlined the multifaceted nature of this security threat. Work was undertaken on implementation of UN Security Council Resolution 1373; the execution of orders to freeze property or evidence; stepping up mutual assistance between police and justice authorities in the member states; bilateral cooperation with the United States; the introduction of anti-terrorism clauses in agreements with third countries (see below); better cooperation between the European police (Europol) and judicial (Eurojust) agencies, updating the list of terrorist organizations;[15] activities to combat bio-terrorism; possible improvements to the Schengen Information System (SIS);[16] and cooperation with external partners.

All these lines of action were grouped together in what became the EU Plan of Action to combat terrorism.[17] A 'road map', based on the Action Plan and comprising some 70 areas of implementation of the action plan, was drawn up. The European Council has periodically updated the Plan of Action. While these updates have been largely of a technical nature, the Plan of Action is currently undergoing a thorough review.

The broad objective was to ensure effective coordination of the EU response to terrorism: to provide a specific EU response in areas falling within EU competence; to extend and enhance the anti-terrorist coalition through political dialogue with other states and in multilateral forums; and, perhaps above all, to strengthen the EU partnership with the United States. In functional terms, the main lines of action could be broken down into four: (*a*) measures aimed at detaining and prosecuting terrorists; (*b*) those aimed at denying them financial and material resources; (*c*) those aimed at encouraging, supporting and technically assisting third countries in tackling terrorism; and (*d*) those aimed at addressing the social and political resources drawn on by terrorist and criminal networks.

---

[15] See 'Council Common Position 2003/651/CFSP of 12 September 2003 updating Common Position 2001/931/CFSP on the application of specific measures to combat terrorism and repealing Common Position 2003/482/CFSP', *Official Journal of the European Union*, L 229 (13 Sep. 2003), pp. 42–45, available at URL <http://europa.eu.int/eur-lex/en/index-list.html>. See also chapter 5 in this volume.

[16] On the SIS see URL <http://www.europarl.eu.int/comparl/libe/elsj/zoom_in/25_en.htm>.

[17] See 'Conclusions and Plan of Action of the Extraordinary European Council meeting on 21 September 2001', Brussels, URL <http://europa.eu.int/comm/external_relations/110901/actplan01.pdf>; and Presidency Conclusions, Seville, 21–22 June 2002, Annex V: 'Declaration by the European Council on the Contribution of the CFSP, including the ESDP, to the fight against terrorism', URL <http://ue.eu.int/en/Info/eurocouncil/index.htm>.

Measures in the field of internal security

The opening of intra-European borders, global markets and global communications have facilitated the activities of both criminal and terrorist networks, enabling people and goods to move with growing ease. The 1997 Treaty of Amsterdam[18] provided for closer police and judicial cooperation against organized crime—although crime within national borders remains under national responsibility. The terrorist attacks of September 2001, subsequent attacks on European targets in Istanbul (Turkey), Morocco and Saudi Arabia, and planned attacks within the European Union have accelerated police and judicial cooperation between member states against all forms of cross-border crime, including terrorism.

The most significant developments include: (*a*) agreement and legislation on a European Arrest Warrant, adopted on 27 December 2001,[19] which will dispense with traditional extradition procedures and expedite the arrest and transfer of suspects (although it has yet to be implemented); (*b*) agreement on a common definition of terrorist offences for criminal law purposes; (*c*) provision for improved joint investigation between national police forces, the creation of an anti-terrorism unit within Europol[20] and strengthened cooperation between anti-terrorist units; (*d*) improved cooperation between the Judiciary and Prosecutors' offices; (*e*) measures to give the intelligence services access to parts of the data of the Schengen Information System, and simplification of procedures to improve use of the SIS in the fight against terrorism; (*f*) enhanced cooperation between member states on a common list of terrorist organizations (Article 4 of the Common Position on terrorists lists),[21] on strengthening external border checks, on exchange of information on visas and on strengthening internal security; and (*g*) closer cooperation with Canada and the United States, including the appointment of liaison officers to the EU from both countries and mutual visits between Eurojust and Canada and the USA. Europol signed a Strategic Cooperation Agreement with the United States on 4 December 2001 and negotiated a second agreement with the USA on 20 December 2002, allowing for the transfer of personal data.[22] The USA has pushed in general for a 'single-stop shop' where it can coordinate with the Brussels authorities on all these matters, and some progress has been made.

---

[18] The 1997 Treaty of Amsterdam Amending the Treaty on European Union entered into force on 1 May 1999. For the treaty see URL <http://europa.eu.int/abc/obj/amst/en/>.

[19] On the European Arrest Warrant see Laeken European Council, 'Extradition will no longer be necessary between EU member states', URL <http://europa.eu.int/comm/justice_home/news/laecken_council/en/mandat_en.htm> and European Union Factsheet, 'The fight against terrorism', URL <http://europa.eu.int/comm/external_relations/us/sum06_03/terror.pdf>.

[20] See the Europol Internet site at URL <http://www.europol.net>.

[21] 'Council Common Position 2001/931/CFSP of 27 December 2001 on the application of specific measures to combat terrorism', *Official Journal of the European Communities*, L 344 (28 Dec. 2001), pp. 93–96, updated in Council Common Position 2003/402/CFSP, 5 June 2003, *Official Journal of the European Union,* L 139 (6 June 2003).

[22] See United States Mission to the European Union, 'US, Europol to sign cooperation agreement', 4 Dec. 2001, Brussels, URL <http://www.useu.be/Terrorism/EUResponse/Dec0401Europol/Agreement.html>.

In some cases, such as the European Arrest Warrant, preparatory work had been done prior to 11 September. In fact, this work was accelerated and repackaged in the weeks following the attacks and further work is under way. Work on the future requirements of SIS II (the next-generation system) includes a new, simpler consultation procedure, in the context of combating terrorism, for alerts issued pursuant to Article 99 of the 1990 Schengen Convention;[23] the possibility of running searches on the basis of incomplete data; access for public authorities responsible for vehicle registration; extended access for the authorities which issue residence permits; and access for Eurojust and for Europol and security services to the SIS.

Other measures related to blocking the international movement of guilty persons and protecting that of the innocent have proved more problematic. To take the case of aviation security, the EU had no trouble in backing the initial US pressure, for example, for better baggage security and passenger screening, which many people felt had already been raised to a higher level in Europe than on most US domestic flights.[24] However, when airlines were hit by rocketing insurance premiums and sought help effectively in the form of reinsurance from national governments, the European Commission was concerned to make sure that any such support measures were time-limited and kept to the minimum to avoid their taking on the character of hidden or competitive subsidies. The Commission also watched carefully to ensure that any European airlines driven to the point of closure by their losses were not bailed out improperly.

By late 2003 the US demands on countries enjoying visa-free access for their citizens to the USA to introduce machine-readable passports with bio-data were causing practical problems for many European governments.[25] US proposals to place armed 'air marshals' on flights and to transfer large quantities of personal data on passengers for US intelligence screening were seen by many as objectionable in principle as well. These issues remain sensitive, and European states have increasingly seen the sense of maintaining a common front through the EU to protect their interests when dealing with them. However, as concern grew within the US aviation sector that business was being adversely affected by tighter aviation restrictions, the US pressure on Europe was softened. Meanwhile, within the EU itself there are debates in progress on land border controls—prompted not just by concerns about terrorist infiltration, but also by illegal migration and the growing flow of asylum seekers—that continue to divide the European countries because of the values and principles involved as well as the practicalities.

---

[23] On the 1990 Schengen Convention, which entered into force in Mar. 1995, and for the signatories see URL <http://europa.eu.int/comm/justice_home/fsj/freetravel/frontiers/wai/fsj_freetravel_schengen_en.htm>.

[24] European Commission, Directorate-General for Energy and Transport, 'Air safety & air security', URL <http://europa.eu.int/comm/transport/air/safety/index.en.htm>. See also the Introduction and chapter 19 in this volume.

[25] See the US–VISIT Program, URL <http://www.dhs.gov/dhspublic/interapp/editorial/editorial_0333.xml>. See also the Introduction and chapter 15 in this volume.

In the area of consequence management after terrorist actions, there are already a number of proposed or existing Community programmes which take into account the need to maintain and restore vital services in situations of crisis affecting the EU itself. Examples are in the sector of transport and energy, the general issue of security of supply and energy stock reserves,[26] the proposal to improve the use of civilian and military airspace in Europe under the concept of a Single European Sky, and the introduction of a European global positioning system (GPS) using the GALILEO satellite system.[27] In these sectors, and perhaps even more so in the information-technology (IT) sector, the issue of protection of critical infrastructure such as telecommunications and the Internet (cyber crime) has been the subject of increasing attention.[28]

Addressing the financial and material resources of terrorism

The European Union accounts for 40 per cent of world gross domestic product and a high proportion of global financial transactions. Tighter controls on these transactions can make a significant contribution to cutting off the financial resources of terrorism. In this field, the EU largely supports the United Nations. In 2001 the Financial Action Task Force on Money Laundering (FATF) of the Organisation for Economic Co-operation and Development (OECD) extended its remit beyond money laundering to include measures against terrorist financing. The FATF Eight Special Recommendations required governments to ratify and implement UN instruments, criminalize the financing of terrorism and associated money laundering, freeze and confiscate terrorist assets, report suspicious transactions, assist third countries with implementation, and review and upgrade domestic legislation in certain areas.[29]

The most important contribution the EU can make is to ensure ratification and implementation of all relevant UN instruments and decisions by its own members and others, and to implement the FATF Recommendations. In this respect, its record is respectable but not exemplary. By mid-2003, only two of the EU's 15 current members were in full compliance with all the FATF Recommendations, a further 11 member states were in full compliance with six recommendations, one was in full compliance with four of the recommendations, and another was in compliance with only one recommendation.[30] Much of the non-compliance is related to a failure to implement UN instruments.

[26] See European Commission, *Green Paper: Towards a European Strategy for the Security of Energy Supply*, 9 Aug. 2002, available at URL <http://europa.eu.int/comm/energy_transport/en/lpi_lv_en1. html>.

[27] On the Single European Sky see European Commission, URL <http://europa.eu.int/comm/transport/air/single_sky/index_en.htm>.

[28] European Commission, 'Activities of the European Union Information Society', URL <http://europa.eu.int/pol/infso/index_en.htm>; and see chapters 16, 17 and 18 in this volume.

[29] See Financial Action Task Force on Money Laundering, 'Special Recommendations on terrorist financing', URL <http://www1.oecd.org/fatf/SRecsTF_en.htm>; and chapters 4, 5 and 8 in this volume.

[30] Financial Action Task Force on Money Laundering (FATF), *Annual Report 2002–2003* (FATF: Paris, 20 June 2003), available at URL <http://www.fatf-gafi.org/pdf/AR2003_en.pdf>.

That said, the EU rate of implementation compares well with that of other states, including the USA, itself not in full compliance with all the regulations. Of greater concern is the fact that several EU applicants assessed for the report showed slow progress towards implementation, and some had severe shortcomings with compliance.

Nonetheless, there has been significant progress, not only towards implementing decisions of the United Nations and the FATF, but also in corresponding measures at the EU level. The November 2001 EU Directive on Money Laundering was upgraded to include terrorist acts, and a regulation regarding the freezing of funds of terrorist organizations was adopted in December 2001.[31] It also made provision for an additional Protocol on mutual assistance in respect of money laundering and financial crime. On 28 February 2002 the Justice and Home Affairs Council reached a common understanding on the draft Framework Decision on the execution in the European Union of orders on the freezing of property or evidence. The purpose was to establish the rules under which a member state was to recognize and execute in its territory a freezing order issued by a judicial authority of another member state. A special committee was set up to review policy at frequent intervals.

Assistance and support to third countries in tackling terrorism

As the world's largest trading partner and its largest provider of development assistance, the European Union is in a very good position to help other governments tackle organized crime and terrorism—and to withdraw assistance from governments which refuse to do so. The EU has taken steps to use its leverage in trade and cooperation with third countries by linking this to implementation of standards for cooperation on terrorism and nonproliferation.

Agreement was reached in 2002 at the Seville European Council on the inclusion of an 'anti-terrorism clause' in the Association and Co-operation Agreements between the EU and other parties, either directly in the agreement itself or in a separate declaration or exchange of letters.[32] This clause has been included in a small number of agreements concluded since then.[33] It provides for cooperation in 'preventing and repressing terrorist acts within the framework of [UN Security Council] resolution 1373' and on sharing information

---

[31] The scope of Directive 91/308/EEC on prevention of the use of the financial system for the purpose of money laundering was extended in Directive 2001/97/EC of the European Parliament and the Council, approved on 19 Nov. 2001 and issued on 4 Dec. 2001. For the new directive see *Official Journal of the European Communities*, L 344 (28 Dec. 2001), pp. 76–82.

[32] See Seville European Council, 21–22 June 2002, Presidency Conclusions, Annex V (note 17).

[33] See Perpiña-Robert, F., 'EU Presidency Statement on Counter-Terrorism: Resolution 1373: Summary: Speaking points for the presentation by the European Union in the meeting of the Counter-Terrorism Committee with the EU', New York, 23 Apr. 2002, URL <http://europa-eu-un.org/article.asp?id=1323>; and 'Report of the European Union to the Security Council Committee established pursuant to resolution 1373 (2001) concerning counter-terrorism', Enclosure, UN Security Council document S/2001/1297, 28 Dec. 2001, available at URL <http://europa.eu.int/comm/external_relations/un/docs/eu1373.pdf>.

and expertise. The anti-terrorism clause is technically regarded as non-essential, however, meaning that it could not lead to suspension of agreements. Its application is further limited 'with respect to international conventions to which [the signatory states] are party, and to their legislation and to their respective regulations'.[34]

The 'non-proliferation clause', agreed at Brussels in December 2003, is potentially much more far-reaching in its effect, as it is an 'essential clause' which could lead to suspension of cooperation in the event of concerns arising which were not addressed through an established dispute procedure.[35] It applies to new agreements. One is currently under negotiation with Syria.

Work has also focused on technical assistance for states' efforts to combat terrorism. Trial projects have been carried out in Indonesia, Pakistan and the Philippines, and more are planned.[36]

A common theme of European responses was the need to tackle the 'sources of terrorism' as well as terrorism itself. Terrorist networks can put down deep roots in weak states and can draw social and political capital from societies where there is unresolved conflict or social upheaval and economic stagnation.

A thread which is common to the analysis and prevention of all new threats is state weakness—or in some extreme cases the absence of any functioning state. Afghanistan's link with both terrorist and crime networks has been well documented. Most of Europe's heroin originates in Afghanistan and enters Europe along trafficking routes through Central Asia and the Western Balkans. Organized crime is a predatory problem that eats away at the fabric of societies, contributing to erosion and collapse from within. The Western Balkans offers a case where the perspective of EU membership has acted as a powerful driver for reform, but it also illustrates how much practical help is needed.[37] The problem does not lend itself to statistical precision. Nonetheless, Balkan criminal organizations are thought to control the distribution of around 70 per cent of the heroin entering Europe.[38] Up to 200 000 women are trafficked through the Balkans for the sex trade each year. According to the International Organization for Migration (IOM),[39] among the 700 000 women who are transported over international borders each year for the sex trade, as many 200 000 are taken to or through the Balkans.[40] In addition, every month 1000 tonnes of illegal cigarettes cross the Adriatic Sea to the European market.

[34] The standard text of this clause is an internal Council document which has not been published.

[35] See '"Non-proliferation clause" to be included in agreements with third countries', URL <http://ue.eu.int/pesc/Armes/Docs/st14997.en03.pdf>.

[36] Commitments to cooperate closely in the fight against terrorism have been included in or agreed alongside new Association Agreements between the EU and Algeria, Chile and Lebanon.

[37] See Caparini, M., 'Security sector reform in the Western Balkans', *SIPRI Yearbook 2004* (note 7).

[38] Interpol statistics, quoted in 'Intervention by Javier Solana at the London Conference on Organised Crime in South Eastern Europe', London, 25 Nov. 2002, URL <http://ue.eu.int/pressdata/ENdiscours/73343.pdf>.

[39] See the IOM site at URL <http://www.iom.int/>.

[40] See Binder, D., 'Bosnia shunning European drive to halt trafficking in women', *International Herald Tribune* (Internet edn), 21 Oct. 2002, URL <http://www.iht.com/articles/74297.html>, citing the IOM.

Clearly, there cannot be any lasting solution to these problems unless the environment is tackled which allows these networks to flourish. Much of the responsibility for this rests with the governments concerned—where there are functioning governments which can act—but the European Union can do much collectively to address this challenge.

At the collective European level, the range of instruments—at least on paper—is formidable. The EU is the world's largest trading partner and the world's largest provider of development assistance. It operates assistance programmes and has structured agreements with most countries. Even if these measures were not primarily designed for or billed as security-building programmes, their effects can militate against the conditions which breed and spread terrorism in a number of ways: by promoting social and economic development, by drawing states into profitable international economic cooperation, by improving education, cultural standards and transparency, and in general by fostering and consolidating democracy and good governance.

The strongest operation of this kind in which the EU has engaged in recent years has undoubtedly been the pre-accession process, which has so far brought 10 states, mostly post-Communist, to the point of qualifying for EU entry and has managed to eliminate interstate conflicts between them (and, at least, ameliorate most of their internal security problems) along the way.

The prospect of EU membership is acting as a powerful incentive for reform in the Western Balkans. The Stabilisation and Association Process (SAP), introduced by the EU for the Western Balkans in 1999,[41] was designed, more explicitly than any previous EU strategy, to bring security problems in the region under control and to pre-empt new conflict through a combination of material aid and political incentives—notably the prospect (albeit long-term) of eventual full EU membership. The prospect of EU membership is also giving new momentum to a settlement in Cyprus which would allow both communities on the island to accede to EU membership.

A strong security rationale can also be found in the EU's Barcelona Process, the latest embodiment of a long-standing Euro-Mediterranean dialogue with states in North Africa and the Middle East.[42]

---

[41] The SAP offers the possibility for the 5 countries of the region (Albania, Bosnia and Herzegovina, Croatia, FYROM, and Serbia and Montenegro) to sign a new kind of agreement, i.e., a Stabilisation and Association Agreement with the EU, opening up concrete EU accession perspectives for the first time, as the EU did for Central and East European countries in 1998 with the launch of the enlargement process and the opening of accession negotiations. See European Commission, 'EU in Southeast Europe: the Stabilisation and Association Process', URL <http://www.eudelyug.org/en/eu_in_see/stabilisation.htm>.

[42] On the Barcelona Process, or Euro-Mediterranean Partnership, see URL <http://europa.eu.int/comm/external_relations/euromed/>. The Euro-Mediterranean Partnership has since 1995 built up a solid and substantial set of cooperation activities, ranging from political dialogue, through trade liberalization, economic reform and infrastructure networks to culture, education and the movement of people. It is based on a comprehensive approach to security and the principle that cooperation and co-ownership are the best way to promote reform and to deal with the root causes of the terrorist threat. It includes EU-financed activities to promote exchange of best practice and training to help the police and judicial authorities in the countries concerned in the fight against terrorism.

Certain capabilities developed in the framework of the ESDP since 1999—especially in the areas of policing[43]—can help to develop local capacities. The first-ever EU crisis-management operation, the EU Police Mission (EUPM), was launched in Bosnia and Herzegovina in January 2003 with a mandate for three years and with the goal of establishing local police enforcement capacities. The EU Police Mission Proxima in the Former Yugoslav Republic of Macedonia (FYROM), with similar aims as well as a focus on efficient border management, was launched in December 2003.[44]

III. Remaining challenges for the EU

The examples above, which are far from exhaustive, show what has been achieved within the EU framework in the three years since the attacks of September 2001. New instruments have been developed—particularly in the area of internal security—and old instruments have been adapted and combined. The speed of the changes is especially noteworthy against a background where the EU, until recently, could not have been seen as a (conscious) security actor. The need to adapt has in itself been a driver of institutional change and development. Nonetheless, the response has been uneven: stronger in some areas than in others. As work is brought forward, a number of issues will have to be addressed.

One of these issues is the role which the ESDP might play in tackling terrorism more directly. A fundamental objective of the CFSP is 'to strengthen the security of the Union in all ways'. For many years, however, there has been more 'foreign' than 'security' in CFSP. Engagement in crises was hampered by the absence of capabilities at the EU level, leaving Europe reliant on the United Nations, NATO or the USA for external security. Even in the foreign policy area, effectiveness was constrained by the shifting focus of rotating six-monthly presidencies, by an emphasis on declamation over action, and by the strong and often competing interests of member states. This has begun to change with the appointment of an EU High Representative for the CFSP and with the progressive development of joint military and police capabilities for crisis management.

The initial stimulus for this development was the 1999 crisis in Kosovo, which created a determination to take a more active role in the challenges of post-conflict reconstruction that Europe faced in the region. This was followed by two years of essentially institutional and doctrinal development before the EU declared itself operational.[45] In 2003, as noted above, the EU launched police operations in Bosnia and Herzegovina and in FYROM, and it has also

---

[43] See Dwan, R. and Lachowski, Z., 'The military and security dimensions of the European Union', *SIPRI Yearbook 2003* (note 12), pp. 213–36.

[44] The EUPOL Proxima mission was launched on 15 Dec. 2003, for an initial period of 12 months. See URL <http://ue.eu.int/arym/pdf/concordia.pdf>; and Dwan and Wiharta (note 7).

[45] 'The Future of the European Union: Laeken Declaration', 15 Dec. 2001, URL <http://europa.eu.int/futurum/documents/offtext/doc151201_en.htm>.

undertaken military missions in FYROM (EUFOR Concordia, March–December 2003) and in the DRC (Operation Artemis, June–September 2003). However, operations have so far been limited to the Petersberg tasks, that is, humanitarian and rescue tasks; peacekeeping; and other tasks of combat forces in crisis management, including peace making. This mission definition is expressly included in Article 17 of the 1992 Treaty on European Union (Maastricht Treaty) and forms the limiting framework as well as the foundation of ESDP.[46] The range of tasks involved in counter-terrorism was not foreseen when it was formulated. Consequently, when the June 2002 Seville European Council meeting examined the issue of ESDP and terrorism, it foresaw two avenues of work.[47] First was the need to identify the military capabilities required to protect forces deployed in EU-led crisis-management operations against terrorist attacks. Second was the need to explore how military or civilian capabilities could be used to help protect civilian populations against the effects of terrorist action.

Even at the height of internal EU disagreement on Iraq, there was a growing convergence of views in the EU on the need for new thinking in the security and defence field on how best to tackle terrorism. At the Le Touquet Summit of February 2003, France and the UK agreed on the need for solidarity in the face of possible terrorist attacks.

Faced with the risks of all kinds, particularly from terrorism, France and the UK commit themselves as from today to mobilise all their available assets in order to provide help and assistance to the other country. We invite our Partners in the EU to join us in this commitment. We support the proposal to include in the Treaty a solidarity clause, in order to cope effectively with the threats we face together, making use of all the instruments and structures of the EU, both civilian and military.[48]

The draft Treaty on a Constitution for Europe currently under negotiation includes a 'solidarity clause',[49] engaging member states to help each other against the consequences of possible terrorist attacks, and a provision for structured cooperation on defence matters. The European Security Strategy that was approved in December 2003, however, foresees a wider spectrum of ESDP missions, including support for third countries in combating terrorism. It also emphasizes the need 'to transform our militaries into more flexible, mobile forces and to enable them to address the new threats'.[50] The European Council has agreed to the establishment of a small military planning cell. While these decisions in themselves will not encroach on the role which NATO is assuming in counter-terrorist actions, they do ensure that ESDP will become a more serviceable instrument for addressing new security threats.

---

[46] For the Maastricht Treaty see URL <http://europa.eu.int/en/record/mt/top.html>.

[47] See Presidency Conclusions, Seville (note 17).

[48] See 'Declaration on Strengthening European Cooperation in Security and Defence', Le Touquet, 4 Feb. 2003, URL <http://www.defense.gouv.fr/dga/fr/pdef/declaration_touquet.pdf>.

[49] Article 42 of the Draft Constitutional Treaty for Europe (note 1).

[50] European Council (note 8).

A second issue that will need to be addressed is threat assessment and intelligence cooperation. Following the September 2001 attacks, assessments were drawn up by EU member states' embassies and Commission delegations in many capitals. These aimed at producing an assessment of the perceived terrorist threat to third countries and the ability and willingness of governments to enforce strict counter-terrorism measures. It remains the case, however, that most intelligence cooperation between EU member states and with third countries takes place outside the framework of the EU institutions.[51] Different perceptions of the threat from Iraq contributed to sharp differences of view among EU member states on military action. This has contributed to the realization that, in the future, common approaches to difficult security-related issues will have to be based on common threat assessments. A better flow of information from member states will be necessary to underpin strategic decisions at the EU level and to facilitate the targeting of EU instruments in accordance with real needs.

A third issue is coordination. The new threat of terrorism has clearly shown that the EU cannot pigeonhole the threats or categorize the challenges to its existence as a liberal democratic polity and a social market economy, according to its own decision-making structures. The terrorism threat cuts across internal and external security; across the competences of member states and the European Union; and across the spectrum of activities ranging from security to trade, development, transport and justice. It is the threat that synthesizes. Like organized crime, terrorism is an issue that pits networks against bureaucracies. As is the case with the USA, NATO and other actors in the fight against terrorism, the EU is being forced to adapt and better integrate itself in response.

As noted above, the EU deals with terrorism under all three of its institutional pillars. It has two working groups of national experts dealing with terrorism. The Terrorism Working Group (TWG) deals with internal security and the Counter-Terrorism Working Group (COTER) deals with external security. While they have developed the practice of periodic joint meetings, interaction is limited, reflecting the coordination problems in many member states. At the senior working level, the Political and Security Committee (known by its French acronym 'COPS') deals with CFSP and ESDP matters, while the Committee of Permanent Representatives (COREPER) has a broader remit and is the traditional filter and preparatory mechanism for decisions by foreign ministers and the European Council.

Like everything else in the European context, the challenge of integration is complex and operates at three different levels.

The first challenge is to pull together elements of policy, funding and action within what is recognized as the span of the EU's external security-related activity. The incompletely realized link between anti-terrorist strategy and the

---

[51] For a partial overview see Keohane, D. and Townsend, A., 'A joined up EU security policy', *CER Bulletin* (Centre for European Reform), no. 33 (Dec. 2003), URL <http://www.cer.org.uk/articles/issue33.html>.

'classic' instruments of ESDP is referred to above. Other developing elements of EU security policy offer similar overlaps and opportunities for synergy. A good example is the EU's policy against the proliferation of weapons of mass destruction (WMD), which developed rapidly in 2003 through the adoption first of a set of guiding principles and an Action Plan, and then the Strategy against Proliferation of Weapons of Mass Destruction, adopted at the Brussels European Council in December.[52] These documents include measures to combat proliferation not only between states but also involving terrorists and other sub-state actors. They require a laborious concertation of many different lines of action and sources of funding (the Commission, the Council, the member states, the European Atomic Energy Community, and so on) and the integration of the WMD theme into a range of different EU external relationships and dialogues.

EU members have already recognized that a step-change in efficiency across the whole field of external action will demand drastic institutional change. That may happen. There are proposals in the draft EU Constitution to create a more powerful EU 'Foreign Minister', double-hatted as Commissioner and supported by a single Foreign Ministry bringing together personnel and resources formerly split between the different EU organs. The appointment of a longer-term President of the European Council and changes in the system of EU collective representation abroad would also be important steps towards greater coherence. However, the Constitution will take time to adopt and ratify. For the moment—and probably for the next four years at least—better integration will have to be achieved by other means.

The second challenge is posed by the link between internal and external security. This is becoming increasingly obvious and is stressed repeatedly in the European Security Strategy. Viewed through the prism of enlargement, what was once external action to promote stability and security is now internal action. The candidate countries already participate extensively in stability building and other 'homeland security' programmes that are identical or similar to those in place for members of the EU. To a more limited but still significant extent, this is also true for cooperation with some other partners close to Europe which are preparing themselves for candidate country status. An example is the JHA programme, which forms part of the Community Assistance for Reconstruction, Development and Stabilisation (CARDS) programme for the Balkans.[53] Conversely, some security-related Community programmes that were developed primarily for use within the Union are increasingly being applied outside the EU, a prime example being civil protection.

The challenge of achieving full coordination and synergy in this field is complicated both by the institutional barriers remaining between external and internal agencies and activities—at the national level and in the EU 'pillars'—

---

[52] EU Strategy Against Proliferation of Weapons of Mass Destruction, Brussels, 12–13 Dec. 2003, URL <ue.eu.int/pressData/en/misc/78340.pdf>.

[53] On the 2002–2006 CARDS programme see URL <http://europa.eu.it/comm/external_relations/see/docs/cards/sp 02_06.pdf.>

and by the problems of attitude and bureaucratic culture. A further dimension is the proper concern of EU governments and citizens not to allow internal security measures, no matter how real the external threats that drive them, to encroach too far on individual liberties and civil rights or to create new suspicion and divisions in multi-ethnic societies.

The planned consolidation of the EU's 'pillar two' resources will not spread to the second pillar–third pillar relationship anytime soon, and for the foreseeable future improvements in this respect will depend critically on governments' internal coherence and on relationships between the EU's new 'foreign minister' and his Commission colleagues.

A third challenge is to achieve coherence between those EU activities related to external and internal security, and other activities carried out in the 'first pillar', generally under the Commission's authority. The Commission has a limited role in security matters (both CFSP and ESDP) and it certainly has no direct role in military affairs. However, its actions contribute to the emergence and strengthening of the EU security policy and have the potential to enhance the success of future operations. Examples are the efforts under way to improve and simplify the regulatory framework for the defence industry within the Union and its capability to compete on the world market, including through more standardization. Some of the more significant shortfalls related to the ESDP military headline goal are directly related to a number of industrial and technological sectors, including aerospace and information technology, where there is no strict demarcation between civilian and military industries. On the more defensive side, it is the Commission within the framework of the Common Commercial Policy that represents the EU in international discussion on the strategic export controls which are now generally recognized to need strengthening, against both 'rogue states' and terrorists. Other first-pillar matters of obvious relevance are energy, international finance and infrastructure protection.

One more general issue is the need for greater interaction between governmental and non-governmental actors, whether these are non-governmental organizations (NGOs) in the field or companies in the private sector with their own risks and their own methods of risk assessment and risk management. This, in turn, will imply the sharing of information with partners hitherto outside the formal security loop. It will also imply greater coordination and therefore greater costs in human and financial resources. It will imply increased state reliance on private security provision, increased training and considerably enhanced public diplomacy to match the required degree of greater government involvement in the private lives of citizens. These are relatively uncharted waters for the EU, but September 2001 boosted both the consciousness of urgency and the mechanisms of inter-sectoral cooperation and integration.

IV. Conclusions

The evolution of the European Union into a new political form has been neither smooth nor steady. It has developed through a kind of 'punctuated equilibrium' with periods of virtual standstill or equilibrium, alternating with rapid
development into new forms.[54] In the words of an initiated observer, Europe is
a 'permanent building site'.[55] The inherent political difficulty of, in particular,
achieving new surrenders of competence to the centre and new harmonization
of national practice means that moments of great crisis and popular emotion
may offer the only chance to jump certain barriers to progress. History is
likely to regard 11 September 2001 as such a case in point.

With the end of the cold war and the subsequent emergence of 'rogue states'
and new and exacerbated forms of international terrorism, it is now widely
recognized that security must be analysed and managed not only between
states but also at the sub-national, regional and global levels. Similarly, the
functional scope of what is included in 'security' has widened from the purely
military to a broader political, economic, social and environmental coverage.[56]
The EU had arguably been developing as a 'post-modern' security system for
some time before the 'post-modern' security philosophy was voiced.[57] Some
within the EU, including some within the European Commission, have
followed these conceptual developments and have for some time recognized
the EU's consequent potential.[58] Since its inception, the EU has had a range of
competence and applicable resources that are wider than those of almost any
other organization, capable of covering all the currently recognized dimensions of security (other than, so far, collective military defence) and more. Its
intrusive regulatory character gives it unique possibilities to address sub-state
dimensions of threat and mobilize sub-state actors for positive ends. Its bor-
der-free internal market both allows and forces it to become adept in transnational remedies. Its tradition of common external negotiating positions
allows it to make coherent, often influential collective inputs to global-level
discussion of universal human challenges.

The September 2001 events brought home to the EU itself and to a range of
external partners the need for cooperation in areas relating to the internal
security of the Union. Some of these areas relate specifically to the security of
citizens, while others relate to critical infrastructure protection (CIP) and the
environment.[59] Still others are important for security in terms of their effects

---

[54] Gould, S. J., and Eldredge, N., 'Punctuated equilibria: the tempo and mode of evolution recon-
sidered', *Paleobiology*, vol. 3 (1977), pp. 115–51.

[55] Delors (note 4).

[56] See, e.g., Krahmann, E., *The Emergence of Security Governance in Post-Cold War Europe*, Economic and Social Research Council Working Paper 36/01 (University of Sussex, Sussex European Institute: Falmer, 2001), URL <http://www.one-europe.ac.uk/pdf/w36krahmann.pdf>, p. 13.

[57] See, e.g., Cooper, R., *The Breaking of Nations: Order and Chaos in the Twenty-First Century*
(Atlantic Books: London, 2003).

[58] See Commission Report to the Ghent European Council, 19 Oct. 2001, URL <http://europa.eu.
int/news/110901/emu.htm>.

[59] See also chapters 16 and 17 in this volume.

on economic life and prosperity: such widely diverse policy areas as development cooperation or the stabilizing effects of the Economic and Monetary Union (EMU) and the single European currency have far-reaching relevance for overall security. How far the European Union itself will succeed in mobilizing this dauntingly wide range of possibilities and resources—or even in keeping track and control of the narrower range of instruments directed against terrorism as such—remains an open question.

Overall, the EU response to international terrorism since 2001 has brought a new realism to EU foreign policy making. Under pressure from a very present threat and from the US responses to it, the EU has had to grapple with the profound link between domestic and international security and with the need to develop new capabilities and new modes of cooperation. The threat of international terrorism and 'hyper-terrorism'[60] has underlined the impotence of the EU's legalistic approach to policy making, with its undue concentration on separating the three pillars of policy making produced by the Maastricht Treaty. This is increasingly acknowledged—in the European Security Strategy, in the provisions of the draft Treaty establishing a Constitution for Europe and in the wide acceptance of the importance of solidarity as a guiding principle in security matters.

The EU remains hamstrung by its own internal procedures, based on the simple but deceptive premise that internal and external security are somehow separable. Some of its 'limbs', especially in the third pillar, have developed a new reach and flexion, although—as any organism experiencing a growth spurt—coordination between the limbs is not yet as good as it should be. The fairest interim verdict may be that the EU's response to new threats—like the EU itself—is still a work in progress, but also that awareness of the threat, and of the EU's potential for tackling it, is greater than ever before.

---

[60] Heisbourg, F., Fondation pour la Recherche Stratégique, *Hyperterrorisme: La Nouvelle Guerre* (Odile Jacob: Paris, 2003).

8. Banking in an international and European framework: the case of Liechtenstein

Georges S. Baur

I. Introduction

As indicated by the title of this volume and as clear from the dominant context after 11 September 2001, security in the world of banking and finance is defined as relating essentially to terrorism and financial crime. This chapter therefore makes only brief reference to other important issues, such as Internet security, arms deals and war crimes, and does not attempt to establish a definition of terrorism.[1]

What changes has the current security agenda brought for banking and more generally the financial industry? In recent years, particularly after the terrorist attacks of September 2001, financial intermediaries such as banks, professional trustees and to some extent asset managers have been exposed to an important change in the attitude to their work. This is also, of course, the case for the banks and other financial intermediaries in Liechtenstein. Money has been discovered to be a good tool for tracing, blocking, and fighting crime and criminals.[2]

The notion of crime has also changed. Money laundering as well as trans-border corruption and tax fraud have recently been included in Europe's criminal codes.[3] While the most important issue has been the fight against money laundering and organized crime, terrorism has kept everyone on the alert and preoccupied with it for over two years. If financial intermediaries in earlier

---

[1] See, e.g., Raymond Aron's definition: 'une action violente est dénommée terroriste lorsque ses effets psychologiques sont hors de proportion avec ses résultats purement physiques' (an act of violence is a terrorist act when its psychological effects are out of proportion to its purely physical effects). Aron, R., *Paix et Guerre entre les Nations* [Peace and war among nations], 6th edn (Calmann-Lévy: Paris, 1968), p. 176. Note also the comment on the notion of 'war' against terrorism in section VI below.

[2] See Financial Action Task Force on Money Laundering (FATF), *Report on Money Laundering Typologies 2002–2003* (FATF: Paris, 14 Feb. 2003), Introduction, para. 1, available at URL <http://www1.oecd.org/fatf/pdf/TY2003_en.pdf>.

[3] See, e.g., the legislation in France—Loi no. 96-392 du 13 mai 1996 relative à la lutte contre le blanchiment et le trafic des stupéfiants et à la coopération internationale en matière de saisie et de confiscation des produits du crime (1) (Law no. 96-392 of 13 May 1996); in Belgium—Law of 11 January 1993 on Preventing Use of the Financial System for Purposes of Laundering Money; in Germany—Act on the Detection of Proceeds from Serious Crimes (Money Laundering Act), 25 Oct. 1993; in Switzerland—Amended Criminal Code of 1 August 1990 (Articles 305bis and 305ter) and Federal Act on the Prevention of Money Laundering in the Financial Sector (Money Laundering Act) of 10 October 1997; in the United Kingdom—Money Laundering Regulation 1993; and in Liechtenstein—Amended Law on Narcotics of 12 November 1992 (Article 20a), Law of 21 March 1996 on the Amendments to the Criminal Code (Absorption of Enrichment, Money Laundering and Prevention of Abusive Exploitation of One's Position as an organ for Unfair Stock Exchange Dealings, and Law of 22 May 1996 on the Professional Due Diligence when Accepting Assets (Due Diligence Act).

times were inclined not to worry too much about what was happening around them as long as business went well, the new international political agendas have increasingly heightened their concern.

II. International initiatives

The initiatives of international organizations and the ad hoc working groups they have established are described in detail elsewhere in this volume.[4] Noteworthy among them are the Group of Seven/Group of Eight (G7/G8) industrialized nations;[5] the Organisation for Economic Co-operation and Development (OECD) and the Financial Action Task Force on Money Laundering (FATF);[6] the Financial Stability Forum (FSF);[7] the United Nations and its Office on Drugs and Crime (UNODC)[8] and Counter-Terrorism Committee (CTC);[9] the European Union (EU); the Council of Europe and its Select Committee of Experts on the Evaluation of Anti-Money Laundering Measures (MONEYVAL)[10] and Group of States against Corruption (GRECO);[11] the Organization for Security and Co-operation in Europe (OSCE); and the International Monetary Fund (IMF). They all deal with issues which are security-relevant in one way or another.

III. New developments in international law

Since the early 1990s there has been a new development in international law. The old system was based purely on intergovernmental negotiations and conferences which sometimes led to bi- or multilateral agreements, primarily binding on states or member states. This system has changed in four important ways.

[4] See especially chapters 4 and 5 in this volume.

[5] See URL <http://www.g8.fr/evian/english/home.html>.

[6] The FATF is an intergovernmental body, established by the Group of Seven in 1989. The seat of its Secretariat is at the OECD, in Paris. It has 33 member states. The development of standards in the fight against terrorist financing was added to the FATF mission in 2001. The FATF works to generate the political will to bring about national legislative and regulatory reforms in the areas of money laundering and terrorist financing. See URL <http://www1.oecd.org/fatf/>; and chapter 4 in this volume.

[7] The FSF was convened in Apr. 1999 to promote international financial stability through information exchange and international cooperation in financial supervision and surveillance. See URL <http://www.fsforum.org/home/home.html>.

[8] See URL <http://www.unodc.org/unodc/index.html>.

[9] The CTC, consisting of representatives of all 15 members of the Security Council, was created through UN Security Council Resolution 1373, 28 Sep. 2001, available at URL <http://www.un.org/documents/scres.htm>. The CTC monitors the implementation of the resolution by all states and tries to increase the capability of states to fight terrorism. See URL <http://www.un.org/Docs/sc/committees/1373/>; and chapter 5 in this volume.

[10] See URL <http://www1.oecd.org/fatf/Ctry-orgpages/org-pcrev_en.htm>.

[11] GRECO was set up in May 1999 as a flexible mechanism to monitor, through a process of mutual evaluation and peer pressure, the observance of the Twenty Guiding Principles for the Fight against Corruption (adopted on 6 Nov. 1997 by the Committee of Ministers of the Council of Europe and available at URL <http://cm.coe.int/ta/res/1997/97x24.htm>) and the implementation of international legal instruments of the Council of Europe adopted in pursuance of the Programme of Action against Corruption. See URL <http://www.greco.coe.int/>.

1. *Globalization.* Since the early 1990s, after the fall of the Berlin wall and the exponential increase in activity on international markets (i.e., globalization in the true sense of the word), issues of financial crime and security have increasingly become international ones. This has happened not least because organized crime became fully globalized before those who fought it did. Of course, where there is money, crime is close at hand. Security in the financial context used to relate to 'simple' crimes: a bank robbery, or hiding the receipts of a fraud. Furthermore, such crimes were seen as something national: even the question of what happened to the money that was stolen, whether obtained through blackmail or produced in another manner by the Mafia, for example, was seen by others as a problem purely for Italy or perhaps the United States.

2. *Action groups.* With the end of the cold war, ideological issues no longer dominated, political blocs were not in opposition to each other, and the most powerful and influential countries have been able to solve many problems in a cooperative manner. The G7/G8 provides the clearest illustration of this. With a view to greater efficiencies, detailed policy making—for instance in the field of standard setting and assessment—has been increasingly handed over to closed 'action groups' with no standing in classic international law.

3. *'Soft law'.* There is a growing role for so-called 'soft law' which does not necessarily respect, and in certain circumstances consciously disrespects, outmoded principles of international law such as the notion of equal application and applicability, peer review, non-discrimination and action on a level playing field—in short, equal treatment in general as well as transparent rules and procedures.

4. *Influence on the private sector.* The above-mentioned rules and activities are, if not formally applicable, at least highly influential for the private sector. As their authors intended, they have a high degree of influence on everyone's behaviour. Remarkably enough, this is mainly not because of any legal threat, but because of such instruments as 'name and shame'—the fear of losing good reputation—and because of plain political pressure.

IV. Liechtenstein as an example

Which laws are particularly important for the private sector with respect to security issues today, and what has Liechtenstein accomplished?

The security question cannot be separated from the general issue of a well-designed system to control the financial centre. The principal issues of diligence and control are generally the same. Nevertheless, in technical terms a whole new dimension has been added with the development of the fight against money laundering and organized crime. The original question was 'where does the money stem from?', whereas now the question must be added 'where does the money go?'[12] In the first case it was a question of turning

---

[12] FATF (note 2), chapter 1, paras 8 and 9.

money obtained from illegal sources into legal funds, whereas in the second case money obtained from perfectly legal sources is often used for illegal purposes.

When the security issue came to the fore, essentially and in its most globally influential form after 11 September 2001, it became vital for countries' financial systems to be able to react quickly and cooperate in a meaningful manner. Liechtenstein was already acting to fight money laundering: all the necessary authorities were in place and sufficiently alert to be able to take up the fight against the financing of terrorism immediately.

At the end of the 1990s, however, Liechtenstein's financial sector was regarded by foreign authorities as insufficiently regulated and was thus blacklisted by groups such as the FATF and the FSF. As an example for similar jurisdictions, it is interesting to note what Liechtenstein has in general terms done to overcome the shortcomings in its financial centre since its inclusion in the FATF's list of Non-Cooperative Countries or Territories (NCCT) for the year 2000.[13]

Liechtenstein has amended and brought up to state-of-the-art standards its legislation on the duty of diligence of financial intermediaries, on the prevention of money laundering,[14] and on mutual legal assistance in criminal matters[15] as well as with respect to the seizure and forfeiture of money of criminal origin.[16] The 1959 European Multilateral Mutual Legal Assistance Treaty[17] has been given more substance in its application, and a Mutual Legal Assistance Treaty was concluded with the United States in 2002.[18] The staffs of the responsible national authorities, such as the police, the prosecutor's office, the courts and the financial surveillance authority, have all been enlarged. New authorities have been created, such as the special police to combat economic crime (Einsatzgruppe zur Bekämpfung der Wirtschaftskriminalität und organisierte Kriminalität, EWOK), the Due Diligence Unit (DDU) and, most important, the Financial Intelligence Unit (FIU).

All these 'formal' acts would not have led to any significant change, however, if Liechtenstein had not made active efforts to apply the new laws, through real-life investigations and proceedings against people who misuse the financial system. Many of the cases involved have been reported in the media,

---

[13] See Financial Action Task Force on Money Laundering (FATF), 'Review to identify non-cooperative countries or territories: increasing the worldwide effectiveness of anti-money laundering measures', 22 June 2000, URL <http://www1.oecd.org/fatf/pdf/NCCT2000_en.pdf>.

[14] Law of 22 May 1996 on the Professional Due Diligence when Accepting Assets (Due Diligence Act), *Liechtensteinisches Landesgetzsblatt (*hereafter *Liechtenstein Legal Gazette)*, no. 116 (22 Aug. 1996), also available at URL <http://www.jeeves-group.li/files/pdf/FLduediligenceact.pdf>.

[15] The Mutual Legal Assistance Act of 11 Nov. 1992; see *Liechtenstein Legal Gazette*, no. 68 (1993).

[16] Criminal Code §20 in its original version of 24 June 1987; see *Liechtenstein Legal Gazette*, no. 37 (22 Oct. 1988), URL <http://www.recht.li/sys/1988037.html>.

[17] The European Convention on Mutual Assistance in Criminal Matters, *European Treaty Series*, no. 030 (20 Apr. 1959), available on the Council of Europe Internet site at URL <http://conventions.coe.int/Treaty/en/Treaties/Html/030.htm>.

[18] Treaty between the United States of America and the Principality of Liechtenstein on Mutual Legal Assistance in Criminal Matters, document 107-16, 8 July 2002, URL <http://www.amicc.org/docs/Liechtenstein_mutualassisantace.pdf>. The treaty entered into force on 1 Aug. 2003.

and in general the FIU's statistics are very encouraging.[19] All this goes along with an intense actual usage of mutual legal assistance, which has helped the country regain credibility with foreign authorities. This has clearly had an impact on the reviews by international organizations such as the FATF and MONEYVAL, and in 2003 by the IMF.[20]

The IMF's report is probably the most complete recent report: it is based on objective criteria, and follows a transparent procedure and the principle of equal treatment. The IMF remarked on Liechtenstein's high level of compliance with international standards for anti-money laundering and combating the financing of terrorism. With respect to the international supervisory and regulatory standards, it noted that financial-sector supervision and regulation were underpinned by a good foundation of modern legislation and regulations that derive from Liechtenstein's membership of the European Economic Area (EEA). The one substantial criticism made by the IMF is that the authorities responsible for bank supervision and supervision of investment companies in particular, but also the supervision of insurance, are in part understaffed. The recommendations it makes for a reorganization of the supervision of the financial market, which should lead to the establishment of an integrated supervisory authority that is independent of the government, are in line with work that has been under way in Liechtenstein since 2001.[21] Liechtenstein has also established a working group on the development of the financial centre, with aims reaching far beyond the limited issues of fighting crime.

Especially with respect to the fight against terrorism, it has proved to be of the utmost importance that a small country like Liechtenstein should be embedded in a solid international network. On the one hand, as a member of the EEA, Liechtenstein is associated with and partly included in relevant activities of the EU, although it is not an EU member state.[22] On the other hand, Liechtenstein has established direct relations with the USA, and these have proved to be very helpful. With respect to fighting terrorism, representatives of the US Administration have praised Liechtenstein highly.[23]

[19] See *Annual Report 2002 of the Financial Intelligence Unit (FIU) of the Principality of Liechtenstein* (FIU: Vaduz, 2003), available at URL <http://llvweb.liechtenstein.li/picsli/poze_liechtenstein/Staat/newsletter/FIU%20Jahresbericht%202002%20englisch.pdf>.

[20] International Monetary Fund (IMF), *Liechtenstein: Assessment of the Supervision and Regulation of the Financial Sector*, IMF Country Report 03/289, vols 1 and 2 (IMF: Washington, DC, Sep. 2003), URL <http://www.imf.org/external/pubs/ft/scr/2003/cr03289.pdf>.

[21] International Monetary Fund (note 20), vol. 1, *Review of Financial Sector Regulation and Supervision*, p. 7.

[22] See, e.g., *The Balance between Freedom and Security in the Response by the European Union and its Member States to the Terrorist Threats* (European Network of Experts on Fundamental Rights (CFR-CDF), European Commission: Brussels, 2003), URL <http://europa.eu.int/comm/justice_home/cfr_cdf/doc/obs_thematique_en.pdf>; Commission Regulation (EC) no. 244/2003 of 7 February 2003 amending for the 11th time Council Regulation (EC) no. 881/2002 imposing certain specific restrictive measures directed against certain persons and entities associated with Usama bin Laden, the al-Qaeda network and the Taliban, and repealing Council Regulation (EC) no. 467/2001; *Official Journal of the European Communities*, L 033 (8 Feb. 2003), pp. 28–29; and Council Framework Decision of 13 June 2002 on combating terrorism, *Official Journal of the European Communities*, L 164 (22 June 2002), pp. 3–7.

[23] See, e.g., the letter of US Undersecretary of the Treasury for Enforcement Jimmy Gurulé of 5 Nov. 2002 to the editor of *The Observer*: Gurulé, J., 'Side by side', *The Observer*, 17 Nov. 2002 (responding

Cooperation between Liechtenstein and the United Nations is also close. As soon as the CTC started its activities by asking for reports on the implementation of Security Council Resolution 1373,[24] Liechtenstein's authorities cooperated by handing in their report ahead of time. Subsequently, Liechtenstein strengthened its efforts to implement this resolution fully, which clearly contains the most important UN directive with respect to Liechtenstein's situation. Moreover, its implementation of the FATF's Eight Special Recommendations to prevent the financing of terrorism is largely complete.[25] A 'package' of anti-terrorism amendments to the Criminal Code, the Criminal Procedure and the Due Diligence Act has been introduced in the Liechtenstein Landtag (Parliament).[26]

Currently, the national system for listing suspicious individuals and/or corporate entities, charities and so forth is based on Article 3, paragraph 1, of the Law of 8 May 1991 on sanctions relative to commercial relations with foreign countries[27] and UN Security Council Resolutions 1076 and 1267.[28] The lists can be found in annex 2 to the Liechtenstein Government ordinance of 10 October 2000 on sanctions against persons and organizations related to Osama bin Laden, al-Qaeda or the Taliban,[29] which is based on the above-mentioned law. The monitoring of these lists and the individuals or institutions listed is undertaken by an ad hoc group which comprises, among others, the Office for Foreign Affairs, the FIU and the Prosecutor's Office. The lists and all the amendments are immediately made known to the relevant associations, and after amendment of the ordinance they are made available to the public. As soon as such a list is conveyed to the financial intermediary, it triggers the duty to report to the FIU or the Prosecutor's Office according to Article 9 of the Due Diligence Act.

V. The private sector

Turning to the private-sector viewpoint, what additional burdens does all this impose on financial intermediaries? There is, of course—and this must not be underestimated—a huge load of formalities, paperwork and extra controls to be carried out, as well as increased costs. For example, where it was enough

---

to the article: Walsh, C., 'Trouble in banking paradise as Uncle Sam's sheriffs ride in', *The Observer,* 27 Oct. 2002, URL <http://observer.guardian.co.uk/business/story/0,6903,819815,00.html>).

[24] See note 9.

[25] Financial Action Task Force on Money Laundering, 'Special recommendations on terrorist financing', 31 Oct. 2001, URL <http://www1.oecd.org/fatf/pdf/SRecTF_en.pdf>.

[26] Act on Amendments to the Criminal Code, the Code of Criminal Procedure and the Due Diligence Act (the 'Anti-Terrorism Package'), in force as of 10 Dec. 2003. *Liechtenstein Legal Gazette,* nos 236, 237 and 238 (2003).

[27] *Liechtenstein Legal Gazette,* no. 41 (1991).

[28] UN Security Council Resolution 1976, 22 Oct. 1996, and Resolution 1267, 15 Oct. 1999, available at URL <http://www.un.org/documents/scres.htm>.

[29] *Liechtenstein Legal Gazette,* no. 186 (2000).

simply to present a passport when travelling in the past, this is no longer sufficient.[30] At least in Liechtenstein, the financial intermediary must establish
and maintain a client profile:[31] in addition to the address and other such information, the profile must contain details about the purpose of the financial relationship. Furthermore, financial intermediaries are required to monitor relationships and accounts on an ongoing basis, and to monitor transactions for
unusual or suspicious activity which indicates that there could be a connection
to money laundering, a prima facie offence or organized crime. Information on
indications of money laundering are provided by the guidelines of the Due
Diligence Unit, which financial intermediaries are expected to follow and
which require implementation of procedures for the monitoring of relationships—preferably through the use of information technology systems—clarification of activities that raise doubts, and mandatory reporting of transactions
and activities when doubts remain. For example, if an account previously used
for payments for the teaching of a child is suddenly used to transfer payment
for huge quantities of cotton, this should trigger the attention if not the suspicion of the financial intermediary.

In future, financial intermediaries will have to be more than well educated:
they will also have to take an interest in international policy, for example, in
order to identify a political figure (Politically Exposed Person, PEP); to check
whose money the person is being asked to manage; or to establish whether a
charity the person is being asked to set up is really just charitable and where
its money is going and coming from.

To put it bluntly, more security for the financial centre leads to more insecurity for the individual financial intermediary. On the one hand, financial
intermediaries have to be more alert than ever before and they must try to
obtain as much information as they can about facts related to their clients,
even while they can never be sure that this will suffice. On the other hand,
they have to accept that anything can happen, any day, and that they will have
to prove that they have fulfilled all their duties. This entails a further erosion
of the principle according to which the burden of proof is on the accuser—
once a legal tradition of this continent. The new legal order will not accept 'I
didn't know' or 'I have been told'. Financial intermediaries—in order not to
be put out of business—must scrutinize their clients and their businesses all
over again.

Assuming that many of the financial intermediaries in Liechtenstein are
trustees which survive not least thanks to the trust of their clients, the basis of
that trust may be increasingly in danger. This is especially the case in a jurisdiction such as Liechtenstein, where privacy is well protected. Clients have to
be better scrutinized. The spirit of Lenin is now hovering over every one of

---

[30] The Due Diligence Act (see note 14) requires that before establishing a relationship the financial
institution must verify the identity of the customer through official documentation and identify and document the ultimate beneficial owner of the account.

[31] Article 6 of the Due Diligence Ordinance, *Liechtenstein Legal Gazette*, no. 236 (2000).

these capitalist dealings: while trust is good, control is better. Moreover, because of the 'name and shame' effect, financial intermediaries may increasingly find themselves exposed in the media regardless of whether a suspicion has or has not been proved correct.

VI. Future developments

What is to come? The fight against terrorism, organized crime and international crime in general continues. Liechtenstein is about to start implementing the second money laundering directive of the EU.[32] At its meeting at Evian, France, on 1–3 June 2003, the G7/G8—alongside the continuing fight against terrorism—focused on weapon trafficking. Some governments have already started to use for other purposes the new legal tools they were given in order to fight terrorism, for instance, to work against certain groups with political agendas or to fight tax fraud.[33]

Without going into detail here, it may be noted that the term 'war against terrorism'[34] is a highly questionable one if it is used for more than mere public relations. As important as it is to fight terrorism—whether old or new—the approach associated with this 'war' is likely to mean that a further step is taken away from the rule of international law and will, as seen in numerous cases since 11 September 2001, increasingly undermine not only essential human rights but also civil rights.

Every day there are stories in the media about political crimes, wars, terrorism and so on. Every day financial intermediaries have to carefully assess the impact that such news could have on their work: for instance, one of their clients may be under scrutiny, or money linked to such an action may be paid into an account for which they are responsible. Today, no one dealing with money (and increasingly with commodities, real estate, art and other valuable objects) can ignore what is happening in the world. The dealer does not want to be involved in a criminal investigation. On the other hand, the client's rightful interests need to be protected, and there should still be a presumption of innocence. Involvement in a criminal action and guilt should need to be proven to establish guilt. Many decisions are imposed on financial intermediaries today which put either their reputation or their client's confidence at risk.

---

[32] Directive 2001/97/EC of the European Parliament and of the Council of 4 Dec. 2001, amending Council Directive 91/308/EEC on Prevention of the Use of the Financial System for the Purpose of Money Laundering, *Official Journal of the European Communities,* C 316 (27 Nov. 1995), pp. 49–57, available at URL <http://www.imolin.org/EUdir01e.htm>.

[33] See, e.g., the new German anti-money laundering legislation (Geldwäschebekämpfungsgesetz: Money Laundering Act in the version of the Act on the Improvement of the Suppression of Money Laundering and Combating the Financing of Terrorism (Money Laundering Act) of 8 Aug. 2002, *Bundesgesetzblatt,* vol. 1, no. 57 (14 Aug. 2002), pp. 3105–10.

[34] See, e.g., Lugar, R. G., 'Strengthen diplomacy for the war on terror', *Foreign Service Journal,* July/Aug. 2003, URL <http://www.afsa.org/fsj/jul03/lugar.pdf>.

Life, and business, has definitely not become easier. This may be the price that has to be paid for more security. However, as important as it is to crack down on terrorism, we need to be aware of this price: in terms not only of economic restrictions, but also of our freedom.[35] For the sake of credibility as well as in order to gain the support of citizens and the business community, we must ensure that there is no opening for political abuse.

[35] See Andersson, T., Cameron, I. and Nordback, K., 'EU blacklisting: the renaissance of imperial power, but on a global scale', *European Business Law Review*, vol. 14, no. 2 (2003), pp. 111– 41.

9. The resources and tactics of terrorism: a view from Russia

Vadim Volkov

I. Introduction

In the two years since the tragic events of 11 September 2001, several states have made huge efforts and allocated significant resources to eliminating international terrorism. Pursuing the goal of destroying terrorist bases, the US-led coalition of states has achieved important military victories in Afghanistan and Iraq. Russia has made military and political progress towards settlement of the Chechen conflict. Israel has overwhelming military superiority in the Middle East region and can boast an impressive list of counter-terrorist operations which eliminated their targets. However, these successes have not resulted in the decline of terrorist activities in the regions concerned, still less worldwide. On the contrary, terrorism has intensified and gained confidence.[1] It has also become more lethal, relying increasingly on suicide bombing and claiming a rapidly multiplying number of military and civilian lives. It is therefore justified to question the adequacy both of the aims and of the means of the war on terrorism. Certain counter-terrorist efforts seem to be producing unintended consequences that outweigh the positive effects. Are counter-terrorist activities and policies well-targeted and well-calculated? Is there a sufficient understanding of terrorism's specific resources, patterns of action and social infrastructure to allow it to be addressed in a systematic way?

With these questions in view, but without any ambition to provide exhaustive answers, this chapter discusses Russia's experience with international terrorism as a background to understanding the threat. It assesses the extent to which the stock of knowledge about terrorism is confirmed by Russian experience; which views this experience does not support; and what new ideas can be distilled from Russia's treatment of the problem of terrorism. Focused on origins, action patterns and resources of terrorism, the chapter advances the following three main arguments.

1. States that are now the primary targets of terrorist groups have in the past contributed to creating and mobilizing those groups.

2. Terrorism is a weak enemy, but weak enemies are more dangerous than strong enemies.

---

[1] In Russia, during the period 1997–2002, the number of terrorist acts increased by a factor of 11. Luneev, V., 'Terrorism I organizovannaya prestupnost' [Terrorism and organized crime], *Organizovannaya Prestupnost', Terrorism i Korruptsiya*, no. 2 (2003).

3. The social resources of terrorism are far more important than its technical resources.

II. The dual role of states

The first lesson which Russian experience confirms is both sad and alarming. As the major source of anti-state violence today, terrorism could not have become so strong without state sponsorship in the past. It is important to recognize that certain state policies, as well as the activities of state intelligence services of the kind that are now being mobilized to counter terrorism, have in the past contributed to the creation and support of nascent terrorist networks. The roots of this phenomenon originated in the period of the cold war when, for obvious reasons, direct warfare between the superpowers was not feasible. One of the major forms of the superpower competition was involvement in low-intensity conflicts at the margins of the global interstate confrontation. Tied by the constraints of the nuclear balance and held back by it from any direct challenge, the superpowers and their allies nonetheless provided support to various insurrectionist guerrilla forces in their efforts to limit their opponent's expansion.

The Soviet Union sponsored guerrilla groups in Central America and terrorists in the Middle East. The Komitet Gosudarstvennoi Bezopasnosti (KGB, or Committee for State Security) provided training and shelter for one of the world's leading terrorists—Ilich Ramirez Sanchez, or 'Carlos the Jackal', who organized the kidnapping of ministers attending the meeting of the Organization of the Petroleum Exporting Countries (OPEC)[2] in Vienna, Austria, in 1975. The United States, through its secret services, supported the Afghan and Pakistani mujahedin Islamic guerrilla fighters in the war in Afghanistan in 1970s and in the process also supported Osama bin Laden, who would later become the USA's 'enemy no. 1'. The purely instrumental logic of supporting the enemies of one's enemies, whoever they might be, has also manifested itself in recent local conflicts and had similarly grave consequences. Shamil Basaev, the major Chechen terrorist in Russia, was trained in the breakaway republic of Abkhazia (Georgia) by Russian military instructors and successfully deployed against Georgian troops in the conflict in 1993. The group led by Ruslan Gelaev, another terrorist, who is now hiding in Georgia, was also trained and equipped by the Russian military in Abkhazia in 1993 for the same purpose as Basaev. When the first Chechen war began, in 1995, both turned against Russia.

Terrorism, as the major anti-state force today, could not have become so strong without past state sponsorship. The short-term pragmatism of states, whereby they created and supported outlaw groups to wage low-intensity wars against their opponents, tended to backfire. It fed international terrorism and made the citizens of these and other states the hostages of short-sighted poli-

---

[2] On OPEC and for its membership see URL <http://www.opec.org>.

cies. The international business community and civil society need to take a more active stance, in the light of these lessons, in evaluating and possibly even demanding specific constraints on state policies, especially those dealing with military interventions and secret operations. How many would-be international terrorists have initially been discovered, trained and covered by state intelligence services for their own special purposes? The reliability and manageability of such terrorists are very low, and the risks are high.

The October 2002 terrorist hostage crisis at the Dubrovka Theatrical Centre in Moscow provides another example. After the special operation, in which all the terrorists were killed and their identities established, it became clear that two of the participant terrorists were Russian Federal Security Service informers who had a record of previous cooperation and were considered reliable. They had not, however, divulged any information whatsoever to the authorities about the preparation of this major terrorist act.[3]

III. Asymmetric warfare

With respect to quantity, firepower and technical equipment, terrorist networks are much weaker than states and state organizations, just as guerrillas are much weaker than regular armies. The sheer fact of their relative weakness determines their pattern of action: the choice of asymmetric tactics, which compensates for the imbalance in strength. However strong states may be, they remain vulnerable to asymmetric warfare—not only because they suffer human and material losses, but also because terrorists constantly threaten to undermine state authority, which rests on the ability to protect the state's citizens.

The asymmetry implied in this type of warfare transcends purely military features, extending into the realm of social organization and behaviour. What does this asymmetry imply? Strong agencies such as states (or even large corporations or media agencies) typically base their strategic action on the following fundamental methods and principles.[4]

1. *The delineation of spatial frontiers that separate the internal domain from the external.* The building of a castle, the creation of a business office, the delimitation of the territorial frontiers of the state and the deployment of the headquarters of an army are all examples of the practice of spatial fixation and delimitation. The possession of one's own place is a precondition for objectifying, knowing and controlling what lies outside it.

---

[3] Author's interview with 'Vladimir', an officer of the Anti-terrorist Division of the St Petersburg Division of the FSB.

[4] The following is based on the work of James Scott and Michel de Certeau: Scott, J., *Weapons of the Weak: Everyday Forms of Peasant Resistance* (Yale University Press: New Haven, Conn., 1985); Scott, J., *Seeing Like a State: How Certain Schemes to Improve the Human Nature Have Failed* (Yale University Press: New Haven, Conn., 1998); and de Certeau, M., *The Practice of Everyday Life* (University of California Press: London, 1988).

2. *The hierarchical organization of the internal domain.* Hand in hand with the creation of an internal space of one's own (or even a national or corporate space) goes the formal differentiation of functions and capacities and the creation of a hierarchical organization suited for the particular realm in which the subject of strategy operates.

3. *The sustaining of a fixed identity.* The production of identity is a vital component of domination and requires dominant authority to have its own name, emblem (a flag or a logo), uniform, slogan, and so on. The specific material symbols to which identity is attached are arbitrary; what is crucial is that it must be fixed and permanent.

4. *The production of a plan or a scheme of action.* Strategic action requires future-oriented representations, or plans. Schemes and diagrams constitute the recurrent moment of domination. There are many sub-types of this key instrument: for a company, figures and diagrams of production and sales; construction schemes; city plans, military maps; grammar books; legal codes and so on—everything that gives ideal, abstract or abridged form to the reality that is to be known, conquered, controlled and transformed by the owner of the strategy.

Conventional types of rivalry between parties or coalitions with comparable strength and chances of success, such as wars between states or competition between large firms in a market, unfolded in a symmetric fashion whereby both parties adopted principles of strategic action, as outlined above. Today the pattern of rivalry is changing. The new global conflict that manifests itself in terrorism, as well as in the rapid growth of various forms of 'shadow economy' and semi-legal markets, is asymmetric in its core features. Asymmetry, in this context, is what gives the weak a chance to survive and sometimes to prevail in a competition with the strong that would otherwise be fatal.

What are the tactics of the weak? The pattern of action of weak and subordinate groups can be understood in terms of an asymmetric response to or reflection of the domination strategy of the strong.

1. *Mobility and rejection of place.* Subjects of tactics avoid spatial fixation, visibility and concentration in one place. They do not have a territory or headquarters of their own. Because they are constantly on the move, weak rivals, such as shuttle traders or guerrillas, do not have a place of their own. 'The space of the tactics is the space of the other . . . Thus it must play on and with a terrain imposed on it and organized by the law of a foreign power'.[5] The weak are those who have to act on the other's territory, including 'territory' in the more abstract sense of rules laid down by the dominant power. Tactics, then, is the art of circumventing, reinterpreting and exploiting the rules without being able openly to overthrow their authority.

2. *Flexible network organization.* The users of such of tactics, especially terrorists or criminal groups, favour short-lived assemblages for concrete pur-

[5] de Certeau (note 4), p. 37.

poses or networks composed of small cells. In such entities all ties are highly personified and particularized, offering opportunities for open-ended recruitment and making it difficult to identify and destroy the whole. Organized crime or terrorist organizations are in fact social forms that deny organization in the conventional sense. Terrorists as well as other outlaw groups, including organized criminals and entrepreneurs in the shadow economy, rely on ways of action and forms of organization that are very different from those of states or legitimate businesses.

3. *Improvisation and manipulation of identity.* Avoiding direct and open warfare with regular army and police units, which would be self-defeating, terrorists rely on opportunism and shifting identity. This involves unforeseeable recombinations, unexpected and surprise timing, exploitation of one-time opportunities, creative adaptations, and so on. Terrorists are masterful in the art of mimicry, taking over many different identities—aircraft or bus passengers, shoppers, orthodox believers, and so on. The Chechen terrorists who took hostages in the Moscow theatre incident transported over 100 kilograms of high explosives inside two of the four high-pressure air containers normally used in the hydraulic system of Kamaz trucks and then used these steel containers as bombs. Suicide bombers are an extreme case and have so far constituted the most powerful weapons of the weak. They exemplify the pure type of asymmetric warfare. Suicide bombers invert the normal human motivation where life and survival are matters of both instinct and value; they exactly personify the tactics of the ever-shifting identity, network organization, and the creative adaptation for their purposes of an array of technical devices, including trucks and aircraft.

A close examination of the asymmetric relationship between states and terrorist networks shows that, when states try to define this type of enemy in terms that reflect their own image, they are likely to fail or waste resources. In asymmetric warfare, the B-52 bomber aircraft is the least efficient weapon. Regular troops can achieve initial success in destroying terrorist regimes in the republic of Chechnya, or in Afghanistan or Iraq, but they are unable to counter guerrilla warfare and to bring sustainable peace. Warfare often helps terrorist networks to recruit new members, while social and economic measures—such as job creation, social services and infrastructure, the local mass media and the preservation of other features of normal life—can produce anti-terrorist effects by blocking the 'reproduction' of terrorist groups and facilitating the social reintegration of their former members.

IV. The social resources of terrorism

Terrorists rely on two types of resource: technical and social. The technical resources include weapons, explosives, transport, means of communication and so on; and the means for acquiring them, namely, money. The social resources include existing social structures—institutions, networks, organizations, and so on—that are instrumentally employed by terrorists for their own purposes. Foundations, banks, organized crime groups and other networks as well as the mass media can temporarily but unexpectedly become vital resources for international terrorism. Social resources complicate counter-terrorist activity, for they make the task of externalizing the enemy—differentiating it from civil society—very difficult.

Much has been written about the drug trade as the source of financial support for terrorists. Russian experience highlights another aspect of the relationship between terrorism and organized crime. Organized crime supplies hiding places, covert channels for mobility, and a pre-existing system of contacts with bribed officials and individuals who are ready to perform certain criminal tasks. It provides a convenient infrastructure that can be adapted for a variety of purposes. Most countries have 'black' and 'grey' labour markets where jobs are provided to illegal migrants, mainly from adjoining or more distant developing countries. In turn, the illegal labour market relies on established migration networks and channels that allow the illegal cross-border trafficking of potential workers and that can be used by international terrorism. Thus, in 1999 the Russian law enforcement authorities uncovered a channel of illegal migration through southern Russia that was being used by members of the Liberation Tigers of Tamil Ilama terrorist organization. Consequently, 34 citizens of Sri Lanka—members of the terrorist organization—were arrested and deported on their way to Western Europe. Another 33 'Tamil Tigers' were prevented from entering Russia on its eastern frontiers.[6]

Apart from providing material and infrastructural support to terrorism, organized crime can act as a subcontractor, as the following example illustrates. In October 2002 the leading Chechen terrorist, Shamil Basaev, set out to organize the kidnapping of a close relative of Yuri Luzhkov, the mayor of Moscow. By so doing he hoped to receive a huge ransom and publicity. Basaev gave the task of organizing the kidnapping to a member of his *teip* (clan), Ruslan Murzabekov, who was residing in Kharkov, Ukraine. In late 2002 Murzabekov travelled to St Petersburg, Russia, to meet Said-Magomed Akhmadov, a Chechen who was a leading member of a local organized crime group specializing in racketeering and robberies. Akhmadov and five other members of the criminal group, who were ethnic Russians, agreed to carry out the kidnapping. According to the plan, having kidnapped the relative of the mayor of Moscow, they would transport him to Novgorod, where the local criminal group was subcontracted to provide a hiding place and a specially equipped truck in which the victim could be transported to the mountain region of Chechnya. The terrorist plan did not work out because all the partic-

---

[6] Vorontsov, S., 'Organizovannaya prestupnost' v Yuzhnom federal'nom okruge kak geopoliticheskii factor, stimuliruiushchii separatism' [Organized crime in the Southern Federal District as a geopolitical factor that stimulates separatism], *Sovremennye Problemy Geopolitiki Kavkaza*, vol. 5 ([no publisher]: Rostov-na-Donu, 2001), p. 166.

ipants in Russia and Ukraine were revealed and arrested by the law enforcement authorities.[7]

The tactics of terrorists involve creative and on-the-spot exploitation of existing social organizations, networks and connections, often without the other individuals involved being aware of the true purpose. The preparation of the terrorist hostage taking in the Moscow theatre involved using bribed state officials who issued false passports to certain members of the Chechen group. The transport of explosives and extensive use of truck-bombs in Chechnya over the past two years would not have been possible without the cooperation of individuals from the Russian military who, for a bribe, let those trucks pass without inspection. Through bribery, organized crime, channels of covert mobility and legal as well as informal money transfer systems, terrorism has infiltrated itself into existing social structures.

Finally, one of the most painful issues in Russia's recent experience with terrorism is the role of the mass media. Terrorist acts are acts of violence that cannot achieve their effects without publicity, which communicates their message to the widest possible audience. For the media, a terrorist act is a sensational, headline-making event. Preparations for a terrorist act therefore often take into account the role of the mass media and the potential reaction. Simultaneously with the hostage taking in the Moscow theatre, the group of Movsar Baraev passed a video tape with a prerecorded public statement to an al-Jazeera news agency correspondent in Moscow, so that the world could get a first-hand message from the terrorists together with reports from the scene. In this way the terrorists hoped to gain control over the way their act would be reported, to determine the public interpretation of the hostage taking and to win the information war. One could even argue that the public relations campaign which the terrorists aspired to launch by making themselves the focus of the world media was the primary goal of the hostage taking, while the actual form of the latter was secondary and instrumental.

In the heat of the crisis, Russian television reported live on the developments in and around the theatre, including the movements of the police force. Terrorists who were inside and watching television had the opportunity to follow developments in close proximity to the theatre. This gave rise subsequently to intense public debate about the need to restrict media coverage, touching on one of the most sensitive democratic freedoms, the freedom of information. Subsequently, the Russian Government initiated amendments to the Law on the Mass Media[8] that provided for restrictions on the coverage and circulation of information in times of crisis.

---

[7] The story is based on a report in *Vash Tainyi Sovetnik*, no. 8 (2003), p. 6, and confirmed by the interview with 'Vladimir' (note 3).

[8] The amendments were passed by the State Duma on 1 Nov. 2002. They specify cases in which the government can withdraw licences for media outlets, such as cases involving the dissemination of information that impedes a counter-terrorist operation or information that threatens the life and health of people. It is also prohibited to reveal special technical details or tactics of operations against terrorists or to spread information that can serve to propagate and justify terrorism and extremism.

V. Conclusions

A successful counter-terrorist strategy must take into account two circum-stances: that terrorism constitutes an asymmetric threat; and that terrorist networks are not only hidden in the mountains or forests, but are also embedded in social structures. What are the implications of these features of terrorism for business and civil society? Asymmetric conflict is not new, but it has now become global. Conflict between states and terrorist networks poses a greater challenge than conflict between states, which was the prevalent type of conflict until the end of the cold war. The dividing line in world politics is being redrawn: states find themselves on one side of the divide, facing asymmetric challenges from various disorganized anti-state forces on the other. Business and civil society should therefore influence governments to encourage closer alliances with other governments against terrorism and, more importantly, urge governments and their secret services to abstain from attempts to use or manipulate terrorists as part of their policies against rival states.

The assumption that terrorism is embedded in and produced by social structures means both that societies produce people who are prepared to engage in terrorist activities, including suicide bombings, and that terrorist networks are intertwined with existing social networks and establishments. This implies that long-term social and economic policies are likely to be more efficient anti-terrorist instruments than military interventions, however successful they may be in the short term. Investments in modernizing education, in communications and in labour markets in terrorist-ridden areas should produce greater effects than huge sums spent on military operations. The business community and civil society should undertake to change government policies accordingly. Finally, anti-terrorist measures should be aimed not just at terrorists themselves, but at their social support infrastructure, since corruption, the shadow economy and other forms of tacitly accepted and tolerated non-transparency can be used by terrorists.

Part III

Business and conflict

Editors' remarks

The connection between business and conflict is as old as the caveman's first purpose-made axe. Its ambiguities, too, have always been with us—as illustrated by the owner of a dynamite company who endowed the Nobel Peace Prize.

In modern conditions, the interweaving of private sector activities with the entire conflict cycle has become more complex than ever. Companies can have decisive influence for good or ill through their actions both in a pre-conflict setting and during post-conflict reconstruction. In active conflict they may provide not just arms, but integrated services and support for the combatants (including private armed forces), financing, and other 'conflict commodities', both legitimate and illicit. The range of possible political, legal and moral evaluations of business's role is equally wide. At one extreme, as discussed in Said Adejumobi's chapter in Part VI of this volume, business can be seen by some victims or parties in a conflict as an enemy, an aggressor, or even a war criminal. In other cases companies are wooed as potential saviours, bringers of wealth and employment, or facilitators of reform and renewal. What is increasingly clear is that business cannot escape the share of responsibility which its major share of influence in conflict processes brings. Private actors must be just as answerable as official ones in key aspects, such as respect for international humanitarian law and the avoidance of war crimes.

Christine Batruch's chapter about an oil company's experiences in Sudan suggests that business's best hope of behaving properly in a conflict environment is not to isolate itself, but to engage and understand better the parties and the processes at work. Dialogue with the locals and with international actors should reduce the risks both of becoming the 'bad guy', and of being unfairly seen as such. Businesses can also anticipate and prepare for such challenges through the private sector's own networks and development of 'codes of conduct', and through processes of mutual learning with qualified non-governmental and official organizations. Gilles Carbonnier's chapter is full of pointers to good practice in this regard.

It is important—as argued in John Maresca's introductory chapter—not to cast business in the role of actual or potential villain. Trends such as the predominance of internal over external conflicts, the ubiquity of transnational terrorism, and also climate change and disease seem bound to increase the proportion of business work that will have to be carried on in hazardous, often conflict-prone environments in future. In a world running out of resources, business will need to be motivated—and supported as necessary—to continue exploring even the most rugged frontiers. Moreover, as argued in Andrew Bone's chapter on 'conflict diamonds', business can offer useful models for the *process* of international cooperation against new security hazards, including those linked with conflict

Conflict will always offer profits to a limited sector of business for a limited time. It will always be the enemy of business as a whole, as well as of security. The strength of the case for public–private sector partnership was recognized in this domain long before 11 September 2001, and the often quite mature models of cooperation described in this part of the volume deserve particular attention as a result.

10. Business investment, humanitarian problems and conflict

John J. Maresca

I. Introduction

With the end of the cold war, the trend towards globalization and the proliferation of information, the role of business in today's world has become the focus
of considerable attention. Most business people are aware of this and are seeking to understand what is expected of them. The overall issue is the appropriate role for businesses at a time when there are new expectations, new
critics and many new standards for business performance. This is what lies
behind the worldwide movement towards greater corporate responsibility: that
is, towards more positive participation by the private sector in the effort to find
solutions to problems of general public concern.

As a part of this general trend, responsible people in businesses, governments, international organizations and non-governmental organizations
(NGOs) have been rethinking the relationship of the private sector to the
world's humanitarian problems. This is only natural and logical, since the
humanitarian problems are growing even while the financial resources available to deal with them are dwindling—by up to 12 per cent per year in real
terms. The problem of dealing with famine, lack of safe water, refugee flows,
poverty, disease and other humanitarian problems is in large part financial:
given sufficient resources, many of them could be resolved. However, public
resources are limited because of taxpayers' reluctance to accept heavier tax
burdens. So the root question is: where will the resources come from to
respond to these vast challenges?

Meanwhile, the private sector remains by far the world's largest allocator of
funds. It is the world's principal engine for economic development, the creation of wealth and jobs, the payment of taxes and the elimination of poverty.
About $1 trillion of new wealth is created each year by the private sector, and
more than half of the world's 100 largest economies are companies.[1] If the
world is to be able to meet its humanitarian needs, it must harness the
resources, energy and creativity of the private sector. This does not mean more
business philanthropy, as some business people fear. Rather, it must entail a
creative alignment of business objectives with the public interest; a far greater
effort to inform businesses about humanitarian needs; and new ways to engage

---

[1] See Wenger, A. and Möckli, D., *Business and Conflict: The Untapped Potential of the Business
Sector* (Lynne Rienner: Boulder, Colo., 2003); and Maresca, J. J., 'The role of the private sector in post-
conflict reconstruction', Presentation to the Business Humanitarian Forum, 28 Mar. 2003, URL <http://
www.bhforum.org/en/documentation/speech_maresca_20030328_webster.cfm>.

them in investments which will meet their legitimate profit-making objectives while at the same time serving the public good.

II. Conflict as the multiplier of humanitarian problems

Conflict is the most dramatic multiplier of all humanitarian problems, whether disease, hunger, homelessness, displacement or lack of education. It is in relation to, and in the aftermath of, conflicts that all these problems grow and become more dramatic. If the world could master the process of conflict prevention and resolution, many humanitarian problems would fade away naturally or would never occur. The area where a more important and positive business role would have the greatest impact is therefore in relation to conflict prevention and transformation and in post-conflict reconstruction.

There is a tendency in some quarters to see business as a contributor to some specific world problems, especially through the negative effects of economic activity on the environment, through the undercutting of human rights, by adding to the potential for corruption and by stimulating the continuation of conflicts. This view sees business as a part of the problem, responsible in whole or in part for humanitarian problems and for the conflicts which multiply them.

The more positive way to view business is to ask how it can contribute to finding positive solutions to humanitarian problems—how market forces and the natural behaviour of business can be used and aligned with efforts to find solutions. This is the rationale which lies behind United Nations General Assembly Resolution 57/265, which mandated the Secretary-General and the Administrator of the United Nations Development Programme (UNDP) to conduct a study of how private resources could be deployed to better support development.[2] Indeed, the UN is now more interested than ever before in public–private cooperation to meet more effectively the goals of the international community. In analysing the link between business and conflict, this positive approach should also be the guideline for attracting the support of the private sector for international humanitarian goals.

III. Differentiating legitimate business from criminal activity

As in every walk of life, there are, of course, unscrupulous business people. However, the overwhelming majority of businesses try hard to respect the law and to adhere to their own codes of behaviour, which are often more stringent than required by law. It is important for the world to recognize this.

---

[2] See UN General Assembly Resolution 57/265, 20 Dec. 2002, On the establishment of the World Solidarity Fund, URL <http://www.solidarity-fund.org/eng/resolution.html>; and UN General Assembly and UN Economic and Social Council, Annex, Progress report on the measures taken for the operationalization of the World Solidarity Fund, Report by the Administrator of the United Nations Development Programme, UN document A/58/72–E/2003/53, 11 Apr. 2003, URL <www.un.dk/doc/A.58.72.pdf>.

Legitimate business activity is sometimes casually lumped together with drug dealing, gun running and other unacceptable practices. For some people, all of this is 'business'. For legitimate business people, illegal activities such as drug dealing, prostitution, exploitation of children or the supply of weapons to warring factions are not business activities—they are criminal activities, and have no place in a discussion of the role of business. Wars are always surrounded by scoundrels, but legitimate business people condemn such criminal activities.

Generally speaking, and leaving aside such war profiteers, business stays away from regions of instability and conflict. The fact is that, when conflicts start, most businesses flee, with the clear exception of resource companies, which must remain where the resources are located. The problem is not keeping business away from war, but rather attracting business investment to areas where stability may be a problem, or bringing businesses back to an area where there has been a conflict so that normal economic life can resume.

IV. Why invest in conflict-torn areas?

A basic question for many people is 'Why do businesses invest in conflict-torn areas at all?' The answer is that all businesses, in all circumstances, ask themselves a relatively simple question: do the possible profits of a prospective investment outweigh the risks involved? Business is about taking risks for financial gain, including the risks of whether the product can be sold and whether the competition can be beaten. There are also political risks involved, such as whether operating in a country run by an unstable or unsavoury regime will undercut the ability to conduct work. Businesses are used to evaluating risks and weighing them against potential gains. They are also used to investing for gains which may only come years into the future. Political risks, including the risks of conflict, are just another form of the risks businesses face every day.

Businesses are not governments, nor are they international organizations or NGOs. Their functions are legitimate and worthy, but they are not the same as the functions of such bodies. It is simply wrong to expect businesses to take on the functions of, for example, governments, as is sometimes suggested. Nor does this somehow imply that business operates on a lesser moral level. Indeed, in some areas, such as modern personnel policies, businesses can give lessons to other sectors of society.

V. The business–humanitarian relationship

Businesses are already involved with humanitarian matters in a number of ways. Business philanthropy is a well established and honourable tradition. Businesses, and foundations established by successful business people, contribute substantial funding to humanitarian causes. Businesses pay taxes which are used in part for humanitarian purposes, and they also sometimes take on contracts to carry out the work of humanitarian organizations. This is happening today in the war-damaged areas of Afghanistan, Iraq, parts of Africa and the former Yugoslavia.

By far the most important role of business in conflict-torn or developing regions is that of an investor. It is business investment that provides the jobs, the economic development and the hope which permits these societies to break out of the circle of poverty and despair. Without prosperity, or at least hope, people become desperate and are more easily led by political demagogues into wasteful and hopeless confrontations. Populations with some hope for a prosperous future are less likely to put their good fortune at risk by supporting conflicts. As President of the World Bank James Wolfensohn has pointed out, 'one of the principal causes of conflict is poverty and inequity'.[3]

A key role for business investment is clearly in post-conflict reconstruction. A post-conflict society may be dependent on emergency aid supplies for a long time but, as stability returns, business investment in the area can bring jobs, economic opportunities and some hope for the future. With the growth of business and economic activity the society can gradually sustain itself and humanitarian aid can be terminated.

One of the key roles of international organizations in the aftermath of conflict is to stabilize a society, and to recreate the framework conditions in which businesses can invest and carry out their normal operations. These organizations usually pay too little attention to the direct problem of attracting business investment, assuming that businesses will come into a post-conflict region when the framework conditions are favourable. However, much more is required to attract business investment, and this is the area where creativity is needed. Businesses focus on specific business opportunities, evaluate them and take their own decisions on investment. New approaches, such as those of the Business Humanitarian Forum (BHF), can promote this process.[4]

VI. The special role of resource companies

Resource development companies, such as oil and mining enterprises, are in an especially sensitive position in relation to unstable or conflict regions. Unlike the manufacturing or trading businesses, resource companies do not have the luxury of relocating when conflicts emerge. They are condemned to developing resources where they can find them or where their investments have already been made.

---

[3] 'Defining new cooperation in the humanitarian agenda', Keynote presentation by James D. Wolfensohn, President, The World Bank, Conference on Defining New Cooperation in the Humanitarian Agenda, 1–2 Nov. 1999, available on the Internet site of the Business Humanitarian Forum at URL <http://www.bhforum.ch/en/partnership/wolfensohn_011199.cfm>.

[4] The BHF was launched in Jan. 1999. Its mission is to build mutual support between humanitarian organizations and the business community through dialogue and projects. It has a formal partnership with the UNDP to enhance efforts to create sustainable economic development projects. The BHF is located in Geneva, Switzerland. See URL <http://www.bhforum.org/>.

This means that some resource companies maintain or even seek investment opportunities in war-torn areas if they appear to warrant the risks. In such cases, in order to move their projects ahead, companies must be prepared to deal as best they can with the local authorities they encounter.

Resource development projects can change the economic prospects of entire peoples from dismal to promising. They can provide jobs, real economic benefits and a variety of spin-offs which benefit broad segments of the population. If the resource is oil or natural gas, for instance, such projects can provide cheap energy for economic development. Moreover, resource projects take years to develop, so the benefits may actually be felt only after the conflict has ended or under a successor regime. In a subsequent post-conflict period, of course, such investment will be desperately needed.

Companies must be careful in dealing with the local authorities in place, so that they do not burn their bridges with other political factions that could accede to power at a later date. They also have no interest in being seen as oppressors themselves; on the contrary, one of the objectives of these businesses must be to win the respect and loyalty of the people. Multinational firms are sometimes sophisticated enough to manage these complex considerations, but not always.[5]

VII. Meeting security requirements

Companies operating in unstable areas need security for their installations and employees. Some companies have managed this requirement intelligently and discreetly, while others have been accused of brutality or of cooperating with unscrupulous local security forces. The objectives of companies are normally limited to protecting their employees and investments, but in conflict situations the implications can be much broader than intended.

Anyone who has been on the ground in a conflict area knows how complicated it can be to try to choose friends. The choices in such situations are usually all unattractive. The principal alternatives for company security are local security forces, which are sometimes corrupt, or private security companies, whose ranks may include former mercenary troops and other soldiers of fortune.[6] Just as a lack of security is unacceptable, these choices can lead to new and equally undesirable problems, including becoming linked with human rights abuses.

VIII. Respect for human rights

In today's world, companies must be alert to, and steadfastly oppose, any infringement of human rights, not only by the company itself but also up and

---

[5] For a detailed discussion of 2 corporations' experience of such challenges see chapters 11 and 12 in this volume.

[6] On private security companies and mercenaries see also chapters 14 and 21 in this volume.

down its business chain. This means that if a company's upstream supplier or its downstream sales agent is responsible for human rights violations, the company must take whatever steps are necessary to oppose those violations. The choice of steps is fairly simple—either the supplier or sales agents stop the human rights abuses, or the company stops doing business with them.

The equation becomes more complicated if the human rights violations are being committed by a government, especially if the company is a resource company. First, as noted above, a resource company cannot simply move its operations elsewhere. Natural resources, whether they are oil or gas fields, or deposits of a valuable mineral, are where they are—their location has nothing to do with the type of government which controls the area.

In addition, when a resource company identifies a commercially interesting prospect, evaluates the technical, economic and political factors, and decides to invest, it must enter into negotiations with the government of the country. Because natural resources are virtually always considered to be a part of the patrimony of the country and thus within the domain of the state, it is the government which must authorize their exploitation.

From the very outset a resource company must deal with the country's government and most likely must enter into complex agreements with the government about access to land, transportation routes, taxes, division of potential profits or outright payments to the government. In this way the government becomes a partner and an integral part of the resource company's business chain.

If it is the government which is responsible for human rights abuses, the choice of how to deal with the situation is not as simple as it is when dealing with another type of business partner. It is not the stark choice described above, under which the partner company either corrects its behaviour or is dismissed.

Governments, even unscrupulous ones, are sovereign. The choice for the company thus becomes one of either seeking positive change in the government's behaviour, or pulling out of the investment and leaving the country. Sometimes both of these options are so bad that the company simply cannot take them without severe business losses. A company caught in such a situation may try to create an 'island of integrity' for its project within the country.

It is easy to criticize such hesitation from the outside, but it is sometimes extremely difficult for even the most conscientious executives, on the inside, to take the necessary decisions. The issue in its most extreme terms can be put this way: should a company put itself out of business over the behaviour of an unscrupulous government? Or can a company somehow separate itself from the governing context in which it works? There are no easy solutions in such situations.

The special position of resource companies, and their exposure to situations in which they can be accused of human rights violations or complicity in such violations, lay behind the joint initiative of the British and US governments, with the participation of private companies, to develop a set of Voluntary

Principles on Security and Human Rights. This initiative was announced on 20 December 2000, and supported by companies such as Chevron, Texaco, Freeport McMoran, Conoco, Shell, British Petroleum and Rio Tinto, as well as by a range of business organizations and NGOs.[7]

The Voluntary Principles initiative is a special undertaking by resource companies in relation to respect for human rights as they seek security for installations in the countries where they work. It reflects the special circumstances in which these companies often find themselves. Certainly, the existence of this set of principles will not make the debate on the role of resource companies go away. The companies themselves are aware that they often find themselves in no-win situations, when they have existing investments in countries where there are human rights violations. They usually do not want to take on responsibilities which are properly those of governments, such as encouraging or pressuring a country to change its policies; companies are organized to make profits, not to influence governments. Most people would agree that businesses should not take on the role of governments, but in the new world of expectations about corporate behaviour this is exactly what many activists expect them to do.

These are good examples of the many situations in which dialogue between companies and humanitarian organizations working in the same country would be mutually beneficial. Companies which maintain such dialogue can often obtain useful insights and advice from their interlocutors, as well as a better understanding of their predicament and possible solutions.

IX. The role of sanctions

Business people generally believe that engagement is a better way to influence unsavoury local regimes than isolation. There is a strong belief among business people that exposure to the standards of international business, coupled with jobs, economic benefits and the simple presence of foreigners, will have a positive moderating influence on undesirable regimes.

Sanctions place complex restrictions on businesses, with a generally negative effect on the companies concerned. As a result, some companies have pulled out of investments in unstable areas, even when these investments may be the only possible source of economic development for the countries concerned, and thus desperately needed. This compounds the problems faced by the peoples of these countries, while at the same time discouraging companies from investing in conflict regions at all. It has not been proven that sanctions can dislodge an undesirable government, but it is clear that they curtail investment and economic development, to the detriment of the populations.

---

[7] For the Voluntary Principles see URL <http://www.state.gov/g/drl/rls/2931.htm>. See also chapters 12 and 13 in this volume.

X. The need for business–humanitarian dialogue and cooperation

Despite an obvious need, businesses, humanitarian organizations and academics do not routinely work together, and in many cases do not even have contact with each other. The reason is that there are deep mutual suspicions on both sides. Humanitarians, international civil servants and many academics tend to view businesses as totally concentrated on making money, cynical and prepared to do anything to benefit their companies. Business people tend to see humanitarian workers, international civil servants and academics as idealistic and self-righteous, and they do not accept that international organizations and NGOs have any mandate to sit in judgement of their behaviour. On the contrary, business people believe that they form a respectable and law-abiding component of society and that they are fully capable of taking responsibility for their own actions. This chasm of misunderstanding must be bridged if the positive potential of the business world is to be harnessed effectively in conflict areas and other regions that need investment and economic development.

Business takes pride in its achievements, even while recognizing that mistakes have been made in the past. For every negative example of business behaviour there are thousands of examples of businesses which have provided worthwhile jobs, stability and hope for the communities in which they work. Business can be an important element in conflict avoidance or post-conflict reconstruction. The sooner this is generally recognized, the sooner there can be creative efforts to engage businesses positively in order to stabilize and bring prosperity to these areas.

11. Conflict diamonds: the De Beers Group and the Kimberley Process

Andrew Bone

I. Introduction

UN Security Council Resolution 1173

The concept of 'conflict diamonds' stems from the conflict in Angola and the failure of the international community to bring a lasting settlement to the civil war there through the combined efforts of the United Nations and a 'troika' of states comprising Portugal, Russia and the United States. In June 1998 the UN Security Council, exasperated by the perceived intransigence of União Nacional para a Independência Total de Angola (UNITA, National Union for the Total Independence of Angola), decided to impose comprehensive economic and political sanctions on the organization and its leadership through the adoption of Resolution 1176, which activated Resolution 1173.[1]

Among other things, Resolution 1173 prohibited the purchase of rough diamonds from UNITA. Only rough diamonds with official government certificates could be exported from Angola.[2]

In the late 1990s, De Beers was engaged in a partnership with the Angolan Government and was active on the open market, buying rough diamonds in several government-held locations in Angola.[3] The company immediately complied with Resolution 1173 and stated its support for the effective implementation of the sanctions.

Conflict diamonds: from security risk to humanitarian issue

Six months after Resolution 1173 was adopted, Global Witness, a British non-governmental organization (NGO) which specializes in the analysis of war economies, highlighted UNITA's ability to fund and perpetuate hostilities against the government through the sale of rough diamonds mined from territory under its control. In December 1998 Global Witness published a report on the role of diamonds in the Angolan conflict and followed this up with an

---

[1] For UN Security Council Resolution 1173, 12 June 1998, and UN Security Council Resolution 1176, 24 June 1998, see URL <http://www.un.org/Docs/scres/1998/scres98.htm>.

[2] Then the government of the Movimento Popular de Libertação de Angola (MPLA).

[3] On the De Beers Group see URL <http://www.debeersgroup.com>.

effective media campaign, which in due course attracted the attention of politicians in both Europe and the United States.[4]

In January 1999 Robert Fowler, Chair of the UN Security Council Sanctions Committee on Angola, was mandated by the Security Council to produce a report on 'sanctions busting' in Angola.[5] At the same time, Gary Ralfe, Managing Director of De Beers, wrote to the UN Secretary-General outlining De Beers' involvement in Angola and reiterating its commitment to the restoration of peace and its adherence to Resolution 1173. In May, Ambassador Fowler appointed two Panels of Experts to investigate violations of the sanctions regime in Angola. As part of the exercise, he held meetings in May (London) and July (Johannesburg) with Nicky Oppenheimer, De Beers' Chairman, and Ralfe. In September, the international NGO Human Rights Watch published a report which assessed the political and military situation in Angola and confirmed the view that UNITA had been funding its war effort largely through the sale of rough diamonds.[6]

By October 1999, Global Witness had stepped up its media activities by joining forces with several other NGOs and launching an umbrella group called Fatal Transactions, whose first action was to distribute information material to jewellery retailers, alerting them to the issue that by then was known as 'conflict diamonds'.[7]

De Beers ceases 'outside buying'

In October 1999, following widespread reports that official government export certificates were being forged, De Beers decided to cease buying Angolan goods[8] on the 'open market'. By the end of 1999 the company had closed down its remaining 'outside buying' operations throughout the world. This was done in spite of the fact that it had never traded in conflict diamonds: the intention was rather to secure De Beers' own channels of distribution comprehensively against any possible infiltration from external sources. Since 1999, the company's only supply of rough diamonds has been from its own mines or from contractual sources, such as the Russian producer Alrosa. At the same time De Beers declared that it had become an absolute necessity to secure confidence in its product.

[4] Global Witness, *A Rough Trade: The Role of Diamond Companies and Governments in the Angolan Conflict* (Global Witness: London, Dec. 1998), available at URL <http://www.globalwitness.org/reports/show.php/en.00013.html>. On Global Witness see URL <http://www.globalwitness.org/>.

[5] The report was presented in Mar. 2000. See 'Letter dated 10 March 2000 from the Chairman of the Security Council Committee established pursuant to Resolution 864 (1993) concerning the situation in Angola addressed to the President of the Security Council', UN document S/2000/203, 10 Mar. 2000, URL <http://www.un.org/News/dh/latest/angolareport_eng.htm>.

[6] Human Rights Watch, 'Angola unravels: the rise and fall of the Lusaka peace process', URL <http://www.hrw.org/reports/1999/angola/>.

[7] Fatal Transactions is an international campaign to influence governments and companies involved in extractive industries to implement effective national and international controls 'to ensure that the trade in natural resources does not finance or otherwise support conflict and economic injustice'. See URL <http://www.fataltransactions.org/home/index2.html>.

[8] The word 'goods' is a diamond industry euphemism to describe parcels of diamonds.

In September 2000, political interest in the issue was further enhanced when US Congressman Tony Hall introduced the bill for legislation which became the Consumer Access to a Responsible Accounting of Trade Act (the CARAT Act).[9] This draft legislation required that diamonds imported to the USA be accompanied by a certificate of origin.

In the meantime, the momentum of the Fatal Transactions campaign appeared to wane after the release of a press statement in November 1999 by former South African President Nelson Mandela, who emphasized the importance of diamonds for the economies of southern Africa and the harm that would be caused by a consumer boycott of diamond jewellery. He stated, 'The diamond industry is vital to the Southern African economy. Rather than boycotts being instituted, it is preferable that through our own initiative the industry takes a progressive stance on human rights issues'.[10] Six months later, President Festus Mogae of Botswana stated, 'We must recognise that the very diamond trade we seek to regulate is also the life-blood of millions across the globe. Diamond revenues support essential programmes of national development in stable, democratic countries such as Botswana, South Africa and Namibia. In fact, the great majority of diamonds in world trade contribute positively to human welfare'.[11] A representative of the Fatal Transactions campaign denied that it had tried to encourage a boycott, stating that raising 'consumer awareness' was its preferred method.[12]

Sierra Leone becomes embroiled

By the end of 1999 media interest in the issue had begun to decline. However, this changed in January 2000 with the publication of a report by the NGO Partnership Africa Canada (PAC) on the role played by diamonds in the civil war in Sierra Leone.[13] Images of children mutilated by factions within the Revolutionary United Front (RUF) rebel movement aroused significant media attention throughout the world. The report was particularly critical of activities in Antwerp, the world's biggest diamond trading centre. De Beers was also criticized even though it had not done any business in, or purchased goods emanating from, Sierra Leone since 1985.

---

[9] The CARAT Act is available at URL <http://www.gpoaccess.gov/bills/search.html>. See also Fisher-Thompson, J., 'US legislators attack war in Sierra Leone with anti-diamond bill: Reps. Hall and Wolf speak after seeing victims of violence', URL <http://usinfo.state.gov/regional/af/security/a9121502.htm>.

[10] See 'Statement by Mr Nelson Mandela on the announcement by De Beers re the sourcing of diamonds from UNITA', 17 Nov. 1999, URL <http://bridge.netnation.com/~debeersc/conflict/index.html>.

[11] See 'Speech by His Excellency F. G. Mogae, President of the Republic of Botswana, on the occasion of the official opening of the ORAPA 2000 Project', Orapa Mine, 20 May 2000, URL <http://bridge.netnation.com/~debeersc/conflict/index.html>.

[12] See Thomas, I., 'Global Witness wages war on "conflict diamonds"', URL <http://manovision online.com/is18ar04.htm>.

[13] Smillie, I. et al., The Heart of the Matter: Sierra Leone, Diamonds and Human Security (Partnership Africa Canada: Ottawa, 2000), URL <http://www.pacweb.org/e/pdf/heart of the matter.doc>. On Partnership Africa Canada see URL <http://www.partnershipafricacanada.org>.

In spite of this fact, and in order to secure confidence in its diamonds, in March 2000 De Beers began issuing guarantees on its invoices, declaring that none of the diamonds in its sales boxes had been purchased from areas where rebels were challenging the legitimate government.[14]

A significant and defining opportunity for De Beers to establish credibility, demonstrate its determination to be 'part of the solution' and regain some of the initiative came in May 2000, when it was invited to provide written testimony to the US House Committee on International Relations.[15] The testimony was presented before the Subcommittee on Africa's hearings on the issue of conflict diamonds. It contained proposals for ending the trade in conflict diamonds, many of which have since found their way into the Kimberley Process certification regime (see section II). The testimony also contained expert evaluation of the value of the trade in conflict diamonds. Claims by civil society and sections of the media that conflict diamonds represented 20 per cent, or more, of annual global rough diamond production were countered by De Beers, which remains the only organization to have quantified the amount of rough diamonds actually available to the RUF and UNITA. De Beers was able to demonstrate in its testimony that, in 1999, this represented no more than 4 per cent of world production, by value approximately $255 million.

This figure was accepted by the UN, by governments and, eventually, by leading NGOs. Having established a more realistic perspective on the volume of the trade in conflict diamonds, De Beers adopted and publicized the view that 'just one diamond dealt with in such a way, is one too many'.[16]

Also in May, and at the invitation of the US Department of State, De Beers attended a conference in Sierra Leone to investigate and discuss measures to rescue the Sierra Leone diamond industry from rebel groups and develop it in the future.

At the same time, a 'technical forum' was convened and hosted by the South African Government in Kimberley. This was the first time that all interested parties had met at the same venue. This meeting initiated the series of conferences that became known as the Kimberley Process.[17]

In its testimony, De Beers defined 'conflict diamonds' as 'diamonds mined or stolen by rebels who are in opposition to the legitimate Government of a country'.[18] Global Witness welcomed this as a 'good working definition'. It was subsequently adopted universally.

[14] See Swindells, S., Reuters, 'De Beers supports diamond embargo on Sierra Leone', 6 June 2000, URL <http://www.clw.org/cat/newswire/nw060700.html>.

[15] See 'Transcript: Written testimony before the United States Congress, House Committee on International Relations, Subcommittee on Africa, Hearings into the Issue of "Conflict Diamonds"', 9 May 2000, available on the De Beers Internet site at URL <http://www.debeersgroup.com/hotTopics/cdActions01.asp#>.

[16] See De Beers, URL <http://www.debeersgroup.com/hotTopics/cdIntroduction.asp>.

[17] On the Kimberley Process see URL <http://www.kimberleyprocess.com>.

[18] See 'Transcript' (note 15), p. 4.

II. The Kimberley Process

The first Kimberley Process meeting was held in a small Dutch Reform Church hall. Only a handful of government representatives, industry leaders—mainly from De Beers—and NGO members, led by Global Witness and the PAC, were present. However, its modest beginnings belied the significance of the gathering. The conference brought clarity to the issue, defined the problem and united the disparate parties in the recognition of a shared objective: an end to the trade in conflict diamonds. The tactics required to reach this objective were, and would continue to be, the focus of intense—and often laborious—negotiation over the next two and a half years.

The Kimberley Process was lent greater momentum in July 2000 at the 29th World Diamond Congress in Antwerp, Belgium, when, following sustained encouragement from De Beers, leaders of the international diamond industry issued a joint resolution declaring 'zero tolerance' towards those who traded in conflict diamonds.[19] Anyone caught doing so would be expelled from the industry, effectively marginalizing them and, as one De Beers executive put it, forcing them to trade 'in the gutter'.

Key among the nine proposals in the resolution was a call for the establishment of a World Diamond Council (WDC) that would represent the entire industry, from mining through to retail companies.[20] The disparate structure and competitive nature of the diamond industry made turning this into a reality an exceptional achievement. De Beers immediately became a member of the WDC, whose executive board spoke on behalf of all the members.

Governments now had the Kimberley Process, chaired by South Africa, in which to negotiate a solution through the establishment of an international certification system. The industry, via the WDC, and leaders of the NGO community were invited to attend each meeting of the Kimberley Process as observers, if not direct participants.

Measures begin to take effect

The Diamond High Council[21] assisted first Sierra Leone and then Angola in creating a certification system that would be the forerunner of the Kimberley Process. In 2003, with these systems in place, including the use of 'unforgeable' certificates provided by De La Rue,[22] Sierra Leone is enjoying a record level of official exports of rough diamonds.

---

[19] See 'Joint Resolution of the World Federation of Diamond Bourses (WFDB) and the International Diamond Manufacturers Association (IDMA)', 19 July 2000, URL <http://www.conflictdiamonds.com/pages/Newsarchive/19_07_00.html>.

[20] On the World Diamond Council see URL <http://www.worlddiamondcouncil.com>.

[21] On the Diamond High Council see URL <http://www.diamondmanufacturer.com/tutorial/council.htm>.

[22] De La Rue is the world's largest commercial security printer and papermaker; in Jan. 2001 it was invited to participate in a policy debate on conflict diamonds. See 'Diamonds', URL <http://www.delarue.com/DLR_Content/CDA/Pages/RevenueDCP/fgsolns/rdpcoddia/0,2241,,00.html>.

In early 2001, De Beers reassessed the value of the previous year's trade in conflict diamonds. It concluded that a combination of measures taken by the UN, the Angolan military and the international diamond industry had significantly reduced UNITA's access to alluvial deposits and its ability to sell its diamonds through legitimate channels. The UN concurred with this view.

UNITA's estimated diamond receipts were revised downward to $75 million from $150 million in 2000. In the meantime, the RUF had retained possession of its territories, as had the rebels in the Democratic Republic of the Congo (DRC). Their revenue from diamonds was therefore assumed to have been maintained at $70 million and $30 million, respectively. The total value for the trade in conflict diamonds in 2000 was estimated to be $180 million, or 2 per cent of world rough diamond production.

In the meantime, De Beers' efforts were recognized by UN Secretary-General Kofi Annan, who said in January 2001, in his address to delegates at the World Economic Forum in Davos, Switzerland: 'De Beers has set an example with its response to criticism of the diamond trade in Africa, and its efforts to ensure that traders and consumers of diamonds will no longer unwittingly help to finance warlords'.[23]

The pace of the intergovernmental negotiations accelerated in 2001. In November a Ministerial Meeting held in Gaborone, Botswana, endorsed the Kimberley Process document put before the UN General Assembly.[24] The document included measures of self-regulation by the diamond industry—a 'system of warranties'—that were adopted unanimously by the WDC and welcomed by the other participants.

US legislation

In November 2001 the US House of Representatives passed a compromise version of the Clean Diamonds Trade Act—supported by all parties, including industry—by a majority vote of 408–6.[25] The legislation had been difficult to pass in the Senate because several senators wanted to strengthen its provisions beyond the point of acceptability to the US Administration.

The WDC stressed that, while enabling national legislation was essential for effective implementation of the Kimberley measures, it should not—as emphasized in the original UN General Assembly mandate—place any undue burden on either governments or industry.

---

[23] See the Secretary-General's address in United Nations Press Release, 26 Jan. 2001, at United Nations Association of the USA (UNA-USA), URL <http://www.unausa.org/news/gcarchives/jan2001.asp>.

[24] The Kimberley Process was mandated to submit its report in UN General Assembly Resolution 55/56, On the Role of Diamonds in Fuelling Conflict, 1 Dec. 2000, available at URL <http://www.un.org/Depts/dhl/resguide/r55.htm>.

[25] This legislation comprises 2 companion bills introduced in the Senate and the House of Representatives. It puts in place the Kimberley Process Certification Scheme. See 'The campaign to eliminate conflict diamonds welcomes passage of the Clean Diamond Trade Act', 9 Apr. 2003, URL <http://www.amnestyusa.org/diamonds/diamonds_act.html>.

The end of the beginning

The Kimberley Process, with its unique collaboration between governments, business and civil society, finally delivered its proposals to the UN General Assembly and received approval at the end of 2002. It was agreed that the measures would be implemented on 1 January 2003. The European Commission, which negotiated on behalf of the European Union member states, issued a regulation directly applicable in all European Community member states on implementation of the Kimberley Process Certification Scheme.[26] More than 50 nations had signed up to the Kimberley Process and each began, with different degrees of speed and success, to initiate its own implementing legislation. However, full and effective implementation was delayed because of legislative difficulties and eventually two further deadlines were set: first February, then finally June 2003.

Governments, the NGO community and industry, in particular, all recognize that the system is not a perfect construct. The Kimberley Process will continue to convene to refine it for as long as is necessary. The business of implementing this process is only the end of the beginning.

At the end of October 2003 the Kimberley Process met in plenary for the second time that year. As with the last plenary, in April,[27] the focus was on how best to acquire a credible system of monitoring. The NGO community had expressed its serious misgivings at the apparent lack of a monitoring system 'with teeth'. Although the diamond industry has lent its full support to civil society for the establishment of a monitoring process that can be seen to work, differences remained on the tactics to secure this objective. The October plenary 'agreed unanimusly to implement a voluntary "peer review" system to ensure the credibility of the Kimberley Process Certification Scheme'.[28]

III. An example well set?

Setting aside the core objective of severely curtailing, if not stopping altogether, the trade in conflict diamonds, what—if anything—does the Kimberley Process offer?

In a world where public confidence in established international institutions such as the UN and the Group of Eight (G8) industrialized nations is fading, the Kimberley Process has provided an alternative model for the resolution of humanitarian and environmental security problems. The combination of inter-

---

[26] Council Regulation (EC) no. 2368/2002 of 20 Dec. 2002, implementing the Kimberley Process Certification Scheme for the international trade in rough diamonds, *Official Journal of the European Communities,* L 358/28 (31 Dec. 2002), URL <www.diamonds.net/kp/EU%20Council%20Regulation %202368.pdf>.

[27] See 'Final communique, Kimberley Process plenary meeting, Johannesburg, 28–30 Apr. 2003', URL <http://www.kimberleyprocess.com/news/documents.asp?Id=51>.

[28] See World Diamond Council, Press release, 'Diamond industry and NGOs hail Kimberley Process breakthrough', 31 Oct. 2003, URL <http://www.worlddiamondcouncil.com/press/wdc%20release%20 103003.html>. For the Kimberley Process Certification Scheme see annex 11A, also available at URL <http://www.debeersgroup.com/hottopics/cdintroduction.asp>.

ested governments with the participation of a global industry and civil society provides 'ownership', responsibility and accountability for all involved. Different needs are addressed along the way, while the structure of such a model ensures that the shared objectives are not ignored.

In the first instance, success will depend on what distinguishes the Kimberley Process from other institutions and endeavours. From the beginning, in addition to the executive powers of government representatives, both the business and NGO communities have been involved as observers. However, this 'observer' status has evolved to allow these communities to contribute significantly to policy formulation in the Process. It is a multilateral approach. The framework of the Kimberley Process presents an opportunity to address specific problems that have regional origins but can have an effect elsewhere. For example, the problem at the root of the conflict diamonds issue was that valuable natural resources were being stolen by rebel groups in Angola, the DRC and Sierra Leone and sold to international markets through legitimate, mainstream channels of distribution.

The role of governments

Governments with a direct interest and stake in developing solutions can become involved and establish ownership. In the case of conflict diamonds, this process has included governments whose interests included diamond mining, diamond polishing and diamond jewellery consumption. For Angola it was the mining aspect that counted; the US interest lay in diamond polishing and consumption; and for South Africa it was all three. Governments approached the issue from different perspectives.

The Kimberley Process is guided by a Chair who, in addition to organizing plenary sessions, coordinates the distribution of policy initiatives, discussion of them at plenary meetings, and the composition and conduct of groups formed to develop and implement them. All agreements are reached by consensus.

Business participation

The involvement of business in such endeavours is enhanced if, as in the case of conflict diamonds, it is united in its efforts. The establishment of the World Diamond Council in September 2000 was critical for the effectiveness of contributions by the diamond industry. The WDC represents the entire industry, from mining through to retail. This has limited the number of industry delegates at meetings, with the positive effect that those who attend have a mandate to present policy proposals for discussion at plenary sessions of the Kimberley Process. In addition, a small, focused WDC team has allowed a flexible and more intimate approach to engagement with the NGO community. This has occasionally led to industry and civil society representatives finding themselves in 'furious agreement' with each other, united in their frustration at governments' intransigence and procrastination.

The WDC and the NGO community have been able to adopt a more pragmatic approach to negotiations as a mutual trust has developed between them. This is a direct result of the flexibility provided by a pan-industry organization and its ability to carry out ongoing and often ad hoc meetings and negotiations with civil society between plenary sessions, in addition to having the mandate to deliver on its promises.

The contribution of civil society

While gathering the support of some 160 other civil society organizations throughout the world, the leading NGOs on the issue—Global Witness and Partnership Africa Canada—have benefited from the establishment of a core team to carry out negotiations with governments and business.

The essential requirements for sucess in addressing issues under the model of the Kimberley Process framework can thus be summarized as: (*a*) bringing together those parties with a direct interest; (*b*) providing relevant expertise; and (*c*) adopting a unified and flexible approach.

An ideal role for the UN Security Council

The fourth player in this framework is the United Nations. There is no doubt that the General Assembly's endorsement of the Kimberley Process provided the validation required to maintain momentum.

The Kimberley Process complemented the various Security Council resolutions which addressed conflict regions, but the two activities were largely conducted without coordination. For example, the interests of the diamond industry—as well as the interests of the people of the DRC—would have been better served if a resolution had been adopted by the Security Council banning the trade in diamonds from the Kisangani region of the DRC. The resolutions on Sierra Leone and, in particular, Liberia were—in the view of the industry—implemented too late. What was required, as the Kimberley Process Certification Scheme was being developed, was clarity on where rough diamonds should not be purchased.

This is the ideal role for the Security Council to play in such a framework. Negotiations and policy formulation are best carried out outside the UN, but with the support of the General Assembly.

In an interview with *The Financial Times*, Kofi Annan said that the time was ripe for a fundamental reassessment of how the UN functions: 'We are living through a crisis of the international system. The emergence of new and nonconventional threats forces us to ask whether the institutions and methods to which we are accustomed are really adequate'.[29] Recent events suggest that they are not, but the inclusive approach taken by the Kimberley Process, which included a supportive and proactive role for the UN, might serve as a model. The UN has stated that the Kimberley Process contributed significantly to the reduction of UNITA's funding, effectively admitting that the Process succeeded in doing in three years what the UN (and the 'troika') had failed to achieve in a decade. It would be wrong to suggest that the Kimberley Process alone brought peace to Angola or Sierra Leone, but it undeniably helped to establish the conditions in which other forces for a durable settlement could operate more effectively.

The G7 also requires reassessment

Other institutions require equally robust reassessment. Jean-François Rischard, World Bank Vice-President for Europe, argued that:

The beleaguered [G7] Genoa Summit in July 2001 . . . cost more than $100 million—yet the crucial discussion on the world economy lasted only ninety minutes . . . Given the complexity of most of the big global issues, the knowledge base of civil servants dispatched into such groupings by governments could never be strong enough without civil society and business. The Group of Seven (G7) industrialized nations still has not found a good way to enlist those other sectors.

Rischard has observed a further drawback with the G7 forum: 'The distance between people at large and the officials in these groupings is very great—the dialogue nil'.[30]

Global issues networks

Rischard also develops a theme of 'inclusivity' by arguing for the establishment of what he calls global issues networks (GINs). The structure he advocates for these networks is almost identical to that of the Kimberley Process. Rischard suggests that the UN would have a role as facilitator, not as a problem solver, in the constitutional phase of launching such networks.

Each network's inception would additionally enlist individuals drawn from three kinds of partners: (1) national governments of developed and developing countries that are especially concerned with, or experienced in, the issue . . .; (2) international civil society organizations that can lend individuals with comprehensive knowledge of the issue and represent other elements of civil society; and (3) firms that . . . pos-

---

[29] See Turner, M., 'New challenges mean time for change at UN', *Financial Times*, weekend edn, 6/7 Sep. 2003, p. 3.

[30] Rischard, J. F., *High Noon: 20 Global Problems, 20 Years to Solve Them* (Basic Books: New York, 2002); and Rischard, J.-F., 'Global issues networks: desperate times deserve innovative measures', *Washington Quarterly*, vol. 26, no. 1 (winter 2002/2003), pp. 17–33, available at URL <http://www.twq.com/03winter/docs/03winter_rischard.pdf>.

sess knowledge of the issue and are able both to represent other businesses and lend highly exprerienced business leaders to the effort.[31]

For this format to succeed, Rischard states that 'a member may have come in as a business, government, or civil society representative, but once in, must think and act as a global citizen. . . . To that effect, the network must make a constant appeal to universal values . . . that are a prerequisite to the global issue at hand.' This is largely reminiscent of the way Kimberley Process participants have conducted themselves over the past three years. It recognizes De Beers' view on the nature of the Kimberley Process negotiations, namely, that although each 'partner' has differing needs, the objectives—and values—are shared.

Whether this fresh approach to dealing with humanitarian issues is called the 'Kimberley Framework' or 'global issues networks' does not matter—although the present author would like to point out that the launch of the Kimberley Process predated Rischard's book. What is important is that such initiatives are not ignored or forgotten.

The abuse of natural resources enslaves a nation in poverty and instability, and can be a threat to international security. In conclusion, the hypothesis that, in the absence of sufficient confidence in existing structures, the Kimberley Process offers a viable alternative to providing solutions on humanitarian issues has been shown to have merit. It is certainly worthy of serious consideration as the UN embarks on a fundamental reassessment of how it functions.

---

[31] Rischard, 'Global issues networks' (note 30), p. 25.

Annex 11A. The Kimberley Process Certification Scheme

Adopted on 5 November 2002 at Interlaken, Switzerland

PREAMBLE

PARTICIPANTS,

RECOGNISING that the trade in conflict diamonds is a matter of serious international concern, which can be directly linked to the fuelling of armed conflict, the activities of rebel movements aimed at undermining or overthrowing legitimate governments, and the illicit traffic in, and proliferation of, armaments, especially small arms and light weapons;

FURTHER RECOGNISING the devastating impact of conflicts fuelled by the trade in conflict diamonds on the peace, safety and security of people in affected countries and the systematic and gross human rights violations that have been perpetrated in such conflicts;

NOTING the negative impact of such conflicts on regional stability and the obligations placed upon states by the United Nations Charter regarding the maintenance of international peace and security;

BEARING IN MIND that urgent international action is imperative to prevent the problem of conflict diamonds from negatively affecting the trade in legitimate diamonds, which makes a critical contribution to the economies of many of the producing, processing, exporting and importing states, especially developing states;

RECALLING all of the relevant resolutions of the United Nations Security Council under Chapter VII of the United Nations Charter, including the relevant provisions of Resolutions 1173 (1998), 1295 (2000), 1306 (2000), and 1343 (2001), and determined to contribute to and support the implementation of the measures provided for in these resolutions;

HIGHLIGHTING the United Nations General Assembly Resolution 55/56 (2000) on the role of the trade in conflict diamonds in fuelling armed conflict, which called on the international community to give urgent and careful consideration to devising effective and pragmatic measures to address this problem;

FURTHER HIGHLIGHTING the recommendation in United Nations General Assembly Resolution 55/56 that the international community develop detailed proposals for a simple and workable international certification scheme for rough diamonds based primarily on national certification schemes and on internationally agreed minimum standards;

RECALLING that the Kimberley Process, which was established to find a solution to the international problem of conflict diamonds, was inclusive of concerned stake holders, namely producing, exporting and importing states, the diamond industry and civil society;

CONVINCED that the opportunity for conflict diamonds to play a role in fuelling armed conflict can be seriously reduced by introducing a certification scheme for rough diamonds designed to exclude conflict diamonds from the legitimate trade;

RECALLING that the Kimberley Process considered that an international certification scheme for rough diamonds, based on national laws and practices and meeting internationally agreed minimum standards, will be the most effective system by which the problem of conflict diamonds could be addressed;

ACKNOWLEDGING the important initiatives already taken to address this problem, in particular by the governments of Angola, the Democratic Republic of Congo, Guinea and Sierra Leone and by other key producing, exporting and importing countries, as well as by the diamond industry, in particular by the World Diamond Council, and by civil society;

WELCOMING voluntary self-regulation initiatives announced by the diamond industry and recognising that a system of such voluntary self-regulation contributes to ensuring an effective internal control system of rough diamonds based upon the international certification scheme for rough diamonds;

RECOGNISING that an international certification scheme for rough diamonds will only be credible if all Participants have established internal systems of control designed to eliminate the presence of conflict diamonds in the chain of producing, exporting and importing rough diamonds within their own territories, while taking into account that differences in production methods and trading practices as well as differences in institutional controls thereof may require different approaches to meet minimum standards;

FURTHER RECOGNISING that the international certification scheme for rough diamonds must be consistent with international law governing international trade;

ACKNOWLEDGING that state sovereignty should be fully respected and the principles of equality, mutual benefits and consensus should be adhered to;

RECOMMEND THE FOLLOWING PROVISIONS:

SECTION I

Definitions

For the purposes of the international certification scheme for rough diamonds (hereinafter referred to as "the Certification Scheme") the following definitions apply:

CONFLICT DIAMONDS means rough diamonds used by rebel movements or their allies to finance conflict aimed at undermining legitimate governments, as described in relevant United Nations Security Council (UN Security Council) resolutions insofar as they remain in effect, or in other similar UN Security Council resolutions which may be adopted in the future, and as understood and recognised in United Nations General Assembly (UNGA) Resolution 55/56, or in other similar UNGA resolutions which may be adopted in future;

COUNTRY OF ORIGIN means the country where a shipment of rough diamonds has been mined or extracted;

COUNTRY OF PROVENANCE means the last Participant from where a shipment of rough diamonds was exported, as recorded on import documentation;

DIAMOND means a natural mineral consisting essentially of pure crystallised carbon in the isometric system, with a hardness on the Mohs (scratch) scale of 10, a specific gravity of approximately 3.52 and a refractive index of 2.42;

EXPORT means the physical leaving/taking out of any part of the geographical territory of a Participant;

EXPORTING AUTHORITY means the authority(ies) or body(ies) designated by a Participant from whose territory a shipment of rough diamonds is leaving, and which are authorised to validate the Kimberley Process Certificate;

FREE TRADE ZONE means a part of the territory of a Participant where any goods introduced are generally regarded, insofar as import duties and taxes are concerned, as being outside the customs territory;

IMPORT means the physical entering/bringing into any part of the geographical territory of a Participant;

IMPORTING AUTHORITY means the authority(ies) or body(ies) designated by a Participant into whose territory a shipment of rough diamonds is imported to conduct all import formalities and particularly the verification of accompanying Kimberley Process Certificates;

KIMBERLEY PROCESS CERTIFICATE means a forgery resistant document with a particular format which identifies a shipment of rough diamonds as being in compliance with the requirements of the Certification Scheme;

OBSERVER means a representative of civil society, the diamond industry, international organisations and non-participating governments invited to take part in Plenary meetings; (Further consultations to be undertaken by the Chair.)

PARCEL means one or more diamonds that are packed together and that are not individualised;

PARCEL OF MIXED ORIGIN means a parcel that contains rough diamonds from two or more countries of origin, mixed together;

PARTICIPANT means a state or a regional economic integration organisation for which the Certification Scheme is effective; (Further consultations to be undertaken by the Chair.)

REGIONAL ECONOMIC INTEGRATION ORGANISATION means an organisation comprised of sovereign states that have transferred competence to that organisation in respect of matters governed by the Certification Scheme;

ROUGH DIAMONDS means diamonds that are unworked or simply sawn, cleaved or bruted and fall under the Relevant Harmonised Commodity Description and Coding System 7102.10, 7102.21 and 7102.31;

SHIPMENT means one or more parcels that are physically imported or exported;

TRANSIT means the physical passage across the territory of a Participant or a non-Participant, with or without transhipment, warehousing or change in mode of transport, when such passage is only a portion of a complete journey beginning and terminating beyond the frontier of the Participant or non-Participant across whose territory a shipment passes;

SECTION II

The Kimberley Process Certificate

Each Participant should ensure that:

(a) a Kimberley Process Certificate (hereafter referred to as the Certificate) accompanies each shipment of rough diamonds on export;

(b) its processes for issuing Certificates meet the minimum standards of the Kimberley Process as set out in Section IV;

(c) Certificates meet the minimum requirements set out in Annex I. As long as these requirements are met, Participants may at their discretion establish additional characteristics for their own Certificates, for example their form, additional data or security elements;

(d) it notifies all other Participants through the Chair of the features of its Certificate as specified in Annex I, for purposes of validation.

SECTION III

Undertakings in respect of the international trade in rough diamonds

Each Participant should:

(a) with regard to shipments of rough diamonds exported to a Participant, require that

each such shipment is accompanied by a duly validated Certificate;

(b) with regard to shipments of rough diamonds imported from a Participant:

• require a duly validated Certificate;

• ensure that confirmation of receipt is sent expeditiously to the relevant Exporting Authority. The confirmation should as a minimum refer to the Certificate number, the number of parcels, the carat weight and the details of the importer and exporter;

• require that the original of the Certificate be readily accessible for a period of no less than three years;

(c) ensure that no shipment of rough diamonds is imported from or exported to a non-Participant;

(d) recognise that Participants through whose territory shipments transit are not required to meet the requirement of paragraphs (a) and (b) above, and of Section II (a) provided that the designated authorities of the Participant through whose territory a shipment passes, ensure that the shipment leaves its territory in an identical state as it entered its territory (i.e. unopened and not tampered with).

SECTION IV

Internal Controls

Undertakings by Participants

Each Participant should:

(a) establish a system of internal controls designed to eliminate the presence of conflict diamonds from shipments of rough diamonds imported into and exported from its territory;

(b) designate an Importing and an Exporting Authority(ies);

(c) ensure that rough diamonds are imported and exported in tamper resistant containers;

(d) as required, amend or enact appropriate laws or regulations to implement and enforce the Certification Scheme and to maintain dissuasive and proportional penalties for transgressions;

(e) collect and maintain relevant official production, import and export data, and collate and exchange such data in accordance with the provisions of Section V.

(f) when establishing a system of internal controls, take into account, where appropriate, the further options and recommendations for internal controls as elaborated in Annex II.

Principles of Industry Self-Regulation

Participants understand that a voluntary system of industry self-regulation, as referred to in the Preamble of this Document, will provide for a system of warranties underpinned through verification by independent auditors of individual companies and supported by internal penalties set by industry, which will help to facilitate the full traceability of rough diamond transactions by government authorities.

SECTION V

Co-operation and Transparency

Participants should:

(a) provide to each other through the Chair information identifying their designated authorities or bodies responsible for implementing the provisions of this Certification Scheme. Each Participant should provide to other Participants through the Chair information, preferably in electronic format, on its relevant laws, regulations, rules, procedures and practices, and update that information as required. This should include a synopsis in English of the essential content of this information;

(b) compile and make available to all other Participants through the Chair statistical data in line with the principles set out in Annex III;

(c) exchange on a regular basis experiences and other relevant information, including on self-assessment, in order to arrive at the best practice in given circumstances;

(d) consider favourably requests from other Participants for assistance to improve the functioning of the Certification Scheme within their territories;

(e) inform another Participant through the Chair if it considers that the laws, regulations, rules, procedures or practices of that other Participant do not ensure the absence of conflict diamonds in the exports of that other Participant;

(f) cooperate with other Participants to attempt to resolve problems which may arise from unintentional circumstances and which could lead to non-fulfilment of the minimum requirements for the issuance or acceptance of the Certificates, and inform all other Participants of the essence of the problems encountered and of solutions found;

(g) encourage, through their relevant authorities, closer co-operation between law enforcement agencies and between customs agencies of Participants.

SECTION VI

Administrative Matters

MEETINGS

1. Participants and Observers are to meet in Plenary annually, and on other occasions as Participants may deem necessary, in order to discuss the effectiveness of the Certification Scheme.

2. Participants should adopt Rules of Procedure for such meetings at the first Plenary meeting.

3. Meetings are to be held in the country where the Chair is located, unless a Participant or an international organisation offers to host a meeting and this offer has been accepted. The host country should facilitate entry formalities for those attending such meetings.

4. At the end of each Plenary meeting, a Chair would be elected to preside over all Plenary meetings, ad hoc working groups and other subsidiary bodies, which might be formed until the conclusion of the next annual Plenary meeting.

5. Participants are to reach decisions by consensus. In the event that consensus proves to be impossible, the Chair is to conduct consultations.

ADMINISTRATIVE SUPPORT

6. For the effective administration of the Certification Scheme, administrative support will be necessary. The modalities and functions of that support should be discussed at the first Plenary meeting, following endorsement by the UN General Assembly.

7. Administrative support could include the following functions:

(a) to serve as a channel of communication, information sharing and consultation between the Participants with regard to matters provided for in this Document;

(b) to maintain and make available for the use of all Participants a collection of those laws, regulations, rules, procedures, practices and statistics notified pursuant to Section V;

(c) to prepare documents and provide administrative support for Plenary and working group meetings;

(d) to undertake such additional responsibilities as the Plenary meetings, or any working group delegated by Plenary meetings, may instruct.

PARTICIPATION

8. Participation in the Certification Scheme is open on a global, non-discriminatory basis to all Applicants willing and able to fulfil the requirements of that Scheme.

9. Any applicant wishing to participate in the Certification Scheme should signify its interest by notifying the Chair through diplomatic channels. This notification should include the information set forth in paragraph (a) of Section V and be circulated to all Participants within one month.

10. Participants intend to invite representatives of civil society, the diamond industry, non-participating governments and international organisations to participate in Plenary meetings as Observers.

PARTICIPANT MEASURES

11. Participants are to prepare, and make available to other Participants, in advance of annual Plenary meetings of the Kimberley Process, information as stipulated in paragraph (a) of Section V outlining how the requirements of the Certification Scheme are being implemented within their respective jurisdictions.

12. The agenda of annual Plenary meetings is to include an item where information as stipulated in paragraph (a) of Section V is reviewed and Participants can provide further details of their respective systems at the request of the Plenary.

13. Where further clarification is needed, Participants at Plenary meetings, upon recommendation by the Chair, can identify and decide on additional verification measures to be undertaken. Such measures are to be implemented in accordance with applicable national and international law. These could include, but need not be limited to measures such as;

a. requesting additional information and clarification from Participants;

b. review missions by other Participants or their representatives where there are credible indications of significant non-compliance with the Certification Scheme.

14. Review missions are to be conducted in an analytical, expert and impartial manner with the consent of the Participant concerned. The size, composition, terms of reference and time frame of these missions should be based on the circumstances and be established by the Chair with the consent of the Participant concerned and in consultation with all Participants.

15. A report on the results of compliance verification measures is to be forwarded to the Chair and to the Participant concerned within three weeks of completion of the mission. Any comments from that Participant as well as the report, are to be posted on the restricted access section of an official Certification Scheme website no later than three weeks after the submission of the report to the Participant concerned. Participants and Observers should make every effort to observe strict confidentiality regarding the issue and the discussions relating to any compliance matter.

COMPLIANCE AND DISPUTE PREVENTION

16. In the event that an issue regarding compliance by a Participant or any other issue regarding the implementation of the Certification Scheme arises, any concerned Participant may so inform the Chair, who is to inform all Participants without delay about the said concern and enter into dialogue on how to address it. Participants and Observers should make every effort to observe strict confidentiality regarding the issue and the discussions relating to any compliance matter.

MODIFICATIONS

17. This document may be modified by consensus of the Participants.

18. Any Participant may propose modifications. Such proposals should be sent in writing to the Chair, at least ninety days before

the next Plenary meeting, unless otherwise agreed.

19. The Chair is to circulate any proposed modification expeditiously to all Participants and Observers and place it on the agenda of the next annual Plenary meeting.

REVIEW MECHANISM

20. Participants intend that the Certification Scheme should be subject to periodic review, to allow Participants to conduct a thorough analysis of all elements contained in the scheme. The review should also include consideration of the continuing requirement for such a scheme, in view of the perception of the Participants, and of international organisations, in particular the United Nations, of the continued threat posed at that time by conflict diamonds. The first such review should take place no later than three years after the effective starting date of the Certification Scheme. The review meeting should normally coincide with the annual Plenary meeting, unless otherwise agreed.

THE START OF THE IMPLEMENTATION OF THE SCHEME

The Certification Scheme should be established at the Ministerial Meeting on the Kimberley Process Certification Scheme for Rough Diamonds in Interlaken on 5 November 2002.

ANNEX I

Certificates

A. Minimum requirements for Certificates

A Certificate is to meet the following minimum requirements:

• Each Certificate should bear the title "Kimberley Process Certificate" and the following statement: "The rough diamonds in this shipment have been handled in accordance with the provisions of the Kimberley Process Certification Scheme for rough diamonds"

• Country of origin for shipment of parcels of unmixed (i.e. from the same) origin

• Certificates may be issued in any language, provided that an English translation is incorporated

• Unique numbering with the Alpha 2 country code, according to ISO 3166-1

• Tamper and forgery resistant
• Date of issuance
• Date of expiry
• Issuing authority
• Identification of exporter and importer
• Carat weight/mass
• Value in US$
• Number of parcels in shipment
• Relevant Harmonised Commodity Description and Coding System
• Validation of Certificate by the Exporting Authority

B. Optional Certificate Elements

A Certificate may include the following optional features:

• Characteristics of a Certificate (for example as to form, additional data or security elements)

• Quality characteristics of the rough diamonds in the shipment

• A recommended import confirmation part should have the following elements:
• Country of destination
• Identification of importer
• Carat/weight and value in US$
• Relevant Harmonised Commodity Description and Coding System
• Date of receipt by Importing Authority
• Authentication by Importing Authority

C. Optional Procedures

Rough diamonds may be shipped in transparent security bags. The unique Certificate number may be replicated on the container.

ANNEX II

Recommendations as provided for in Section IV, paragraph (f)

General Recommendations

1. Participants may appoint an official co-ordinator(s) to deal with the implementation of the Certification Scheme.

2. Participants may consider the utility of complementing and/or enhancing the collection and publication of the statistics identified in Annex III based on the contents of Kimberley Process Certificates.

3. Participants are encouraged to maintain the information and data required by Section V on a computerised database.

4. Participants are encouraged to transmit and receive electronic messages in order to support the Certification Scheme.

5. Participants that produce diamonds and that have rebel groups suspected of mining diamonds within their territories are encouraged to identify the areas of rebel diamond mining activity and provide this information to all other Participants. This information should be updated on a regular basis.

6. Participants are encouraged to make known the names of individuals or companies convicted of activities relevant to the purposes of the Certification Scheme to all other Participants through the Chair.

7. Participants are encouraged to ensure that all cash purchases of rough diamonds are routed through official banking channels, supported by verifiable documentation.

8. Participants that produce diamonds should analyse their diamond production under the following headings:
- Characteristics of diamonds produced
- Actual production

Recommendations for Control over Diamond Mines

9. Participants are encouraged to ensure that all diamond mines are licensed and to allow only those mines so licensed to mine diamonds.

10. Participants are encouraged to ensure that prospecting and mining companies maintain effective security standards to ensure that conflict diamonds do not contaminate legitimate production.

Recommendations for Participants with Small-scale Diamond Mining

11. All artisinal and informal diamond miners should be licensed and only those persons so licensed should be allowed to mine diamonds.

12. Licensing records should contain the following minimum information: name, address, nationality and/or residence status and the area of authorised diamond mining activity.

Recommendations for Rough Diamond Buyers, Sellers and Exporters

13. All diamond buyers, sellers, exporters, agents and courier companies involved in carrying rough diamonds should be registered and licensed by each Participant's relevant authorities.

14. Licensing records should contain the following minimum information: name, address and nationality and/or residence status.

15. All rough diamond buyers, sellers and exporters should be required by law to keep for a period of five years daily buying, selling or exporting records listing the names of buying or selling clients, their license number and the amount and value of diamonds sold, exported or purchased.

16. The information in paragraph 14 above should be entered into a computerised database, to facilitate the presentation of detailed information relating to the activities of individual rough diamond buyers and sellers.

Recommendations for Export Processes

17. A exporter should submit a rough diamond shipment to the relevant Exporting Authority.

18. The Exporting Authority is encouraged, prior to validating a Certificate, to require an exporter to provide a declaration that the rough diamonds being exported are not conflict diamonds.

19. Rough diamonds should be sealed in a tamper proof container together with the Certificate or a duly authenticated copy. The Exporting Authority should then transmit a detailed e-mail message to the relevant Importing Authority containing information on the carat weight, value, country of origin or provenance, importer and the serial number of the Certificate.

20. The Exporting Authority should record all details of rough diamond shipments on a computerised database.

Recommendations for Import Processes

21. The Importing Authority should receive an e-mail message either before or upon

arrival of a rough diamond shipment. The message should contain details such as the carat weight, value, country of origin or provenance, exporter and the serial number of the Certificate.

22. The Importing Authority should inspect the shipment of rough diamonds to verify that the seals and the container have not been tampered with and that the export was performed in accordance with the Certification Scheme.

23. The Importing Authority should open and inspect the contents of the shipment to verify the details declared on the Certificate.

24. Where applicable and when requested, the Importing Authority should send the return slip or import confirmation coupon to the relevant Exporting Authority.

25. The Importing Authority should record all details of rough diamond shipments on a computerised database.

Recommendations on Shipments to and from Free Trade Zones

26. Shipments of rough diamonds to and from free trade zones should be processed by the designated authorities.

ANNEX III
Statistics

Recognising that reliable and comparable data on the production and the international trade in rough diamonds are an essential tool for the effective implementation of the Certification Scheme, and particularly for identifying any irregularities or anomalies which could indicate that conflict diamonds are entering the legitimate trade, Participants strongly support the following principles, taking into account the need to protect commercially sensitive information:

(a) to keep and publish within two months of the reference period and in a standardised format, quarterly aggregate statistics on rough diamond exports and imports, as well as the numbers of certificates validated for export, and of imported shipments accompanied by Certificates;

(b) to keep and publish statistics on exports and imports, by origin and provenance wherever possible; by carat weight and value; and under the relevant Harmonised Commodity Description and Coding System (HS) classifications 7102.10; 7102.21; 7102.31;

(c) to keep and publish on a semi-annual basis and within two months of the reference period statistics on rough diamond production by carat weight and by value. In the event that a Participant is unable to publish these statistics it should notify the Chair immediately;

(d) to collect and publish these statistics by relying in the first instance on existing national processes and methodologies;

(e) to make these statistics available to an intergovernmental body or to another appropriate mechanism identified by the Participants for (1) compilation and publication on a quarterly basis in respect of exports and imports, and (2) on a semi-annual basis in respect of production. These statistics are to be made available for analysis by interested parties and by the Participants, individually or collectively, according to such terms of reference as may be established by the Participants;

(f) to consider statistical information pertaining to the international trade in and production of rough diamonds at annual Plenary meetings, with a view to addressing related issues, and to supporting effective implementation of the Certification Scheme.

12. Oil and conflict: Lundin Petroleum's experience in Sudan

Christine Batruch

I. Introduction

Lundin Petroleum[1] obtained the rights to explore for and produce oil and gas in concession Block 5A, Unity State, Sudan, in February 1997; it sold these rights in June 2003.

During the period in which the company was active in Sudan, it operated in the belief that oil could benefit the economic development of the area and the country as a whole, and that this would have a catalysing effect on the peace process. The problems which it encountered in the area, however, led the company to constantly reassess its activities, role and responsibilities there.

This chapter examines the reasons why Lundin decided to operate in Sudan, the challenges it faced in the course of its activities, the steps it adopted to satisfy both its commercial objectives and ethical concerns, and its efforts to promote a peaceful resolution of the conflict.

II. Sudan's war

Sudan has been embroiled in a civil war that began shortly after it gained independence from the United Kingdom in 1956. It is one of the longest and most tragic wars of modern history: fighting has taken place for nearly 50 years, with a single reprieve between 1972 and 1983.[2] The Government of Sudan and the Sudan People's Liberation Movement/Army (SPLM/A), led by rebel leader John Garang, are the main protagonists in the conflict which resumed in 1983, although armed militias in different parts of the country have also been involved at various times. The fighting has taken place chiefly in the southernmost parts of the country although other areas, such as the Nuba

---

[1] On the independent Swedish oil and gas exploration and production company Lundin Petroleum AB—hereafter referred to as Lundin, or the company—see URL <http://www.lundin-petroleum.com/>. Lundin was the operator of Block 5A on behalf of the consortium which included OMV (Sudan) Exploration GmbH, Petronas Carigali Overseas Sdn Bhd and Sudapet. For a map showing the location see URL <http://www.lundin-petroleum.com/eng/sudan3.shtml>.

[2] For an account of recent developments in this conflict see Wiharta, S. and Anthony, I., 'Major armed conflicts', *SIPRI Yearbook 2003: Armaments, Disarmament and International Security* (Oxford University Press: Oxford, 2003), pp. 101–104. At the time of writing, peace negotiations held under the auspices of the Intergovernmental Authority on Development (IGAD) were in their final phase and a comprehensive agreement was expected to be signed by the end of the year. On the peace process see 'Sudan: peace talks, humanitarian action', URL <http://www.irinnews.org/webspecials/sudan/default.asp>; and Powell, C. L., 'An opportunity for peace in Sudan', 28 Oct. 2003, URL <http://www.sudan.net/news/posted/7274.html>.

Mountains region, Unity State and more recently the Darfur region of western Sudan, have also witnessed periods of intense combat.

It is difficult to ascertain the root causes of the war and the contributing factors over such a long period of time. Nonetheless, certain elements have, at various times, played a role in the conflict. They include: (*a*) the country's extreme poverty—Sudan is ranked among the poorest nations of the world;[3] (*b*) the religious/racial divide—northern Sudan is mainly Arab and Muslim, while southern Sudan is African and animist or Christian; (*c*) the competition for power—political opponents seek a greater participation in power, while regions seek greater autonomy from the central government; and (*d*) the competition for resources—southern regions contest the government's control over national resources such as water and oil, which originate in the south.

When peace is achieved, it will be easier to determine which of these elements played the decisive role in the conflict and its eventual resolution. What is clear, however, is that the war began years before the presence of oil was even suspected, and it was only after oil was produced that a material basis for a sustainable peace was seen to have been achieved. It is only then that an active, internationally mediated peace process began.[4]

Until that time, Sudan's war had been largely ignored, except from a humanitarian perspective. The conflict was regarded as another typical African war: over local issues and involving local parties. The situation seemed insoluble because of the many problems to be resolved and the slight foundations for sustainable peace. However, in the course of the 1990s a number of developments brought the world's attention to Sudan.

The early 1990s had seen the rise of Islamic fundamentalism, which figured prominently in the Sudanese Government; the harbouring of renowned terrorists such as Ilich Ramirez Sanchez, known as 'Carlos the Jackal', and later Osama bin Laden; and the suspicion that Sudan was linked to the 1995 assassination attempt on Egyptian President Hosni Mubarak. At this stage, Sudan was considered a 'rogue state' which had to be isolated from the community of nations.[5] In the latter part of the 1990s, however, the government adopted certain progressive measures, which the international community interpreted as signals of impending reform and of Sudan's interest in shedding its pariah status. The steps taken by Sudan included the handover of Carlos to French authorities, the expulsion of Osama bin Laden, the purging of key Islamic fundamentalists from the government, allowing the return of political opponents from abroad, the signing of the 1997 Khartoum Peace Agreement with south-

---

[3] For a discussion of Sudan's economy and the positive impact of oil in the past few years see the US Department of Energy Internet site at URL <http://www.eia.doe.gov/emeu/cabs/sudan.html>.

[4] The current phase of peace negotiations originated with the activities of Senator John Danforth, who was appointed by President George W. Bush as Special Envoy for Peace in Sudan on 6 Sep. 2001. See Danforth, J. C., 'Report to the President of the United States on the outlook for peace in Sudan, April 26, 2002', at URL <http://www.sudan.net> (under 'Latest news', 'Press releases and commentary', posted on 14 May 2002). The oil issue and the means for resolving the conflict are also discussed there.

[5] Because of Sudan's perceived connection with international terrorism, the UN and the USA imposed sanctions against Sudan, the former through a travel ban on Sudanese officials and the latter in the form of a ban on the conduct of business in the country by US companies.

ern opposition groups (see section III), improved relations with neighbouring countries, and the adoption of a new Constitution and Bill of Rights.

Whereas the United States was reluctant to recognize these efforts immediately, the European Union (EU) decided to engage in a constructive dialogue with the Sudanese Government because it believed that this approach was more likely to bring results than keeping Sudan isolated. Thus, when Lundin acquired the rights to explore for and produce oil and gas in Block 5A, world opinion regarding Sudan was beginning to change.

III. Lundin in Sudan

The company's primary concern when considering a new area for activities is geological. If an area presents the required geological profile—that is, if it is assumed to contain oil reserves—Lundin proceeds to study the technical and commercial feasibility of exploiting the oil. In the case of Sudan, the main risk identified in the course of the company's risk analysis was financial. The company decided, however, that the estimated potential oil reserves were important enough to justify the significant investments required for the venture, in particular investments in infrastructure development. It did not identify any legal risks—there were no international or EU sanctions against Sudan that prohibited a European company from doing business there—or political risks—there were no SPLA forces in the concession area, as the civil war was proceeding further south.

The company therefore engaged in negotiations to obtain a licence to explore for and produce oil and gas in Block 5A. As in most countries, mining rights in Sudan belong to the central state. Negotiations were therefore held with representatives of the Sudanese Ministry of Energy and Mining (MEM). The terms of the agreement were standard for the trade, with an initial period for oil exploration—in exchange for a work commitment and the carrying of costs—followed by a period of oil production, with cost recovery sought after initial production. The only terms that were specific to the exploration and production sharing agreement (EPSA) concerned the 'Sudanization' of the operations. At the request of the MEM, the company committed itself to hire and train Sudanese with a view to their constituting 50 per cent of the staff within 5 years of the commencement of operations and 80 per cent within 10 years. There was also a provision that the company would carry the costs of its Sudanese partner, Sudapet, which had a 5 per cent interest in the venture.

On its first visit to the concession area, Lundin met with key representatives of the local community, who welcomed oil activities as the only way to promote long-term economic development in their area.[6] They also committed themselves to providing a safe environment in which the company could oper-

---

[6] The company met with Dr Riek Machar, who, pursuant to the 1997 Khartoum Peace Agreement, was Vice-President of Sudan and President of the South Sudan Co-ordinating Council (the government representative for the south); with Taban Deng Gai, the Governor of Unity State; and with representatives of the local factions.

ate. This commitment arose out of the terms of the Khartoum Peace Agreement, which they had signed with the Sudanese Government and which set out the parties' respective rights and responsibilities in the area.[7]

Security, however, proved to be elusive. The prevalence of arms, coupled with the division of tribes into various factions, contributed to making the situation volatile.[8] Within a few years, instances of fighting started to increase. While the company was not directly affected by the fighting at the time, it was nevertheless worried about the safety of its staff and its operations. It was also concerned because of the criticisms that were being directed against an oil consortium situated in a nearby concession. To better understand these developments, Lundin decided in 1999 to commission a socio-political assessment of the area.

The study, conducted both at the Lundin head office in Geneva and in Sudan, was based on an analysis of reports on the political and human rights situation in Sudan, on interviews with company representatives in the head office and in Sudan, and on meetings with members of the Government of Sudan and humanitarian organizations. It also included a visit to the concession area.

The report's conclusion was that, despite the lack of evidence of a direct link between the sporadic fighting that had taken place in the concession area and company activities, there was a potential risk of deterioration if the local communities ceased to perceive the role of oil companies as beneficial. The report also noted that in view of the limited positive benefits of the oil activities at the time—revenues were not expected for a number of years, since activities were at the exploration stage—there was a distinct possibility that the local communities would grow disgruntled.[9] The report's main recommendations were that the company should continue to monitor socio-political developments in the concession area and reinforce its existing relationship with the local community.

Community relations

From the time it started its activities in Block 5A, Lundin adopted a proactive approach to community relations. The company not only met with representa-

---

[7] The text of the Khartoum Peace Agreement, signed in Apr. 1997, is available at URL <http://www.sudani.co.za/Documents%20and%20Issues/Khartoum%20Peace%20Agreement.htm>. It was signed between the Government of the Sudan, the South Sudan United Democratic Salvation Front (UDSF)—comprising the South Sudan Independence Movement (SSIM) and the Union of Sudan African Parties (USAP)—the SPLM, the Equatoria Defence Force (EDF), and the South Sudan Independents Group (SSIG).

[8] The main tribe in the area is the Nuer tribe, which has 5 sub-groups: the Bul, Lek, Jikany, Jagei and Dok Nuer. In turn, these groups are affiliated with local militia.

[9] Oil exploration and production are by nature a long-term activity: it takes a number of years before oil is found, and several more before it is brought into production and sold. It therefore takes years for revenue from oil to accrue to an area, which, in the meantime, has observed construction activity, equipment being brought in, and teams of people going back and forth. In many areas of the world, this poses no particular problem, but in an area like southern Sudan, where the majority of the population live in very precarious conditions, this issue requires special attention.

tives of the local community but also sought to show goodwill towards the population by hiring local staff and improving the infrastructure in the area.[10] The company believed that, if the local population obtained tangible benefits from oil activities, they would be even more supportive of these activities. However, given the lack of required skills locally, the number of people who were hired was minimal and the impact of this effort was limited. Similarly, while infrastructure developments such as bridge and road building increased local mobility, because they had been carried out for operational purposes the company did not consider them as community projects.

The company therefore sought ways to make a more direct contribution to the local community. It initiated a number of projects, which later became an integral part of the company's Community Development and Humanitarian Assistance Programme (CDHAP). The projects had three main objectives: (a) to promote better health, hygiene, education and general quality of life for the current and future inhabitants of the concession area of Block 5A, Unity State; (b) to contribute to the economic and social development of the area; and (c) to reinforce relationships between the local community and the company.

Through this programme, the company also wished to demonstrate to the local and central authorities that it was concerned with the interests and welfare of the population and was prepared to make significant contributions, despite the fact that it would not obtain any revenues from its activities for a number of years.

In order to ensure that its projects were relevant, Lundin had consulted with a number of local actors, in particular non-governmental organizations (NGOs) that were active in the area. With their assistance, it identified areas of need where it felt it could make a contribution, such as fresh water supply, health, education and capacity building.

In the three years Lundin ran CDHAP, it spent over $1.7 million on its various projects. These ranged from the delivery of fresh water by trucks, to the drilling of water wells and the construction of a water filtration unit. In the field of education, Lundin started by supplying educational materials to existing schools and orphanages, then built schools with local materials, and eventually constructed a permanent building to accommodate several hundred children. Through a team of five Sudanese doctors, assisted by local nurses, Lundin provided medical assistance in mobile tent clinics, temporary straw clinics and eventually in a fully equipped permanent clinic which it had built. Similarly, it relied on two veterinarians and local para-veterinarians whom it had trained to tend to local cattle in a vet station and in mobile vet clinics. The capacity-building projects included the creation of a mobile brick factory, a women's development centre and a nursery as well as a programme for train-

---

[10] The uniqueness of Lundin's approach did not go unnoticed. Indeed, in a meeting with representative of an international NGO, Dr Riek Machar, who had then defected from the Government of Sudan, stated that Lundin was different in that it had consulted with the local people and tried to involve them in its activities.

ing local people as midwives, para-veterinarians, nurses, bricklayers, vector control specialists, computer analysts, and so on. In times of emergency brought about by climatic or security conditions, the company provided ad hoc humanitarian assistance by supplying people with water containers, soap, blankets, mosquito nets and medical services.[11]

From its inception, CDHAP was a constant element of the company's presence in Unity State. Not only were CDHAP staff members often the first to go to projected areas of activities and the last to be pulled out when the security situation deteriorated, but they stayed there even when operations were suspended. During the company's temporary suspensions of activities in 2001 and 2002, services to the community continued to be rendered in the two main towns of the area, Rubkona and Bentiu, and in surrounding villages. Maintaining its presence in the area through CDHAP was the company's way of demonstrating its long-term commitment to the local community and the area.[12]

If CDHAP was the company's most tangible way of showing its concern for the people in the area, it was by no means the only way. Outbreaks of fighting, coupled with allegations that these conflicts were related to oil, led Lundin to reassess its role and responsibilities and seek ways of exercising a positive influence on the protagonists in the conflict.

Internal review

In the latter part of 1999, civil rights activists started to question the role of the Greater Nile Petroleum Operating Company (GNPOC) oil consortium in the conflict.[13] This consortium, which was operating in a concession area adjacent to Lundin's, had participated in the construction of a pipeline linking the southern oilfields of Unity State to the northern city of Port Sudan and was beginning to produce oil. Activists claimed that human rights violations, such as population displacement, had taken place in order to pave the way for the consortium's activities. The consortium consistently refuted these claims. The activists also believed that the revenues obtained by the Sudanese Government from GNPOC operations would be used to build up its military arsenal and quash the rebel SPLA.[14]

There was a marked discrepancy between Lundin's first-hand experience in its concession area and reports about what was being alleged to have taken

[11] For a review of CDHAP activities in 2001–2002 see URL <http://www.lundin-petroleum.com/eng/comdev.shtml>.

[12] This commitment has been passed on to Petronas Carigali Overseas Sdn Bhd, Lundin's successor in the area, which has decided not only to pursue projects initiated by Lundin but also to expand the activities under CDHAP.

[13] The GNPOC was at the time a consortium of Canadian, Chinese, Malaysian and Sudanese companies.

[14] The consortium contested these allegations. It provided evidence of population growth in the area and divulged the nature of its discussions with the government regarding the use of its facilities for military purposes.

place in the neighbouring GNPOC concession. The report commissioned by Lundin confirmed that many elements distinguished the two operations. First, the GNPOC concession area was sparsely inhabited, which gave credence to the claim that population displacement had taken place prior to the commencement of operations, even though this was disproved by satellite images.[15] Second, the local community there was partly of Dinka origin, the main tribal group behind the SPLA; it was therefore conceivable that there could be clashes between them and government forces. Finally, GNPOC operations had started generating revenue for the government, of which little, if any, appeared to be reinvested by the government in the area.

Despite these differences, Lundin recognized that negative perceptions of the effects of oil operations could also come to be applied to its area and therefore decided to set out, in a Code of Conduct, the conditions under which it was prepared to operate.

The Lundin Code of Conduct

The process of development of the Code of Conduct was important for Lundin, as it required the company to assess the role of its business from a different perspective. Lundin's management had always regarded (and continues to regard) itself as making a positive contribution to economic growth by providing a necessary source of energy. It had also witnessed how oil revenues in undeveloped areas acted as a catalyst for economic development, paving the way for other businesses and international loans.[16] Lundin was aware of the potential negative impacts of its operations on the environment, and took mitigating measures to address them. The socio-political dimension of its activities, however, was not something the company had had particular reason to consider before the Sudan experience. It believed that these were issues beyond its field of competence.

When faced with the possibility that its activities could have a negative impact on the conflict in Sudan, senior management re-examined the company's role from this wider perspective. Lundin established its objective to play a positive role not only directly, in the economic field, but indirectly in the socio-political field as well. As stated by its chairman, the company's 'aim is not only to find oil and gas, we are also committed to developing this valu-

---

[15] The Canadian company in the consortium hired Kalagate Imagery Bureau, a British company specialized in the analysis of satellite images, to ascertain population patterns in its concession area in the 1980s and 1990s. The conclusions were that there was no evidence of appreciable population migration from the area.

[16] It had felt this way about Sudan, and in many ways it turned out to be right. Over a period of 5 years Sudan shed its pariah nation status and became an attractive place for the international business community (sanctioned by the International Monetary Fund).

able resource in the best socio-economic manner possible for the benefit of all our partners, including the host country and local communities'.[17]

The Code of Conduct was developed after the company had consulted documents in the field of corporate responsibility[18] and after discussions with members of the Board of Directors as well as senior corporate and country-based management. The Code was adopted as a consensus document which served as a guide for the company's activities worldwide.

The Code set out the company's values, responsibilities and the principles by which it was guided. The company recognized that it had specific responsibilities towards its shareholders, employees, host countries and local communities, as well as to the environment. It committed itself to act in a fair and honest way, to observe both national and international laws, and 'to act in accordance with generally accepted principles on the protection of human rights and the environment'.[19] After the Code of Conduct had been adopted by the Board, Lundin disseminated it to its employees in Geneva and in Sudan, and to the company's affiliates. It became an integral part of the company's contracts of employment.

The adoption of the Code was followed by other initiatives, such as the publication of the company's policies on health and safety, the environment and community relations. The company also arranged for an awareness session on human rights and developed a human rights primer, explaining the origins of and guiding principles for the protection of human rights and how they relate to business. The company's security liaison personnel in Sudan were provided with information regarding human rights and security, to sensitize them to such issues in conflict situations, and were encouraged to report any violations they witnessed.[20]

The internal dissemination of the Code of Conduct was necessary in order to ensure that the staff understood what the company stood for and what was expected of each and every one of them. It also became the basis for discussions with stakeholder groups in Sudan.

---

[17] Code of Conduct, 'Message from the Chairman'. The text of the Lundin Code of Conduct and related documents are available at URL <http://www.lundin-petroleum.com/Documents/ot_lupe-code_e. pdf>.

[18] These include the Caux Principles, the Global Sullivan Principles, the UN Declaration of Human Rights, the International Labour Organization's Tripartite Declaration of Principle concerning Multinational Enterprises and Social Policy, the Organisation for Economic Co-operation and Development's Guidelines for Multinational Enterprises, Amnesty International's Human Rights Code for Companies, the Prince of Wales Business Forum on Operating in Conflict Zones, and so on.

[19] Code of Conduct (note 17).

[20] The relevant personnel received information about the Voluntary Principles on Security and Human Rights for the Extractive Sector, available at URL <http://www.amnesty.org.uk/business/newslet/spring01/principles.shtml>; Amnesty International's 10 Basic Human Rights Standards for Law Enforcement Officials, URL <http://web.amnesty.org/aidoc/aidoc_pdf.nsf/Index/POL30004l998ENGLISH/ $File/POL3000498.pdf>; the 1990 UN Basic Principles on the Use of Force and Firearms by Law Enforcement Officials, URL <http://www.unhchr.ch/html/menu3/b/h_comp43.htm>; and the 1979 UN Code of Conduct for Law Enforcement Officials, URL <http://www.unhchr.ch/html/menu3/b/h_comp 42.htm>.

Stakeholder engagement

In the course of developing its Code of Conduct, the company defined more precisely who its stakeholders were in relation to its activities in Sudan. In the first few years of its operations in Sudan, it had cultivated friendly relations with business partners, government representatives at the central and local levels, and community representatives. It also had informal relations with other oil companies and NGOs active in the area. However, it decided, that in view of the competing claims being made about the impact of oil in the region, it needed not only to widen the scope of these contacts but also to alter the content of its discussions to include socio-political issues.

The company's early consultations with central and local authorities had revealed a shared view that oil represented a momentous opportunity for the development of the country and the area. Even the humanitarian and development organizations it had consulted at the time recognized this potential, but they remained more reserved as to whether the wealth produced would be properly shared among the population.

This general consensus began to erode, however, when representatives of the local communities whom Lundin had met at the outset accused the Sudanese Government of reneging on its commitments under the Khartoum Peace Agreement and decided to resign from their governmental posts. Their decision, coupled with the defection of a local tribal faction to the SPLA, represented a turning point both in the conflict and for the company. Interfactional fighting escalated into a conflict which pitted against each other militias that were backed by the two contenders in the civil war—the Government of Sudan and the SPLA.

Judging the situation as representing an undue risk to the safety of its staff—the SPLA having then indicated that it considered oil operations and staff as legitimate military targets—Lundin decided to temporarily suspend its operations. It made its resumption of activities conditional upon a peaceful environment, noting that this could only be achieved with the support of the local community.

Lundin also decided to enhance its knowledge of the situation by consulting not only those with whom it had formal relations, such as its partners in the consortium and the government, but also those with particular knowledge of, or interest in, the conflict in Sudan. The purpose of these discussions was to share information and opinions about the conflict and to establish what was required for company operations to resume.

The institutions with which the company met included the following.

The Sudanese Government (host government) and the Government of Unity State (local government)

Discussions with the Sudanese and local governments focused on the means to render the area conducive to oil operations. The company expressed its view that the long-term security required for sustainable oil activities could only be achieved with the support of the local community. Lundin made it clear that, in its view, military action—except for defensive purposes—was not an acceptable option.

The Nuer opposition (local community)

In its discussions with representatives of the Nuer opposition, the company attempted to convey its view that oil business presented the best opportunity to achieve sustainable peace and growth in the area and encouraged them to seek a peaceful way to assert their rights to the area.

The Swedish Ministry for Foreign Affairs (home government)

It was important for Lundin, as a Swedish company, to share with the Swedish Ministry for Foreign Affairs (MFA) its views about the situation in Sudan and its approach there. Given the allegations about wrongdoings committed in its area of operations, the company kept the MFA informed of its first-hand experience in the area and the steps taken to address local needs and concerns. As a member of the European Union, Sweden had adopted a policy of constructive engagement in Sudan: the activities of the company fell within this approach, in so far as it ensured that its activities were not affecting the conflict negatively.

United Nations relief organizations (the humanitarian community)

UN organizations were present in Sudan mainly to deliver humanitarian assistance under the umbrella organization Operation Lifeline Sudan (OLS).[21] Set up both in Khartoum to service government-controlled areas and in Lokichoggio, Kenya, to service parts of the country under SPLA control, the OLS had witnessed the unbearable toll of the war on civilians. Its main concern was to have full access to all areas of the country in order to be able to provide humanitarian relief in the case of crises. As the company had itself offered assistance to internally displaced people fleeing from areas of natural or man-made catastrophe, it shared the view of the OLS that unrestricted humanitarian access was required and raised this issue in its meetings with government and Nuer representatives.

The United Nations Commission on Human Rights

The UN Commission on Human Rights had two representatives for Sudan: an in-country representative, whose role was to promote respect for human rights by the Sudanese Government and in government-controlled areas; and a

---

[21] At that time, the OLS was comprised of 42 intergovernmental and non-governmental development and humanitarian organizations, among which were the UN Children's Fund (UNICEF), the UN Office for the Coordination of Humanitarian Affairs (OCHA) and the UN Development Programme (UNDP).

Special Rapporteur on the Situation of Human Rights in Sudan, whose role was to assess and report on the human rights situation throughout the country. In 1999 the Special Rapporteur claimed that oil activities had exacerbated the conflict, although he had not visited the oilfields or even consulted with the oil companies. Lundin therefore contacted him to inform him of its first-hand experience and knowledge of the situation in the area and invited him to visit the oilfields instead of relying on secondary, sometimes biased, sources. The eventual visit of the Special Rapporteur to the area took place at such a time and was of such short duration (a mere three hours) that he could not conduct an in-depth inspection. In the course of discussions with company representatives, however, he admitted that the civil war was the cause of the human rights problems and that oil production, if properly channelled, could contribute to a sustainable peace.

Non-governmental organizations

The NGOs with a focus on Sudan may be categorized in two broad groups: (a) those which have a permanent presence in Sudan, and assist the population through local humanitarian or development projects; and (b) those which are based outside Sudan, and promote special interests such as human rights, religious rights, development rights, and so on. Lundin was in contact with both groups to exchange views about the situation in Sudan and means to improve it. Not surprisingly, it found that organizations with a humanitarian focus were generally supportive of the company's efforts to contribute to the local communities in its area of operations. They were prepared to talk to company representatives and even work with them on certain projects. When the stigma surrounding oil activities became significant, most chose not to be publicly associated with the company and therefore only a few cooperative ventures continued, on a confidential basis.

Lundin's experience with special-interest NGOs was more difficult. In many cases, views about the situation in Sudan were so different that discussions rarely went beyond each side trying to convince the other of the correctness of its views. This was particularly true with respect to religious-based organizations, which characterized the conflict as an attempt by Muslims to eradicate the Christian population in the south of Sudan in order to gain access to the oil there. Although the company responded to their claims, in discussions and in writing, it felt that not much would be gained from this effort. These NGOs believed that the cessation of oil activities was a means to achieve peace, while the company believed that oil activities would be the basis for peace.[22]

There were two notable exceptions in Lundin's relations with special-interest groups: Amnesty International, particularly the Swedish branch; and the Church of Sweden. Both organizations believed in the benefits of con-

---

[22] In Mar. 2001 Lundin posted a report on its Internet site 'Lundin in Sudan' which described company activities to date and responded to allegations regarding the nature of the conflict in its area of operations.

structive engagement with companies operating in Sudan and met with Lundin on a number of occasions. Lundin invited their representatives to visit its concession area, but because of its suspension of oil activities and later sale of the asset the visits never materialized. Nonetheless, some of these groups' views and recommendations were taken into consideration and, where appropriate, were integrated into Lundin's business conduct.[23]

Think tanks

The think tanks which had been following and reporting on Sudan for a number of years also considered how oil could act as an incentive for peace in Sudan.[24] Above and beyond the obvious positive benefits of oil for the overall economic performance of the country, they were interested in ascertaining whether oil could be used as a peace incentive. Discussions with representatives of think tanks were dedicated to a review of oil exploration, production and revenue distribution schemes. It was generally accepted that a fair distribution of oil resources was a necessary condition for peace, and in this regard the company drew their attention to the equitable sharing scheme laid out in the Khartoum Peace Agreement.

The media (representing public interest)

When allegations of a possible connection between the war and Lundin's operations surfaced in the press, the company decided that the best way to respond was to invite both Swedish and international journalists to visit its concession area. Until that time, journalists who had reported from the field had been able to do so only with the support of rebel forces; their reports therefore presented only one side of the story. The company believed that if they had the opportunity to visit the area without support or interference from either rebel or government forces, they would have a more balanced and realistic view of the situation. A number of journalists took up the company's suggestion and visited the area in 2001 and 2002. They produced articles for the press as well as video recordings that were aired on both Swedish and Swiss television.

Peace negotiators

As a principle, Lundin refrains from getting involved in the political affairs of a country; it believes that it cannot make a meaningful contribution in this sphere and prefers to restrict itself to its commercial mission. The situation it encountered in Sudan, however, was exceptional, and the company needed to

---

[23] Amnesty International had issued recommendations for oil companies operating in Sudan; these were circulated among relevant company staff, as were copies of the 10 Basic Human Rights Standards for Law Enforcement Officials (note 20).

[24] Two US-based think tanks devoted particular attention to this issue: the Center for Strategic International Studies (CSIS), Washington, DC; and the Carter Center Peace Program, Atlanta, Georgia.

make clear to the protagonists in the conflict that it saw peace as the best means to ensure sustainable oil operations. In this endeavour it relied on the skills and competence of Carl Bildt, a member of Lundin Petroleum's Board of Directors, whose experience as the UN Secretary-General's Special Envoy for the Balkans in 1999–2001 was particularly relevant. In a series of trips to Brussels, Cairo, Khartoum, Nairobi and Washington, Bildt met with high-level representatives of the Sudanese Government, including the President, his peace adviser, the Minister of Energy and Mining, the Minister of Foreign Affairs, and the main representative of the Nuer community (later deputy chairman of the SPLA), as well as with representatives of the key nations acting as peace mediators, such as Kenya, Norway, the UK and the USA. Bildt delivered the same message to all: oil represented an incentive for peace in so far as oil activities could not be pursued in a war context. He also underlined how oil provided the material basis for a sustainable peace. The company's repeated suspensions of activities were a proof that oil activities could not flourish in a conflict situation, and experience in various other countries demonstrated that a conflict of this nature could not be resolved militarily. In Bildt's view, the parties had to determine for themselves their minimum, not maximum, requirements for the achievement of peace. The mediators' role was to help the parties achieve this compromise by offering them support, in the form of international monitoring and monetary assistance for purposes of reconstruction.

IV. Lessons learned

During the seven years in which it acted as operator of Block 5A in southern Sudan, Lundin was faced with a constantly changing environment. The company learned that, despite its desire to restrict itself to a commercial role, it could not ignore either the socio-political developments in its area of operations or the claims—even if unfounded—of a possible connection between its activities and the conflict.

A reaffirmation of its values in a Code of Conduct, a greater involvement in community life, stakeholder engagement and the suspension of activities were the tools adopted by the company in response to the challenges it faced.

In the spring of 2003, the company sold its interest in Block 5A at a profit. The transaction was satisfying not only from a commercial perspective but also from the perspective of corporate responsibility. At the time the company left, active peace negotiations were under way and its community development programme was maintained by its successor. This reinforced Lundin's belief that it is possible for business to pursue commercial objectives while meeting ethical concerns, even in areas of conflict.

13. The role of humanitarian organizations: the case of the International Committee of the Red Cross

Gilles Carbonnier

I. Introduction

The 1990s saw a great deal of progress in the field of corporate social respon-sibility. After the United Nations world summit meetings in the first half of the decade,[1] top executives of multinational companies began to focus their efforts on environmental and social concerns. In recent years, the business com-munity has also started to examine its role and responsibility in conflict-prone areas, where companies face increasingly complex challenges. This applies in particular to the business of raw material extraction, where investment deci-sions are dictated by geological factors rather than by political risks. When extractive industries look for new deposits in ever more remote areas or con-tinue operating in countries undergoing fragile democratization processes, they need to learn how to manage risks related to armed violence and conflict in a new environment where they are expected to act as responsible corporate citizens.

Humanitarian organizations have learned that any intervention in a conflict-prone area, even with the best intention to assist victims, can do more harm than good if the overall impact of this intervention is not carefully assessed. Development cooperation agencies have elaborated new methods to conduct so-called peace and conflict impact assessments before starting a project in sensitive, unstable places.[2] Similarly, private companies have been asked to devote much more attention to these issues so that their production activities and the ensuing revenue generation and distribution do not raise tensions or aggravate the local political situation. In addition to the 'do-no-harm' approach, business is increasingly expected to consider how to contribute to conflict-prevention and peace-building processes. Corporations are thus increasingly addressing issues that were formerly considered the exclusive concern of governments, multilateral organizations and non-governmental organizations (NGOs). It is clear, however, that business cannot provide a

---

[1] On the UN Conference on Environment and Development (UNCED, or the Earth Summit), held in Rio de Janeiro in 1992, see URL <http://www.un.org/esa/sustdev/documents/UNCED_Docs.htm>; and on the World Summit for Social Development, held in Copenhagen in 1995, see URL <http://www.un.org/documents/ga/conf166/aconf166-9.htm>.

[2] On these assessments see, e.g., 'Peace and conflict impact assessments', in 'Peace in the millen-nium', Alliances for Africa Online Bulletin, no. 3 (1 Jan. 2000), URL <http://www.alliancesforafrica.org/print.asp?news=198&width=500>.

cure-all for the world's ills. Governments, humanitarian organizations and private companies each have different objectives. They also have different responsibilities, the boundaries of which have yet to be clarified and reaffirmed.

The International Committee of the Red Cross (ICRC) is a humanitarian organization born out of war 140 years ago.[3] Its mandate is to promote international humanitarian law and to provide war victims with assistance and protection. In order to carry out its activities, the ICRC maintains relations with those who exert a direct or an indirect influence on armed conflicts. After World War I, it established formal contacts with liberation movements and guerrilla groups in its capacity as a neutral intermediary in war. It later expanded its network of contacts to include formers of public opinion, the media, trade unions, religious leaders and other groups in order to promote greater respect for international humanitarian law.

With the globalization process now under way, the business community is playing an ever more important role in international relations, including in war-prone countries. The ICRC has consequently decided to develop its contacts with the private sector in the belief that the plight of the children, women and men affected by an armed conflict is likely to be addressed more effectively if the business community is involved in a constructive manner, rather than being excluded simply because of its corporate motives. The goals of companies have not suddenly become humanitarian in nature. Profitability obviously remains their top priority, but they are realizing that it is in their best interest to contribute to the preservation of basic humanitarian principles.

II. Business and the economy in conflict prevention

Research has shown that abundant natural resources can be more of a curse than a blessing for communities located in resource-rich areas.[4] For example, the risk of war seems to be higher in these than in other countries,[5] and fair revenue distribution within a society may reduce the probability of armed conflict. The international community is involved in several initiatives to fight corruption and promote transparency, one example of which is the Extractive Industries Transparency Initiative (EITI).[6] However, transparency alone is not

---

[3] See the ICRC Internet site at URL <http://www.icrc.org>, especially Carbonnier, G., 'Corporate responsibility and humanitarian action: what relations between the business and humanitarian worlds?', *International Review*, vol. 83, no. 844 (Dec. 2001), URL <http://www.icrc.org/Web/eng/siteeng0.nsf/htmlall/57JRLN/$FILE/0947-0968_Carbonnier.pdf>. Much of this chapter is based on this document.

[4] Karl, T. L., *The Paradox of Plenty: Oil Booms and Petro-States*, Studies in International Political Economy 26 (University of California Press: London, 1997).

[5] Collier, P., *Breaking the Conflict Trap: Civil War and Development Policy*, World Bank Policy Research Report (World Bank and University Press: New York, 1 June 2003).

[6] The EITI was launched by British Prime Minister Tony Blair at the World Summit on Sustainable Development in 2002. Its objective is 'to increase transparency over payments and revenues in the extractive sector in countries heavily dependent on these resources'. See 'Extractive Industries Transparency Initiative (EITI), London Conference, 17 June 2003, Statement of Principles and Agreed

enough. The International Monetary Fund and the World Bank are also trying to improve revenue allocation mechanisms so that entire populations benefit from natural resource exploitation (e.g., in the Chad–Cameroon region and in Azerbaijan). Transparency and revenue allocation are thus important ingredients of conflict prevention. It is true that the ultimate success of recent initiatives in this area will depend on governments and international organizations, but they cannot succeed without the strong support and cooperation of the business community.

War economies

The role of business in conflict prevention or peacebuilding cannot be considered without taking into account war economies and their specific characteristics. In many countries with a fragile peace process, the major obstacles along the road to economic recovery are insecurity and lack of investor confidence (e.g., Iraq today). In addition, when economic governance is weak and the population has developed survival strategies outside the formal sector, the informal financial sector is often larger than the 'official' economy. In the direct aftermath of a protracted conflict, this development seriously reduces the government's revenue and tax base, and hence the capacity of the state to deliver essential public services and maintain basic infrastructure.

The judiciary system of states with war economies is also often weak, and corruption is rampant. As criminal actors enjoy impunity, illegal economic activities thrive without any serious risk of sanction, which attracts international criminal networks. As a result, part of the politico-economic elite is often discredited. In such an environment, it is not easy for a company to operate in the formal economy and still abide by high standards of business behaviour. However, even in war-torn countries such as the Democratic Republic of the Congo and Somalia, many national and foreign business people manage to maintain day-to-day activities in the communities despite this environment. They help to preserve or rebuild a minimal social capital, without which reconstruction efforts are highly unlikely to succeed.

Several recent initiatives reflect the growing interest of the international community in better understanding and tackling the economic dynamics underlying civil wars. The Kimberley Process—created to curb the flow of 'conflict diamonds'—is a prime example,[7] as is the work of panels of experts mandated by the UN Security Council to produce reports on the illegal exploitation of natural resources in African countries at war.[8] Consequently,

Actions', URL <http://www.worldbank.org/wbi/corpgov/csr/econferences/publicpolicy/pdf/eiti_stat_of_principles.pdf>.

[7] The Kimberley Process originated in 2000 through the decision of southern African diamond producing countries to take action to stop the flow of conflict diamonds to markets while at the same time protecting the legitimate diamond industry. See URL <http://www.kimberleyprocess.com/>. See also chapter 11 in this volume.

[8] For recent reports of UN panels of experts on natural resources and conflict see the Internet site of the Global Policy Forum at URL <http://www.globalpolicy.org/security/natres/docsindex.htm>. The

today no one would deny that economic factors may contribute to fuelling conflicts, sometimes with dramatic humanitarian consequences.

How do humanitarian organizations position themselves in this environment? The economic actors who are outlawed by these new initiatives feel under increasing scrutiny when working in war zones. They may thus oppose any external presence—sometimes violently—including that of humanitarian organizations. This carries serious security risks for these organizations and may impede their access to a population caught in the midst of a conflict. For this reason, the ICRC often has to reaffirm that it is not in any way associated with the monitoring or reporting of economic activities and to make it clear that its sole purpose, as a humanitarian organization, is to assist and protect the victims of armed conflict.

III. Challenges for business in conflict areas

When operating in a conflict area, companies must take measures to ensure the security of their personnel and facilities while at the same time avoiding any association with violations of internationally recognized norms of behaviour. A bad decision by management concerning security can have disastrous consequences for the company's reputation. It may also result in legal action, as is presently the case for many major oil and mining companies in the United States.

International humanitarian law

In this context, where does the 'humanitarian responsibility' of a company begin and end? The primary responsibility for respecting as well as ensuring respect for human rights and international humanitarian law rests with states. The states parties to the Geneva Conventions of 1949, for example, have made such a commitment.[9] This does not mean, however, that international humanitarian law does not place any constraints on economic actors. It applies to all those involved in the conduct of hostilities during an armed conflict, government and non-state actors alike. Companies can be held accountable for violations of international humanitarian law if they are directly involved in the hostilities, for example, through military personnel whom they have hired for that purpose.

There is a lively debate on the notion of complicity, notably in connection with crimes covered by the Rome Statute of the International Criminal Court (ICC), with particular reference to Article 25 on individual criminal responsi-

Forum monitors policymaking at the United Nations, promotes accountability of global decisions, educates and mobilizes for global citizen participation, and advocates on vital issues of international peace and justice.

[9] See Article 1 common to the 4 Geneva Conventions of 12 Aug. 1949: 'The High Contracting Parties undertake to respect and to ensure respect for the present Convention in all circumstances'. The Geneva Conventions are available at URL <http://www.icrc.org/Web/Eng/siteeng0.nsf/htmlall/party_gc>.

bility.[10] Several analysts have drawn attention to the fact that the Statute's accomplice liability provision could create international criminal liability for corporate employees and managers.[11] Companies could thus be prosecuted for crimes against humanity through the *individual liability* of their staff or directors. In the specific case of a breach of the 1949 Geneva Conventions,[12] for example, a perpetrator's superior would be held accountable if this person knew, or could conclude, that the subordinate person was going to commit such a breach and did not try to prevent it. Attempts to include the principle of *corporate liability* in the ICC Statute have been unsuccessful, even though several states provide for such a form of criminal responsibility in their national legislation.

The case of private military or security firms deserves specific mention, as there is a clear trend towards the privatization of some military functions, including combat support, logistics and training.[13] In principle, national legislation should regulate the practice of security companies, and penal sanctions for violations of international humanitarian law should be included in national legislation. In practice, however, private military companies are often contracted to work in places where there is little respect for the rule of law and where the state is unable to offer a sufficient level of security, which is why those who can afford to do so opt for private security companies in the first place. It is thus not exceptional to find private military and security firms operating in places with weak legal infrastructure and an inefficient or paralysed judicial system. They often pursue their activities in a 'legal vacuum'. Further reflection is needed on the appropriate regulatory tools and enforcement mechanisms to ensure effective compliance with international humanitarian law in such cases.

Voluntary initiatives

Many companies have adopted voluntary codes of conduct to address the risks associated with operating in conflict areas.[14] NGOs and advocacy organizations have expressed concern that these voluntary initiatives should not become substitutes for fulfilling the legal requirements of intergovernmental agreements.[15] They have instead called for binding regulations to ensure that companies respect international law. It seems that some business leaders are beginning to share this view, since binding rules might contribute to fair competition conditions—'a level playing field'—between those companies that

---

[10] For the Rome Statute see URL <http://www.un.org/law/icc/>. See also Wiharta, S., 'The International Criminal Court', *SIPRI Yearbook 2003: Armaments, Disarmament and International Security* (Oxford University Press: Oxford, 2003), pp. 153–66.

[11] See, e.g., Nyberg, M., 'At risk from complicity with crime', *Financial Times*, 27 July 1998.

[12] Article 86 of 1977 Protocol I Additional to the 1949 Geneva Conventions (see note 9).

[13] On private military companies see also the introduction and chapters 14 and 21 in this volume.

[14] See also chapter 12 in this volume.

[15] See, e.g., Utting, P., UN Research Institute for Social Development, 'UN–business partnerships: whose agenda counts?', *Transnational Associations*, no. 3 (2001), pp. 157–65, available at URL <http://www.uia.org/uiata/utting.htm>.

commit themselves to promoting transparency and respect for international law, and those that do not.

Companies operating in war-prone areas have established voluntary norms, such as the Voluntary Principles on Security and Human Rights for the Extractive Sector, adopted in December 2000 by a number of multinational oil and mining firms together with the US State Department, the British Foreign and Commonwealth Office, Amnesty International, Human Rights Watch, International Alert and labour unions.[16] The guiding principle is that governments should adopt the Voluntary Principles before the extractive industries and NGOs based in their countries can adhere to them. The Netherlands and Norway joined in 2002, and additional countries may follow suit in the near future. The Voluntary Principles process involves regular plenary meetings and, perhaps more importantly, efforts to implement the Principles in the field, where they obviously matter most and would make a real difference to the host communities.

The participants of the Voluntary Principles recognize the importance of the promotion and protection of human rights and the constructive role that business and civil society can together play in advancing these goals. More specifically, they state that while 'governments have the primary responsibility to promote and protect human rights and that all parties to a conflict are obliged to observe applicable international humanitarian law, [they] recognize that [they] share the common goal of promoting respect for human rights . . . and international humanitarian law'.

IV. Dialogue between companies and the ICRC

As is often the case with voluntary codes of conduct referring to internationally recognized norms, the main challenge for companies is to translate general policy statements into operational reality. The ICRC aims to assist companies in identifying concrete steps to put into practice the 'common goal of respecting and promoting respect for international humanitarian law'. It has thus established a dialogue with companies, which focuses on the relevance of fundamental humanitarian principles in the countries where they operate. In doing so, the ICRC remains faithful to its traditional *modus operandi,* developing these exchanges in the framework of a confidential and constructive dialogue, as with any other stakeholder in war zones. For the ICRC, the dialogue further represents an opportunity to share specific humanitarian concerns and to better understand the rationale and views of economic actors in complex emergencies.

A major objective of the ICRC is to strengthen its capacity to assist and protect communities affected by war by inculcating respect for basic humanitarian

---

[16] The Voluntary Principles were developed to guide companies in the areas of risk assessment, relations with public security and relations with private security. See US Department of State, Bureau of Democracy, Human Rights, and Labor, Fact sheet, 20 Feb. 2001, URL <http://www.state.gov/g/drl/rls/2931.htm>. See also chapters 10 and 12 in this volume.

principles to companies operating in conflict-prone settings. Among these basic principles, embodied in international humanitarian law, are the following:[17]

1. *The distinction to be made at all times between civilians and combatants.* The obligation to distinguish between civilian objects and military targets is of specific interest to companies that do not want their facilities to be used for military purposes by parties to a conflict so that they will not become objects of attack.

2. *The prohibition of forced movement of civilians.* The implication for private companies is obvious when displacement of people is caused by their own operations (for example, in the case of construction of a pipeline or exploitation of natural resources).

3. *The protection of objects indispensable for the survival of the civilian population, especially goods such as food and water and access to these goods.*[18]

4. *Respect for and protection of detained persons.*

Three additional principles apply in particular to companies hiring security forces:

1. Under the principle of proportionality, it is forbidden to use means and methods of warfare which may cause superfluous injury or unnecessary suffering, or widespread, long-term and severe damage to the natural environment.

2. Indiscriminate attacks are forbidden.

3. Medical services and other facilities displaying the Red Cross or Red Crescent emblems must be respected.

For the ICRC, it is essential to continuously assess the potential impact of technological innovations and new weapons vis-à-vis the risk of indiscriminate attacks and the principle of proportionality. In 2002 the ICRC launched the Initiative on Biotechnology, Weapons and Humanity.[19] While biotechnological innovation brings enormous potential benefit for humanity, important advances in science and technology may also be put to hostile use.

The ICRC Initiative on Biotechnology, Weapons and Humanity was prompted by the need to reduce the risk of biotechnology being used to the detriment of humanity. It is intended to promote serious reflection on the risks, roles and responsibilities related to advances in this area. The initiative appeals to governments, the scientific community, the military, industry and civil

---

[17] See, e.g., the 1997 Convention on the Prohibition of the Use, Stockpiling, Production and Transfer of Anti-Personnel Mines and on their Destruction (Preamble); the 1998 Rome Statute of the International Criminal Court (Article 7, para. 2); and 1977 Protocol (I) Additional to the Geneva Conventions of 12 August 1949, and Relating to the Protection of Victims of International Armed Conflicts (Article 54 and Article 75, para. 3).

[18] There is also a rule that combatants must refrain from attacking works and installations containing dangerous substances.

[19] On this ICRC initiative see URL <http://www.icrc.org/Web/eng/siteeng0.nsf/htmlall/bwh?OpenDocument>.

society to work together to strengthen the commitment to the norms of international humanitarian law, which prohibit hostile uses of biotechnology, and to impose effective controls on potentially dangerous biological knowledge and agents.

The ICRC believes that it is only through the establishment of an effective network of prevention—bringing together the private sector, governments and the research community—that advances in biotechnology will be firmly harnessed for the benefit of humanity. The ICRC has established a dialogue with states and the academic community, and it encourages industry to join the dialogue in order to strengthen the prevention network.

The potential and limits of dialogue

The ICRC is, of course, aware that the prime objective of business is and remains the generation of profit. It is, however, convinced of the importance of building relations with the corporate sector and believes that it is in the mutual interest of business and humanitarian organizations to promote exchanges on issues of common concern. For the ICRC, the ultimate objective is to expand its outreach in order to provide enhanced protection and assistance to people suffering the consequences of armed conflicts. The new dialogue is promising, but the future will show whether exchanges with the business community will lead to effective improvements for those who suffer violations of international humanitarian law.

The private sector has a pivotal role to play in the rebuilding of war-torn societies. Corporate involvement is required to help restore basic infrastructure and to create jobs and opportunities, in particular for demobilized combatants and refugees or for internally displaced people after they have returned home.

During the transition from war to peace, the ICRC has had several positive experiences in handing over some of its programmes to companies engaged in the reconstruction process. This was the case in Kosovo, where responsibility for helping the authorities to provide water in urban areas was transferred to the local water board.[20] In addition, companies that have facilities and material available in the field can sometimes make a decisive difference in saving lives by supporting humanitarian organizations with logistics and other means necessary to launch an emergency relief operation. Nonetheless, corporate managers must understand that a humanitarian organization such as the ICRC often needs to be very prudent—some would say overcautious—in considering exchanges with companies. Rumours are often more powerful than facts in war situations, and humanitarian organizations have to carefully monitor how the belligerents perceive their relations with private firms. Local actors sometimes consider multinational companies as allies of the enemy or the government, or believe that they are acting as proxies for foreign powers. The ICRC

---

[20] See 'Kosovo: clean water for Gjilan/Gnjilane', *ICRC News* 03/13 (27 Jan. 2003), URL <http://www.icrc.org/web/eng/siteeng0.nsf/iwpList464/7F60F85BFE42AA77C1256CBB005534B1>.

not only has to act as a neutral, impartial and independent organization, but also must ensure that it is perceived as such.

V. Conclusions

Bridges between the business and humanitarian communities have the potential to improve the plight of those suffering the consequences of armed conflict. The ongoing dialogue is promising, but it is too early to tell whether it can bring about better compliance with international humanitarian law. The ICRC strongly believes that it is worth giving this dialogue a chance but is also mindful that states must bear the primary responsibility for promoting greater respect for basic humanitarian principles by all those who have real influence in armed conflict. To this end, the ICRC is committed to strengthening its dialogue with both states and private companies.

Part IV

Preserving the legitimate economy and critical infrastructure

Editors' remarks

The focus in this part of the volume is on the private sector both as a factor of, and as a contributor to, the security of nations and communities. The first two chapters make the case that business may sometimes be the best judge of the relative importance of threats facing it, and hence of the choice of remedies (many of which are, in turn, available today in the form of commercial services). Hasty or excessive government intervention—in this field as in others— may do more harm than good. Crispin Black goes further, to point out that familiar government institutions of today, such as police and intelligence services, arose out of models first developed by the private sector. He argues that some of the recently revealed deficiencies of governmental intelligence might be remedied (and the cause of transparency and objectivity better served) by drawing business experts and expertise into the assessment process. One might add that certain aspects of the *modus operandi* of modern transnational terrorism are closer to the private sector's way of exploiting the globalized environment than to anything within governments' own experience: it is therefore not illogical to look for help and new thinking from business sources, at the conceptual and analytical as well as the practical level.

The remaining chapters of this part turn the spotlight back on to the vulnerability of a certain class of business assets and actions, namely, those involved in the supply of various forms of energy, other utilities, and information technology and communication services. This subject is currently the focus of growing public and institutional concern and of a growing body of research, under the general heading of critical infrastructure protection (CIP). The authors explore the meaning of this concept and of its important subdivisions dealing with information infrastructure and energy supply infrastructure, respectively. The security significance of CIP is easy to appreciate given the intense dependence of modern armed forces, governments and ordinary citizens on the uninterrupted supply of all the services concerned. At the same time, the increasingly transnational and networked nature of supply arrangements creates a host of new vulnerabilities, by no means originating only from terrorists and by no means affecting only the most high-technology components (*vide* the amount of petroleum products still delivered by ship and barge). Consideration of remedies is still at quite an early stage in the international community, not least because the great part of the operations concerned are now in private hands and no one can believe that simple 're-nationalization' would help. The three authors writing here all review possible ways forward, both practical and analytical—and, in the latter context, Jan Metzger's plea for a new marriage of the social and natural sciences could well be applied to the handling of the whole 'new threats' agenda.

14. The security of business: a view from the security industry

Crispin Black

I. Introduction

Private security companies have been in existence for a long time—at least as long as, or longer than, the modern concept of government's role in the provision of security. Just one example may be cited which is topical on both sides of the Atlantic at the time of writing in view of the visits of US President George W. Bush to London and Baghdad in the autumn of 2003. In 1861, while investigating a railway case in Baltimore, Maryland, the Pinkerton private detective agency uncovered a plot to assassinate President-elect Abraham Lincoln when he passed through Baltimore on his way to Washington for his inauguration. Allan Pinkerton himself warned Lincoln, who changed cars in the middle of the night for the final leg of his train journey.[1] A core of private security agents surrounding Pinkerton later formed the embryo of the US Secret Service and the forerunner to the Federal Bureau of Investigation.

Having laid the foundations in many parts of the world for police forces and intelligence agencies, private security companies subsequently passed on the primary responsibility to the state. In a nice historical irony, a significant part of these functions and responsibilities seems in the early 21st century to be drifting back to the private sector. Modern Western states need help in providing the security that their citizens want and need.

A typical modern security company provides services across a spectrum. Most companies have both an analytical/intelligence arm and a 'hands-on' physical security arm—usually operating in close concert. The physical security arm in a British company is normally staffed by former members of the military establishment, many with experience in the Special Forces. The types of service offered can further be subdivided into 'consulting services', where the security company acts as an expert adviser, and 'specialist security services', where the security company actually provides a physical service.

This chapter provides, in section II, further details of the range of services now available from the private security sector; it then discusses (section III) the historic interplay of governmental, private and military actors in security emergencies. It ends with some personal reflections on the United Kingdom's experience of intelligence gathering and assessment and on a possible new role for the private sector (section IV). Brief conclusions are presented in section V.

---

[1] On this incident see URL <http://en2.wikipedia.org/wiki/Allan_Pinkerton>.

II. The services available

The consulting services available from private security companies typically include the following types.

Security intelligence gathering. Private firms have a requirement to gather and then analyse intelligence to support either particular projects for clients or their own general operations. Such intelligence-gathering activities can be either defensive or offensive in aim. Some security firms also offer a general business intelligence service involving 'due diligence' searches prior to deals, mergers or acquisitions.

Threat assessment and security risk analysis. Security provision in the modern world requires a sound intellectual and conceptual basis. It is only through a thorough analysis of the threats and vulnerabilities facing a commercial enterprise that a plan can be put together to mitigate them. In view of the current globalized terrorist threat, the process of comprehensive security risk analysis—including projections of future risks—is being increasingly understood and used by private companies.

Security survey and audit. This process involves a detailed inspection of premises and staff activity in order to identify physical or electronic vulnerabilities. As part of such an audit, or separately, security companies can offer assessment and advice on information technology (IT) security and cyber risk management; security training (for those responsible for security and/or all personnel); help with contingency planning; and advice and help with security crisis management.

Penetration testing. This involves covertly testing vulnerabilities in security management systems, either by exploiting weaknesses in physical and information system security, or by exposing gaps in procedures and training of staff and contractors. Such tests, carried out by members of specialized security companies, allow company risk managers to understand the specific vulnerabilities in their systems by observing them being exploited.

Specialist security services typically include the following activities.

High-risk operations. This entails the provision of a full range of protective and training security services to allow a commercial enterprise to carry out its business in hostile circumstances. There is a worldwide requirement for this kind of service, particularly in the states members of the Commonwealth of Independent States (CIS)[2] and in the regions of Africa, Latin America and the Middle East. Currently, the companies helping to rebuild Iraq are mostly protected by private security companies.

Close protection. This service is increasingly in demand for the protection of key individuals or those carrying out necessary duties in particularly threaten-

[2] The CIS member states are Armenia, Azerbaijan, Belarus, Georgia, Kazakhstan, Kyrgyzstan, Moldova, Russia, Tajikistan, Turkmenistan, Ukraine and Uzbekistan.

ing environments. In addition to 'close' bodyguarding skills, this service usually involves the gathering of protective intelligence.

Surveillance and counter-surveillance. Counter-surveillance in particular is
becoming an increasingly important part of the private security business. Most
serious crimes and nearly all terrorist attacks require some form of detailed
reconnaissance in advance, which is usually apparent to a surveillance professional and often apparent to the layman with some surveillance-awareness
training. British companies are particularly strong in this area because of the
British military's extensive experience of counter-terrorism in Northern Ireland.

Employee screening. Screening programmes identify dishonest or incompe-
tent candidates for employment and minimize employee-related risk.

Confidential investigations. When internal fraud or information leaking are
suspected, security companies provide the human and technological investigative services required.[3]

III. Survival planning: never a state monopoly?

Survival planning is not new. The ancestors of those living in today's highly
developed countries of Western Europe and North America took such activity
for granted in a world that was much less predictable than today's. The effort
to meet and mitigate risk runs deep in both business and human culture, and
people have rarely if ever been able to devolve the whole responsibility for
providing it upon the state. In early modern Europe, things were often the
other way round: it was private finance houses that supported both independent merchants, and national leaders and their armies, against the costs of
operation and the financial consequences of failure. The principles of prudent
risk calculation were the same as today, as was the danger that the exceptional,
odds-against event would bring calamity to even the best prepared societies.
Typically, in modern circumstances as well as the past, it is a string of
unrelated but cumulative unlucky circumstances that generates the worst disasters.[4]

New human and animal epidemic diseases are often reckoned among
today's worst threats to orderly commerce and government and to 'human
security' in general, but there is nothing particularly novel about such
'plagues' either. The recent experience of Hong Kong and several countries
with severe acute respiratory syndrome (SARS) reminded the world that,
within living memory, people in highly developed countries had to confront
the threat and terrible effects of infectious disease. The scourge of poliomyeli-

---

[3] This listing stops short of combat and combat-related services, which are defined as the purview of
private *military* companies.

[4] The merchant Antonio in Shakespeare's play *The Merchant of Venice* was nearly ruined by the
effects of weather in the English Channel despite what many would still see as a sensible risk mitigation
strategy. As the character Shylock commented in this play, Antonio had spread his investment over several different ships on different routes, but: 'ships are but boards, sailors but men' (Act I, Scene III,
lines 15–20).

tis, for instance, was not eradicated in the western hemisphere until 1994, and even later in Europe.[5] Any person living and working in the British Empire would have encountered or suffered from an array of communicable diseases which had to be endured or managed without the benefits of antibiotics.

An earlier medical emergency in Hong Kong—the Plague of 1894—also has lessons which are relevant today. The Hong Kong government of the day struck a special medal for all those seen to have done signal service to the colony, and most of the medals went to officers and men from the King's Shropshire Light Infantry, a military regiment in the British imperial garrison. They had undertaken palliative and hygienic measures in an attempt to stop the ravages of the plague. This was at a time before antibiotics and even before doctors understood how the disease was transmitted but, crucially, after the Western medical community had begun to understand the importance of hygiene and antisepsis. Of the 300 men from the regiment involved in the operation, only seven died as a result.[6] We see therefore that people near to us in history were able to bring under control diseases which inspire the deepest fear today, armed only with courage, sound decision making and a good deal of disinfectant. The other point of the story—also relevant today—is the way in which local administration drew upon the resources of those most able to help, who happened to be military personnel stationed for quite a different purpose. Just as the private sector may today penetrate into areas of security provision formerly reserved for state organs, state assets such as armed forces may have a potential that is still largely unexplored for solving various acute problems of human and 'homeland' security.

Another apparently eternal principle is that one man's crisis is another's opportunity. At any point of crisis evolution when people feel a shortfall of security but still have money in hand, there are business opportunities to be seized by both responsible and unscrupulous traders. Modern examples would be the rush on gas masks, emergency supplies and private shelters after the events of 11 September 2001, or the lively and often controversial competition for reconstruction contracts after the occupation of Iraq in 2003. An older instance would be the Great Fire of London in 1666 and the observations of contemporary diarist (and business survival planner) Samuel Pepys. His diary entry for 5 September 1666 records a visit to an area just outside the city that was crammed with poor refugees who had lost everything. The diarist is deeply distressed by their plight and the damage to his beloved city, but his lamentations are cut short by the laconic entry 'paid two-pence for a plain penny loaf'.[7] The lesson is clear: survival planning can represent a business opportunity. Somehow, a baker had managed to keep producing his goods, and doubled his price in the process.

---

[5] See, e.g., the Internet site of the US Advisory Committee on Immunization Practices at URL <http://www.cdc.gov/mmwr/preview/mmwrhtml/rr4905a1.htm>; and the World Health Organization Internet site at URL <www.who.int/gb/EB_WHA/PDF/WHA52/ew8.pdf>.

[6] On the King's Shropshire Light Infantry consult URL <http://www.lightinfantry.org.uk>.

[7] Pepys, S., eds R. C. Latham and W. Matthews, *The Diary of Samuel Pepys,* vol. 7 (1666), (Harper Collins: London, 1995), p. 277.

IV. Terrorism and intelligence

Terrorism is not new—not even for the United States, although 11 September 2001 was a serious break from the past. Outsiders had not attacked the continental United States since the War of 1812, but the mindset and methods behind the attacks by Islamicists on that day changed the world in one crucial respect. For the first time since the 1962 Cuban missile crisis, the collection and analysis of intelligence became crucial to the safety of every man, woman and child living in the democratic West.

Although efforts for intelligence collection go back at least as far as the existence of organized states, it is only comparatively recently that this work has been understood and treated as a state monopoly. As mentioned above, private detection agencies were the ancestors of public ones in the USA, and in the UK there has long been a cultural predisposition for private individuals to become involved in this sector. During World War II, in the UK, the breaking of the German Enigma codes (used in one form or another for all military communications) was largely entrusted to a mix of civilians, university lecturers, crossword and chess enthusiasts, and clever undergraduates recruited by word of mouth[8] and brought together at Bletchley Park in Hertfordshire. In this heterodox environment, private individuals with no military background achieved brilliant success. The 'Double-Cross System'—the code name for a sustained series of operations which captured nearly every German spy despatched to the UK and then turned many of them into double agents—was the creation of Oxford don and detective novelist J. C. Masterman.[9] What such outsiders brought, and what the operation needed, was mental nimbleness, abilities unconstrained by standard training and a willingness to 'think outside the box'. Such qualities are still a necessary part of the mix for good intelligence work today.

After the war, in the UK the highest responsibility for intelligence assessment—carefully kept distinct from the business of intelligence collection—devolved upon the Joint Intelligence Committee (JIC), which had been created in 1936.[10] The members of the JIC, which is technically a sub-committee of the Cabinet of Ministers, are senior representatives of the Foreign and Commonwealth Office, the Ministry of Defence and other departments; the heads of the three intelligence and security agencies; and normally a representative of the Prime Minister's staff. The secretariat for the JIC is provided by the Cabinet Office Assessments Staff, manned by civil servants and military officers recruited from the whole range of government departments by open competition. This personnel structure was expressly designed to protect the JIC

---

[8] In late 1941 they were recruited through a crossword competition organized by *The Daily Telegraph.* Smith, M., *Station X: The Codebreakers of Bletchley Park* (Channel 4 Books: London, 1998).

[9] Masterman, J. C., *The Double-Cross System in the War of 1939–1945* (Yale University Press: New Haven, Conn., 1972).

[10] See Cradock, P., *Know Your Enemy: How the Joint Intelligence Committee Saw the World* (John Murray: London, 2002); and 'Iraq's chemical, biological, nuclear and ballistic missile programmes', URL <http://www.number-10.gov.uk/output/Page273.asp>.

and its staff from inbuilt bias towards any individual intelligence agency and from excessive interference from any policy-driven ministry. It reflects a traditional desire to keep the British civil service impartial and separate from elected politicians and their appointees—very different from the 'spoils system' prevailing in the USA, where the national security adviser is a personal nominee of the president. Through the national intelligence priorities which it sets, its overview of intelligence cooperation with other nations, and the analytical papers which it approves on the basis of drafts from the Assessments Staff, the JIC aims to provide to the Crown, ministers, the armed forces and senior officials an agreed and bias-free national assessment on weighty intelligence matters.

So far, so good in principle: but events since 11 September 2001 have brought the impartiality and efficiency of the British, as well as the US, national intelligence apparatus into question. In the first place, there is the issue of why these systems were unable to anticipate or warn of the attacks. The Joint Inquiry by the Senate Select Committee on Intelligence, and the House Permanent Select Committee on Intelligence, into the activities of the US intelligence community in connection with the attacks goes to the heart of the problem in its systemic finding number 5.

Prior to September 11, the Intelligence Community's understanding of al-Qa'ida was hampered by insufficient analytic focus and quality, particularly in terms of strategic analysis . . . there was a dearth of creative, aggressive analysis targeting Bin Ladin and a persistent inability to comprehend the collective significance of individual pieces of intelligence. These analytic deficiencies seriously undercut the ability of U.S. policy makers to understand the full nature of the threat, and to make fully informed decisions.[11]

Criticizing intelligence failures with hindsight is, of course, easier than predicting events in the future or making sense of piecemeal intelligence. However, there was little sign that the lessons of September 2001 had been learned when, in a later phase of the crisis, British and US forces prepared together to defeat the forces of Saddam Hussein and to occupy Iraq. The question that the British and US intelligence establishments appear to have been asking themselves and answering at that stage was: how easy would it be to win the war? A more sensible question might have been: given that formal military resistance to a US-led combined arms offensive in Iraq would be both suicidal and ineffective, how will Iraqis who are loyal to Saddam Hussein (and others) seek to force the US allies out of Iraq after the war has been won? More serious reflection on this question, and on other worst-case contingencies, might have spared the occupying forces and the people of Iraq many of the unpleasant surprises that faced and still face them in the attempt to 'win the peace'.

---

[11] United States Congress, *Joint Inquiry into Intelligence Community Activities before and after the Terrorist Attacks of September 11, 2001: Abridged Findings and Conclusions* (US Government Printing Office: Washington, DC, 2002), p. xvi.

This was not, by far, the only apparent failure of crisis-linked or terrorism-linked intelligence in modern times. The collapse of the Soviet Union, on which the bulk of the British and US intelligence effort had been focused, came as a surprise to most. Famously, in the history of the British intelligence community, the JIC failed to anticipate the Argentinian invasion of the Falkland Islands in 1982, despite clear evidence that it was in the offing.[12] Add this to the recent failures over Islamist extremism, and it might suggest that there is a cultural or organizational factor at work rather than any ad hoc reason for failure—or at the very least, that serious intelligence gathering and analysis operates at the edge of human intellectual and judgemental capabilities.

These concerns are deepened by the recent indications, also linked to the Iraq crisis, that the intelligence communities on both sides of the Atlantic may have come under irresistible political pressure to publish assessments that made the strongest possible case for a pre-emptive attack on Saddam Hussein. Whatever the final verdict may be on the extent of and responsibility for specific distortions of the evidence,[13] it already seems clear that Prime Minister Tony Blair and his advisers gave the JIC and its products a more 'instrumental' role than had ever before been thought proper in making their policy case to the nation. According to the accounts so far available, the Chairman of the JIC seems to have been too willing to accommodate the government's presentational and substantive concerns by allowing changes to the wording in a key document about Saddam's weapons of mass destruction (WMD) capability.[14] The episode has awakened serious concerns in all parts of the British political spectrum about the reliability of the present assessment system, the JIC's relations with the executive branch, and the larger question of the extent to which major state decisions involving the use of force can be based on intelligence alone.[15]

It need hardly be underlined that any actual or perceived weakening of the JIC system in the UK—or the intelligence equivalent in any Western state—is a matter of more than ephemeral political concern. The reliability of intelligence assessments is important not just for the success of the country's exter-

---

[12] West, N., *The Secret War for the Falklands: The SAS, MI6, and the War Whitehall Nearly Lost* (Little Brown and Co.: London, 1997), pp. 25–57, provides a full account of the role of the JIC before and during the 1982 Falklands/Malvinas War.

[13] An official enquiry under Lord Hutton was appointed to look into the circumstances surrounding the death of Dr David Kelly—a British civil servant who had been reported in the press as saying that an intelligence-based dossier had been 'sexed up' for public presentation—and the final report is still awaited at the time of writing. On the Hutton Inquiry see URL <http://www.the-hutton-inquiry.org.uk>.

[14] See Kampfner, M., *Blair's Wars* (Free Press: London, 2003).

[15] Former British Foreign Secretary Lord Owen was vituperative in his comments in a speech at the London School of Economics on 9 Oct. 2003: 'I do not need to await Lord Hutton's verdict to judge that the joint intelligence committee machinery, which I have known well and respected, was corrupted in a way which will leave damage for decades to come . . . It is impossible to believe that Sir Anthony Duff, Sir Percy Cradock or Dame Pauline Neville Jones, to name but three heads of the JIC with whom I have worked, would ever have conducted themselves as John Scarlett did with Jonathan Powell and Alastair Campbell over amending the statement on Iraqi weapons of mass destruction.' Lord Owen, 'The Ever Growing Dominance of No. 10 in British Diplomacy since 5 April 1982', Lecture at the London School of Economics and Political Science on 8 Oct. 2003, available at URL <http://www.lse.ac.uk/collections/LSEPublicLecturesAndEvents/events/2003/20030915t1227z001.htm>.

nal policy, but for the confidence held by internal constituencies in the correctness of the government's judgement. (The impact of any proven bias in British intelligence assessments on Iraq would hardly be helpful, for instance, in rallying the UK's own moderate Islamic community to support the anti-terrorism effort.) In the UK, the JIC's analytical skills have also been an important bulwark of the British–US intelligence relationship, given that the amount of 'raw' intelligence that British agencies can contribute to the partnership is relatively small. Just as the USA became reluctant to share intelligence with the UK after a series of British double agents working for the Soviet Union were exposed in the 1950s and 1960s, the fact that US intelligence has been exposed to its own share of criticisms after 11 September 2001 will not necessarily prevent it from raising questions about British judgement and reliability.

Bring in the private sector?

When the state is seen to be failing in the provision of an important service, it is often natural to turn to the private sector for help. Either there is something inherently inefficient about the current system—in which case it should be adapted and changed—or the whole enterprise is so inherently difficult that it needs to draw on the widest possible pool of talent and experience. On either view, there could be merit in turning to the private security sector and exploring the possible contributions of business more widely. Private experts could contribute both analytical and human intelligence resources from areas which the official system does not reach. They are more likely to provide 'out of the box' thinking, informed by the foresight and nimbleness characteristic of private risk assessment at its best. More generally, opening up the assessment process to new actors representing an important part of British society ought to serve the same aims of balance and comprehensiveness which the JIC's original creators had in mind. Putting intelligence in touch with the British public and *vice versa* is not in itself an ignoble aim, any more than the idea of publishing intelligence-based 'dossiers' on important security issues of the moment is wrong per se. The nub of the issue is how to make sure that the information is as credible as it is accessible.

Specifically, one could consider opening up the process of recruitment to the Cabinet Office Assessments Staff, which actually drafts the papers for the JIC. The organization already recruits through open competition from all those holding the appropriate rank in government service. It would be simple to expand its catchment area. If large British companies, or private firms or academic institutions engaged in the business of intelligence analysis, were allowed to second talented individuals for two-year postings to the Cabinet Office, a considerable body of intelligence expertise and experience of Whitehall could be built up over time within the private sector. Those who proved their worth in both fields could eventually be qualified to hold more senior posts within the central intelligence structure. It is no secret that some of the best and brightest British graduates become analysts of one sort or another in the City of London, where the essence of their work is to act on imperfect data and to try to look into the future, in order to make money. Why not bring their skills to bear on more important matters?

The benefits that could be gained from private-sector involvement are not limited to analytical skills. One of the effects of globalization has been the creation of companies with a literally worldwide reach, allied with a truly global culture. Their senior employees are no longer drawn exclusively from the 'motherland' but from a range of different regions and cultural backgrounds. Often, the only collective culture to which they owe true loyalty is that of the firm in which they work. At the grass-roots operational level, meanwhile, these companies extend their tentacles into nearly every corner of the world, making their employees—both local and expatriate—uniquely well placed to assess local moods, attitudes and politics.

The best collection principle for human intelligence is to make use of everyone, or at least everyone who is on your side. This notion lies behind the best designed anti-criminal and anti-terrorist information campaigns. In such cases the authorities believe that members of the public, alert and properly briefed, have a much greater chance—if only because of their numbers—of picking up indications of a criminal enterprise or terrorist attack than do the official organs themselves. The same argument can be made for the added value to be gained from private intelligence collection. Private firms are more numerous and very often have greater cultural penetration than formally structured intelligence services. Senior officials of important global firms invariably hold high social positions in the community and cultural life of the cities in which they are stationed and, in capital cities especially, are likely to be well integrated into the business and government elite. They are thus ideally placed to gather intelligence: if only a way can be found to enlist and make use of their efforts that does not conflict with their own principles, and with the prime commercial purpose of their activity.

V. Conclusions

Other contributions to this volume focus on the business sector's own vulnerabilities and the options for its protection.[16] This chapter draws attention, rather, to the long-standing traditions of public-sector dependence on private-sector expertise and assistance, which can apply as much in the security field as in any other.

The events of September 2001 and their aftermath have exposed at several points the difficulty faced by traditional state security policies and intelligence systems in adjusting to the reality of an age when whole societies, not just national borders, are under attack. Universal vulnerability makes the accuracy

---

[16] See in particular chapter 15 in this volume.

of intelligence a universal concern, yet the latest attempts by intelligence specialists and their political masters to reach out to the public have been a mixed success at best. The private sector has not precisely been excluded from the picture, but in public perception has often provided added reason for confusion and concern—*vide*, for example, the conspiracy theories that business interests were behind the choice of Iraq as a target in 2003 and/or that they have profited improperly from the aftermath of the war.

Drawing private-sector expertise, including that of professional security companies, more systematically into the business of threat identification and assessment as well as into the provision of remedies is certainly no panacea. If successfully done, however, it could bring a double benefit. Not only would private experts be likely to bring a genuine accretion of information, analytical skill and new policy thinking, but the establishment of an open and systematic partnership between them and the state authorities could also be an important victory for transparency and a step towards the restoration of public trust.

15. Survival planning for business: a view from Nokia

Urho Ilmonen

I. Current threat assessment

Nokia produces telecommunications equipment, which is a non-military, neutral and universally beneficial technology.[1] Good communications are important for democracies and dictators alike. Accordingly, the company believes that it neither poses a threat to anyone nor is a specific target for anyone except ordinary criminals. On current company analysis, non-state assailants should not have any interest in harming the company.

Nokia believes that security can be created by sound business practices and careful processes. The company's threat scenarios include as the worst root causes of threats: (*a*) employees who are careless and over-trusting; (*b*) subcontractors who also work with the company's competitors and implement lax security measures; (*c*) poor information security that compromises data; (*d*) industrial espionage by competitors, either alone or with the assistance of state investigation agencies; (*e*) 'social engineering' specifically as a means of industrial espionage;[2] and (*f*) specific environments in the so-called emerging markets which pose new threats to personnel security, such as kidnappings and ransom activities, and can give rise to large-scale armed robbery of valuable cargoes.

II. What has changed after 11 September 2001?

The attacks of 11 September 2001 were a tragic act committed against innocent people by a new player in the international league of aggression. The action came as a shock, especially because of the surprise and generally perceived injustice, and because it happened in a country that had not experienced domestic warfare for a very long time. Such an attack would not have come as such a shock for people in Grenada, Israel, Kosovo, Lebanon or similar places, or indeed in Europe, which was ravaged by war and massive bombings not such a long time ago. For the risk assessments of non-US companies, not much changed as an immediate result of the attacks. Co-location with offices of large US companies was considered a risk, and defence and other industries that were considered high-risk targets became more alert. However, politically

---

[1] See the Nokia Internet site at URL <http://www.nokia.com>.

[2] On the social engineering methods of compromising computer security see, e.g., the Computer Emergency Response Team (CERT) Internet site at URL <http://www.cert.org/incident_notes/IN-2002-03.html>.

a great deal changed in the world, including the role of the United Nations, and this will change our lives dramatically for a long time to come.

III. Why is security needed and what is the focus?

Security is a basic need of all people. According to the Maslow hierarchy of basic human needs, security is ranked just below air, food and water.[3] Business entities also need security to be able to carry out their activities with as little interference from criminals, terrorists or the authorities as is possible and feasible. Important changes in this equation have occurred after September 2001, and some of them are more welcome than others.

The main focus of corporate security activities remains on the threat scenarios mentioned above. Awareness training should tackle the problem of careless employees and fend off most of the risk of social engineering. Sound, well-enforced processes should be able to meet most of the information security challenges. Efficient, well-applied emergency response plans and business continuity plans can help in preparing for and minimizing the effects of crises. Nokia sees this as its primary task. On the other hand, federal security requirements tend to steer the focus of corporate security towards sometimes costly actions which have only a limited effect on general domestic security and sometimes dramatic effects on business. This is not necessarily the focus the private sector would like to have.

IV. Vulnerabilities and attacks increase

The world has become increasingly dangerous, not least with regard to the security of information systems. Research conducted by the Computer Emergency Response Team Coordination Center (CERT/CC) of Carnegie Mellon University shows that incidents breaching information security systems have increased exponentially, from under 10 000 in 1999 to 76 404 in 2003 (and still rising), while known system vulnerabilities increased over the same period from under 500 to 1993 (albeit currently on a declining trend).[4]

The complexity of systems and the vast deployment of global data networks have put both the public and private sectors in a new situation. So far we have not seen proof of deliberate, coordinated terrorist-initiated attacks on data systems. Should terrorists exploit these abundant vulnerabilities—and it seems likely that they may soon—our society will find itself in a new, challenging situation.

---

[3] On the theory of Abraham Maslow's hierarchy of basic human needs see, e.g., URL <http://web.utk.edu/~gwynne/maslow.HTM>.

[4] CERT is a worldwide network of national and regional teams for the collection and dissemination of computer security threats, vulnerabilities, incidents and incident response. CERT/CC is operated by the Software Engineering Institute of Carnegie Mellon University, Pittsburgh, Pennsylvania. On CERT/CC see URL <http://www.cert.org/>. See also chapter 2 in this volume.

V. Emergency response and business planning

Crises occur because of disasters of a natural, political and terrorist nature, and society must be prepared for them. The private sector has to shoulder its responsibility vis-à-vis its employees, their families, its stakeholders and its customers. This requires contingency planning—preparing for the unforesee-able. However, preparations can only be taken up to a level deemed reasonable in the light of the current threat assessment.

During the war in Iraq in 2003, Nokia had Emergency Response Plans (ERPs) drafted and tested in all the countries affected. A special support team with intimate knowledge of all the sites, all the people and all the plans was made available to follow the situation closely, 24 hours a day and 7 days a week. Deployment of the ERPs was decentralized. Each country manager had an independent right to pull out his or her people, and had the financial means and arrangements for this at his disposal at all times. Business Continuity Plans (BCPs) remain in place and are continuously updated.

VI. Partnership with the authorities?

There is truth in the saying that the road to hell is paved with good intentions. This should be kept in mind when contemplating responses to the post-11 September 2001 security situation, if actions are to be avoided that could in any way support the disruptive goals of terrorists.

Pressing requests are being made to business to participate in the fight against terrorism. As an example, the US Customs–Trade Partnership Against Terrorism (C-TPAT)[5] is being promoted as a voluntary programme to improve logistics security. From the point of view of the private sector, it is not voluntary, it is costly, and it leaves the private sector's own security situation unchanged. Corporations thus perceive no advantage with this system, not least because it is being pursued without extra funding and with only negative incentives for participation. Is this the way for the public sector to motivate the private sector? Is this the way to promote true partnership? What started as an initiative to improve logistics security in the delivery channels for imports to the United States has amounted to something bordering on an illegal obstacle to the free movement of goods.

Business operates by business principles. Shareholder value and profit are important, as are continuity and corporate social responsibility. Is not business entitled to a reasonably safe operating environment in exchange for the taxes it pays? Companies tend to become concerned if they are faced with strict meas-ures and demands for partnership that do not make indisputable sense from the standpoint of sound cost–profit analysis.

---

[5] On the C-TPAT see URL <http://www.customs.ustreas.gov/xp/cgov/import/commercial_enforcement/ctpat/>, and chapter 19 in this volume.

VII. Conclusions

This brings the discussion back to the opening remarks. First, it should be acknowledged that governments are generally acting in the best and noblest interests. The parts of the private sector which are engaged directly in their efforts, as security contractors, are obviously acting in their own best business interests and as such need to be controlled by their principals. How good a job the regimes involved make of this has an immense effect on the public perception of the efficiency of the partnership. Everyone travelling to and within the United States by air has been experiencing the immense effort to maintain air travel security. How efficient this really is, and at what cost in terms of both finance and civil liberties, remains to be seen once the system starts to work in the way it was intended. What remains puzzling is why the USA cannot learn from the experience in Europe, where full luggage screening is carried out reasonably cheaply and efficiently, and without infringing on civil liberties.

The solution proposed here is a partnership based on equality. What is needed are truly efficient public-sector measures that do not unduly infringe on civil liberties or on the freedom of business. The public–private sector partnership must be based on give and take, equality, trust and mutual respect. This is surely feasible: it already works in many countries with very good effect. More work is needed, and everyone needs to participate. The private sector cannot lean back and say 'you do it, we will pay taxes', and the public sector cannot lean forward and say 'you have to do it, we have determined that this is in your own best interest'. A real discussion, real controls, real incentives and, above all, *reasonableness* is what is needed.

16. Defending against cyber terrorism: preserving the legitimate economy

Olivia Bosch

I. Introduction

The main thesis of this chapter is that the means used to defend against the many commonly occurring cyber incidents can provide a strong foundation for dealing with the effects of the less frequent acts of cyber terrorism. Daily cyber security 'housekeeping' by businesses, government departments and individuals will not prevent cyber incidents, but good information security policies and business continuity plans (BCPs) for disaster recovery can mitigate the effects when such incidents do occur. Further research is required to determine how much the state, which has both the responsibility and the tools to address national security issues, can protect information assets beyond those that are owned directly by government.

This chapter examines what is meant by cyber *terrorism* and how it compares with other cyber *incidents*, how issues of attribution and BCPs could be addressed, and what kind of information security vulnerabilities are arising from new developments in the activities of business and others in the private sector.

In the latter half of the 1990s, when widespread use of the Internet and computer connectivity were still relatively new, minor computer disruptions were often deemed to be acts of cyber terrorism or the result of hacker attacks when they were not. Today, computer disruptions occur so frequently that reactions have shifted towards the other extreme, of treating them as routine occurrences and responding to them in a blasé or lax manner. These reactions often confuse or complicate analysis of what has happened and distort judgements on the choice of policies for the protection of electronic information assets.

II. Cyber terrorism

Cyber terrorism can be defined as the actual use of, or the threat to use, attacks by and on computers and related electronic information networks to intimidate or kill civilians or to cause large-scale disruption or destruction for primarily political objectives. This form of terrorism includes the use of computers and related equipment to cause mass disruption in the flow of information or services, with intent to induce fear or undermine public confidence in essential public services and critical national infrastructure.[1] This definition of cyber terrorism is primarily derived from the definition of terrorism in general. Although there is no commonly agreed definition of terrorism, it is often described as the intentional use, or threat to use, violence to intimidate or kill civilians or incur large-scale destruction for political purposes.[2] Examining some of the characteristics of terrorism can provide insights, leading to a better understanding of the context in which cyber terrorism might occur. Unlike traditional terrorism, however, cyber terrorism has occurred so infrequently that Richard Clarke, US Special Advisor for Cyberspace Security, stated that he prefers not to use the term, favouring instead a focus on the broader concept of 'information security' or 'cyberspace security'.[3]

Concerns evoked by cyber terrorism are based on an assumption that its targets are most likely to be a state's critical information infrastructure: that is, assets which the state has a strategic responsibility to protect. Critical infrastructure consists of the essential human-built assets related to energy, communications and water supply that underpin a state's survival and well-being.[4] Critical *information* infrastructure consists of the electronic information network components of these essential assets as well as their connectivity with other essential industry and service sectors, such as transport and banking.[5]

Non-cyber terrorists have traditionally relied on the use of conventional weaponry, primarily explosives, guns and mortars. These instruments tend to have familiar and calculable effects that are readily reported by the media. As the number of media outlets has increased worldwide and with the increased span and immediacy of reporting since the late 1990s, these acts have received more public attention. Media scrutiny has not, however, prevented non-state groups, such as al-Qaeda, from carrying out terrorist acts. Nor has media attention hindered them from finding effective ways to evade counter-terrorist operations: through changing their goals and alliances (including partnerships or links with criminal groups), by creating leaderless cell structures and— since the mid- to late 1990s—by taking advantage of Internet communication and the alienating effects of globalization.[6]

---

[1] See, e.g., Soo Hoo, K., Goodman, S. and Greenberg, L., 'Information technology and the terrorist threat', *Survival*, vol. 39, no. 3 (autumn 1997), pp. 135–55.

[2] There is an extensive literature on terrorism. See, e.g., Hoffman, B., *Inside Terrorism* (Columbia University Press: New York, 1998); Slater, R. O. and Stohl, M. (eds.), *Current Perspectives on International Terrorism* (Macmillan Press: Basingstoke, 1988); Wardlaw, G., *Political Terrorism: Theory, Tactics, and Counter-measures*, 2nd edn (Cambridge University Press: Cambridge, 1989); and Wilkinson, P., *Terrorism and the Liberal State*, 2nd edn (Macmillan Press: Basingstoke, 1986).

[3] Clarke, R., 'Administrative oversight: are we ready for a cyberterror attack?', Briefing to the Senate Judiciary Committee Subcommittee on Administrative Oversight and the Courts, 13 Feb. 2002, reported in US Department of State, International Information Programs, Wynne, J., 'White House advisor Richard Clarke briefs Senate panel on cybersecurity', 13 Feb. 2002, URL <http://usinfo.state.gov/topical/pol/terror/02021409.htm>.

[4] On critical infrastructure protection see chapter 17 in this volume, and on critical energy system infrastructure see chapter 18.

[5] On banking see also chapter 8 in this volume.

[6] Stern, J., 'The protean enemy', *Foreign Affairs*, vol. 82, no. 4 (July/Aug. 2003), pp. 28–35.

If cyber-terrorist attacks were to occur and result in large numbers of casualties or mass disruption and destruction, they would not go unnoticed by the media. Attempted cyber-terrorist acts that have been thwarted through successful intelligence, on the other hand, would normally not be reported.

Traditional, politically motivated terrorists have tried to conduct their destructive activities on a scale that is large enough to draw media attention to their goals and to induce overreaction by governments, but not so large as to undermine any public support their group may enjoy or to provoke destructive retaliation. Terrorism is seldom the main mode of operation, but rather a tactic used in support of broader operations.[7] The scale of casualties has varied, however, depending on such factors as the objectives and conduct of the terrorist operations. For example, some cults or apocalyptic groups and groups which carry out suicide bombings may have organizational goals that require them to aim at inflicting particularly high casualties. Where cyber terrorism lies in the spectrum of the more commonly occurring types of terrorist attack is still an open question. Given the low frequency of cyber terrorism so far, it is suggested that types of electronic attack that are not obviously terrorist in intent might be used instead to *support* the more commonly occurring conventional terrorist attacks, or indeed other forms of violent conflict.

Types of cyber incident

The objective of this chapter is not to show that cyber terrorism will not occur or has not been attempted, but rather to place this relatively low-probability (albeit high-impact) event into better perspective vis-à-vis the great majority of computer and network incidents that occur from other causes. As cyber terrorism has been infrequent, it is worth noting the main causes of computer incidents. The following is a general breakdown of various types of 'incident', a term that is neutral as to cause. Further research is needed to produce a more exact breakdown which would facilitate the understanding of the dynamics of cyber incidents.

At least half of all computer incidents are not caused deliberately. These include not only accidents but also the unintentional effects of vulnerabilities arising from the mismanaged configuration of networks, software flaws (which also open the way for computer viruses), improper or poor technical or administrative implementation of information security policies (e.g., failing to update anti-virus protection or software patches), inadequately trained computer users and human error. About 75 per cent of all large information technology (IT) projects are delayed, run over budget and do not work as intended, indicating the high degree to which inadequate IT project management is likely to contribute to inadequate IT security.

---

[7] On terrorism as a mode of operation in violent conflicts see Stepanova, E., *Anti-terrorism and Peace-building During and After Conflict,* SIPRI Policy Paper no. 2 (SIPRI: Stockholm, June 2003), available at URL <http://editors.sipri.se/recpubs.html>.

The remaining incidents are caused by individuals with malicious, criminal or political intent, the great majority of whom are disgruntled employees—in this context also called 'insiders'.[8] Many policy and corporate decision makers or directors either do not admit to having many cyber incidents or describe a computer network disruption as the result of cyber terrorism when it is not.[9] While this may be more convenient than acknowledging the existence of bad management and consequent dissatisfied employees, it causes confusion and misguided perceptions of what is required to improve information security.

A small proportion of malicious activity is carried out by cyber criminals seeking to steal or manipulate data directly for financial gain. They rely on the critical information infrastructure being intact so as to be able to conduct their activities without risk of detection. It can also be expected that some malicious cyber activities will aim to cause disruption in support of other criminal objectives, such as extortion and blackmail (which is sometimes considered a form of terrorism, depending on the definition chosen). Violence and intimidation are increasingly being used to recruit hackers or to obtain computer passwords from employees.[10] In these cases, terrorism is, and is treated as, a criminal act.

There is also a smaller group of 'hactivists' (who conduct civil protest online) and hackers (who obtain unauthorized access to networks primarily for the sake of intellectual challenge). These groups exploit the Internet to attract media or other public attention. Unlike cyber terrorists, who also seek media attention, their intention is not to kill or cause severe damage in the pursuit of their activist or civil protest goals.[11]

The term 'cyber warfare' describes cases in which electronic computer attacks are the means used to cause disruption, destruction or casualties in time of armed conflict. However, these actions would be subject to the laws of armed conflict, which include observing the principles of non-combatant dis-

---

[8] See, e.g., the annual Computer Crime and Security Surveys of the US Computer Security Institute (CSI), with the participation of the San Francisco Federal Bureau of Investigation (FBI) Computer Intrusion Squad. They report that 60–80% of incidents have been caused by employees. For information on the 2003 edition of *Computer Crime and Security Survey* see URL <http://www.gocsi.com>. On lax employees and security, see chapter 15 in this volume. Recent CSI–FBI surveys show a rise in computer attacks from outside enterprises. Such attacks have become more numerous as connectivity to the Internet has increased and 'attack' tools have become automated. The number of incidents caused by insiders has not necessarily declined and may become more significant as 'insider knowledge' of networks is acquired by outsiders with malicious intent.

[9] Computer incidents known to result from cyber terrorism are reported to be *c.* 1% of all incidents. See Saita, A., 'Searching for cyberterrorism', Aug. 2002, at URL <http://infosecuritymag.techtarget.com/2002/aug/news.shtml>, which refers to Belcher, T. (co-author), *Internet Security Threat Report,* Symantec/Riptech, June 2002, available at URL <http://www.riptech.com>.

[10] Bell, R. E., 'The prosecution of computer crime', *Journal of Financial Crime*, vol. 9, no. 4 (Apr. 2002), pp. 309–10.

[11] Denning, D. E., 'Activism, hactivism, and cyber terrorism: the Internet as a tool for influencing foreign policy', Paper for the Workshop on the Internet and International Systems: Information Technology and American Foreign Policy Decisionmaking, Nautilus Institute and World Affairs Council of Northern California, 10 Dec. 1999, San Francisco, Calif., available at URL <http://www.nautilus.org/info-policy/workshop/papers/denning.html>.

crimination, proportionality of force used to achieve military objectives, and other related norms.[12]

An adequate understanding of cyber terrorism requires interaction between computer programmers, who have not hitherto needed to be experts on terrorism; experts in such fields as explosives and law enforcement; and security analysts, who have not hitherto required knowledge of the intricacies of computer software programming and electronic information networks. At some organizational or policy level, different disciplines need to share insights when analysing the impact of cyber terrorism in relation to other types of cyber incident.

III. Attribution and business continuity planning

Because many types of threat may arise and many types of vulnerability become apparent when a computer incident occurs, it is often difficult to pinpoint, or attribute, its cause or origin. Sabotage by a disgruntled employee, a wire gnawed through by a rodent, a dislocated plug-in, certain weather conditions and cyber criminals are all examples of different sources or causes of the same type of outage or incident. An analogy might be made with a simplified description of an aircraft accident investigation process. There may be up to four types of team that visit the scene of such an incident: one team is sent by a manufacturer to assess a component defect in the case of liability claims; one team comes from a law-enforcement agency to investigate whether a criminal act has been committed; one team might be sent from intelligence agencies to assess whether the incident was a terrorist act; and alongside them a team from the emergency services works to rescue casualties and restore local order, sometimes disturbing or inadvertently destroying evidence that might be useful to the other teams. Although they may all be doing their professional best, the cause of the accident may be difficult to discover in a timely manner. The efforts made to avert and monitor computer breakdowns at the time of the turn of the millennium provided a dry run of the various processes available to distinguish 'millennium bug' incidents from those arising from hacking or other causes.

The mis-labelling of cyber incidents as cyber terrorism distorts the assessment of policies which should be pursued for anticipating and managing the disruptions that occur. Assuming that terrorists, and hence also cyber terrorists, seek or require media attention in order to publicize their cause, it is log-

---

[12] The laws of armed conflict—a body of international law with a history dating back to the past century—basically stipulate 'that weapons and war tactics must, in their application, be confined to military targets; that they must be proportional to their military objectives as well as reasonably necessary for the attainment of these objectives; and that they should not cause unnecessary suffering to the victims or harm human beings and property in neutral countries'. Goldblat, J., SIPRI and International Peace Research Institute, Oslo (PRIO), *Arms Control: The New Guide to Negotiations and Agreements* (SAGE Publications: London, 2002), chapter 17, 'Restrictions on the methods of warfare', pp. 279–98. For a list and the texts of agreements from the 1860s to the 1990s see University of Minnesota, Human Rights Library, 'Law of armed conflict', URL <http://www1.umn.edu/humanrts/instree/auoy.htm>.

ical to assume that incidents caused by cyber terrorists would be relatively likely to be brought to public attention. If terrorists repeat such incidents, the perpetrators and their method of attack could thus eventually be determined. Critical information infrastructure can be expected to be a likely target for cyber terrorists since it comprises the related national energy and communications assets that underpin state survival, the ultimate protection of which lies with government, whose policies, in turn, terrorists aim to influence.

The degree to which potential terrorist incidents can be identified beforehand should be a function of the work of the intelligence community, an asset of the state which contributes to maintaining national security. In the past, knowledge of threats to the security of a nation's infrastructure, particularly in times of crisis or conflict, would have been conveyed informally by government to the owners and operators of energy and communications infrastructure, who in turn could take precautionary protection measures. The degree to which such an information flow should now be institutionalized or made more formal is still an open question, especially if cyber terrorist acts remain relatively infrequent within the wide range of computer incidents that occur. It can be expected that the state has computer assets and technologies designed to try to thwart potential cyber terrorists, in the same way as the state has assets to try to prevent other types of terrorist incidents. Further research is needed to assess how these assets might be made available to, or developed in association with, the private sector with a view to predicting cyber incidents or at least being able to monitor them in real time.

Since it is not possible to prevent all types of terrorism or the many other types of computer incident that occur, and given that attribution of the cause or origin of a cyber incident may be delayed or difficult, business continuity plans and their implementation are a means by which to mitigate the effects of cyber incidents. As an aspect of senior management functions, BCPs could be prepared in advance and then implemented upon notice of, during or after an incident to restore essential corporate or government services. Mechanisms for early warning and detection of incidents can be part of BCPs in order to minimize the time between detection, incident and reaction. Computer emergency response teams (CERTs) are already in place to monitor and report incidents, such as those caused by computer viruses and their potentially worldwide propagation.[13]

Through setting in place early-warning mechanisms for triggering BCPs, methods to assess the origins, type and development of incidents, and plans to restore essential services until fuller recovery occurs, local authorities and central government can put themselves in a better position to respond and recover not only from the less newsworthy and more commonly occurring computer incidents but also from a cyber terrorist act. Governments, however, have the additional responsibility of dealing with the injuries and accidents which result from the public panic that a terrorist act is intended to create.

---

[13] On CERTs see also chapters 2 and 15 in this volume.

The design and implementation of BCPs, including early-warning and information-sharing mechanisms, present their own difficulties and risks. These include shortages of skilled staff who are already struggling to perform basic services; poor installation and maintenance of large computer projects, making it difficult to locate the problem; and the need to deal with data and services that have been outsourced abroad. The potential effects of cyber incidents, moreover, vary in different parts of a country, or across regions of the world, in part because of variable standards of living and emergency services support as well as the diversity of geographical circumstances (e.g., locations susceptible to particular natural disasters or sites of critical infrastructure assets). Small and medium-sized enterprises and many developing countries with a lack of resources often do not have BCPs and instead rely on an often implicit strategy of reacting to an incident after it has occurred.

At the corporate board or senior government policy level, security management can be linked to business continuity planning, especially when dealing with critical infrastructure. Companies and governments need to assess not only threats but also vulnerabilities arising from connectivity and interdependencies. One of the most important interdependencies is that between the communications and utilities sectors, recognized most acutely at the millennium shift. The degree of interconnectedness, however, can also be viewed as an asset. For example, the utilities' transmission and distribution systems in mainland Europe are highly integrated, enabling arrangements for alternative provision when one country faces an outage. In Asia, however, historical and geographical factors have forced countries to rely solely on national means of electricity provision. These two different sets of circumstances are illustrative of the varying requirements for business continuity planning, not only among companies within the energy sector which have to provide services, but also among users whose BCPs need to cover the choice of alternative supply.

A holistic approach in both business continuity planning and security management is required. It must include protection of not only information and services but also the infrastructure on which data and services are transmitted, and vetting of the personnel handling sensitive employee or proprietary data. IT security issues can no longer be dealt with solely by a technical person in a back office or within a compartmentalized subdivision of management.

IV. Globalization and the role of business in cyber security

The rhetoric about cyber terrorism galvanizes awareness of the need for information protection, but this rhetoric can also have a distorting effect. When companies ask government to advise them on the severity of the cyber terrorism threat and receive a nebulous response, corporate decision makers may then argue that they do not need to pay for more security. Yet, as the business sector becomes more aware of the causes of non-cyber terrorist incidents, business can no longer afford to delay in implementing information security measures. It can be expected that the corporate sector, including infrastructure owners, should pay for security measures to deal with the risks which they know may affect their sector—now including those arising from IT projects and networks.

As owners of infrastructure become aware of these new risks, they can budget for the protection of their information as well as for the implementation of BCPs in the event of a cyber incident. Corporate liability and responsibility are gradually becoming codified and institutionalized for dealing with these relatively new security requirements, and are increasingly becoming a corporate budget line-item. In the UK, the 1999 Turnbull Report provides guidance to directors and other managers of companies listed on the London Stock Exchange for their requirement to identify, evaluate and manage their significant risks. They must review on a regular basis reports on the effectiveness of the system of internal control in managing key risks and make annual assessments.[14] Such types of guidance and international standards for IT security management, such as ISO 17799,[15] enable more widespread and consistent implementation of IT security policies, facilitating more secure economic transactions, which in turn stimulates business and commerce.

While regulations and standards have roles in promoting good IT security, the uncertainty about the economics of IT and networks worldwide also strengthens the impetus for business to implement IT security management processes, as these uncertainties lie beyond any one entity's local corporate control.[16] Internet-based remote access to sites for routine maintenance may reduce personnel costs, but these systems also give rise to opportunities for interception and data manipulation. Internet-based or -accessible products or services may stimulate new revenue streams, but if improperly implemented or secured they may also lead to security incidents and potential loss of reputation. Many companies, including those in the financial services sector, write off a considerable amount of their losses from computer incidents, whatever the cause, because this is cheaper than improving management and staff satisfaction or hiring and training skilled personnel to implement adequate information security policies. BCPs often include mechanisms for reputation management, which may be cheaper than overhauling an IT security system.

Within the context of globalization and the spread of IT, new vulnerabilities have arisen. While the spread of new technologies is not new in itself, concerns arise from the rate at which new IT technologies and applications have appeared over the past decades and from the unevenness of the global spread of IT, often referred to as the 'digital divide'. However, the digital divide

---

[14] Institute of Chartered Accountants in England & Wales, 'Internal control: guidance for directors on the Combined Code (The Turnbull Report)', Sep. 1999, available on the Institute's Internet site, URL <http://www.icaew.co.uk>.

[15] International Organization for Standardization, 'The ISO 17799 Service & Software Directory', URL <http://www.iso17799software.com/index.htm>. See also the ISO Internet site at URL <http://www.iso.org>.

[16] Frye, E., 'Information-sharing hang-ups: is antitrust just a cover?', *CIP Report*, vol. 1, no. 8 (Feb. 2003), p. 7, available at URL <http://techcenter.gmu.edu/programs/cipp/cip_report.html>.

encompasses more than just uneven IT spread or absorption: it also reflects more deep-rooted disparities in a country's income distribution and in its education and employment opportunities. Understanding the new vulnerabilities in IT for any given environment thus requires knowledge of a country's overall infrastructure. Because much technology spreads via the corporate, commercial or business sector, not by governmental routes, uncertainties about its use abound.

Three trends concerning globalization and business developments can be identified to help provide a wider context for IT security concerns. One perception of globalization is that the largest companies in the world, which tend to be firms in the United States, are destined to remain in control of advances in IT technology. While some anti-globalization protesters dislike this perception of control, the spread of IT by multinational companies can bring with it the spread of common IT infrastructure, and along with it the spread of 'good practice' in the fields of IT project development and cyber security. Second, globalization raises awareness of 'the local'. Given that about 60–80 per cent of the gross national product of most countries is derived from small and medium-sized enterprises, the spread of IT means that more local and regional businesses are stimulated and encouraged as new ideas and processes come into the region. However, these opportunities are sometimes opposed by strong vested interests which see technology as reducing both jobs and the scope for the corruption that some regard as a necessary 'enhancement' of their otherwise meagre incomes. IT security concerns may be greatest in such cases if a lack of resources necessitates reactive rather than proactive approaches to BCPs and security management. Third, globalization has resulted in the creation of 'virtual companies', based on highly integrated information networks that bring together and then distribute knowledge, skills, labour resources and production facilities—wherever and whenever they are required. This process highlights the business drivers and the pressure for new sources and streams of business revenue, but it also points to the new security risks arising from bringing together people and networks with varying degrees of IT capability and knowledge of security. These three modes of IT transfer and absorption represent a dynamic range of business or economic developments that require strategic thinking about how best to devise security management in the face of international IT vulnerabilities and threats.

V. Conclusions

Further research needs to be carried out on the extent to which a potential terrorist would choose cyber means rather than explosives to achieve the large or spectacular impact associated with terrorism. The complexities of the often proprietary electronic networks of critical information infrastructure, and the increasingly strong authentication procedures for access, suggest that it is very difficult for those outside a large corporate enterprise to launch a successful cyber attack on it without 'insider' knowledge of its networks. Outside the critical infrastructure sectors, however, the fact that so many businesses are not yet properly implementing even the most basic security policies implies that anyone, including a cyber terrorist, could have an opportunity to manipulate data or bring down a network without insider knowledge.

Putting into place protection and intrusion-detection systems, minimizing technical vulnerabilities, assessing computer connectivity with the Internet and implementing good management of IT projects, including software upgrades and contingency and recovery plans, would all contribute either to the prevention of cyber incidents in general or to better emergency response action. They would also go a long way towards protecting against or mitigating the impact of cyber-terrorist acts. This is not to argue for complacency on matters of cyber terrorism, but rather to place into better perspective the questions of what types of security effort are required and where.

The degree to which the private and public sectors cooperate on critical infrastructure protection and how they do so are important. Most analysts agree on the need for more information sharing between the public and private sector, but the more debatable issue is how and where this cooperation might be institutionalized or codified. Given the importance of ensuring that critical infrastructure provides a reliable service, governments have traditionally shared relevant intelligence information about impending threats to such infrastructure with owners and operators, albeit on an informal basis.

The strategic impact on issues of cyber security of new technologies and their global spread requires further analysis. The 1990s brought new developments in IT which companies, governments and individuals throughout the world understandably were keen to use. New communications and computing technologies were introduced into daily operations to reap the benefits of reducing operational costs, facilitating remote access and processing, and enabling new business models, such as electronic commerce, to produce new revenue streams. However, more research is needed on how global developments in commerce and business, such as outsourcing, may give rise to uncertainties which require a greater focus on data and infrastructure protection measures.

17. The concept of critical infrastructure protection

Jan Metzger

I. Introduction

The US Department of Homeland Security (DHS) was established on 1 January 2003, following the largest administrative restructuring undertaken in the United States since World War II. The task of the 170 000 DHS employees, in over 20 agencies and under the leadership of Secretary of Homeland Security Tom Ridge, is to protect the nation against the threat of terrorist attacks. A sizeable portion of the budget for fiscal year 2003 of nearly $38 billion will be allocated to the area of Information Analysis and Infrastructure Protection, one of the four main DHS directorates. A major task of the Assistant Secretary for Infrastructure Protection, Robert P. Liscouski, will be to conduct a comprehensive analysis of critical infrastructures and to put in place a national protection plan.[1]

What does critical infrastructure protection (CIP) entail? Is CIP a feasible concept for the pursuit of traditional security policy goals, such as 'independence', 'territorial sovereignty' and 'national security'?[2] This chapter begins by defining the term CIP. It then assesses the concept, applying the following criteria: (*a*) linguistic usage compared with actual practice (the operational perspective), and (*b*) analytical and terminological precision (the conceptual perspective).

II. CIP from an operational perspective

The concept of 'critical infrastructure' was the subject of political debate in the United States even before the current focus on terrorism. There was a lively debate on infrastructure security in the 1980s, but there was no generally accepted definition or common understanding of the term.[3] The 1997 report of

---

[1] The Department of Homeland Security was established on 1 Jan. 2003. See the DHS Internet site at URL <http://www.dhs.gov>. On the Information Analysis and Infrastructure Protection Directorate see URL <http://www.dhs.gov/dhspublic/display?theme=13>.

[2] For the Swiss context see Article 2 (Purpose) of the Swiss Federal Constitution, available on the University of Bern Internet site at URL <http://www.oefre.unibe.ch/law/icl/sz00000_.html>; and *Security through Cooperation: Report of the Federal Council to the Federal Assembly on the Security Policy of Switzerland*, no. 97.667e, 7 June 1999, URL <http://www.vbs-ddps.ch/internet/vbs/en/home/publikationen/berichte.html>. Other security policy goals, such as 'solidarity' or 'stability and peace beyond the borders', are deliberately excluded in this context.

[3] 'With no standard or agreed definition, the concept of infrastructure in policy terms has been fluid, as it appears to be today.' Moteff, J., Copeland, C. and Fischer, J., *Critical Infrastructures: What Makes an Infrastructure Critical?*, Report for Congress (Library of Congress, Congressional Research Service:

the President's Commission on Critical Infrastructure Protection (PCCIP) presented a broad definition of critical infrastructures, reflecting a multitude of requirements and perspectives.[4] After a process of policy transposition— that is, after transferring and adapting a political paradigm to a different national context—many countries launched CIP initiatives that focused more or less exclusively on the Internet or cyber communications.[5] For example, efforts to meet the requirements for a US national CIP plan included a strategic Internet security plan which was presented in 2000, although it largely neglected physical infrastructure protection.[6]

It is important to distinguish between the protection of critical infrastructure in general and the protection of critical information and telecommunication infrastructures—critical information infrastructure protection, CIIP—as a subordinate task. The distinction is often not obvious or easy to make because of the crucial role of CIIP in an overall CIP strategy. In official publications, both terms are often used to refer to CIIP. However, it is important to note that CIP comprises *all* critical sectors of a nation's infrastructure, while CIIP is only a subset of a comprehensive protection effort.[7]

The *International CIIP Handbook* defines CIIP as 'a subset of CIP. CIIP focuses on the protection of systems and assets including components such as telecommunications, computers/software, Internet, satellites, fiber optics, etc., and on interconnected computers and networks, and the services they provide'.[8] This task is particularly important for three reasons: first, as an economic sector, these infrastructures represent a major component of economic value creation. Second, they act as a crucial interconnecting link between other areas of infrastructure. Even under normal conditions, they are essential for the proper functioning of all other infrastructures. Third, in a crisis situation they are a crucial tool for managing risk factors and re-establishing normal conditions.[9]

Washington, DC, Updated 29 Jan. 2003), p. CRS-1, available at URL <http://www.fas.org/irp/crs/RL31556.pdf>.

[4] *Critical Foundations: Protecting America's Infrastructures, The Report of the President's Commission on Critical Infrastructure Protection*, Oct. 1997, URL <http://www.ciao.gov/resource/pccip/PCCIP_report.pdf>.

[5] See Wenger, A., Metzger, J. and Dunn, M. (eds), *International CIIP Handbook: An Inventory of Protection Policies in Eight Countries* (Swiss Federal Institute of Technology, Center for Security Studies: Zurich, 2002), available at URL <http://www.isn.ethz.ch/onlinepubli/publihouse/misc/ciip>.

[6] *Defending America's Cyberspace: National Plan for Information Systems Protection, Version 1.0, An Invitation to a Dialogue* (The White House: Washington, DC, 2000), available at URL <http://www.ciao.gov/publicaffairs/np1final.pdf>. For the more recent version of Feb. 2003, see the US Department of Homeland Security Internet site, 'The National Strategy to Secure Cyberspace', URL <http://www.dhs.gov/interweb/assetlibrary/National_Cyberspace_Strategy.pdf>.

[7] Dunn, M. and Wigert, I., *The International CIIP Handbook 2004: An Inventory of Protection Policies*, eds A. Wenger and J. Metzger (Swiss Federal Institute of Technology, Center for Security Studies: Zurich, forthcoming 2004), Introduction.

[8] See Wenger, Metzger, and Dunn (note 5), glossary of key terms, p. 178.

[9] Wenger, A., Metzger, J. and Dunn, M., 'Critical information infrastructure protection: eine sicherheitspolitische Herausforderung' [A challenge for security policy], eds K. R. Spillmann and A. Wenger, *Bulletin zur Schweizerischen Sicherheitspolitik* [Bulletin on Swiss security policy] (Swiss Federal Institute of Technology, Center for Security Studies: Zurich, 2002), pp. 119–42 (in German).

Clearly, the observable tendency to reduce CIIP (or even CI) to an issue of computer security—with its attendant exclusive focus on isolated, often technological aspects, as illustrated by terms such as 'cyber terrorism', 'cyber crime' and 'cyber warfare'—is problematic and short-sighted. Terrorists do not tend to restrict their range of options or to operate solely in one dimension of threat. The perpetrators of political violence are not exclusively 'cyber' terrorists but choose the particular area or specific tool with which they can best achieve their political objectives. In order to combat the challenge of terrorism successfully, Western information societies must endeavour to think like the perpetrators of terrorist attacks—and hence to think not illogically, but according to the logic of terrorists. It is the nature of the threat, not the instruments through which the threat manifests itself (physical, network-based or biological agents), which must be taken as the basis for analysis and should serve as a guidance for institutional preparedness and defence.

Several features make CIIP a special case of CIP, meriting modern societies' serious concern and attention. For one thing, the system characteristics of the emerging information infrastructure differ radically from those of traditional structures, including earlier information infrastructures: in terms of scale, of connectivity and of dependencies. This is especially important because understanding them will require new analytical techniques and methodologies. Second, the subject of cyber-network security is evolving rapidly in terms of technological capabilities and modern societies' vulnerabilities.[10] The cyber threat has thus become a prototype for studying the asymmetric nature of 'new' or 'emerging' risks and institutional response policies.

Moreover, several driving forces are likely to aggravate the problem of critical information infrastructures in the future: namely, the interlinked aspects of market forces, technological evolution and emerging risks.[11] On the one hand, the dynamic globalization of information services, combined with technological innovation (e.g., localized wireless communication), will result in a dramatic increase in the level of connectivity, lead to poorly understood systems behaviour and create new vulnerabilities. Added to this is the fact that security has never been a driver of design. Since pressure to reduce the time from designing a product or service to marketing it is intense, a further dramatic increase in computer and network vulnerabilities can be expected. There is therefore a risk of the potential emergence of infrastructures with built-in instabilities, critical points of failure, and extensive interdependencies. In addition, increasingly large parts of the critical infrastructure of a given territory will be in the hands of the private sector, or even another state, since the injection of sufficient capital and cost-effective development is a prevailing market driver.[12]

[10] Dunn and Wigert (note 7).

[11] Dennis, I. and Conroy, R., *New Technology as a Threat and Risk Generator: Can Countermeasures Keep Up with the Pace?*, ed. G. Jervas (Swedish Defence Research Agency: Stockholm, Mar. 2001).

[12] Dunn and Wigert (note 7).

This forward-looking perspective points clearly to a need to distinguish conceptually between the CIP and CIIP concepts. However, the two concepts cannot and should not be completely isolated from each other. As stated above, CIIP is an essential part of CIP. An exclusive focus on cyber threats that ignores important traditional physical threats is just as dangerous as neglecting the aspect of cyber-network security. What is needed is sensible handling of both concepts as interrelated but conceptually separate.[13]

III. CIP from a conceptual perspective

If there is no general, standardized usage and broad-based mutual understanding of the term CIP, what can be said about its analytical and terminological precision? In order to answer this question, the terms 'infrastructure', 'critical' and 'protection' must be examined more closely.

The term 'infrastructure' describes the underlying basis of an organization or system, for example, a country. Information and telecommunications systems; banking and financial institutions; water, electricity, oil and gas supplies; transportation and logistics structures; and health and emergency services are all essential infrastructures.

The essential nature of these infrastructures also presents a central problem. If it is assumed that security policy, as a 'policy for extraordinary circumstances' or as a policy for existential threats, is something removed from the realm of everyday politics—or at least represents a special form of policy—a purely practical question of definition arises: when is critical infrastructure protection an issue of maintaining 'business continuity' for an individual, corporate or local actor and when is it the subject of national and, where necessary, even international security policy?[14] The problem of distinguishing between everyday operations and regulatory policy, on the one hand, and defence and security policy, on the other hand, is further exacerbated by the fact that many of the above-mentioned infrastructures are privately owned and controlled, in some cases from abroad. Some may not even be located within the territory of the state in question.

The fact that CIP is a multifaceted issue of high relevance to many different, very diverse and often overlapping communities is a major obstacle to academic and practical dialogue. Because different groups do not necessarily agree on what the problem is or what needs to be protected, the actual meaning ascribed to critical information infrastructure depends to a great extent on the group. To complicate the picture, the boundaries between the different perspectives are by no means clear-cut.

The following list presents the most important perspectives as ideal types and in simplified form.[15]

[13] Dunn and Wigert (note 7).
[14] Buzan, B., Weaver, O. and de Wilde, J., *Security: A New Framework for Analysis* (Lynne Rienner: London, 1998), p. 24.
[15] Dunn and Wigert (note 7).

The system-level, technical perspective: CIP is approached as a question of information technology (IT) security or information assurance, with a strong focus on Internet security.

The business perspective: CIP is seen as a question of 'business continuity'.

The law-enforcement perspective: CIP is seen as a question of protecting society against (cyber) crime.

The defence perspective: This perspective is centred on either military or civil protection.

The regulatory policy perspective: The smooth and routine operation of infrastructures and questions such as privacy, or hardware and software standards, must be regulated.

The national and international security policy perspective: This perspective is addressed in this chapter.

Thus infrastructures are viewed as objects to be protected against crime, as competitive advantages in the private sector, as technical/operative systems, as defence-relevant strategic assets, and as objects that are relevant for the formulation of national and international security policy. One final aspect—and one that is frequently ignored—is that infrastructures are also objects of individual cognition and of public reflection and perception. As objects of both historical consciousness and contention in current political debates, they are inextricably associated with such notions as 'risk', 'threat', 'trust', 'crisis', 'disaster' and 'catastrophe'.

If the perspective is widened accordingly, a fundamental question must be asked: whether it is primarily the actual infrastructures that need to be protected. In fact, the real focus of interest in protection is the services, the physical and electronic flows of information as well as their role and function, and in particular the core values symbolized by infrastructures. Whereas infrastructures are constructed, maintained and operated by people, and have relatively clear organizational and institutional hierarchies, it is much more difficult to represent and comprehend the services, flows and especially the core values they give rise to because of their intricate significance and interconnections. In order to take into account the system dynamics involved and interests in protection, it would make more sense to speak of 'critical services robustness' or 'critical services sustainability' rather than CIP.

IV. Criticality

The word 'critical' is more appropriate than 'infrastructure' for making a conceptual distinction between normal operating procedures and strategic security policy. For example, the German Federal Office for Information Security distinguishes between protecting 'critical infrastructures' and protecting 'business-critical infrastructures'.[16]

Is this also appropriate for the distinction between everyday routines and crisis situations? There are two trends: first, in the public perception, there are increasingly fewer genuinely 'natural' catastrophes about which we can do nothing. Such events are more often seen as the result of policy failure, or the failure of politicians, and personal responsibility is increasingly called for. Second, the criterion for what constitutes 'good' policy is changing: the future career of political decision makers is not determined by their administrative competence during routine periods, but by their management efficiency before, during and after a crisis.

The definition of 'critical' is highly dependent on the author of the definition, but the concept itself is also undergoing constant change. A survey of the literature on critical infrastructure protection, and of the general definitions for and lists of critical infrastructures, shows a great variety. The main reason is that the criteria for qualifying infrastructures as critical have expanded over time; the PCCIP, for example, defined critical infrastructures as assets whose prolonged disruption could cause significant military and economic dislocation.[17] Today the term also includes national monuments where an attack might cause a large number of casualties or adversely affect the nation's morale. This development permits a typology of two different but interrelated ways of understanding criticality.

Criticality as a symbolic concept. An infrastructure is inherently critical because of its role or function in society. This means that an existential security policy objective, such as territorial sovereignty, cannot be achieved in the event of the collapse of or damage to the infrastructure. In this case, it is basically the national interest, rather than the infrastructure itself, that is critical. In theory, the question whether, or to what degree, the infrastructure is interconnected with other areas is irrelevant—the inherent symbolic meaning of certain infrastructures per se makes them potential targets. For example, the US Congress building and the White House represent attractive targets for various groups of terrorists because they are symbols of national power.[18]

Criticality as a systemic concept. An infrastructure is critical because of its *structural positioning* in the whole system of infrastructures, especially when it is an important link between other infrastructures or sectors. Electric power

---

[16] See the Internet site of the Bundesamt für Sicherheit in der Informationstechnik (Federal Office for Information Security) at URL <http://www.bsi.bund.de/fachthem/kritis/index.htm>, and in English: 'BSI IT security topic briefing: critical instrastructures in state and society', at URL <http://www.bsi.bund.de/literat/faltbl/kritis_e.htm>.

[17] *Critical Foundations: Protecting America's Infrastructures* (note 4).

[18] For an example of this view of a 'criticality' assessment, without reference to the aspect of networking, see US General Accounting Office (GAO), *Homeland Security, Key Elements of a Risk Management Approach*, Statement of Raymond J. Decker, Director, Defense Capabilities and Management, Testimony before the Subcommittee on National Security, Veterans Affairs, and International Relations, House Committee on Government Reform (GAO: Washington, DC, 2001), p. 6, available at URL <http://www.gao.gov/new.items/d02150t.pdf>.

and information/telecommunication networks are of special importance in terms of interconnection and dependability. Accordingly, in its final report of 1997, the PCCIP defined infrastructures as 'a network of independent, largely private-sector owned, technical (man-made) systems and processes.'[19]

The concept of symbolic criticality allows non-networked and non-technical objects, systems and processes to be integrated into protection and emergency planning. Human targets, such as the president of a country, or national heritage sites with a strongly symbolic character are 'critical' targets not because of their networking significance, but because of their function and importance for national pride, that is, for their significance for the identity of a people as a nation.

The typology described above is of course an idealized, even artificial one: in reality, infrastructures can rarely be separated from one another. Energy generation is dependent on transport, while transportation methods are, in turn, dependent on energy; both require functional information networks, while information networks are dependent on energy, and so on. The example of the New York World Trade Center (WTC) shows how different types of criticality are likely to be combined in certain objects. In the case of the attacks of 11 September 2001, there was an accumulation of different 'criticalities': the importance of the WTC within the financial system as a juncture of global monetary flows, as a large workplace, as an administrative centre and tourist site, and for its symbolic significance as *the* World Trade Center.

It would be fair to say that the systemic understanding of criticality, with its understanding of infrastructures as 'complex, adaptive systems', provides a more satisfactory representation of everyday reality in all its complexity. It is also more amenable than symbolic criticality to an empirical analysis based on statistical data. Security policy analysts hold that systemic criticality has a disadvantage in that it is more difficult to make a distinction between optimizing routine emergency management and a 'policy for existential threats', whereas symbolic criticality is, by definition, placed in a security policy context. This approach allows the national security analyst and researcher to define relevant assets more easily than the systemic one, because it is not the interdependencies as such that are definitive in a socio-political context, but the role, relevance and symbolic value of specific infrastructures.

A key problem is that the notion of 'critical infrastructure' has over the past few years moved away from a technical scientific or at best system-theory expert level, and has been introduced into the political agenda, without intellectually adapting the CIP concept to this very different socio-political context. The term 'critical' is etymologically related to the word 'crisis'. Crises are, by their very nature, social events: they affect individuals, a group, an

---

[19] *Critical Foundations: Protecting America's Infrastructures* (note 4).

organization, a society and/or a state. They are characterized by the very fact that 'critical' decisions are (or must be) taken when they arise.[20]

It is possible to measure system criticality, resilience and robustness with a certain degree of objectivity: first, as part of the process of 'optimizing the normal case'; and second, at the level of technical infrastructure. At the security policy level, however, risks, threats and crises can be neither quantified nor objectively compared with one another. Given the degree to which criticality manifests itself in every crisis, there is little point in excluding non-technical and non-networked items requiring protection. It is not the networking aspect, but rather the significance of the infrastructure per se that is the decisive criterion for categorizing an infrastructure as 'critical' on a security policy level. Crises with relevance for security policy are *by definition* critical and complex events, in terms of when and where they take place, the interaction between the institutions involved on a vertical (federal, state and municipal) and horizontal (inter-ministerial) level, the identification of the problems that arise, and the information needs and surpluses that are revealed.[21]

Even where quantitatively exact measurement is not possible, this does not necessarily mean that the situation is of no importance, and this certainly does not prevent its being dealt with by means of preventive risk reduction measures based on risk awareness. One example illustrates this well: at the individual level, the risk of being hit by an automobile represents one of the most extreme events of all. There are detailed statistics on how many pedestrians are run over each year in different countries, but the average citizen is unaware of these empirical data. Yet, every day, people perceive this risk as relevant and adopt an appropriate risk-reduction strategy by using pedestrian crossings. This example illustrates that the statement 'you can only improve what you can measure' is false. It is not primarily a quantitative but rather a qualitative knowledge of risks and vulnerabilities that is needed, not only to protect pedestrians and other road users, but also to protect infrastructures against terrorist threats. Recently, three risk analysts asserted: 'Understanding and reducing vulnerability does not demand accurate predictions of the incidence of extreme events'.[22]

For security policy analysis, the task ahead is not so much to measure crises precisely, but rather to determine under what circumstances they *start, develop and end*. Taking a broad contextual and a methodologically interdisciplinary approach, the characteristics of crises, the detailed structural circumstances that lead to them and their consequences must be revealed. Extreme events are created and characterized *by their context*:

---

[20] On the definition of 'crisis' see Stern, E. K., Crisis Management Europe Research Program, *Crisis Decisionmaking: A Cognitive–Institutional Approach* (Swedish National Defence College: Stockholm, 2001), pp. 4–6.

[21] Stern (note 20), pp. 14–16.

[22] Sarewitz, D., Pielke, R. and Keykhah, M., 'Vulnerability and risk: some thoughts from a political and policy perspective', *Risk Analysis,* vol. 23, no. 4 (Aug. 2003), p. 807, URL <http://www.cspo. org/products/articles/Vulnerable.pdf>.

The character of an extreme event is determined not simply by some set of character-istics inherent in the physical phenomena (e.g., a hurricane, or monsoon rains), but by the interaction of those characteristics with other systems . . . A focus on vulnerability management would require a clear-eyed view of the limits of predictive science to guide the way to an uncertain future and instead focus on the design of healthy deci-sion processes flexible enough to learn from experience and intelligent enough to assess alternative approaches to vulnerability management.[23]

In contrast to technical infrastructure analysis, security policy research is less concerned with identifying objective crisis thresholds than with investigat-ing *actors* and *events*, as well as *when, in what context, how and with what result* a crisis occurred. This is based on the conviction that the principal con-cern of strategic policy direction must be *not to overlook* any risk, rather than to *precisely measure* those risks that have already been identified. People, and also collective groups of people such as states, do not react directly to an objectively constituted environment, but rather according to their own percep-tion of reality. For that reason, it is not helpful, either politically or analyti-cally, to attempt to identify 'real security' in isolation from a political con-text.[24] In German-speaking countries, the difficulty of distinguishing between a technically operational CIP analysis and a socio-political one is exacerbated by the fact that *Sicherheit* can be translated as both 'safety' and 'security'.

The question of the criticality of an infrastructure is inseparable from the issue of how the impact on an infrastructure is politically perceived, capital-ized, dealt with and exploited. When does the image of a threat become a security policy issue, and when does it not? Eriksson and Noreen cite various factors that influence individual perceptions of threat images. Taken as a whole, these factors to some extent determine whether threats appear on the political agenda, disappear from it, persist or are even given higher priority. They include the crisis experiences of a community, aspects of identity, the political and institutional context and the influence of public opinion.[25] In this context, it is interesting to note that different political parties place priority on different threat images. Typically, political parties oriented on environmental issues tend to have a broader concept of security, while the perception of con-servative parties traditionally focuses on military threats.

This aspect is also of crucial importance in the current debate over the fight against terrorism. Terrorism could be said to be primarily, although not exclu-sively, a form of communication. The actual goal of terrorists is not primarily to commit acts of violence against their victims per se, but to influence the

[23] Sarewitz, D. and Pielke, R., 'Vulnerability and risk: some thoughts from a political and policy per-spective', Discussion paper prepared for the Columbia–Wharton/Penn Roundtable on Risk Management Strategies in an Uncertain World, 4 Apr. 2002, p. 4, URL <http://www.ldeo.columbia.edu/res/pi/CHRR/Roundtable/Pielke_Sarewitz_WP.pdf>; and Sarewitz, D. and Pielke, R., 'Extreme events: a research and policy framework for disasters in context', forthcoming in *International Geology Review*, URL <http://www.cspo.org/products/articles/xepaperfinal.pdf>.
[24] Buzan, Weaver and de Wilde (note 14), p. 31.
[25] Eriksson, J. and Noreen, E., *Setting the Agenda of Threats: An Explanatory Model*, Uppsala Peace Research Paper no. 6 (Uppsala University, Department of Peace and Conflict Research: Uppsala, 2002), pp. 12–15, available at URL <http://www.pcr.uu.se/publications/UPRP_pdf/uprp_no_6.pdf>.

consciousness of a broad spectrum of the public who witness their attacks in their 'theatre of operations'.[26]

It follows that CIP studies on a security policy level should focus primarily on the subjects of political culture, political debate and political (party) constellation. CIP research seen in this way is first and foremost an analysis of the political context in which infrastructures can be identified, analysed and protected. It is not the CIP analyst but rather the political actors, and especially the general public, who determine whether a threat is accepted as 'critical'.

It is important to note that this political context also includes the politically motivated perpetrator or terrorist who consciously and deliberately attacks an infrastructure. Many infrastructure studies use a largely 'intra-system' determination of criticality, by considering which infrastructures are linked to one another, and how and where. The approach of the German Federal Office for Information Security is an example of a problematic approach: its analysis consciously looks at vulnerabilities 'independently of the type of threat'.[27] However, vulnerabilities manifest themselves only in their particular context, in other words in relation to the threats relevant for decision making. This analytical approach thus needs to be extended if criticality is to be determined not purely by structure, but also by violence and symbolism. As Doron Zimmermann explains, terrorism is a 'people business' that is intrinsically non-quantifiable. 'We should first know who (actors, motives and objectives) and what (organizations and capabilities) we are dealing with, before jumping to conclusions, comparing and referencing with a known, but possibly inapplicable, body of knowledge and committing resources to protect and counteract on that basis.'[28]

Even though criticality cannot be measured objectively, indicators can be established to determine whether damage to an infrastructure is critical or not. For example, US Presidential Decision Directive 63 (PDD-63) of May 1998 states that: 'Any interruptions or manipulations of these critical functions must be brief, infrequent, manageable, geographically isolated and minimally detrimental to the welfare of the United States'.[29]

In addition, the criticality of an infrastructure can also be analysed in terms of another factor: the measure of loss of *trust* suffered by the state when a

---

[26] Hoffmann, B., *Inside Terrorism* (Columbia University Press: New York, 1998), available in German translation as *Terrorismus: Der unerklärte Krieg, Neue Gefahren politischer Gewalt* [The undeclared war: new dangers of political violence], (Fischer: Frankfurt am Main, 2001), p. 48.

[27] Blattner-Zimmermann, M., 'Schutz Kritischer Infrastrukturen in Deutschland' [Protection of critical infrastructures in Germany], Speech at the Lucerne meeting on information security (Luzerner Tage für Informationssicherung, LUTIS), 24 June 2003, Transparency 7, URL <http://www.infosurance.ch/de/lutis_downl.htm> (in German). See also Bundesamt für Sicherheit in der Informationstechnik, 'Kritische Infrastrukturen' [Critical infrastructures], URL <http://www.bsi.bund.de/fachthem/kritis/kritis.htm>.

[28] Zimmermann, D., *The Transformation of Terrorism: The 'New Terrorism', Impact Scalability and the Dynamic of Reciprocal Threat Perception*, Zurich Contributions to Security Policy and Conflict Research no. 67 (Swiss Federal Institute of Technology, Center for Security Studies: Zurich, 2003), p. 61.

[29] 'The Clinton Administration's Policy on Critical Infrastructure Protection: Presidential Decision Directive 63', White Paper, 22 May 1998, section III, A national goal, URL <http://www.fas.org/irp/offdocs/paper598.htm>.

service is disrupted. This is a useful yardstick in that public demands for government to take responsibility, even in cases involving private sector control of ownership, are a clear indication that a vital service has been affected. Despite the fact that baggage controls for domestic flights were largely the responsibility of private companies at US airports on 11 September 2001, public opinion blamed the terrorist attacks on negligence on the part of federal authorities and thus, by extension, the government. In other words, it is the perception of risk and the reaction to risk on the part of the public, and not the analyst, that ultimately determines whether an event represents a catastrophe, whether an attack triggers an existential crisis and whether an infrastructure or service is 'critical'. From this perspective, the criticality of an infrastructure cannot be determined in a preventive manner, based on empirical data, but only on an *ex post facto* basis as the result of a normative process.

The term 'protection', creating a mental image of 'all or nothing', is also not appropriate for addressing the complexity of modern infrastructure vulnerabilities, because it is impossible to ensure full protection. For this reason, it would be better to use a word from the vocabulary of the natural sciences, such as 'robustness' or 'resilience', and in general to use the terms 'survival capability' or 'regenerative capability', 'availability', 'stability' or 'reliability'.

It thus becomes apparent that CIP describes a natural, age-old, ultimately biological phenomenon—not a new technical phenomenon. For example, trees undergo a process in the autumn that could also be described as critical infrastructure protection: they reduce their activities to the minimum level required to survive a period of stress, the winter. This is also a familiar concept from military contexts: Switzerland's defence strategy in World War II, withdrawal to the 'Alpine recess' (*réduit*) was based on the same strategy and philosophy.

V. Conclusions and recommendations

'Critical infrastructure protection' is an unfortunate term: it is often used incorrectly and analysed from inappropriate perspectives. The main problem is that it originated in the technical–scientific context of closed systems. Since 1996, CIP has been used indiscriminately in the security policy debate and without regard to the different contexts of open systems. As a result, infrastructure analysis is still often understood as a precise instrument, which largely ignores the socio-political and cognitive context of the power relationships, actors, cultures and interests involved. For example, the threat of terrorism is often either excluded—because it cannot be measured—or considered as a 'black box', without any attempt to draw on the expertise of intelligence services to verify the plausibility of attacks from a terrorist actor's point of view. A British Government report came to a similar conclusion: some applications of the risk management concept were too mechanical and were insufficiently adapted to decision making at the highest strategic level. The higher the assessment of the risks was, the more difficult it was to identify and quantify them, the more destructive the effects and the more unstable the situation. Accordingly, the report recommended that risk identification, or 'horizon scanning', should be broadly defined, and that risk analysis should be based more on judgements than on empirical facts.[30] Extreme events or 'mega-risks', also known as 'wild cards' in scenario technique terms, combine low probability with large-scale damage: they represent existential risks, by definition; and they are typically unforeseeable events. For this reason, and specifically in relation to the threat of terrorism, infrastructure may be critical for strategic protection and defence planning even when the risks cannot be measured exactly.

Over the past few years, a series of methods have been developed for the analysis of critical infrastructure interdependencies. For example, Rinaldi, Peerenboom and Kelly use a conceptual framework with six dimensions: (a) the infrastructure characteristics (organizational, operational, temporal, spatial); (b) the type of interdependency (physical, network-based, logical and geographical); (c) the environment (political/social, technical, legal, economic); (d) the characteristics of the dynamic feedback; (e) the type of disruption; and (f) the state of operation.[31]

Owing to the fact that there is effectively no limit to vulnerabilities, risk analyses are by definition never complete or exact. Even Yacov Haimes, of the US Society for Risk Analysis, points out in his textbook on risk analysis: 'To the extent that risk assessment is precise, it is not real. To the extent that risk assessment is real, it is not precise'. According to Haimes, this applies in particular to the risk of extreme and catastrophic events, which should not be assessed in the same way as high-probability, low-consequence events.[32]

In the field of counter-terrorism, a fundamental asymmetry can be discerned between terrorists' apparent ability to strike anywhere and at any time, and the inability of security forces to protect every imaginable target.[33] However, this situation does not mean that it is impossible to prioritize infrastructures in relation to the terrorist threat, but it requires a national and international comprehensive risk analysis and management dialogue.[34]

Effective protection for critical infrastructures calls for holistic and strategic threat and risk assessment at the physical, virtual and psychological levels as the basis for a comprehensive protection and survival strategy. This makes

[30] British Cabinet Office, Strategy Unit, *Risk: Improving Government's Capability to Handle Risk and Uncertainty*, Strategy Unit Report, Nov. 2002, p. 29, URL <http://www.number-10.gov.uk/SU/RISK/REPORT/01.HTM>

[31] Rinaldi, S. M., Peerenboom, J. P. and Kelly, T. K., 'Identifying, understanding, and analyzing critical infrastructure interdependencies', *IEEE Control Systems Magazine*, Dec. 2001, pp. 11–25.

[32] Haimes, Y. Y., *Risk Modeling, Assessment, and Management* (Wiley-Interscience: New York, 1998), p. 45. On the Society for Risk Analysis see URL <http://www.sra.org/>.

[33] Hoffmann (note 26), p. 76.

[34] E.g., the Comprehensive Risk Analysis and Management Network (CRN), run by the Center for Security Studies of the Swiss Federal Institute of Technology, in cooperation with several international partner institutions. URL <http://www.isn.ethz.ch/crn>. See also Braun, H., 'The non-military threat spectrum', *SIPRI Yearbook 2003: Armaments, Disarmament and International Security* (Oxford University Press: Oxford, 2003), pp. 33–43, which describes the Comprehensive Risk Analysis Switzerland project.

partnerships essential. Close public–private sector partnerships are frequently encouraged at present, and rightly so, because they are an important prerequisite for such a strategy. Less often discussed, either in practice or in specialist literature, is the need for partnerships between the social and natural sciences. Based on the understanding that absolute security does not exist, lessons must be learned from unfamiliar fields of knowledge, and also from the past. If the study of history is to present options instead of ruling them out, it must be remembered that many of the consequences associated with specific events seem plausible today only because those events actually occurred. Decades before September 2001, Kahn and Wiener held that future events need not always be taken from the restricted list of what is possible, and that we must be prepared for further surprises.[35] Bearing this in mind, there are lessons to learn just as much from the future as from the past in the current fight against terrorism—the key notion being the 'scenario technique'. This approach calls for institutional and individual creativity, bearing in mind that creativity, as opposed to knowledge, has no limits.

Specifically, we must ensure that infrastructure analyses are no longer carried out without an understanding of the motive, the potential and the modus operandi of politically motivated actors.

Recent US Congress policy papers also conclude that analyses of threats, vulnerability and criticality should not be performed separately, but should complement one another as part of a comprehensive risk management approach.[36] This necessitates a modification to the analytical approach, which must assess different aspects not so much on the basis of their measurability as of their relevance to decision making, whether they are of a quantitative or a qualitative nature. There are many such analyses, but very few comprehensive studies on a strategic level. This point is also made by Gebhard Geiger: namely, that the research and development task for international security, and ultimately for security policy, is not to create a new applied research discipline, but to apply existing approaches, models and methods in an appropriate manner to the problems of social infrastructure protection.[37]

---

[35] Kahn, H. and Wiener, A. J., *Ihr werdet es erleben: Voraussagen der Wissenschaft bis zum Jahre 2000* [You will live to see it: predictions on science up to the year 2000], (Oldenburg: Vienna, Munich and Zurich, 1967), p. 254.

[36] See, e.g., 'A good risk management approach includes three primary elements: a threat assessment, a vulnerability assessment, and a criticality assessment.' US General Accounting Office (note 18), p. 1.

[37] Geiger, G., *Information und Infrastruktursicherheit: Grundzüge eines sicherheits- und technologiepolitischen Forschungs- und Entwicklungsprogramms* [Information and infrastructure security: outline for a security and technology policy research and development programme], (Stiftung Wissenschaft und Politik, Forschungsinstitut für Internationale Politik und Sicherheit: Ebenhausen, May 2000), p. 33.

18. Critical energy system infrastructure protection in Europe and the legitimate economy

Kevin Rosner

I. Introduction

On 14 August 2003 there was a catastrophic breakdown in the transmission of electricity in North America, affecting at least 50 million consumers and spanning an area as far west as the US automobile capital of Detroit, Michigan, as far north as Canada's largest city, Toronto, and as far east as the US financial centre of New York.[1] In late August and early September, several other incidents throughout the world involved interruptions in energy systems: power outages in the south of London, stranding hundreds of thousands of rail passengers; a terrorist attack on a vital Iraqi pipeline; attempts to kidnap Western oil executives in the South Caucasus region; and further guerrilla attacks on Colombia's power supply and delivery network. The lesson to be learned from these events is clear. At a minimum, the replication of debilitative events with an impact on critical energy system infrastructure (CESI) integrity in Europe is an established reality. At the other extreme, a repetition of similar events designed by sinister actors is at least a distinct possibility.

New integrated energy enterprises, power developers, regulated transmission and distribution companies, unregulated enterprises, municipal power authorities, oil and gas exploration and production companies, gas transmission companies, pipeline developers, local distribution companies, industry associations, investors, financial institutions and above all the 450 million people in an enlarged European Union (EU) of 25 states are all exposed to the primary or cascading effects of the debilitation or destruction of CESI. On the low-intensity, asymmetric side of the equation are low-probability but high-risk attacks, for example on congested transmission lines in densely populated areas, to cyber attacks on the information systems that regulate electric power and pipeline throughput. The only certainty regarding these threats from human factors is that they are changing in a way that could allow such attacks to be carried out without a high risk of detection or interdiction.

Javier Solana, the EU High Representative for Common Foreign and Security Policy, has pointed out that 'the European Union is, like it or not, a global

---

[1] On this event see, e.g., the Internet site of the Office of Electric Transmission and Distribution of the US Department of Energy at URL <http://www.electricity.doe.gov/2003_blackout.htm>.

actor; it should be ready to share in the responsibility for global security'.[2] A major disruption in the supply of vital natural resources, and the debilitation or destruction of CESI for the generation, refinement, storage, transport and distribution of these resources, would cause severe, cascading economic and human hardships for not only for the directly affected national infrastructures and populations but also for regional or even global security. Recent emphasis on the threats to energy supply and CESI have focused on up- and mid-stream infrastructures in the Gulf region, the Caspian Sea Basin and the South China Sea. However, attention must also be drawn to terrorist threats to mid- and downstream CESI in the European theatre. These hazards should be incorporated into the process of building comprehensive and transnational strategies for dealing with the security challenges of the 21st century.[3]

Observations made by Paul Ionescu, State Secretary of Romania, help to put in context several important considerations regarding threats to energy system infrastructure in an enlarged European theatre. With respect to conflict prevention and threat assessment, Ionescu made the following statement.

The twentieth century has left us with what some experts have called 'a symptom of conceptual uncertainties'. We must recognize that globalization has presented us with a new state of affairs which compels us to rethink our security strategies. Our core problem is that we knew well the world we left behind, but we are still unclear on how to manage the security of the world we are now entering. In a globalizing world it is not only prudent but necessary to try and identify the global consequences of threats, irrespective of their 'national' or 'local' character. We have already learned that transnational threats cannot be fought successfully with national means alone. In this regard, it is sufficient to remind ourselves of the tremendous change in the character of threats since the Cold War—from traditional to non-traditional, from national to transnational—and the required change in our manner of dealing with them. Accepting the changed nature of the terrain in which we operate, we must now concentrate our attention on the accurate and thorough identification of developing threats and emerging crises.[4]

II. Implications of the new European security framework

Several observations on the evolving new European security framework are worth particular consideration in the context of energy infrastructure.

1. An enlarged European Union implies increased responsibilities for the European Security and Defence Policy (ESDP), with a corresponding increase

---

[2] Javier Solana, EU High Representative for the Common Foreign and Security Policy, 'A secure Europe in a better world', European Council, Thessaloniki, 20 June 2003, URL <http://www. statewatch.org/news/2003/sep/solanasec.pdf>, p. 3.

[3] In this context the terms up-, mid- and downstream refer to the entire energy cycle, from exploration and extraction through transport, storage and distribution.

[4] Ionescu, P., 'Procedural interoperability', Paper presented at the NATO Advanced Research Workshop (ARW) on Future NATO Security: Addressing the Challenges of Evolving Security and Information Systems and Architectures, 8–10 Mar. 2003, Prague, Czech Republic (on the NATO ARWs see URL <http://152.152.96.1/science/calendar/2003/arw-srcs-2003.htm#Mar>).

in threats from non-traditional, transnational actors to CESI integrity in an enlarged European theatre.[5]

2. An enlarged European Union will worsen the already bleak state of EU dependence on the import of energy. On a national basis, European import dependence is an established fact: 9 out of 33 European countries are more than 95 per cent dependent on imports, and only 5 are either self-sufficient or net exporters.[6] Fossil fuels account for four-fifths of total EU energy consumption, and almost two-thirds of these fuels are imported. Natural gas from Russia alone represents 20 per cent of EU consumption and made up one-third of the EU's gas imports in 2000. By the EU's estimate, this figure is expected to double by 2020. The EU's own energy supply covers barely half of what it needs, and it is estimated that, in the absence of effective mitigating actions on the part of EU member states, European energy imports will be much higher in 30 years' time, amounting to 70 per cent of total consumption. Ninety per cent of oil is likely to be imported.

The associated vulnerabilities of a continuous EU energy flow, which depends directly on CESI integrity, have been addressed in a number of EU policies that rely heavily on demand management, the introduction of renewable energy-generating capacity, and the creation of an integrated, flexible internal market for power. However, EU hydrocarbon supplies must often transit numerous highly volatile regions with individuals, cells, groups and movements that constitute threats of a non-traditional nature. These regions are external to and still largely beyond the reach of the EU itself. The Azerbaijan–Georgia–Turkey (AGT) corridor[7] for the delivery of both oil and gas from the Caspian Sea to Ceyhan, Turkey, is but one in a long list of ongoing energy supply development projects that could provide additional hydrocarbon supply for Europe. Yet the political risk profile of the states involved is largely high, given their historic legacy of internal separatist and terrorist movements.

Enhancing energy supply and the networks that deliver it is but one aspect of an overall CESI protection plan. In short, a Common Security and Defence Policy for the EU should comprehensively assess and develop response mechanisms to these fluid, external physical threats to CESI integrity and not rely simply on 'market mechanisms' to provide a comprehensive matrix of solutions to CESI protection, debilitation or destruction.

3. Globalization itself presents extreme challenges for CESI integrity, particularly for new EU member states in economic transition. The CESI in many of these states dates largely from the Soviet era, with a poor level of safety and monitoring equipment, coupled with an often complete lack of comprehensive planning, control and response policies on the part of CESI transition partners against attacks on CESI from 'rogue', human-incited causal factors. Global-

[5] See also chapter 7 in this volume.

[6] Stern, J., *Security of European Natural Gas Supplies: The Impact of Import Dependence and Liberalization* (Royal Institute of International Affairs: London, July 2002), available at URL <http://www.riia.org/pdf/research/sdp/Sec_of_Euro_Gas_Jul02.pdf>.

[7] See 'Azerbaijan, Georgia, Turkey Pipelines Project: Azerbaijan section, International Fact Finding Mission: Preliminary Report', Sep. 2002, URL <http://www.bicusa.org/eca/AzerbaijanFFMreport.htm>.

ization, and the competition policies it promotes, is partly responsible for this situation because it prioritizes debt reduction and high asset valuations (against the backdrop of the privatization of public utilities), both of which could be put at risk if the need for investment in safety and security technologies was recognized and met.

4. To the extent that threats to CESI emanate from non-traditional, non-state actors, why is there no comprehensive database which could serve to model, track and assess the impacts, both in human and non-human terms, of known or potential attacks on CESI, for which information could be drawn from global, open sources?[8]

5. To the extent that European CESI is an interdependent, transnational network of power grids, pipeline networks, and distribution routes and facilities, it is by definition beyond the protective capacity of any single national security, defence, regulatory or coordinating institution to oversee and control. Hence, methodologies, vulnerability assessment criteria and counter-terrorism measures should be driven by international collaboration reflecting the transnational character of CESI.

Before taking steps to assess the threats to CESI and develop counter-terrorism strategies for its protection, an inclusive definition of what CESI constitutes is required. CESI could be defined as encompassing the entire cycle, from energy production to consumption. While energy supply is a critical element of CESI, it is but one element in a much broader system. A RAND Corporation paper defined critical infrastructure (CI) as 'transportation and energy systems, defense installations, banking and financial assets, water supplies, chemical plants, food and agricultural resources, police and fire departments, hospitals and public health systems, government systems'.[9] However, this is no more than a list of hard- and soft-target assets, and it does not prioritize them. CESI could also be defined as the 'core value' on which all other CI assets largely depend, regardless of any given national CESI configuration. It is both gratifying and paradoxical that much national and international research, planning and emergency response work has been carried out on critical information infrastructure protection (CIIP),[10] while the main determinant for continuous operation of critical information infrastructure systems (excluding cyber terrorism) is continuous energy flow—a core CESI value.

[8] For a proposal for such a database see chapter 2 in this volume.

[9] Don, B. and Mussington, D., 'Protecting critical infrastructure', *RAND Review*, vol. 26, no. 2 (summer 2002), available at URL <http://www.rand.org/publications/randreview/issues/rr.08.02/infrastructure.html>.

[10] See, e.g., Wenger, A., Metzger, J. and Dunn, M. (eds), *International CIIP Handbook: An Inventory of Protection Policies in Eight Countries* (Swiss Federal Institute of Technology, Center for Security Studies: Zurich, 2002), available at URL <http://www.isn.ethz.ch/onlinepubli/publihouse/misc/ciip>.

III. Developing CESI protection models and strategies

Many of the country-specific efforts to analyse and evaluate various aspects of CIIP, and the methods developed for CIIP vulnerability assessment, are extremely valuable for considering evaluative, vulnerability and prevention/protection strategies for CESI. One pragmatic first step towards developing transnational CESI protection models and strategies might thus be to launch an effort, based on the exemplary collaboration of the Swiss Federal Institute of Technology and the Swedish Emergency Management Agency, for CIIP evaluation and analysis. The desired output in this case would be a series of national studies on CESI protection, and threat assessment measures that would lead to the elaboration of a better understanding of the entire issue. Policy planners could begin by identifying high-risk critical energy infrastructure assets on a national basis. National energy resources (from natural endowments), the types of generating facilities, and resource import dependencies will obviously vary from country to country, but the overall objective of establishing a baseline for a better understanding of CESI issues on a nation-by-nation basis should hold good.

A second step would be to detail the interdependencies of national CESI assets on a transnational basis. This data-gathering activity would allow individual states, regions and the EU as a whole to assess CESI along the up-, mid- and downstream supply continuum referred to above. These two steps would then form the bedrock for further steps in overall CESI protection in an effort to deny 'rogue', non-state actors the ability to generate crises in CESI networks.

Even when extensive analyses of transnational interdependencies of CESI are undertaken, there may be financial or even geographic barriers to the effective introduction of sufficient redundancy systems for energy supply and delivery. One example is drawn from the Central European Pipeline System (CEPS) managed by the Central Europe Pipeline Management Agency (CEPMA) of the North Atlantic Treaty Organization (NATO).[11] CEPS is a vintage cold-war energy supply and distribution system which begins approximately 100 kilometres east of Munich, running south along the Mediterranean coast, north as far as Hamburg, and west to Rotterdam, Le Havre and Dunkerque. It is a comprehensive, 10 000-km system on which both military and civilian aircraft and their respective airports depend for jet fuel delivery. The Brussels National and Luxembourg airports, for example, depend on CEPS for 100 per cent of jet fuel deliveries. The Frankfurt International Airport, a key hub for both military and civilian aviation, depends on this system for 50 per cent of its jet fuel. However, despite extensive scenario building and contingency planning, including redundancy systems for fuel deliveries by

---

[11] On the CEPS and the CEPMA see, e.g., NATO, *NATO Logistics Handbook,* Oct. 1997, chapter 15, 'Fuels, oils, lubricants and petroleum handling equipment', URL <http://www.nato.int/docu/logien/1997/lo-1506.htm>.

pipeline, land-based transport and barge along the Rhine River, incidents have occurred which highlight the vulnerabilities in this system. During the extensive heat wave in the summer of 2003, fuel barge deliveries were severely hampered on the Rhine owing to the reduction of the river's depth. Further vulnerabilities or challenges are created by NATO enlargement. For example, the Czech Republic, which like most other Central and East European states has a well-founded historic aversion to increasing its fuel dependency on Russia, is not yet connected to the CEPS grid. Extending the CEPS network to supply the Czech Republic's needs is at the present time considered financially untenable.

In general, the defining task for CESI protection in the legitimate economy is to develop and refine a comprehensive strategy for anticipating and pre-empting, intervening and reacting, and ultimately for ensuring prompt recovery after interruptions to supply and delivery.

A rigorous planning system must: (*a*) catalogue and define high-risk CESI; (*b*) analyse the costs and effects of proposed solutions; (*c*) construct pragmatic modalities for prevention and response mechanisms, particularly on a transnational basis; (*d*) adapt solutions and investments as necessary, based on peer dialogue; and (*e*) identify best practices related to CESI that have already been implemented in Europe and elsewhere.

The formulation and implementation of a strategy must be long-term in vision and holistic in approach. Cooperation with organizations focused on energy transport security, such as GUUAM (Georgia–Ukraine–Uzbekistan–Azerbaijan–Moldova)[12] and the Shanghai Cooperation Organization (SCO),[13] while positive, is insufficient. The key to success in protecting CESI is the development of a continuous planning system (CPS) that will remain relevant in the face of constantly changing circumstances. Benign cooperation must be augmented with active, constant collaboration against new threats. The use of computational techniques and models for the process of prioritizing infrastructure vulnerabilities can improve resource allocation and enable better analysis of interdependencies among critical systems.

A second strand for formulating strategies for the protection of CESI should include an analysis of the activities undertaken by those states outside the European community to protect their energy assets. An assessment of the security measures taken by a number of states in the Persian Gulf region may point to energy transport and distribution protection strategies that have not been properly considered by other nations.

CESI is a fundamental building block of all modern societies because its assets, systems and functions are vital to national security. By definition, all CESI faces some level of risk, but the question must be asked: What risks are

[12] See the GUUAM Internet site at URL <http://www.guuam.org>.
[13] On the SCO see, e.g., the Internet site of the Ministry for Foreign Affairs of Kazakhstan at URL <http://missions.itu.int/~kazaks/eng/sco/sco01.htm>; and Bailes, A. J. K. *et al.*, *Armament and Disarmament in the Caucasus and Central Asia*, SIPRI Policy Paper no. 3 (SIPRI: Stockholm, July 2003), especially chapter 4, available at URL <http://editors.sipri.se/recpubs.html>.

unacceptable, and to whom? The answer must be based on a variety of assessment criteria.

However, physical asset protection is but one aspect of a comprehensive CESI plan. In a sense, just as the revolution in information technology has transformed global markets and those who control these markets—financial intermediaries which evaluate, administer and execute currency trade, commodity purchases, and financial asset management over loan and portfolio investment—so, too, has control over energy protection been ceded to cyberspace. Advanced, post-industrial societies and economies are critically dependent on the linked computer information and communication systems which serve as the foundation for economic activities in all modern, market-based economies. Control over these networks is far from secure, however. Cyber-attack strategies directed against CESI can be a highly effective 'asymmetrical' technique for small states and non-state actors, not least because of the relatively modest cost of waging cyber war.[14]

IV. Conclusions

The potential weaknesses in CESI in Europe and the problems of its protection are numerous and complex. These problems are vastly greater than the existing architectures for ensuring the continuous flow of energy to states in this region. A number of recommendations are therefore proposed below.

A small combined joint task force of technical, scientific, economic and political officers, perhaps within the framework of the EU–NATO dialogue process or within a broader framework incorporating the Organization for Security and Co-operation in Europe, the EU, NATO and the research community, should work to: (a) collaborate with European states, allies and partners in cataloguing high-priority CESI; (b) identify critical weaknesses leading to system vulnerabilities and suggest best practices for protecting CESI based on peer-to-peer dialogue; (c) focus on the downstream impact of breaches in energy supply and of CESI debilitation and disruption on critical defence, industrial and financial infrastructures; (d) measure the economic and human costs of CESI debilitation and destruction; (e) estimate the time required for real-life CESI recovery; and (f) launch a continuous planning system based on active collaboration with EU member states and with NATO members, partners and allies.

---

[14] Shimeall, T., Williams, P. and Dunlevy, C., 'Countering cyber war', *NATO Review*, vol. 49, no. 4 (winter 2001), pp. 16–18, available at URL <http://www.nato.int/docu/review/2001/0104-04.htm>.

Part V

The economic consequences of terrorism: can we afford to be safe?

Editors' remarks

In economic terms, security is not a fixed quantity but a trade-off. It can never be absolute, and when efforts are made to approach absolute security the costs—both direct and indirect—are liable to grow exponentially. The price for security measures taken by the state or by intergovernmental organs will eventually be paid either by the taxpayer, or in the form of enlarged fiscal deficits. For measures taken by the private sector, the costs will eventually be passed on to the consumer through prices. There are, however, often also indirect costs and impediments to wealth-creating economic activity inherent in the attempt to defend that same activity against attack or exploitation by hostile elements. Many of the ways to trace and block terrorists and criminals involve tighter controls on the movement of people and goods. Pre-emptive actions against such foes, as well as the actions taken by them, can create conflicts which disrupt normal economic intercourse. Such actions also divert resources from the civilian economy to the security sector, with uncertain implications for overall growth prospects. Last but not least, security strategies developed without economic advice may compromise the free play of competition and comparative advantage on which the efficiency of the global market depends.

Patrick Lenain's chapter surveys the costs both of terrorist outrages, and of actions taken since 11 September 2001 to counter them. Somewhat counter-intuitively, he concludes that the (negative) impact of these factors both on the private sector's balance sheet and on the US budget and trade deficit in the past two years has been relatively slight. As he also points out, however, these are proportional judgements reflecting the fact that other, more or less 'untypical' factors were at work at the time. It is too early for conclusions about the economic rationality (and longer-term sustainability) of the policy choices made after September 2001 by the USA and the free-market community in general. Business and consumer confidence has been an important factor and may, overall, have proved unusually robust during this period. New terrorist attacks, or new Western interventions, could still change the picture.

The issue which gives clearest cause for unease is that of insurance. The viability of the existing world insurance system is under threat from terrorism and from its knock-on effects on economic activity, but also from several other quarters. Climate change is increasing the frequency of costly natural calamities. Numerous other risk factors are making a growing number of countries and regions 'unsafe for business' to some degree.* The insurance sector is already signalling that another major disaster could push it to the point of collapse, unless governments help by (as Lenain puts it) becoming 'insurers of last resort'. If they do this, however, it will raise questions both about reintroducing state ownership through the back door, and about their own ability to cope. Deciding which government should reinsure a multinational company (say, an energy provider) will not be as simple as it has been since 2001 in the case of (still largely national) airlines. This whole issue needs more serious international attention, also from security experts, than it has received up to now.

---

* Control Risks Group (CRG), *RiskMap 2004* (Control Risks Group: London, 2003). See URL <http://www.crg.com>.

19. The economic consequences of terrorism

Patrick Lenain

I. Introduction: the shock of the new

The most shocking aspect of the 11 September 2001 terrorist attacks in the United States was the tragic loss of lives. The attacks also, however, caused serious economic disruption: financial markets did not operate for some days; a large part of southern Manhattan, where Wall Street stock exchanges and major investment banks are located, was destroyed; and communication links were inoperative. All US airport commercial flight operations were halted, and border crossings and ports were subject to intense scrutiny. In October, letters filled with concentrated anthrax spores were mailed to US news media and politicians, causing postal mail to be disrupted in a large part of the country. For the first time, terrorist events hampered the free movement of persons, merchandise, mail and money in the United States. Although these disruptions were temporary, they heralded a new era in which the protection of people and property from terrorist attacks could no longer be taken for granted anywhere. The US homeland was no longer considered a sanctuary, and the United States' economic recovery, eagerly awaited after a period of recession, was considered to be in jeopardy.

Large firms already knew that the safety of properties, employees and merchandise could not be taken for granted. In fact, since the early 1980s private-sector spending on security in the USA had quintupled and the number of security companies had grown almost fourfold. Companies realized that they had to protect themselves against theft, fraud, crime, hackers and eavesdropping. They had established security departments for this purpose, but they did not believe that they would be the targets of devastating terrorist attacks, nor that the smooth flow of industrial inputs and outputs on which they relied could be disrupted. They were not expecting their supply chains, now based on deliveries with extremely narrow time margins, to be interrupted. Cross-border operations, for example companies with plants in both Canada and the USA linked by fast transportation lines, no longer felt like a safe bet.

This chapter examines the consequences of terrorist threats for the functioning of modern economies and how economic agents—investors, consumers, companies and markets—reacted to the new threat. Was there a 'flight to safety' in the business community? Have companies spent more money to protect their premises and employees? Has insecurity inhibited risk-taking behaviour, an indispensable component of economic growth in market-based economies? Have measures enacted to tighten security been economically harmful? Section II discusses the economic consequences of the attacks and section III the business sector's own reaction to the elevated security threat. The specific problems in the insurance sector are addressed in section IV, and section V discusses the economic consequences of government measures for secure cross-border transfers of merchandise. Section VI examines the consequences of the rise in budgetary spending on homeland security and military operations that followed the al-Qaeda attacks. Section VII presents the conclusions.

II. A less safe world

Terrorists had struck at North American and European interests before 11 September 2001. The United States itself had been attacked on its own soil: in 1993, when a large bomb was detonated in an underground car park of the New York World Trade Center, killing six people and injuring more than 1000; and in 1995, when the Murrah Federal Building was bombed in downtown Oklahoma City, killing over 160 persons. However, at the time these were seen as non-recurring events (in the first case caused by Islamic fundamentalists with broadly anti-US motives and in the second by anti-government extremists). There were many incidents in Europe but, again, for the most part with identifiable and nation-specific causes. For example, the United Kingdom suffered casualties from bombings linked to the Irish Republican Army (IRA), such as the explosion in the centre of Manchester in 1996 which injured over 200 people. In the latter half of the 1990s France was hit by a wave of bombings and an Air France aircraft hijacking linked to civilian unrest in Algeria, and Spain suffered from a series of incidents related to the situation in the Basque region. In the 1980s several passenger aircraft were attacked, most notably the bombings of flight PanAm 103 over Lockerbie in 1988 and of flight UTA 772 over Chad in 1989.

The terrorist acts of September 2001 were of another dimension. They were carried out by terrorists who were determined, organized, well funded and ready to give their lives for their ideals. They not only inflicted heavy losses but also succeeded in causing widespread fear. The attacks generated a dramatic rise in the general feeling of insecurity: people felt that the environment of relative safety that had previously been taken for granted was no longer guaranteed.

The economic consequences of this sudden rise in fear and uncertainty quickly became clear.[1] Indicators of business and consumer confidence plunged. US consumer and business surveys showed a drop in overall levels of confidence. Economic forecasters projected that investment and consumer spending would be hit hard and downgraded their projections for growth. The

---

[1] See also Lenain, P., Bonturi, M. and Koen, V., *The Economic Consequences of Terrorism,* Economics Department Working Paper no. 334 (Organisation for Economic Co-operation and Development (OECD), Economics Department: Paris, 17 July 2002). This chapter is based largely on this document, as updated in 2003. The OECD Working Papers are available at URL <http://www.oecd.org/eco>.

hope that the US economy would rebound from its recession faded away. Equity prices tumbled. Financial markets trembled worldwide. The gap between corporate and government bond yields widened, as did those between emerging market and US bond index yields. Several business sectors were particularly hard hit. The insurance industry (particularly the reinsurance industry) faced the largest reimbursement claims ever submitted, with additional claims still subject to litigation.[2] The airline industry in the USA and elsewhere suffered because passengers no longer felt that air travel was safe. Aircraft manufacturers almost immediately saw their orders curtailed. Spending on tourism fell sharply, affecting hotel chains and cruise operators. For the first time, a terrorist attack was forecast to have major consequences not only for security and political stability but also for the economy in virtually every region of the world.

Re-establishing confidence was important for promoting economic recovery. Confidence is a key factor in market-based economies because without it firms do not invest, employers do not create jobs and banks do not lend. Aggregate demand shrinks, with the risk of dragging the economy into recession. Positive expectations are essential for output growth and employment creation. Governments therefore acted quickly after the September 2001 attacks in an attempt to dissipate the feeling of uncertainty before it affected the economy. In order to strike at the sources of the terrorist threat, President George W. Bush declared the aggression to be an act of war and in early October 2001 military action commenced in Afghanistan, the country harbouring the al-Qaeda terrorist network which was responsible for the attacks. This was presented as the first phase of a broader and possibly protracted war against global terrorism.

In addition to military action, the US crisis management policy also encompassed economic policy. The US Federal Reserve indicated that it stood ready to inject virtually unlimited amounts of liquidity to avoid payment failures and cascading defaults. It made a series of aggressive cuts in interest rates: the federal funds target rate (FFTR) was cut by 50 base points, and over the subsequent weeks by another 125 base points. On 14 September 2001, the US Congress cleared a $40 billion supplementary appropriation for an emergency spending package. At least half of the money was to be used for relief related to the destruction in Manhattan, at the Pentagon and in Pennsylvania. Ten billion dollars were available immediately for emergency rescue and rebuilding efforts; for tightening security at airports and other transportation centres and in public buildings; for investigating and prosecuting those involved in planning and executing the attacks; and for enhancing national security. The Department of Homeland Security (DHS) was established on 1 January 2003 to coordinate the government's efforts against terrorism.[3]

---

[2] On the insurance problem see section IV.

[3] On the US Department of Homeland Security see URL <http://www.dhs.gov/dhspublic>.

The enhancement of security is costly. Government spending on homeland security and military operations requires budgetary appropriations that have to be financed either by borrowing or by increasing taxes. Similarly, private corporations' security departments represent a business cost, in terms of staff resources, external services and equipment. There are also less visible costs resulting from border security requirements. Bringing merchandise across borders involves complying with a number of formalities required by customs officials which are costly and cause delays. Faced with less predictable supply chains, companies need to hold larger inventories of inputs and therefore carry additional costs. Rising insurance premiums represent another additional cost, reflecting a revaluation of risks as well as a need for insurance companies to replenish their reserves. All of these additional security costs have the potential to diminish returns on investment, lower productivity, reduce capital formation and undermine economic growth.

While the quest for enhanced security was a rational reaction to the destruction caused by terrorism, the question must be asked: Has the effort to increase security gone too far and put economic prosperity at risk?

III. Is the private sector spending more on security?

After the September 2001 attacks in the United States, it was expected that the security departments of private corporations would be strengthened and the 'security economy' would be boosted. Only limited data are available on recent developments. A 1999 study estimated that the USA spends about $40 billion annually on private security.[4] Nearly half of total spending on security by the private sector is composed of a single category—security guards and other protective service employees. The rest is on items such as alarm systems, computer security, locks, safes, fencing, surveillance cameras, safety lighting and guard dogs. The total amount is considerable: it is comparable to what the US Government spends on the federal, state and local police (excluding the armed forces).

The anticipated increase in corporate security was also expected to increase the US labour force. Companies were expected to hire more security guards and contract new security services, but it was also feared that this additional labour force would reduce the level of labour productivity. Like spending on the reduction of pollution, private efforts to enhance security may improve welfare but do not produce output in the sense in which it is traditionally measured. Other security measures, such as extra controls at airports and borders, were also seen as lowering productivity because, for instance, they would require business travellers to spend more time going through airport security controls.

---

[4] Anderson, D., 'The aggregate burden of crime', *Journal of Law and Economics*, vol. 42, no. 2 (1999).

The medium-term impact of a sharp increase in private security spending was generally gauged to be small. A study prepared by the US Council of Economic Advisers estimated that a doubling of private security spending would reduce the level of potential output by 0.6 per cent after five years.[5] A more recent study suggests that a doubling of private sector security spending and additional airport delays would reduce labour productivity by 1.12 per cent and multi-factor productivity by 0.63 per cent.[6] Seen against the strong rise in labour productivity currently observed in the United States, however, these are small impacts.

So far, the private sector does not appear to have increased its spending on security as a result of the al-Qaeda attacks. A recent survey of 331 large companies by the Conference Board found that spending on security had increased by only 4 per cent since 2001, and that most of this increase was in the form of higher insurance premiums.[7] The passive reaction of the US corporate sector to the increased risk of terrorism seems confirmed by the stability of employment in security-related jobs. The US Department of Labor even reports a small decline in the number of private security guards in 2002 over the previous year, to slightly fewer than 1 million.[8] If these trends are confirmed, this would suggest that the corporate sector has resisted making large increases in security-related spending—perhaps by reorienting the priorities of existing programmes. This may leave private companies vulnerable to costly disasters, especially if, as discussed below, their insurance coverage against terrorist risk has shrunk. On the other hand, this may also imply that even the small deterioration of labour productivity which had been expected to result from the hiring of security personnel and the enforcement of greater controls in private premises will now not become a reality.

IV. The insurance problem

The insurance sector was directly affected by the attacks on the New York World Trade Center. Insurance claims for damages and losses resulting from the attacks in various classes of business (e.g., liability and workers' compensation) are currently estimated at $40 billion.[9] As noted above, the precise amount is subject to a high degree of uncertainty because litigations are still pending; the process of assessing claims may well extend beyond 2004 (especially for aviation). The attacks represented the largest insurance event in

[5] US Council of Economic Advisers, *Economic Report of the President* (US Government Printing Office: Washington, DC, 2002).

[6] Hobijn, B., 'What will homeland security cost?', *Economic Policy Review* (Federal Reserve Bank of New York), vol. 8, no. 2 (Nov. 2002).

[7] Armstrong Whiting, M. and Cavanagh, T. E., *Corporate Security Management: Organization and Spending Since 9/11*, Conference Board Research Report no. R-133-03-RR (Conference Board: New York, July 2003).

[8] See the 2002 National Occupational Employment and Wage Estimates, available on the Internet site of the US Department of Labor at URL <http://www.bls.gov>.

[9] Swiss Re, 'Reinsurance: a systemic risk?', *Sigma*, no. 5 (2003), URL <http:www.swissre.com/sigma>.

recent history, dwarfing the $21 billion in losses incurred when Hurricane Andrew hit Florida in 1992. In terms of non-life insurance premiums, only the San Francisco earthquake of 1906 was more damaging.[10] In spite of the magnitude of these payments, no major bankruptcies have occurred in the industry, in part because the risk was spread over a number of companies and countries. It is estimated that reinsurers, most of them European, incurred over half the losses.[11] The capital base of many insurance and reinsurance companies has been severely hit because the shock came on top of a series of other recent disasters (including a number of major storms) and portfolio losses associated with stock market declines.

Following the attacks in 2001, primary insurers and reinsurers raised their premiums and curtailed or dropped altogether coverage for terrorism-related risk. The rises in insurance premiums have hit several industries. Aviation has been hit the hardest, but other sectors—including transport, construction, tourism and energy generation—have also been affected. Overall, reinsurance rates are estimated to have increased globally by about 85 per cent between 2000 and 2003.[12] The rapid increase in premiums of 2001–2002, however, slowed down considerably in 2003.

An important channel through which the insurance sector can affect the economy is the reduction in coverage. After the attacks, insurers and reinsurers adopted the approach of generally excluding terrorism losses from coverage for major risks. Insurers offered clients a limited re-inclusion of such losses in the coverage against payment of an additional premium. The reduction in risk coverage was in large part the result of the difficulties which insurance firms had in putting a price on large-scale terrorist attacks: it required reducing exposure and making it controllable. Aviation insurers, for instance, cancelled coverage for war hazards in October 2001 and granted new third-party liability coverage with an upper limit of $50 million per year. This limit prevented airlines from flying because, by doing so with insufficient coverage, they would have contravened leasing and other agreements as well as government regulations.

In response, the US Government decided to provide insurance coverage for a limited period. In November 2002, as provided for in the Homeland Security Act,[13] the government addressed the insurance needs of the US domestic airline industry that were not met by the commercial insurance market. Air carriers were offered third-party war risk liability insurance coverage beyond $50 million per occurrence and expanded war risk coverage for aircraft hulls, passengers, crew and property liability. Thus government became an insurer of last resort for the aviation industry.

---

[10] The losses from the 11 Sep. 2001 attacks account for c. 11% of US non-life net premiums; the San Francisco earthquake came to 35% of US primary insurance premiums at the time. Swiss Re (note 9).

[11] See Jenkins, P., 'Munich Re warns of losses', *Financial Times*, 26 Nov. 2003.

[12] See *The World Catastrophe Reinsurance Market: 2003*, Guy Carpenter Special Report, Sep. 2003, at URL <http://www.guycarpenter.com/portal/extranet/publications/white/whitep.html?vid=57>.

[13] See section 1202 (Extension of insurance policies) of the Homeland Security Act of 2002, available at URL <http://www.dhs.gov/interweb/assetlibrary/hr_5005_enr.pdf>.

Similarly, the US Government set up a special programme to cover the terrorist peril, with the passage of the Terrorism Risk Insurance Act (TRIA) in November 2002.[14] The programme pre-empts and nullifies most pre-existing terrorism exclusions. It is triggered when an event meets the definition of an act of terrorism committed on behalf of a foreign person or interest. The act requires mandatory participation in the programme and the provision of terrorism coverage by all insurers providing commercial property and casualty insurance. The act provides only a short-term solution, however, because it will terminate on 31 December 2005. Each participating insurance company will be responsible for paying out a certain amount in claims—known as a 'deductible'—before federal assistance becomes available. For losses above a company's deductible, the federal government will cover 90 per cent, while the company will contribute 10 per cent. Losses covered by the programme will be capped at $100 billion. Above this amount, the US Congress is to determine the procedures for and the sources of any payments.

Government-sponsored schemes to help maintain coverage against terrorism risk were also introduced in other countries. For instance, in Germany the Extremus AG scheme offers terrorism coverage for properties and business interruption policies up to €25 million, and the French GAREAT insurance pool provides similar coverage.[15]

V. Tighter border controls and their costs

The costs of running corporate security departments and paying insurance premiums are two economic consequences of terrorism. In addition, the business sector is also indirectly affected by government measures aimed at better control of the flow of persons and merchandise, notably at border crossings.

In the days following the 11 September 2001 attacks, the US authorities undertook to monitor border crossings more carefully. Both passengers and merchandise were subject to heightened control procedures. This caused temporary but severe disruptions to the transportation systems. The most severe bottlenecks occurred at the US–Canadian land border, where on average half a million vehicles and $1.4 billion in bilateral trade cross each day. Although the exceptional security measures were gradually lifted, US borders were still considered to be porous and the USA consequently vulnerable to further terrorist attacks. Permanent, tighter screening procedures were deemed necessary. Maritime transport was seen as particularly important because 20 million cargo containers enter US ports every year with very little or no screening. On average, customs officers inspect only 2 per cent of incoming containers.

---

[14] For the TRIA, 27 Nov. 2002, see URL <http://www.ustreas.gov/offices/domestic-finance/financial-institution/terrorism-insurance>.

[15] On Extremus Versicherungs-AG see URL <http://www.extremus-online.de> (in German); and on GAREAT see Raoul, B., 'The French GAREAT—first post-WTC terrorism insurance pool', *Exposure*, no. 10 (Jan. 2003), p. 4, URL <http://www.ercgroup.com/gpc/resource_center/exposure/archive/no_10/expo10_e.pdf>.

Box 19.1. New cargo inspection procedures

The *Container Security Initiative* (CSI) involves inspection in foreign ports of containers destined for the United States. US customs officers posted overseas inspect containers before they are loaded on to ships. Agreements have been signed with authorities responsible for 20 large ports that account for two-thirds of the volume of containers shipped to the USA. This involves improved procedures and technology, requiring significant capital investment in ports, ships and containers. Cargo originating in one of these ports is able to go through more expeditious custom procedures when entering the USA, effectively creating an 'express lane' for shipping.

The *Custom–Trade Partnership Against Terrorism* (C-TPAT) is a voluntary supply-chain security programme requiring certification from the customs administration. Under this programme, businesses must conduct comprehensive self-assessments of their supply chain using the security guidelines developed jointly with the Customs Service, and they must familiarize companies in their supply chain with the guidelines and the programme. These businesses must provide to the authorities specific relevant information about their trucks, drivers, cargo, suppliers and routes. As C-TPAT members, companies may become eligible for expedited processing and reduced inspections. Companies that do not participate face various consequences such as stricter scrutiny of cargo, increased audits and examinations, and requests for information, and they have no guarantees for cargo processing time.

Finally, a *24-hour notification requirement* was introduced in December 2002. Shippers are required to submit a detailed cargo declaration 24 hours before cargo is loaded aboard a vessel in a foreign port. Given the processing time involved, this means that carriers typically have to impose cargo cut-off time, ranging from 72 to 96 hours. Carriers also impose surcharges to cover the cost of preparing manifests.

Observers feared that containers could easily be used to carry weapons of mass destruction (WMD) into the United States.

Several border agencies were merged to form a new body, with 40 000 employees, in charge of overseeing border crossings—Customs and Border Protection, or CBP—within the DHS.[16] The department is responsible for all issues related to border crossings of passengers and merchandise, from arresting terrorists and searching for WMD to collecting import duties. The department has put in place a number of new procedures aimed at tightening the inspection of cargo imported into the United States while at the same time facilitating trade (see box 19.1).

It was feared at the time that all these new security measures, although necessary to secure borders, would significantly increase shipping costs and thus hurt international trade. The declining trend in international transportation costs has been a key driving force behind the process of globalization, contributing to the increase in productivity levels and potential output. Reversing the trend towards more affordable transportation costs, and tightening border

---

[16] See URL <http://www.customs.ustreas.gov/xp/cgov/toolbox/about/mission/cbp.xml>.

crossings indiscriminately, would risk scaling back openness and could have a long-lasting negative impact on growth for both the member states of the Organisation for Economic Co-operation and Development (OECD) and the non-member economies. Quantitative studies of international trade have indeed shown that imports and exports are highly sensitive to transportation costs and that permanently higher costs could affect future trade decisions.

The available evidence suggests, however, that the additional costs of these measures are currently limited. A microeconomic study of the Port of Seattle suggests that these costs are relatively small.[17] If this is extended to the entire USA, the results of the study imply an increase in shipping costs of only $2 billion, equivalent to 0.2 per cent of the value of non-energy imports of goods. Similarly, US balance-of-payments statistics show that the cost of freight and port services increased from 3.37 per cent of imports in 2001 to only 3.54 per cent in the first half of 2003.[18] Indirect costs may also be involved, including the impact of having to retain merchandise in ports, which entails carrying costs. However, the available evidence does not suggest that these costs will have long-term detrimental effects on international trade.

Immediately after 11 September 2001, a trade-off between security and efficiency of border crossings was anticipated. In the event, this trade-off seems to have been resolved without major consequences. New security measures have been formulated in a way that does not unduly diminish the efficiency of merchandise border crossings. International cooperation and partnership between the public and private sectors seem to have helped to make security measures more efficient, while reducing their potentially negative impact on trade flows.

VI. The impact of growing security and military spending: has the 'peace dividend' been reversed?[19]

Although private-sector spending on security does not appear to have risen sharply, governments have significantly increased their security and defence budgets, especially in the United States. Immediately after the attacks, the US Administration and (to a lesser extent) other OECD governments increased public spending for reconstruction and to strengthen domestic security and combat terrorism. These additional appropriations resulted in a sharp increase in general government spending in the fourth quarter of 2001, which helped support aggregate demand and avoid a decline in domestic output. Such a tem-

---

[17] Babione, R. et al., 'Post 9/11 security cost impact on port of Seattle import/export container traffic', Paper presented in the Global Trade, Transportation and Logistics Studies programme of the University of Washington: Seattle, Wash., 4 June 2003, URL <http://depts.washington.edu/gttl/SecurityCost ImpactonPortofSeattle.pdf>.

[18] These figures are calculated on the basis of data on the US balance of payments from the US Bureau of Econoomic Analysis, available at URL <http://www.bea.gov>.

[19] For figures on US military spending see also Sköns, E. et al., 'Military expenditure', SIPRI Yearbook 2003: Armaments, Disarmament and International Security (Oxford University Press: Oxford, 2003), especially pp. 307–12.

Table 19.1. US Government spending on national defence, fiscal years 2000–2003

Figures are in US$ billion.

Fiscal year	Expenditure
2000	295
2001	306
2002	349
2003 (estimate)	376
Change 2000 to 2003	
Defence spending	+ 81
Overall fiscal balance	– 486

Source: US Executive Office of the President, Office of Management and Budget, *Historical Tables: Budget of the United States Government Fiscal Year 2004* (US Government Printing Office: Washington, DC, 2003).

porary increase is not unusual after large catastrophes or natural disasters, such as the 1995 Kobe earthquake in Japan or the windstorms that struck part of Europe in December 1999.

The US President requested from Congress several expansions of security-related programmes in the context of successive budgets. The Department of Homeland Security was created by merging a number of existing agencies—such as the Federal Emergency Management Agency (FEMA), the Customs Administration, the Coast Guard and the Secret Service—and by increasing its overall budget. The president's fiscal year (FY) 2003 budget request included $38 billion to boost homeland security activities, up from $29 billion in FY 2002 and from $17 billion in 2001.[20]

The aim of annual expenditure on homeland security is to improve the preparedness of 'first responders' (firefighters, police and rescue workers), to enhance defences against biological attacks, to secure borders and improve information sharing.

Because the DHS was created by a merger of existing agencies, its current spending can be compared with the aggregate spending of its predecessors in order to gauge the increase in overall homeland security spending. With the recent additional appropriations, the DHS disposes of budgetary authority equivalent to about 0.35 per cent of gross domestic product (GDP). While this represents a large increase, the additional budget authority represents only a quarter of a percentage point of US GDP, a very small amount in comparison with the sharp deterioration in US public finances during the period 2000–2003.

---

[20] See Office of Homeland Security, *National Strategy for Homeland Security*, July 2002, p. 64, URL <http://www.whitehouse.gov/homeland/book/nat_strat_hls.pdf>. These figures include supplemental funding.

By contrast, US Department of Defense expenditure has increased considerably since the attacks of 11 September 2001. Defence spending increased from about $300 billion before the terrorist attacks to an estimated $376 billion in FY 2003 (see table 19.1). A large part of this increase was for the military operations in Afghanistan and Iraq as part of the campaign against terrorism. At constant prices, military spending increased by some 28 per cent between mid-2001 and mid-2003, bringing it back to levels recorded at the end of the cold war. The costs of replenishing weapon stocks and the cost of transporting soldiers and their equipment to battlefields have been rising particularly fast.

Measured as a share of GDP, however, the increase is less considerable. Data suggest that military spending increased from about 3.1 per cent of GDP before the terrorist attacks to about 4 per cent of GDP at the time of the war in Iraq in 2003. While the US federal budget balance has moved from a comfortable surplus to a sizeable deficit over the same period, this is not mainly due to defence spending. Other factors that caused the fiscal deterioration include the tax cuts proposed by the US Administration, the cyclical downturn and the evaporation of exceptional tax revenue during the stock-market 'bubble' (such as taxation of capital gains and stock options).

While defence spending is currently substantial in the United States, it is still below levels recorded during the cold war when measured in terms of GDP. During the 1970s and 1980s defence spending fluctuated between 5 and 6 per cent of GDP—well above the 2003 level of some 4 per cent of GDP. This apparent inconsistency between the sharp increase in constant prices and the relative stability in relation to GDP is explained by the considerable expansion of the US economy since the end of the cold war: real GDP increased by 47 per cent, providing the USA with ample economic power and budgetary resources, and allowing it to muster an impressive military force at a relatively limited cost to the economy. Other countries have made only relatively small additions to their military budgets.

All of this suggests that the so-called 'peace dividend'—the economic benefit of ending the cold war—has been somewhat reduced since the turn of the 21st century, but also that societies continue to benefit from it to a large extent.

Even though the increase in US military spending may not entirely explain the increase in the federal deficit, and although defence expenditure may not have returned to cold war levels, the increase is considerable. The impact of military spending on economic growth is important and has been the topic of theoretical and empirical research, because the peace dividend associated with the end of the cold war was expected to result in positive welfare gains. Some analysts suggest that military spending affects medium-term growth negatively through several channels (such as lower capital accumulation, a reduced civilian labour force and losses resulting from capital reallocation). Other analysts claim that these negative impacts are counterbalanced by the contribution to technological innovation made by research and development in military industries.

Empirical studies have produced ambiguous results.[21] Econometric studies typically have difficulties identifying the impact of military spending on growth because such spending boosts growth in the short run, even though it may lower it after a time lag. Although a 1996 study using panel data estimation found that military spending had a significant negative impact on growth,[22] a 2001 study found no strong relationship between military expenditure and either investment or growth. Overall, the conventional wisdom is that military build-ups are likely to have a detrimental long-term impact on economic growth, but this impact is likely to be small, and in any case much smaller than other traditional determinants of growth. Smith and Dunne, for instance, calculate that, based on commonly accepted parameters, an increase in military spending by one percentage point of GDP is likely to reduce potential output growth by 0.25 per cent during a transition period.[23]

VII. Conclusions

Until 2001, many societies took security for granted. The dissolution of the Soviet Union eliminated the threat of an intercontinental nuclear conflict. The world prospered in a new environment of security. This encouraged the removal of border controls, boosting external trade and investment. As nations became increasingly interdependent, globalization contributed to worldwide prosperity. Governments gradually dismantled their military might, which promised to bring a welcome peace dividend.

The terrorist attacks of 11 September 2001 brought back the realities of violence and fear. With the emergence of organized and well-funded terrorist groups, citizens no longer felt that the world was safe. After having settled claims of unprecedented size, the insurance industry decided that the coverage of terrorism involved incalculable risks. It also decided to drop or drastically reduce the coverage of liabilities caused by terrorist events. Governments stepped in to provide time-limited support, which allowed businesses to resume their activities without having to pay astronomical insurance premiums or spend considerable amounts on their own security. Governments also entered into partnership agreements both internationally and with business groups to devise border control procedures that tightened security and facilitated trade. While these new procedures initially raised some concerns, there is currently little evidence to suggest that the cost of trading internationally has significantly increased.

---

[20] See Knight, M., Loayza, N. and Villanueva, D., 'The peace dividend: military spending cuts and economic growth', *IMF Staff Papers*, vol. 43, no. 1 (1996), pp. 1–37; Ramey, V. and Shapiro, M., 'Costly capital reallocation and the effects of government spending', *Carnegie–Rochester Conference Series on Public Policy*, vol. 48, no. 1 (1998), pp. 145–94; and Smith, R. and Dunne, P., 'Military expenditure growth and investment' (mimeo), Birkbeck College and Middlesex University Business School, Apr. 2001.

[22] Knight, Loayza and Villanueva (note 20).

[23] Smith and Dunne (note 20).

Governments are paying a relatively high cost for the provision of security in a world where terrorists can strike at any time. By becoming reinsurers of last resort, they face a large contingent liability. By reinforcing law enforcement and homeland security departments, they are increasing their spending. By seeking to deter the origin of the terrorist threats through military action, they are contributing to a reversal of the peace dividend. At a time when many governments are facing popular pressure to reduce tax burdens, it is not clear how these new programmes will be paid for. Security-related spending is contributing to larger budget deficits, increased indebtedness and additional borrowing—even though it is not the only cause of the recent deterioration of fiscal balances. If societies are not willing to pay for their security, they risk transferring this burden to future generations.

Part VI

The security–economy linkage in a global perspective

Editors' remarks

Most of the contributions to this volume are based on shared assumptions about the legitimacy of the free-market, competitive world trading system and the phenomena of 'globalization' to which it gives rise. They see terrorism as a weapon of the weak and excluded, which strikes at both the economic and the political foundations of developed democracies and which, on both counts, deserves an annihilating response.

These views are not universally shared. Many official authorities and individual analysts, in developing countries in particular, see the existing international trade system as being unfairly biased against the interests of less powerful participants, both in its rules and in its effects. Many also favour a broader definition of 'terrorism' to include cases of shocking and illegal violence used by the strong against the weak. On this view, which is expounded in detail in Said Adejumobi's chapter, it is possible to define certain kinds of business (including but not limited to private military activities) as having 'terrorist' effects or even constituting 'terrorism' in themselves. The overwhelming priority which the leaders of the developed world have demanded should be given since 11 September 2001 to combating the kind of 'super-terrorism' represented by al-Qaeda may be seen as a partial and selfish 'rich man's agenda'—or, even worse, as a cover for further onslaughts on the interests of other regions and civilizations.

In actuality, many of the steps taken to combat threats of terrorism and those related to weapons of mass destruction since 2001 have drawn remarkably wide support from developed and developing, 'Northern' and 'Southern', nations. The international climate has provided both moral and material incentives for players of all kinds to avoid being stamped as terrorists or as condoning terrorism. Regional organizations in the South as well as the North have hastened to adopt new, and more effective, anti-terrorism and anti-proliferation policies of their own. Their reaction has logic in so far as a world thrown into disorder by terrorism (and by violent responses to it) would be even less likely to produce remedies for economic inequality and underdevelopment than is the existing global order—however imperfect. Nevertheless, anyone who wishes to set anti-terrorism policy and the protection of legitimate commerce on sound and lasting footings needs to pay serious attention to the arguments—and the feelings—associated with what might be called 'the poor man's agenda'.

Saad Alfarargi's and Said Adejumobi's chapters are based on talks which introduced a valuable element of balance in this respect at the Liechtenstein Conference, and they do so in this volume as well. A supplementary contribution by Phyllis Bonanno notes that the restrictions on human movement introduced by the United States for anti-terrorist purposes after September 2001 may be counterproductive not only in commercial terms but also in impeding the education of developing-country students in US institutions and US ways. This may turn out to be only one of many contradictions inherent in defending an open model of society and the economy by means that tend to curtail the openness of both.

20. A view from the League of Arab States

Saad Alfarargi

I. Introduction

Against the background of the current threats and the 'security agenda', the following issues have been defined for reflection in this volume: (*a*) how can the private sector cooperate with governments in order to arrest the progress of 'the bad'?; and (*b*) do governments need to make a greater effort to protect 'the good'? To address these questions properly it is necessary to pose others. Is the task limited to tracking down 'the bad' and 'the terrorists' and punishing those who resort to violence regardless of their motivations? Or is it also to fight the causes of terrorism and violence and thereby tackle the roots of the problem?

What often leads to erroneous answers, and consequently to ineffectual (and at times counterproductive) solutions, is recourse to generalizations that leave the issues even more confused. The correct approach is to characterize the objective and then to define the task. It is prudent to agree first on terminology and to determine who the enemy is before we open fire and end up shooting ourselves in the foot.

Before the collapse of the Berlin wall and the end of the cold war, the 'enemy' was confined within known borders and had specific characteristics. At times the enemy was encountered outside those borders, in other arenas, but at least the enemy and the way to contain the enemy were known. Now these circumstances have changed. The enemy is no longer confined within borders and has no discernible features. The enemy has no physical form to shoot at. In this elusive state, an enemy has emerged to threaten the security and safety of humans throughout the world. The enemy has become 'a meaning' without a visible structure and 'a description' without an evident corporal form. The enemy has become fanaticism, rejection of the other, hatred and violation of human rights. It is also the anger and the frustration of those who have lost faith in the legal system of justice and decided to take the law into their own hands through violence.

It is important, when determining the terminology, to avoid confusion: it must be clear what is meant by 'terrorism' and care should be taken not to confuse it with the legitimate right of peoples and nations to resist occupation. It is important to be consistent and avoid aiming at the wrong target. It is also essential to recognize that the principles of human rights must encompass all humans, without distinction or discrimination.

In some cases, especially in the Middle East, the right to citizenship and to settle in a given country has been conferred on foreigners who arrive without even having visited the country before, without any family roots there. They may become citizens of the new country, while others have been forced out of their homes. We are continuously faced with double standards and a profound confusion as to the definition of the right to self-defence. This happens even in countries with established systems of democracy, justice and security, where there is still strong opposition to the disarming of individuals on the ground that citizens have the right to self-defence if the systems of justice and security fail them. At the same time, these very people oppose the right of other peoples to resist occupation and demand that the resistance be disarmed prior to the commencement of peace negotiations.

The question is: How can we construct a just system with any fair notion of good governance in the world—a world which has become very small thanks to impressive scientific and technological advances, a world where all parts are affected by occurrences in any single part? Who sets the rules? Who will enforce or implement them? Are there any exceptions to the set rules? The situation today does not evoke much optimism in the Arab and broader Islamic world because of the deep sense of anguish and fear felt by many there about the shape of the future. Nor are such fears confined to the small countries of the developing world. There is also a growing European sense of concern regarding certain developments: concerns recently reflected in the positions of some countries in Europe vis-à-vis certain international events. Within many intellectual circles shaping public opinion, a movement has developed which strives to shape a global system of governance based on justice and the acceptance of a form of globalization that would be in the interest of all.

II. Obstacles to a just system of collective global security and governance

The obstacles in the way of this endeavour start with the current tendency towards marginalizing the United Nations, especially after it 'failed' in 2002 to provide a mandate for a war based on unsubstantiated doubts—since proven groundless—regarding threats to international peace and security. Many fear that this reflects the determination of the most powerful to impose their views on the world and their reluctance to submit to international legitimacy. The powerful have decided to lay down their own criteria for the application of legitimacy and the law.

More dangerously, the United Nations, under pressure, has concluded international conventions while making exceptions for certain nations. By openly exempting them from abiding by the criteria governing responses to the threat of weapons of mass destruction (WMD), which endanger international peace and security, it has created a precedent for selective application. The mere suspicion that some countries might have military nuclear programmes was sufficient to point fingers of accusation, launch wars and start an effective state of occupation. Meanwhile, the fact that other countries do have such programmes was overlooked, the only apparent justification being that those countries could be described as democratic. Thus the noble quest for democracy was distorted by making it a justification for the acquisition of WMD. All of the above constitutes a threat to the universal aspiration for global peace and the strengthening of international security through cooperation.

The problem now is that, because the East–West ideological clashes subsided during the last decade of the 20th century, there has been a persistent and precipitous move to 'invent' a 'new enemy'. The parties to the classic conflict between East and West have been replaced by the parties to the conflict between the eastern and the western side of the Atlantic Ocean and the eastern and the western side of the Pacific, as seen at the United Nations and in the World Trade Organization. This is a matter of concern since it drives wedges between ostensible partners and allies. What is the lesson to be learned here by the South?

Relations between the North and the South have also undergone general transformations, shifting from a context of international and regional cooperation to one of a confrontation between classes, ideologies and interests. In the process of inventing 'a new enemy', there has been an egregious and outrageous confusion between violence and poverty, Arabs and oil, Islam and terrorism. A negative perception of the Arabs, the Muslims and the future of oil has been propagated, without due attention to some basic facts. Poverty is not the only source of violence: those who practice violence play rather on the strings of poverty and exploit the suffering of the poor. Oil is the most important of Arab riches, and it is in the interest of the Arabs that oil should flow and be sold. However, the Arabs have no intention of wasting their resources nor of allowing them to be plundered. The rest of the world should consider that their real aim may be to attain a just price rather than to disrupt the supply of oil.

Historically, there has never been animosity between Islam and Christianity as religions per se. This developed rather as a result of attempts by the North to invade the South, to seize resources and trade routes. The crescent and the cross were utilized merely as symbols to rally supporters on both sides.

Many of the writings of Western orientalists have contributed to explaining Islam and have made important contributions to its study. They have shown that the Muslim truly believes that Islam was revealed to complement the message of preceding monotheistic religions, not to oppose them.

III. Rich men's and poor men's agendas

By examining the real agenda of the 'rich man' of the North and the real agenda of the 'poor man' of the South, it should be possible to assess the chances of arriving at a common and unified agenda. The following issues are at the forefront of the rich man's agenda.

Terrorism. The rich countries fear that their interests will be exposed to terrorist actions. There is growing common ground on what is meant by 'terrorism'. However, the world community still needs, as argued above, to agree on a definition and on the terminology to be used. There is, in fact, still no complete agreement on a definition of terrorism, even between the members of the North Atlantic Treaty Organization. There is confusion between the definitions of terrorist acts of violence and what constitutes legitimate resistance against the illegitimate and foreign occupation of land and the denial of self-determination of peoples. A definition is needed which does not confuse those issues. Voices from the South were the first to draw attention to the dangers inherent in the rich men's countries giving shelter and asylum to terrorists and providing them with a protected status on the basis of some distorted application of human rights criteria.

Organized crime. The revolution in telecommunications has caused borders to fade, giving rise to new forms of threats including money laundering and narcotics (most of which are supplied by the South, particularly Latin America). The poor man's agenda can certainly encompass the fight against organized crime, as long as the rich North realizes that this fight involves development. The European Union (EU) should, for example, be commended for its initiative to expand the opportunities for Latin American farmers to gain access to markets for horticultural and floral produce, in an effort to encourage them to abandon the production of narcotics.

Illegal immigration. The USA and many European states have had to receive large numbers of immigrants to balance the decline in natural population growth. However, the issue of illegal immigration is causing a great deal of internal controversy in the rich countries. The argument revolves around whether it is preferable to challenge immigration or to challenge the causes of immigration, that is, the necessity to develop the South. It is worth noting here that the South is willing to cooperate unrestrainedly *if* this will result in the increased access of its products to rich men's markets as a substitute for the infiltration of its citizens into those countries.

Importing the disputes of the poor. The rich man fears the impact of regional disputes on his interests, and the possible threats they bring to transportation routes, oil and energy supplies. The South strives for Europe's acceptance by allowing it to participate in the construction of regional security in the form of cooperative (common) institutions. The EU has accepted that the Barcelona Process and the Euro-Mediterranean cooperation[1] cannot be completely divorced from the peace process in the Middle East; hence the EU is assuming a larger political role in the peace process and continuing its role as the major donor to the Palestinian economy.

---

[1] On the Euro-Mediterranean Partnership and the Mediterranean Partners see URL <http://europa.eu.int/comm/external_relations/euromed>.

An examination of the poor man's agenda may show that the common points it shares with the agenda of the rich man outnumber the points of difference. These may be summarized in the following list of priorities.

The need for development and integration into the world economy. The South needs to adjust to international developments with the aid of the North as a partner, committed to supporting its economic capabilities, modernizing its scientific research and infrastructure and developing its human resources. The South is appreciative of the development assistance that it receives from the donor countries. It must be noted, however, that the donors also benefit through trade promotion for their exports and the creation of stability, peace and security through aid. The goal should be the further opening of markets accompanied by corresponding assistance and the restriction of short-sighted protectionist policy practices. Those who call for international free trade must accept the same principles when dealing with the exports of the South to their countries. It is worth noting here the increasing comparative significance of the EU and its trade with the Arab world, where Europe is now regarded as the main trade partner.

A more active role in the settlement of regional conflicts. World security, especially security in the Middle East, relies on a just and peaceful resolution of disputes accompanied by a narrowing of the differences in income levels between the North and the South, where unemployment and poverty add to the pressure for population movements and immigration to the North. The problem is aggravated by the absence of an effective common EU foreign and security policy. Related to this are the Arab–Israeli conflict, the Western Sahara dispute, and the Cyprus and Balkans issues, which are primarily European concerns.

A better understanding of the political and social conditions in the South. This should teach the North to avoid excessive criticism of features and characteristics which are the product of a certain cultural heritage and specificities possibly not shared by the North.

IV. The way to a common agenda?

The way should be open for a common agenda between the poor and the rich, focusing on the following priorities.

First, a North–South dialogue needs to be launched. The North needs to acquire a deeper knowledge of the culture and the traditions of the South. People in the Middle East are adherents of Islam, Christianity and Judaism. These religions form our historical and confessional foundation. We reject the theories that posit a clash of civilizations. We believe that we belong to the same human civilization. The dialogue must be initiated on the basis of a realization of world relations in the form of values and principles which add up to a more just and more balanced international organizational framework. The framework must be one in which the rules of the game would apply to everyone, and in which all accept that the existence of conflicts in interest or in cultures must not constitute an obstacle to the continuation of dialogue with the participation of all.

Economic and social development is essential to achieve a balance between classes, to close the gap between rich and poor, and to encourage movement towards a widely drawn democracy, both regionally and internationally. Dialogue on democracy must be characterized by inclusiveness and openness among the societies of the South and the North. All must be committed to dialogue and persuasion, not to coercion or the denial of the rights and interests of others. Otherwise, democracy will become a tool for organizing the internal affairs of the rich states but will be left aside when it comes to relations with other states.

The creation of any peaceful, stable world system has to be based on the realization of benefits for all players without one losing out to the other. Inequalities must be reduced, notably by developing institutions and a system of international trade which assist developing countries by increasing their export potential; by drawing upon the regional cooperation experiences of the North to encourage development initiatives between the states of the South; and by reaching the Official Development Assistance targets,[2] reforming international financial institutions, and harnessing political and economic resources to eradicate extreme poverty.

The United Nations system and international financial institutions need reform to serve all parties in a more equitable manner. The UN must be encouraged to play its part in peace processes, since the small powers of the South will choose to draw apart from the rich world to protect their national interests unless the world system takes their interests into consideration. Vigilance is needed to ensure that the growing role of the international system does not lead to a concentration of power in the hands of a single superpower which can then control the system. A 'world democracy' must be designed to take into consideration the interests of all in order to avoid double standards which ultimately lead to, among other things, terrorism.

It must be recognized that there is a crisis of faith in the South on the subject of the work of international economic organizations, as well as a strong sense that the international trade and financial institutions do not operate to benefit the poor. There are also justified impressions that the world is being governed unjustly to serve the interests of the larger powers. These perceptions exist due to the unbalanced decision-making process on international issues, which may lead the poor states to follow inferior choices.

---

[2] See, e.g., United Nations, 'Millennium indicators: goals, targets and indicators', URL <http://millenniumindicators.un.org/unsd/mi/mi_dict_xrxx.asp?def_code=468>.

Last but not least, a shared agenda for rich and poor must include the combating of terrorism through various means. The most important of these is development assistance using methods which respect the law, and which recognize that poverty does not create violence but rather that violence exploits the poor. The rule of law, conditions of democracy, human rights and human development must be guaranteed. Otherwise, financing and poverty problems will continue to increase in the South even while the North becomes more affluent.

21. A view from Africa

Said Adejumobi

I. Introduction

The attacks of 11 September 2001 introduced a new configuration into the international political economy: they have increasingly shaped issues, interests, alliances, coalition building and the focus of global politics. Some have described the attacks as the most significant and shattering event since the end of the cold war and a watershed in global history.[1] The attacks certainly constituted an epochal event that was to set its stamp on the beginning of the new millennium and on the direction of global politics in the 21st century.

The use of terror or terrorist acts is not a new phenomenon, but a means by which states and groups have sought to pursue their interests when they could not do so through conventional political processes. There are basically three new features of the events of 11 September. First is the site of the attacks. The United States, as the sole superpower, has carried an aura of invincibility and presented an impenetrable wall of security that terrorists were not expected to be able to breach. The attacks thus shocked the entire world and raised the question of security higher on the agenda, even for the most developed countries with sophisticated security technology. As Eric Hershberg and Kevin Moore noted, the USA 'was suddenly no longer invulnerable, its power no longer unassailable'.[2]

The second new feature of these events is their significance as signalling that globalization has permeated not only the economy, politics and culture but also the planning and execution of violence, criminality and terrorism. The increasing 'privatization' of terrorism, perpetrated with a high level of sophistication and precision, is one of the manifestations and side effects of globalization. Information technology, global finance and integrated networks have become available to both honest and unscrupulous individuals and non-state groups. Globalization is characterized by both progress and subversion.

The third new feature of the 11 September events is the object of attack. The choice of the New York World Trade Center and the Pentagon as targets—clear symbols of the preponderance of capitalism and globalization, and of the global military power of the USA that backs them—reflects a protest against

---

[1] See, e.g., Debiel, T., 'Privatised violence and the terror of September 11: challenges to foreign, security and development policy', eds T. Debiel and A. Klein, *Fragile Peace: State Failure, Violence and Development in Crisis Regions* (Zed Books: London and New York, 2002), p. 191.

[2] Hershberg, E. and Moore, K. W., 'Introduction: place, perspective, and power—interpreting September 11', eds E. Hershberg and K. W. Moore, *Critical Views of September 11: Analyses from Around the World* (New Press: New York, 2002), p. 3, available at URL <http://www.ssrc.org/sept11/essays/CriticalViewsIntro.pdf>.

the hierarchy of the global system. This criminal protest may not necessarily reflect a clash of culture, civilization or religion, but it could be a reaction to the spatial dimension of economic dispersion and power in the global arena.

After the attacks, the 'war on terrorism' proclaimed by the USA proceeded on a large scale. Afghanistan and Iraq have been the first two victims of the war, and Africa has been identified as a possible base for terrorism. According to Susan Rice, a former US Assistant Secretary of State for African Affairs, 'Africa is the world's soft underbelly for global terrorism . . . Africa is an incubator for the foot soldiers of terrorism . . . Al Qaeda and other terrorist cells are active throughout East, Southern and West Africa, as well as North Africa'.[3] Porous borders, weak economies and poverty are among the factors Rice identifies as qualifying Africa as a site of refuge for terrorist activities. Her prescription is that Africa's security apparatus and economy must be strengthened in order to prevent the continent from becoming a terrorist lair.

The intention here is not to contest Rice's argument, which is indeed contestable, but to address two other issues. First, this chapter addresses the notion of terrorism from an economic perspective. It raises the issue of whether the terms 'economic terror' or 'business as terror' are in fact valid. In other words, can businesses overtly or covertly facilitate terrorism? Second, it raises the issue of Africa's own main security concerns and considers how the war on terrorism is linked to and affects them. It argues that there is another potential agent of political terrorism and insecurity: the activities of business actors. These economic agents may overtly or covertly reinforce the political terrorism perpetrated by state or non-state organizations, thereby exacerbating disorder, instability, conflict and chaos, in Africa as elsewhere. Last but not least, the question of security in Africa also needs to be seen in relation to the notion of human security, for it is human insecurity that provides the context in which terrorist acts can most easily be carried out.

II. Terrorism: the political and economic dimensions

Since the attacks of 11 September 2001, the concept of terrorism has been the subject of considerable debate and of attempts to define it. Most conceptual approaches have focused on the political dimension. What appears to be an official US Government definition of the concept of terrorism is contained in a Congressional Research Service report prepared by Raphael Perl in 2001.[4] The report defines terrorism as politically motivated violence perpetrated against non-combatant targets by sub-national groups or clandestine agents. A terrorist group is defined as a group which practices—or which has sufficient sub-

---

[3] Rice, S. E., 'The Africa battle', *Washington Post*, 11 Dec. 2001, p. A33.
[4] Perl, R. F., *Terrorism, the Future and US Foreign Policy*, CRS Issue Brief for Congress, Updated 23 Mar. 2001 (Library of Congress, Congressional Research Service: Washington, DC, 2001), available at URL <http://www.globalsecurity.org/security/library/report/crs/IB95112.pdf>. (The version of this report as updated on 11 Apr. 2003 is available at URL <http://www.fas.org/irp/crs/IB95112. pdf>.)

groups practising—terrorism. Some have challenged this view of terrorism, arguing that it does not need to encompass the element of civilians and non-combatants as targets. Terrorist acts can be inflicted on combatants as well.[5]

Achin Vanaik defines terrorism as 'the calculated or premeditated use, or threat of use, of violence against an individual, group, or larger collectivity in such a manner that the target is rendered physically defenceless against the attack or against the effects of that violence'. It is the political intent implicit in a terrorist act that makes it different from a criminal act such as murder. The 'defencelessness' of the target can result from surprise attack outside a battle or war zone, its nature (e.g., a civilian target), the types of weapons used, and the enormous disproportion in the violence exercised between sides within a battle or war zone.[6] Vanaik's conception of terrorism is sufficiently elastic to accommodate a wide range of contexts and terrorist acts.

Three factors are central to the notion of terrorism: (*a*) civilian casualties, (*b*) the element of surprise and the use of extreme force, and (*c*) the high level of insecurity that the act engenders.

Political terrorism has a specific agent, context and focus. It may involve state or non-state actors and be domestic or international in nature, as well as overt or covert. In the context of state terrorism, the essential objective is to intimidate the opposition, to promote a sense of fear and to undermine the cause that the opponent may be pursuing. The distinguishing feature is that the state machinery is placed at the service of such actions. Examples include the terrorist acts of the Sani Abacha regime (1993–98) in Nigeria, in which state agents went on a rampage, assassinating political opponents and civil society actors, bombing cars and persecuting groups that did not support the succession policy proclaimed by the dictator. In Angola, the example of the United States' support during the cold war for groups such as União Nacional para a Independência Total de Angola (UNITA, National Union for the Total Independence of Angola), offering military assistance and logistics to an organization that inflicted heavy collateral damage on the country's people, represented a covert means of perpetrating terrorism. The bombing of the US embassies in Kenya and Tanzania in 1998 was a non-state manifestation of terrorism. Political terrorism is the continuation of politics by other means through armed force and a culture of fear.

Economic networks may also be linked to acts of terrorism. This may happen when economic or financial networks provide resources for terrorist organizations—for without funds terrorist groups cannot function—or when business firms, in pursuing their own private interests, cultivate or provide support for terrorist groups. Both phenomena could be correctly described as *economic terrorism*. In the former, an economic network is geared towards political purposes; in the latter, the economic or profit motive remains central but is achieved through political processes of terror. Economic terrorism may

---

[5] Vanaik, A., 'The ethics and efficacy of political terrorism', eds Hershberg and Moore (note 2), p. 27.
[6] Vanaik (note 5), p. 28.

thus be defined as the conduct of activities by business interests or firms which directly or indirectly inflict large-scale damage and loss of lives in a community or society, or which support political organizations, groups or states that undertake reprisals against defenceless civilian populations, either directly on behalf of the firms or in the indirect pursuit of the firms' interests.

In these scenarios the main features of terrorism are present—civilian casualties, the application of force or violence, and fear and insecurity. Economic terrorism may also be overt or covert, just like its political counterpart. The agency of economic terror may be 'legitimate' or otherwise: that is, it may be a duly registered business organization, or one that exists illegally and operates underground.

Only when a nuanced view of terrorism is conceptualized, taking into account both the political and the economic dimension, can the dynamics of insecurity in the global system be understood from the perspectives of the developed and the developing countries.

III. 'Business as terror' in Africa

The scenario of instability, conflict and crisis which plagues the African continent has made it a veritable magnet for various types of businesses which rarely adhere to the rules, norms and ideals of responsible corporate behaviour. Indeed, some of these corporate entities thrive on the instability and insecurity of the region and covertly or otherwise perpetrate acts of terror. In conflict situations in Africa, an intricate network of illegal arms dealers and brokers, private military companies (PMCs) and drug traders often facilitates the perpetration of terror. For these businesses, political instability in Africa has become a market indicator which they have positioned themselves perfectly to exploit.[7] In addition, certain well-established businesses such as the multinational oil corporations also tap into the weak political structures of African countries and the social cleavages inherent in those societies to covertly perpetuate terrorism. Such activities exacerbate insecurity and impoverish the people and society.

The issues of small arms and PMCs resonate in many conflict spots in Africa. 'In July 2001 the US government estimated that small arms are fuelling conflicts in 22 African countries that have taken 7–8 million lives. In Africa, guns are not just the weapons of choice but also weapons of mass destruction.'[8] In West Africa, over 7 million small arms are circulating in the sub-region and have been central to the conflicts in the Manor River Union of Liberia, in Sierra Leone and in Guinea. In South Africa, there are about

[7] Harding, J., Transcript of Radio National (Australia) Programme 'Background Briefing', 'The diamond mercenaries of Africa', 4 Aug. 1996, p. 12, cited in Musah, A.-F. and Fayemi, J. 'K. (eds), *Mercenaries: An African Security Dilemma* (Pluto Press: London, 2000), pp. 4–5, available at URL <http://www.abc.net.au/rn/talks/bbing/stories/s10759.htm>.

[8] Fleshman, M., 'Small arms in Africa: counting the cost of gun violence', *Africa Recovery*, vol. 15, no. 4 (Dec. 2001), p. 18, available at URL <http://www.un.org/ecosocdev/geninfo/afrec/vol15no4/154 arms.htm>.

4 million small arms in the hands of civilians. In Mogadishu City alone (the capital of Somalia), it is estimated that about 1 million small arms are circulating among a population of 1.3 million people. In Mozambique, with a population of 15 million, an estimated 10 million small arms are held throughout the country. In some African countries small arms, particularly the AK-47 rifle, are as cheap as $6 and can be bartered for a chicken or a sack of grain.[9]

Small arms are not the root cause of conflict but they exacerbate it. As Abdel-Fatau Musah and Niobe Thompson observed, small arms are a catalyst of violence. They 'transform fragile democracies containing ethnic and communal antagonisms into hollow and administratively ineffective states racked by violence and civil war'.[10] In addition, small arms prolong wars, impose severe suffering on the people, destroy infrastructure and dislocate societies. The end of the cold war was expected to slow down the production and sale of small arms and reduce their availability in the developing countries that served as proxies in the superpower confrontation. However, this did not happen, mainly because of two factors. First was the increasing commercialization and privatization of the arms industry, which compelled the industry to push for higher profit margins.[11] Second, after the disintegration of the Soviet Union there was a large stockpile of small arms in the former Soviet bloc. Private interests in those countries moved aggressively and often illegally to market them abroad, especially in areas of conflict. The effect was that a network of arms dealers and brokers, including PMCs, swamped Africa, selling weapons to all the warring parties—both rebels and governments—and exacerbating war and human suffering on the continent. These dealers became allies in the perpetuation of terrorism and focused largely on profit or on obtaining natural resources in return for arms sales.

The business network tied to the arms trade includes the dealers, air cargo companies, financiers and local agents. For instance, in the case of Sierra Leone, air transport firms such as Ibis Air, Soruss, Sky Air and Occidental were involved in the illegal shipment of arms to the rebel forces—the Revolutionary United Front of Sierra Leone (RUF)—who perpetrated acts of savage terror on the people.[12] PMCs, such as Executive Outcome (EO), and mercenaries were also involved in the arms deals.

PMCs sell the services of foreign professional soldiers to both state and non-state actors purely for profit motives. They act chiefly in conflict situations and provide consultancy, training, asset protection and combat services to those who can pay for them. Although they project the image of a modern business enterprise that markets technical and military expertise, they are in

[9] Fleshman (note 8); and Musah, A.-F. and Thompson, N., 'A commonwealth of conscience? light weapons violence and human rights', eds A.-F. Musah and N. Thompson, *Over a Barrel: Light Weapons and Human Rights in the Commonwealth* (Institute of Commonwealth Studies: London, 1999).

[10] Musah and Thompson (note 9), pp. 8–9.

[11] Sköns, E. and Weidacher, R., 'Arms production', *SIPRI Yearbook 2002: Armaments, Disarmament and International Security* (Oxford University Press: Oxford, 2002), pp. 323–53.

[12] Musah, A., 'Small arms and conflict transformation in West Africa', eds Musah and Thompson (note 9), p. 124.

fact modern forms of mercenaries who have merely changed their nature and mode of operation. These firms have been established or are run mainly by retired military personnel with extensive networks in the state establishment, and some of them enjoy covert diplomatic and political backing from their home states. Among them, Military Professional Resources Incorporated (MPRI), based in Alexandria, Virginia, has a database of over 2000 soldiers and officers who are available for contract work, and wields political leverage in the USA.[13] In the UK, ArmorGroup has close links to the British military establishment.[14] As Kevin O'Brien noted, 'many of the PMCs operating out of western countries today were, and in many cases continue to be, closely aligned with and supported by the intelligence services of the countries in which they originate. This can clearly be seen today in the cases of the United States, Great Britain and France'.[15]

The logic of globalization and the market ideology has given rise to the increasing commercialization of security and privatization of war. PMCs are regarded by many as more efficient, better organized and able to deliver security services more promptly than the state. Just as extreme market ideology tends to delegitimize the state, private and non-state actors are seen as the answer to state failure as they increasingly take on the state's traditional roles.

The striking characteristic of these modern mercenary activities is that they often enmesh themselves in war-torn economies and engage in the expropriation of the natural resources of those countries. These firms have interlocking relationships with natural resource companies and sometimes trade their services in exchange for mining concessions or oil contracts. For example, in the case of Angola, the contract signed by the government with EO 'is believed to have included a diamond concession awarded to their subsidiary, Branch Energy. In total, the contract is said to have been worth US$40 million'. Similarly, in Sierra Leone, the Government of Valentine Strasser was said to have awarded contracts to EO worth $50 million in cash and mining concessions.[16] On the side of the rebels, contracts with PMCs are not documented since they are essentially 'secret deals' and are generally more extensive than contracts with governments. Angola and Sierra Leone were reputed to have been major business centres for PMCs which offered their services to the warring parties, to private companies seeking protection and security, and to international agencies operating in conflict regions. By far the most profitable part of their activities is the assistance offered to warring parties. By mid-1997 it was esti-

---

[13] Musah and Fayemi (note 7), p. 18. On the MPRI see URL <http://www.mpri.com/channels/home.html>.

[14] Fayemi, J. 'K., 'Africa in search of security: mercenaries and conflicts—an overview', A.-F. Musah and J. 'K. Fayemi, *Mercenaries: An African Security Dilemma* (Pluto Press: London, 2000), p. 18. ArmorGroup formerly operated as Defence Systems Limited (DSL); see URL <http://www.armorgroup.com/services/security.htm>.

[15] O'Brien, K., 'Private military companies and African security 1990–98', Musah and Fayemi (note 14), p. 44.

[16] Fayemi (note 14), pp. 23–24.

mated that no fewer than 90 PMCs were operating in Africa, most of them in Angola.[17]

Essentially, PMCs have transformed conflicts into markets and supported terrorist groups in perpetrating horrendous crimes against civilian populations in Africa. Conflicts in Africa have taken a debilitating human toll, retarded economic and social progress, destroyed institutional capacity, perpetuated poverty and increased human suffering. The World Bank estimates that civil wars currently lower per capita income by 2.2 percentage points a year in Africa.[18] The 1999 Report of the United Nations Special Rapporteur on the Use of Mercenaries established a clear linkage between the mercenary phenomenon and terrorism.

A mercenary is a criminal; he acts not out of altruistic motives, but to earn money in exchange for his tactical and strategic skills and his handling of weapons and explosives. In this regard, the material connection between a mercenary's activity and the commission of terrorist acts has been established through many terrorist attacks in which the perpetrator was proven to be one or more mercenaries hired to commit the crime. . . It must be remembered that terrorism is also a criminal activity in which mercenaries participate for payment, disregarding the most basic considerations of respect for human life and a country's legal order and security.[19]

Attempts to regulate the activities of the 'merchants of death' (PMCs as well as arms dealers and brokers) have so far proved rather futile owing primarily to the reluctance of the home countries of these firms. Mercenaries have been prohibited in several international agreements: for example, 1977 Protocol I Additional to the 1949 Geneva Conventions outlaws the use of mercenaries;[20] and the 1977 Convention for the Elimination of Mercenarism in Africa.[21] Nonetheless, mercenaries are still thriving today. The same scenario of futile attempts at regulation applies to the problem of small arms proliferation and trafficking. These are clear instances where businesses have aided terrorism in Africa, thereby obstructing the continent's development process.

Private firms have also aided local terrorism in Africa through the activities of the oil multinational corporations (MNCs), especially in the Niger Delta

[17] O'Brien (note 15), p. 51.

[18] World Bank, *Can Africa Claim the 21st Century?* (World Bank: Washington, DC, 2000), p. 57, available at URL <http://www.worldbank.org/html/extdr/canafricaclaim.pdf>.

[19] United Nations Economic and Social Council, Commission on Human Rights, The Right of Peoples to Self-determination and its Application to Peoples under Colonial or Alien Domination or Foreign Occupation, Report on the question of the use of mercenaries as a means of violating human rights and impeding the exercise of the right of peoples to self-determination, UN document E/CN.4/1999/11, 13 Jan. 1999, paras 56 and 57.

[20] 'A mercenary shall not have the right to be a combatant or a prisoner of war': 1977 Protocol (I) Additional to the Geneva Conventions of 12 August 1949, and relating to the Protection of Victims of International Armed Conflicts, Article 47, para. 1, available at URL <http://www.hri.ca/uninfo/treaties/94.shtml>. Mercenaries were also banned by UN General Assembly Resolution 3314, 14 Dec. 1974, on the Definition of Aggression (Article 3), available at URL <http://www.un.org/documents/ga/res/29/ares29.htm>.

[21] This convention was opened for signature by the Organization of African Unity (OAU)—now the African Union (AU); see URL <http://www.africa-union.org/Official_documents/Treaties_%20 Conventions_%20Protocols/Convention_on_Mercenaries.pdf>.

region of Nigeria. Apart from the poor environmental standards and ecological disaster that their activities have brought to the area, destroying the livelihood of the communities and their health—leading to 'death by instalment' for the people—some of these oil firms covertly support state terrorism against the people of the area. During the military regimes of Generals Ibrahim Babangida and Sani Abacha (1985–98) the Nigerian state, on behalf of the oil MNCs, unleashed tremendous terror on the people. The entire Niger Delta was militarized, with an army of occupation based in the area to protect the operation of oil firms. The oil companies, especially Shell, supported the government's actions by providing ammunition and logistics for these repressive activities of the state: in the words of Claude Ake, this was a case of the 'militarisation of commerce'.[22] In a report released in 2001, Sokari Ekine captured it succinctly: 'Shell and the other oil companies, especially Elf and Chevron, have shown their open hostility and disregard for local communities by working hand in hand with the Nigerian military, providing them weapons, transport, logistical support and financial payments in order to commit acts of violence against people and property. In return the military serve as a personal security force to oil workers'.[23]

The high point of the terror against the Niger Delta people was in 1994, when an Internal Security Task Force led by Major Paul Okuntimo was established and stationed in the Delta, mainly in Ogoniland. Its task was to occupy the area and maintain the conditions for unfettered exploitation by the oil MNCs. Shell was reputed to have supported the task force with arms, finance and logistics.[24] The Task Force imposed a reign of terror on the people, in which communities were raided, burned and destroyed, hundreds of people were killed and maimed, a large number of people were detained indefinitely, and women and children were attacked repeatedly. The Civil Liberties Organisation (CLO), a prominent human rights group in Nigeria, described the episode as 'terror in Ogoni',[25] while Ken Saro Wiwa called it 'genocide'.[26] The activities of the oil MNCs in the Niger Delta still anger the people and have led to a movement of counter-militarization among the youth of the area. The cycle of violence, militarism and insecurity is thus being perpetuated in the area.

Several issues arise from the above discussion of businesses engaged in the covert or overt support of terrorism in Africa. First, it raises the issue of the use of terror as a political and an economic resource. Second, it touches on the international conception of what a business is and what its standards should

---

[22] See 'Shell's promises and practice', Interviews by Andy Rowell, *DELTA no. 3* (Oct. 1997), URL <http://www.oneworld.org/delta/3_news6.html>, p. 8.

[23] Ekine, S., *Blood and Oil: Testimonies of Violence from Women of the Niger Delta* (Centre for Democracy and Development: London, 2001), p. 19.

[24] Ekine (note 23); see also Civil Liberties Organisation (CLO), *Ogoni: Trials and Travails* (CLO: Lagos, 1996).

[25] Civil Liberties Organisation (CLO), *'Terror in Ogoni', Action Report* (CLO: Lagos, 1 Aug. 1994). See also Civil Liberties Organisation (note 24).

[26] Wiwa, K. S., *A Month and a Day: A Detention Diary* (Spectrum Books: Ibadan, 1995).

be. Third is the linkage between business, terrorism and insecurity; and fourth is the issue of international law, sanctions and their enforcement to ensure minimum standards of good business behaviour. Finally, the discussion raises the issue of corporate responsibility and business ethics.

IV. Prioritizing security in Africa

Since the attacks of 11 September 2001, the war on terrorism has captured world attention and redirected international policy. The foreign and domestic policies of many countries are now judged largely by the extent to which they support the war on terrorism. Countries are compelled to pass anti-terrorism legislation, reform their security machinery and be on the alert for terrorists on their territory. Erstwhile 'pariah' states are reclassified as allies, while those that do not conform to the United States' standards are regarded as 'enemies' or as part of an 'axis of evil'. International economic support and aid, especially for developing countries, are now determined by where a nation stands on the war on terrorism. The USA has pursued the war on the basis of a maximalist ideology of 'you are either with us or against us'. Defence budgets have been increased in many developed countries, and special financial allocations are being made to prosecute the war on terrorism. The US defence budget for fiscal year 2003 was proposed to increase by $48 billion, or by 14 per cent. A special financial allocation called the Defence Emergency Reserve Fund (DERF), for which $20.1 billion was requested for 2003, is dedicated to the counter-terrorism campaign. This includes $9.4 billion to cover costs for the war on terrorism, and $10 billion as a contingency reserve fund for future wars on terrorism in other countries. The financial allocation for internal security in the USA, now called 'homeland security', has also increased as a response to the war on terrorism, and over $37 billion was earmarked for this in 2002.[27] Other countries, such as Canada and Germany, have reoriented their budgets to respond to the war on terrorism. The military industrial complex has resurfaced.

Countries such as Georgia, Pakistan and Uzbekistan have benefited economically from the war on terrorism. Pakistan, which was a ready ally of the USA in the fight against terrorism in Afghanistan, has been handsomely rewarded. The flow of economic aid to Pakistan as a result of the war was estimated at $1 billion, primarily from the USA but also from the European Union (EU) and Japan.[28] In Africa, countries that supported the US military campaign against Iraq, such as Ethiopia and Uganda, are also expected to benefit from US economic aid.

What are the implications of this for Africa? How does it affect security priorities on the continent? First, given the linkage between the war on terrorism, security and economic aid, African countries are likely to reorient their secur-

---

[27] Sköns, E. et al., 'Military expenditure', SIPRI Yearbook 2002 (note 11), pp. 242–43.
[28] Sköns et al. (note 27), p. 241.

ity policies and spending patterns to conform to the requirements for the war on terrorism. The pressure for them to do so is all the greater because organizations based in Africa now rank high on the US Terrorist Exclusion List (TEL).[29] The pressure and incentive for African countries to redesign their security policies to address this problem are therefore enhanced. Second, and related to this, defence and security spending is likely to rise in this region as elsewhere. Military budgets in Africa have been increasing since 1996 in response to internal armed conflicts, the threat of new conflicts and national defence modernization programmes.[30] The war on terrorism is likely to lead to further increases in military and internal security spending.

The third implication for Africa is that security sector reform, currently advocated mostly by civil society and grudgingly pursued by a number of states, will suffer a significant setback. These reforms are centred on accountability and the democratic control of security forces. The pressures of the war on terrorism mean that secrecy, off-budget spending and poor accountability are likely to continue in the security sector.[31] Fourth, the war on terrorism may induce internal repression as civil liberties are increasingly curtailed through new security legislation. It may be convenient for governments to simply classify any internal opposition as a terrorist act to be ruthlessly dealt with. Fifth, the disproportion between spending on security and on social welfare is likely to be exacerbated. As more resources go to the security sector, education, health and agriculture are likely to receive less funding. This will increase poverty, slow economic growth and exacerbate the upward spiral of conflicts on the continent.

While it is important to combat terrorism, Africa's own security problems and priorities lie less in the realm of military and more in the realm of human security. Human security entails ensuring the fulfilment of the basic human needs of education, health, employment, food and infrastructure, which in turn facilitates development. At the heart of all the conflicts, wars and instabilities in Africa is the problem of underdevelopment and poverty, which engender marginalization, political agitation and grievances. Africa's development challenge is its major security concern. Among all the regions of the world, Africa represents the poorest of the poor. Its socio-economic indices rank as the lowest in the world. In 2000, the World Bank reported that in 1997—despite the signs of progress in many countries in the early 1990s—average per capita income for sub-Saharan Africa (excluding South Africa) was $315. 'The region's total income is not much more than Belgium's, and is divided among 48 countries with a median gross domestic product of just over $2 billion—about the output of a town of 60 000 in a rich country. More than 40 percent of its 600 million people live below the poverty line of $1 per day,

---

[29] See US Department of State, Office of the Coordinator for Counterterrorism, 'Terrorist Exclusion List', 15 Nov. 2002, URL <http://www.state.gov/s/ct/rls/fs/2002/15222.htm>, which lists 39 organizations designated on 5 Dec. 2001 and 9 new ones designated on 18 Feb. 2003.

[30] Sköns et al. (note 27), p. 245.

[31] See Omitoogun, W., Military Expenditure Data in Africa: A Survey of Cameroon, Ethiopia, Ghana, Kenya, Nigeria and Uganda, SIPRI Research Report no. 17 (Oxford University Press: Oxford, 2003).

with incomes averaging \$0.65 a day in purchasing power parity terms.'[32] Infant mortality is very high: in many countries, 200 of every 1000 children born die before the age of 5; over 250 million Africans do not have access to safe drinking water and 200 million have no health care services.[33] This grim picture of underdevelopment is a major source of insecurity on the continent. It fuels crime, violence and inter-communal conflicts, and aids corruption.

The best approach to addressing the security and terrorism question in Africa would therefore be to invest not in armaments but in the people and the future of the continent. Economic development creates popular empowerment, allays resentment against regimes—local and international—and creates legitimacy for both local and international political and economic order. It is when people are hungry and frustrated that they see the gun as the only alternative for protection of their social livelihood. It is then that they can be enlisted for suicide missions, hijackings and other terrorist acts. It would be strategic and expedient for the USA and other developed countries to invest a large part of the resources they earmark for the war on terrorism for the eradication of poverty and underdevelopment in the developing countries. This would achieve two things. First, it would create a new partnership between the developing countries, especially Africa, and the developed world—one that would change the negative stereotype of 'imperialist and exploitatively ruthless' countries which dominates popular perceptions and images of the Western world in Africa and many other developing regions. Second, it would keep those whom Susan Rice calls the 'foot soldiers' of terrorism—children and youth engaged as soldiers—out of the reach of terrorism.

V. Conclusions

The linkage between the economy, security and terrorism points in two directions in Africa. The first connection is related to how business firms facilitate acts of terrorism on the continent, either overtly or covertly. The 'merchants of war' include arms dealers and brokers as well as private security companies and their auxiliary agencies, which regard areas of conflict and war as profitable markets. Their activities often prolong wars, increase human suffering and devalue life, as well as blocking the process of development and deepening insecurity. In a sense, they constitute an agency of terrorism. The second connection is related to how security itself should be defined and pursued in Africa in order to deter terrorism. Security in Africa must be conceived largely in human terms: in terms of the basic needs of education, health, food, infrastructure and decent standards of living, all of which are intimately connected with the process of economic development and social redistribution.

---

[32] World Bank (note 18), p. 7.
[33] World Bank (note 18), p. 10.

There are two ways in which human security can be promoted. The first is to redirect a significant part of the funds allocated to support of the war on terrorism to the development of African countries. The second is to re-examine the neo-liberal economic policies of market economy which tend to disempower the state and privatize social welfare. The state must play a role in the world of business and be made functional and effective in the promotion of social welfare. A weak or failed state perpetuates insecurity.

Annex. A comment on immigration controls and education in the United States

Phyllis O. Bonanno

The passage of the USA Patriot Act the month after the 11 September 2001 terrorist attacks on the United States has had an unintended impact on many sectors.[1] One of these sectors is higher education: the tightening of US immigration laws is having an effect on the 600 000 students who come to the USA every year to study.

The importation of students into the US higher education system is a large industry for the United States. Because of the restrictions imposed by the changes in immigration laws, the question for the USA now is whether it should be 'importing students' or concentrate on 'exporting' higher-education services. Countries such as Australia and the United Kingdom have made the decision to do the latter: in 2002 each nation generated revenues of over $4 billion from education services abroad, up from almost zero in 2000.[2]

New information technologies, international trade liberalization, and an unprecedented demand for education and training have changed the global market for these services. The link between education and standard of living as well as its importance for economic competitiveness have been realized at all levels. Together, these forces have combined to increase the global demand for higher education and training. The sector is experiencing unprecedented expansion and diversification in terms of both the number and variety of providers of higher education and training as well as the array of services they offer. Higher education is coming to be seen increasingly not only as a national public service but also as an international commodity.

Education and training rank fifth in terms of the USA's export earnings from service branches, bringing almost $13 billion into the US economy in 2002.[3] This figure primarily arises from international students studying in the USA and does not capture the receipts from the growing number of branches, and other ventures, established overseas by providers of US education services.

As a result of new security concerns and the tightening of visa restrictions, international students are having trouble entering the United States to pursue opportunities for higher education. Many educators fear that this may result in a loss of international market share. The United States' primary competitors in education services—Australia, Canada and the United Kingdom—are making concerted efforts, with the assistance of their governments, to take advantage of this extremely high level of global demand. As a result, US providers of these services will need to look

---

[1] For the Uniting and Strengthening America by Providing Appropriate Tools Required to Intercept and Obstruct Terrorism Act of 2001 (the USA Patriot Act of 24 Oct. 2001) see URL <http://www.epic.org/privacy/terrorism/hr3162.pdf>.

[2] See the Internet site of the US National Committee for International Trade in Education (NCITE) at URL <http://www.tradeineducation.org/general_info/frames.html>.

[3] NCITE (note 2).

to reach these students in their home countries, whether by creating a branch campus, a joint venture, or through distance learning.

Throughout the world, there is a growing middle class. Their children will want to have access to higher education, and if economic growth and prosperity are to continue, a higher education will become more and more of a necessity. In an article in *The Chronicle of Higher Education*, Goldie Blumenstyk points out that, in areas or countries of the world such as South-East Asia, Latin America and India, governments are finding that there is not enough space for students in their own public institutions.[4] She goes on to say that 'about 60% of India's population is 25 or younger'. She further notes that in Brazil, in 2002, 80 000 students applied for the 4000 available spaces in the public university, and by the year 2010 Mexico will need 2 million more university places. The needs in China are just now being quantified.

What does the new transnational higher education look like? The old model was that US citizens studied abroad, while students from abroad came to the USA. Today's new modes are the establishment of branch campuses of existing universities; twinning between US and foreign educational institutions; 'bricks and mortar'; distance education; and the use of traditional educational facilities for corporate training programmes.

A number of other possible barriers to the international trade in education have been noted by the World Trade Organization (WTO).[5] They include: the introduction of national legislation restricting imported activities, already in place in countries such as Greece, Malaysia, Singapore and Spain; limitations on the recognition of foreign credentials by qualified authorities (Israel, Japan and Sweden); problems created by customs regulations (Hungary and Russia); obstacles to the free movement of persons (Denmark, Greece and Japan); and limitations on foreign ownership, for instance in Mexico and Thailand.

The issues and challenges this creates for a country like the USA are numerous. Should visas be restricted for international students and should these students be denied access to Western-style, high-quality education? Does 'exporting' these educational services, instead of 'importing' the students, provide a real alternative? How do you replace the cultural experience of living in another country, which is key to people's understanding and acceptance of each other? Where should this issue be debated internationally—at the WTO, the Organisation for Economic Co-operation and Development or the United Nations?

The issue should be of especial concern to the United States because the most prestigious US institutions of higher education are private, not public. These institutions do not want the US Government to set policy. The whole problem may be linked with a wider dilemma over immigration controls and the balance between their two possible functions: to keep out the bad, but also to let through the good. The agenda is one which should be of serious concern to 'rich men' and 'poor men' alike.

[4] Blumenstyk, G., 'Spanning the globe: higher-education companies take their turf battles overseas', *Chronicle of Higher Education*, 27 June 2003.

[5] For WTO documents on education services see URL <http://www.wto.org/english/tratop_e/serv_e/education_e/education_e.htm>.

Appendices

Editors' remarks

The appendices constitute, so far as the author is aware, a unique compilation of material. These introductory remarks are designed to clarify the motive for compiling them, to explain the criteria for the inclusion of the sources, and to highlight some important findings of the connected research.

The challenges of compiling this information have illustrated the difficulties analysts face when seeking to create a defining framework for research on the business–security relationship. The contributions in this volume have brought out the complexity of the subject. They also underline that, while systematic public–private sector consultation and partnership are needed to tackle present-day security challenges, neither the principles nor the comprehensive mechanisms for such cooperation have been identified. Against this background, the purpose of the appendices is to offer new reference material to help in the further exploration of this important subject without prejudging any of the issues or the policy and practical choices involved. The appendices can be used as a factual directory and at the same time as a suggested framework for analysis of the relevant topics.

The first appendix provides an overview of the main institutions active in the field of security that are at the same time active in or interested in the public–private sector interface. It lists international institutions, including both governmental and non-governmental organizations (NGOs), along with academic and research bodies. In the second appendix the focus lies, conversely, on private-sector organizations and institutions interested in or active in the area of business and security. It presents a selective review of private-sector engagement in this field. The third appendix is a select bibliography, which lists a variety of books and articles covering the broad range of issues linked to the business–security relationship.

The three appendices are the product of one person's review of the available resources, and make no claim to completeness. They do not necessarily include all the sources mentioned in the text and footnotes of the chapters in this volume. Another important limitation of these findings is the necessarily West-centric approach (constrained i.a. by language knowledge) that was taken during the research. Most of the resources are online findings. They cover various manifestations of private–public sector interface, communication and partnership, such as action projects and programmes, dialogue and networking initiatives, 'code setting' and 'best practice' initiatives, international regulations, declarations providing a basis for debate, and other measures for information exchange, building networks and collaboration. The appendices aim to identify what has been achieved in this field up to now and what kind of resources exist, but it also draws attention to some sources in which the author sees potential for further kinds of public–private engagement and, in particular, for more cooperative action.

One of the general findings is that there are few comprehensive resources available for researchers interested in pursuing the various aspects of the relationship between the corporate world and the world of security. Even fewer are the findings regarding active public–private partnerships in these fields. Only a few organizations and institutions have research projects or programmes that directly link up with corporations as responsible actors for enhanced security and conflict prevention. International Alert, for example, has been promoting private-sector engagement in the field of conflict prevention, peace-building and crisis-management policies since 1999, focusing on partnerships between transnational corporations and multilateral agencies, governments and civil society. In general, policy and research institutions have most often analysed the impact of business on society in connection with development aid, humanitarian assistance and sustainable development, rather than linking it directly to 'hard' or 'traditional' security issues. Another topic that has often drawn institutional attention is business responsibility as part of business ethics, since more and more corporations see a need to pay particular attention to corporate social responsibility (CSR) and good governance (codes of conduct). While these findings do not exactly fit into the question of the private-sector relationship to the 'new security agenda', which dominates the rest of this volume, they are, however, relevant to the general security requirement for stable countries and efficient, functioning economies. Progress in these areas would support a broader approach to conflict prevention and would contribute to a more secure global environment.

The large number of official and institutional listings in appendix 1 illustrates that the responsibility and the role of the business sector in the field of security are, at least, now generally acknowledged by the security community. Most international organizations, such as the United Nations Organization (UNO), the World Bank, the European Union (EU), the Organization for Security and Co-operation in Europe (OSCE), the Organisation for Economic Co-operation and Development (OECD), the New Partnership for Africa's Development (NEPAD) and development banks, research centres and NGOs are included because they have, as a minimum, taken some kind of position on the issue.

The findings set out in appendix 2 show a more fragmented picture of private-sector activities explicitly addressing security, ranging from risk-management consul-tancies, business councils and business round tables, to online security services and other Internet-based tools. As noted above, however, the limited results of this search are not necessarily representative, *inter alia* because they deliberately leave out busi-ness activities that may be more indirectly or 'unconsciously' relevant. An overall finding is that there is no major specialized organ on the multilateral level which would allow corporations to assess and prioritize their own security needs, targets, impacts and investments, and at the same time to be informed about their potential role and responsibilities in the general security environment. Despite many long-standing platforms for businesses, such as the World Trade Organization (WTO), the International Chamber of Commerce (ICC) and more specialized business networks and trade, employers' and business policy organizations—and despite existing multi-lateral initiatives such as the UN Global Compact and the Global Reporting Initiative (GRI)—no existing body devotes itself specifically and exclusively to business-relevant security topics or provides a framework for organized cooperation to address them.

That the private sector affects, and is affected by, the recent and continuing devel-opments in the security environment can no longer be in doubt. What is still required is a comprehensive effort to handle the implications of this growing interface and interdependence, and to allow private actors to contribute to better security in its broadest sense—not least so that they can better protect themselves from various threats in their own best corporate interest.

Inclusion in these thematic appendices does not imply an endorsement by the edi-tors or by SIPRI in general of the views expressed in any of these sources. If you wish to correct the information presented, or believe that relevant sources of information have been omitted, please contact director@sipri.org.

Appendix 1
Institutions in the field of security, active or interested in the public–private sector interface: government and international institutions, academic and research bodies, and non-governmental organizations

Isabel Frommelt

African Development Bank (ADB)

URL <http://www.afdb.org>
Established in 1999; location: Abidjan, Côte d'Ivoire

Members: Algeria, Angola, Benin, Botswana, Burkina Faso, Burundi, Cameroon, Cape Verde, Central African Republic, Chad, Comoros, Congo, Côte d'Ivoire, Democratic Republic of the Congo, Djibouti, Egypt, Equatorial Guinea, Eritrea, Ethiopia, Gabon, Gambia, Ghana, Guinea, Guinea-Bissau, Kenya, Lesotho, Liberia, Libya, Madagascar, Malawi, Mali, Mauritania, Mauritius, Morocco, Mozambique, Namibia, Niger, Nigeria, Rwanda, Sao Tome and Principe, Senegal, Seychelles, Sierra Leone, Somalia, South Africa, Sudan, Swaziland, Tanzania, Togo, Tunisia, Uganda, Zambia, Zimbabwe

Description: ADB is a multinational development bank supported by 77 nations. As Africa's first development financial institution, it is often approached for assistance in efforts to promote conflict resolution and prevention. Where tensions have not escalated into violence, ADB also engages in peace-making through policy analysis and dialogue together with other stakeholders. It plays a significant role in post-conflict situations and in rebuilding institutions and infrastructures.

Disaster and Business Continuity Preparedness

URL <http://www.afdb.org/about_adb/tra_tn/disaster_bcp_7apr2003.doc>
Established in 2000

The contingency planning of ADB aims to protect the interests of all key stakeholders of the ADB. A key organ in the implementation of the plan is the Crisis Management Committee, which closely monitors developments affecting ADB and advises on measures for the mitigation of relevant risks.

Strategic Plan 2003–2007

URL <http://www.afdb.org/knowledge/publications/pdf/adb_strategic_plan2003-2007e.pdf>

ADB's strategic planning includes the private sector, regional economic integration and post-conflict reconstruction, since it aspires to play a leadership role in improving the business and investment climate for public–private partnerships (PPPs) in infrastructure and social services. In 2003 the ADB issued the private-sector brochure *Development Objectives and Strategy of ADB Private Sector Operations*, available at

URL <http://www.afdb.org/knowledge/publications/pdf/opsd_brochure_may2003e. pdf>.

Aid and Trade

URL <http://www.aidandtrade.com>
Established in 1999; location: Hadleigh, UK

Description: International Aid & Trade Conferences are exhibitions of goods and services by companies that work with multilateral organizations, such as the United Nations and the World Bank, as well as NGOs, such as the International Committee of the Red Cross (ICRC) and others. The conferences bring together the heads of UN agenci315executive officers, and government and NGO representatives to work more effectively to meet the challenges of man-made and natural disasters and to provide emergency humanitarian and development aid. The conferences are co-organized by the Winchester Group (URL <http://www.wingrp.com>) and the United Nations Office for Project Services (UNOPS; see URL <http://www.unops.org>).

The *International Aid & Trade Europe 2004 Conference on Integrated Aid and Development Solutions: The Role of the Private Sector* (Jan. 2004) featured an opening debate on the significant role of the private sector in the provision of emergency aid and development. The forum focused on the key donors' views on the power of the private sector to effect change, its role in aid and development, and the need for its greater engagement with the major implementing aid agencies (the UN, the ICRC and NGOs). It also defined the responsibilities of business and ways in which it can contribute to poverty alleviation and socio-economic development. See URL <http://www.aidandtrade.com/iat/europe/ov.asp>.

Amnesty International (AI)

URL <http://www.amnesty.org>
Established in 1961; location: London, UK

Description: Amnesty International is a worldwide campaigning movement to promote the human rights enshrined in the Universal Declaration of Human Rights and other international standards. In its campaign on *Economic Globalisation and Human Rights,* AI encourages companies and international financial institutions to be accountable for the human rights impact of their activities; to take into account the human rights impact of all aspects of their operations; to prevent human rights abuses in their own operations; and to use their legitimate influence to support human rights in all the countries in which they operate. AI's *Business and Economic Relation Network (BERN)* comprises coordinators and volunteers who form business groups or are otherwise engaged in dialogue with companies to encourage them to support and promote human rights in their sphere of influence. Within this network AI continues to put pressure on governments and the diamond industry to include a monitoring and statistics-gathering system in the Kimberley Process. The *Amnesty International UK (AIUK) Business Group* was established in 1991 as a small group of individual AIUK members with business or industrial experience. In recent years it has become increasingly active in influencing both the debate on business and human rights and the behaviour of leading British companies on these issues. See URL <http://www.amnesty.org.uk/business>.

Asian Development Bank (ADB)

URL <http://www.adb.org>

Established in 1966; location: Manila, the Philippines

Members: Afghanistan, Australia, Austria, Azerbaijan, Bangladesh, Belgium, Bhutan, Cambodia, Canada, China, Cook Islands, Denmark, Fiji Islands, Finland, France, Germany, Hong Kong (China), India, Indonesia, Italy, Japan, Kazakhstan, Kiribati, Korea (South), Kyrgyzstan, Laos, Luxembourg, Malaysia, Maldives, Marshall Islands, Micronesia, Mongolia, Myanmar, Nauru, Nepal, New Zealand, Norway, Pakistan, Palau, Papua New Guinea, Philippines, Portugal, Samoa, Singapore, Solomon Islands, Spain, Sri Lanka, Sweden, Switzerland, Tajikistan, Taiwan (China), Thailand, Netherlands, Timor-Leste, Tonga, Turkey, Turkmenistan, Tuvalu, UK, USA, Uzbekistan, Vanuatu, Viet Nam

Description: ADB is a multilateral development finance institution with 63 members. It has expanded its private-sector activities for the fight against poverty in Asia and the Pacific Region. It supports the development of the private sector by: encouraging reforms and policy environments that establish the right conditions for businesses to flourish; promoting public–private sector partnerships; and providing financial assistance to private enterprises and financial institutions. The key premises for ADB's work are that private-sector development is crucial for economic growth, that sustainable economic growth creates jobs and can reduce poverty, and that the private sector is the largest source of investment and employment. See URL <http://www.adb.org/PrivateSector/default.asp>.

Through its *Private Sector Department (PSD)*, ADB provides direct assistance to private-sector projects with a clear development impact but which may have limited access to capital. See URL <http://www.adb.org/PSOD/default.asp>.

Berne Declaration (Erklärung von Bern, EvB)

URL <http://www.evb.ch>

Established in 1968; location: Zurich, Switzerland

Description: The Berne Declaration is an NGO which campaigns on development issues at the national and international levels for more just and environmentally sustainable North–South relations in politics, economics, culture and food. It coordinates an international conference, *The Public Eye on Davos*, as a joint project of a coalition of NGOs, held at the same time as the World Economic Forum (WEF) annual meeting. The purpose of the conference is to make the WEF more open, transparent and representative and to serve as a forum for critical analysis of the 'neo-liberal' globalization promoted by the largest multinational corporations, calling for more equitable and sustainable world economic policies.

Bonn International Center for Conversion (BICC)

URL <http://www.bicc.de>

Established in 1994; location: Bonn, Germany

Description: BICC promotes and facilitates the processes whereby people, skills, technology, equipment, and financial and economic resources can be shifted away from the defence sector and applied to alternative civilian uses. BICC's project on *The Role of External Actors in Civil War Economies in Sub-Saharan Africa* (Apr.

2003–Mar. 2005) focuses on the role and function of external economic actors which are based outside conflict zones, but which support conflict parties through economic interaction in civil war economies (Angola, the Democratic Republic of the Congo, Guinea, Liberia, Sierra Leone, Somalia and Sudan). This includes corporations which trade with conflict parties and foreign armed forces whose intervention in a conflict is motivated by economic interests, as well as arms dealers. See URL <http://www.bicc.de/projects/ongoing_projects/111_ecwarend_english.html>.

The conference *Money Makes the War Go Round? The EU and Transforming the Economy of War in Sudan* (June 2002), co-organized with the European Coalition on Oil in Sudan (ECOS), addressed such themes as how resources are mobilized for war; how local, regional or global economic structures and incentives act as impediments to peace; and how European actors can help to transform the economy of war in Sudan. See URL <http://www.bicc.de/events/sudanws/index.html>.

British American Security Information Council (BASIC)

URL <http://www.basicint.org>
Established in 1987; locations: London, UK, and Washington, DC, USA

Description: The objective of the BASIC *Transatlantic Security Program,* is to advance the long-term goal of cooperative security in the Euro-Atlantic region by: developing and promoting ideas for arms control and conflict resolution through the EU, NATO and the OSCE; contributing to a broader definition of European and transatlantic security and a re-evaluation of the roles of international security organizations; monitoring and pressing for conflict prevention in potential regions of conflict; offering a critique of destabilizing policies; and proposing options for improving confidence and understanding among states. See URL <http://www.basicint.org/europe/euroindex.htm>.

Brookings Institution

URL <http://www.brook.edu>
Established in 1927; location: Washington, DC, USA

Description: The Brookings Institution carries out research on several topics relating the private sector to (US) homeland security, such as *Critical Infrastructure Protection and the Private Sector: The Crucial Role of Incentives* (2003). In *Homeland Security and the Private Sector* (2003), Peter R. Orszag claims that, given the significance of the private sector in homeland security settings, structuring incentives properly is critical and should therefore be supplemented with stronger market-based incentives in several sectors. He also argues that a mixed system of minimum regulatory standards, insurance and third-party inspections would better harness the power of private markets to invest in homeland security in a cost-effective manner. See URL <http://www.brook.edu/views/testimony/orszag/20030904.htm> and URL <http://www.brook.edu/views/testimony/orszag/20031119.htm>.

The central role of the private sector in counter-terrorism is also emphasized in *Information Exchange between the Public and Private Sector for Homeland Security* (testimony before the Technology and Privacy Advisory Committee by J. Steinberg, 2003), in which corporations are regarded as collectors and holders of information, stewards of critical infrastructure and material that could be used in an attack, and as important actors in preventing and responding to attacks. It points out that the goal of a working group of the Markle Foundation Task Force is to identify information that exists in the private sector and is valuable for homeland security and counter-terrorism efforts, and to develop a strategy that will give government the ability to access and use it effectively. See URL <http://www.brook.edu/views/testimony/steinberg/20030619.htm>. For further information see 'Building an effective, sustainable partnership between the government and the private sector', Markle Task Force on National Security in the Information Age, Working Group II, Dec. 2003, at URL <http://www.brook.edu/views/papers/steinberg20031202.pdf>.

Brookings organized a workshop on *Protecting the Homeland: The Need for a Public/Private Partnership* (2003), which focused on sharpening the capability to achieve an improved state of organizational effectiveness in critical times and on how public–private partnership can maximize effectiveness. See URL <http://www.brook.edu/execed/open/homeland.htm>.

See also *Terrorist Financing: Report of an Independent Task Force* (2003), URL <http://www.brook.edu/press/books/terroristfinancing.htm>.

Business and Human Rights Resource Centre

URL <http://www.business-humanrights.org>

Location: London, UK

Description: The Centre's online library covers over 1000 companies, over 160 countries and over 150 topics. It provides news releases and links to issues involving security, conflict and business. The site is composed of links to a wide range of materials published by companies, NGOs, governments, intergovernmental organizations, journalists and academics, including reports on corporate policies, accusations of misconduct and positive codes of conduct as well as security issues in conflict zones. The purpose of the website is to promote greater awareness and informed discussion of important issues relating to business and human rights. An overview of the subcategories of companies is available at URL <http://www.business-humanrights.org/Categories/Companies>.

See also the sites on *Security Issues and Conflict Zones* and on *Conflict Prevention and Resolution* at URL <http://www.business-humanrights.org/Categories/Issues/Security>.

Carnegie Endowment for International Peace

URL <http://www.ceip.org>

Established in 1910; location: Washington, DC, USA

Description: The Carnegie Endowment is dedicated to advancing cooperation between nations and promoting active international engagement by the United States. Its interests span geographic regions and relations among governments, business, international organizations and civil society, focusing on the economic, political and technological forces driving global change. The project on *The Public Role of the Private Sector* explores the emerging relationship between business and government and new strategies for managing the public–private nexus, with special focus on the role of business as an international policy actor. See URL <http://www.ceip.org/files/projects/rps/rps_descrip.ASP>.

Center for Contemporary Conflict (CCC)

URL <http://www.ccc.nps.navy.mil>

Established in 2001; location: Monterey, California, USA

Description: CCC conducts research on current and emerging security issues and conveys its findings to US and other NATO policy makers and military forces. Its analysts compile 'strategic insight' assessments of current developments in key regions and issue areas. The following, by Robert E. Looney, are of particular interest: *Strategic Insight: Economic Costs to the United States Stemming From the 9/11 Attacks* (2002) and *Following the Terrorist Informal Money Trail: The Hawala Financial Mechanism* (2002), available at URL <http://www.ccc.nps.navy.mil/rsepResources/si/aug02/homeland.asp> and URL <http://www.ccc.nps.navy.mil/rsep Resources/si/nov02/southAsia.asp>.

Center for Defense Information (CDI)

URL <http://www.cdi.org>

Established in 1972; location: Washington, DC, USA

Description: CDI is dedicated to strengthening security through international cooperation, to reducing reliance on unilateral military power to resolve conflict, and to reducing reliance on nuclear weapons through prudent oversight of defence programmes and related spending. In the framework of its *Terrorism Program* it investigates terrorism and security-related issues, such as reactions to evolving threats, anti-terrorist finances, terror and oil in Central Asia, and port and maritime security in the United States. See URL <http://www.cdi.org/program/index.cfm?ProgramID=39>.

Center for Global Development (CGD)

URL <http://www.cgdev.org>

Established in 1910; location: Washington, DC, USA

Description: CGD is a think tank dedicated to reducing global poverty and inequality through policy-oriented research and active engagement on development issues with the policy community, the private sector and the public. In its research project *Weak States and National Security* research is conducted on more effective policies to engage the poorest countries as part of the US efforts in the global war on terrorism, and to reduce the short-, medium- and long-term threats emanating from the developing world. See URL <http://cgdev.axion-it.net/Research/?Page=Research%20 Projects>.

Center for Security Studies (Forschungsstelle für Sicherheitspolitik, FSK)

URL <http://www.fsk.ethz.ch>

Established in 1986; location: Zurich, Switzerland

Description: FSK, based at the ETH Zurich (Swiss Federal Institute of Technology Zurich), specializes in the field of national and international security studies and has developed two relevant electronic information services: the *International Relations and Security Network* and the *Comprehensive Risk Analysis and Management Network*.

The aim of the *International Relations and Security Network (ISN)*, a Swiss contribution to the NATO Partnership for Peace, is to link professionals working in the security community and to facilitate information exchange, dialogue and cooperation. The network maintains close relationships with over 80 international partner institutes. See URL <http://www.isn.ethz.ch>.

The Comprehensive Risk Analysis and Management Network (CRN) develops methodological expertise for the identification, evaluation and analysis of national collective risks that modern society faces in a Euro-Atlantic context. It is an electronic platform for promoting dialogue on risk profiling, including risk-specific issues such as cyber security threats, natural disasters, technological risks, terrorism and extremism. See URL <http://www.isn.ethz.ch/crn>.

FSK's research in the field of international security policy and conflict prevention covers issues such as security-related aspects of nations' foreign policy, transatlantic relations and the architecture of European security, qualitative analysis of critical information infrastructure protection (CIIP) policies, crisis management and biological terrorism. The Center also conducts basic research on the rise of violence and armed conflict, its dynamics, and the theory and practice of constructive conflict resolution. See URL <http://www.fsk.ethz.ch/research/research_isp.cfm>.

Of special interest is the publication *Conflict Prevention: The Untapped Potential of the Business Sector* (A. Wenger and D. Möckli, 2003), which examines the qualities the business sector could bring to the prevention of deadly intra-state conflict. It also proposes specific ways in which businesses could engage in prevention efforts, and demonstrates that the business sector has both the means and the motivation to ensure the long-term success of conflict-prevention efforts in its own as well as the general interest.

Center for Strategic and International Studies (CSIS)

URL <http://www.csis.org>
Established in 1962; location: Washington, DC, USA

Description: CSIS helps to develop national and international public policy by assessing political risks and examining international security and stability, in particular by analysing new and unfamiliar threats as well as residual dangers and conflicts. CSIS develops responses to threats and dangers to help government and business leaders to react quickly to changing conditions. The *International Security Program* focuses on areas such as homeland defence, global hotspots, the nuclear threat, and re-thinking alliances and partnerships in the 21st century, and on issues related to security, technology and bio-terrorism. In the framework of the *Transnational Threats Initiative (TNT)* more than 150 experts from the public and private sectors comprise seven task forces, ranging from chemical, biological and nuclear terrorism and future cyber threats to financial crimes and money laundering. The Initiative aims to anticipate emerging transnational threats and provide cross-cutting policy recommendations. See URL <http://www.csis.org/tnt/threatsrc.cfm>. At the February 2003 annual *Corporate Security Officer Conference*, chief security officers from major US corporations discussed how the private sector can interact more effectively with the federal government on terrorism risks and how to compare perceptions and current strategies to reduce threat vulnerabilities. CSIS has also launched a comprehensive series of seminars to address the urgent critical infrastructure issues facing the United States. See URL <http://www.csis.org/tech/cips/index.htm>.

See also *Play to Win: Final Report of the Bi-partisan Commission on Post-conflict Reconstruction* (2003) and *Cyberthreats and Information Security: Meeting the 21st Century Challenge* (2001).

Center for the Study of Global Governance (CSGG)

URL <http://www.lse.ac.uk/Depts/global>

Established in 1992; location: London, UK

Description: CSGG, at the London School of Economics and Political Science, focuses on the increased understanding and knowledge of global problems and the interaction between academics and policy makers. Its project on *Oil and Conflict* analyses the roles and responsibilities of multinational oil companies and global powers in oil-dependent countries and the interaction between them. Special attention is devoted to the responsibility of multinational oil companies, with the view that they are not only the main private economic actors but also the main political brokers in many oil-dependent countries. See URL <http://www.lse.ac.uk/Depts/global/Other Projects.htm#>.

Center on International Cooperation (CIC)

URL <http://www.cic.nyu.edu>

Established in 1996; location: New York, N.Y., USA

Description: CIC has established several programmes on conflict-related issues in which the capacities for effective multilateral action in the run-up to and aftermath of violent conflict are examined. One of CIC's first projects, *Pledges of Aid for Conflict Recovery*, led to a major policy initiative—*The Strategic Recovery Facility*. CIC has extended this work to a particular case through the project on *The Reconstruction of Afghanistan,* which monitors assistance and provides analysis on key issues of the country's reconstruction. See URL <http://www.cic.nyu.edu/conflict.html>, URL <http://www.cic.nyu.edu/conflict/conflict_project3.html> and URL <http://www.cic. nyu.edu/conflict/conflict_project4.html>.

Centre for Defence and International Security Studies (CDISS)

URL <http://www.cdiss.org>

Established in 1990; location: Lancaster, UK

Description: CDISS conducts research to raise awareness and stimulate debate on a wide range of defence and security issues relevant to the UK and the international community. CDISS's *Terrorism Programme* aims to identify major trends in international political violence, explaining the background to currently active terrorist groups and their objectives, tactics and weapons, as well as commenting on emerging trends. See also the database on *Terrorist Incidents 1945–1998* at URL <http://www.cdiss.org/terror.htm>.

Commonwealth Association for Corporate Governance (CACG)

URL <http://www.cacg-inc.com>

Established in 1998; location: Marlborough, New Zealand

Members: See URL <http://www.cacg-inc.com/html/about.html#members>

Description: CACG was established by 24 Commonwealth countries to promote the best available international standards of corporate governance through education, consultation and information throughout the Commonwealth as a means to achieve global standards of business efficiency, commercial probity, and effective economic and social development.

Conflict Prevention and Post-Conflict Reconstruction Network (CPR)

URL <http://www.cpr-network.org>
Established in 1998; location: at the World Bank Conflict Prevention and Reconstruction Unit, Washington, DC, USA

Description: CPR was established after a meeting of post-conflict/transition and emergency units of multilateral and bilateral organizations, convened by the World Bank. The participants considered it critical to improve networking and coordination among the various organizations working on complex emergencies, with the support of a platform for knowledge sharing. The CPR Network brings together 29 organizations which are operationally active in conflict prevention, to improve effectiveness in conflict prevention and post-conflict reconstruction; see URL <http://www.developmentgateway.org/node/118839/atn?>. Its objectives include operational coordination, knowledge-sharing, collaborative mobilization and deployment of human and financial resources, the identification of countries and situations for joint interventions and improved capacity to respond.

Council of Europe (CoE)

URL <http://www.coe.int>
Established in 1949; location: Strasbourg, France

Members: Albania, Andorra, Armenia, Austria, Azerbaijan, Belgium, Bosnia and Herzegovina, Bulgaria, Croatia, Cyprus, Czech Republic, Denmark, Estonia, Finland, France, Georgia, Germany, Greece, Hungary, Iceland, Ireland, Italy, Latvia, Liechtenstein, Lithuania, Luxembourg, Malta, Moldova, Netherlands, Norway, Poland, Portugal, Romania, Russian Federation, San Marino, Serbia and Montenegro, Slovakia, Slovenia, Spain, Sweden, Switzerland, Former Yugoslav Republic of Macedonia (FYROM), Turkey, UK, Ukraine

Description: The CoE is the continent's oldest political organization, grouping together 45 states and 5 with observer status (Canada, the Holy See, Japan, Mexico and the USA). Originally created to achieve greater unity between its members, the Council's current aims are to defend human rights, democracy and the rule of law; to standardize social and legal practices; and to assist in carrying out and consolidating political, legal and constitutional reforms in parallel with economic reforms.

Conventions on the suppression of terrorism

Fighting terrorism is a priority for the CoE. Its plan of action is to update legal instruments and reinforce international cooperation, particularly by identifying the financial sources of terrorism, improving investigative methods, adapting judicial systems and supporting the victims of terrorism.

Combating organized crime, money laundering and corruption is covered by European standards such as the 1999 Criminal Law Convention on Corruption; the 1999 Civil Law Convention on Corruption; and the 1990 Convention on Laundering,

Search, Seizure and Confiscation of the Proceeds from Crime. See URL <http://conventions.coe.int>.

Theme File on Terrorism

URL <http://www.coe.int/T/E/Com/Files/Themes/terrorism/default.asp>
This CoE website contains a collection of documents, including several conventions on combating terrorism, information on specialized conferences and Internet links on the sources of terrorism. The most significant developments in the area of legal action against terrorism relate to the work of the *Multidisciplinary Group on International Action against Terrorism* (Groupe multidisciplinaire sur l'action internationale contre le terrorisme, GMT). GMT was set up by the Committee of Ministers in 2001 with the tasks of identifying priorities for future action and reviewing the relevant CoE international instruments, in particular the 1977 European Convention on the Suppression of Terrorism. Following the expiry of the GMT mandate, the Committee of Ministers set up the *Committee of Experts on Terrorism (CODEXTER)*, responsible for coordinating and following up the counter-terrorist activities of the CoE. Progress in the implementation of the priority activities was reported to the October 2003 25th Conference of European Ministers of Justice in Sofia, Bulgaria, which addressed the topic of terrorism and how to improve the legal response to it.

Group of States against Corruption (Groupe d'États contre la corruption, GRECO)

URL <http://www.greco.coe.int>
Members: See the Internet site
Special organs such as GRECO aim to improve their members' capacity to fight corruption by monitoring the compliance of states with their undertakings in this field. GRECO contributes to identifying deficiencies and insufficiencies of national mechanisms against corruption, and to prompting the necessary legislative, institutional and practical reforms in order to prevent and combat corruption. This includes, in particular, the 1997 *Twenty Guiding Principles for the Fight against Corruption* (see URL <http://cm.coe.int/ta/res/1997/97x24.htm>) and implementation of the international legal instruments adopted in pursuit of the Programme of Action against Corruption (PAC).

Fighting cyber crime

URL <http://conventions.coe.int/Treaty/en/Treaties/Html/185.htm>
The CoE's efforts to fight cyber crime have led to the adoption of the *Convention on Cybercrime* (2001) and the *Additional Protocol* to criminalize racist or xenophobic acts carried out via computer networks (2003).

Ethics Resource Center (ERC)

URL <http://www.ethics.org>
Established in 1977; location: Washington, DC, USA

Description: The vision of ERC is a world where individuals and organizations act with integrity. ERC promotes ethics around the world and assists local ethics institutions to develop the necessary capacity and technical expertise to provide a wide range of business and organizational ethics resources. Since 1995 ERC has offered a broad platform for dialogue and cooperation and works with small businesses and business associations to combat corruption.

Ethos Institute of Companies and Social Responsibility

URL <http://www.ethos.org.br>

Established in 1998; location: São Paulo, Brazil

Description: The Ethos Institute NGO was founded in Brazil by a group of business people from 11 companies. Today the institute is an association of hundreds of corporations of all sizes and sectors that are interested in developing their activities in a socially responsible manner. Its mission is to spread business social responsibility by helping businesses to understand and incorporate the concept of socially responsible business behaviour; to contribute to the achievement of long-term sustainable economic success; and to identify innovative and effective ways of acting in partnership with communities in the construction of a common welfare.

European Bank for Reconstruction and Development (EBRD)

URL <http://www.ebrd.org>

Established in 1991; location: London, UK

Description: EBRD was set up to support former communist countries in Central and Eastern Europe and former Soviet republics, *inter alia* by nurturing a new private sector in a democratic environment. As the largest single investor in the region the Bank helps to build market economies and democracies in 27 countries and to mobilize foreign direct investment. Despite its public-sector shareholders, the Bank invests mainly in private enterprises together with commercial partners. Through its investments, it promotes structural and sectoral reforms, privatization and entrepreneurship, infrastructure development needed to support the private sector and the adoption of strong corporate governance.

Corporate policies and the Anti-terrorist Statement

EBRD performs 'due diligence' on the integrity of prospective clients, including verification checks that no client is on the UN Security Council lists of entities and individuals suspected of supporting terrorist activities (see the *Anti-terrorist Statement*, at URL <http://www.ebrd.org/about/index.htm>). EBRD's Chief Compliance Office promotes good governance and ensures that the highest standards of integrity are applied to all activities of the Bank in accordance with international best practice. In particular, it deals with conflicts of interest, corruption, confidentiality and money laundering.

European Centre for Development Policy Management (ECDPM)

URL <http://www.ecdpm.org>

Established in 1986; location: Maastricht, the Netherlands

Description: In collaboration with International Alert, ECDPM developed a discussion paper (no. 31, 2001) entitled *The EU's Response to Conflict Affected Countries: Operational Guidance for the Implementation of the Cotonou Agreement*, which asserts that brokering a public–private dialogue and partnership are prerequisites for a sustainable approach to crisis and conflict affected countries.

European Corporate Governance Institute (ECGI)

URL <http://www.ecgi.org>

Established in 2002; location: Brussels, Belgium

Description: As the successor of the European Corporate Governance Network (ECGN), ECGI provides a forum for debate and dialogue between academics, legislators and practitioners, focusing on major corporate governance issues and promoting best practice.

European Peacebuilding Liaison Office (EPLO)

URL <http://www.eplo.org>

Established in 2001; location: Brussels, Belgium

Description: EPLO was set up by a network of 17 European NGOs (see the website) which are active in conflict prevention and peace-building. The members seek to promote peace-building policies among decision makers in Europe and aim to improve EU awareness of the contribution NGOs can make to conflict prevention and peace-building. Conversely, EPLO informs its member NGOs about EU structures, policies and personnel, institutional and policy developments, EU instruments for conflict prevention and EU-funded peace-building programmes.

European Platform for Conflict Prevention and Transformation

URL <http://www.euconflict.org>

Established in 1997; location: Utrecht, the Netherlands

Description: The European Platform, hosted by the European Centre for Conflict Prevention, is an open network of 150 key European organizations (see 'key contacts' on the website) working in the field of the prevention and resolution of violent conflicts in the international arena. Its mission is to contribute to conflict prevention and resolution by facilitating information exchange and by stimulating cooperation and synergy. Its comprehensive website contains information on conflicts, conflict prevention and peace-building; efforts by non-state actors to prevent or resolve conflicts; profiles of international and local organizations; contact details for national and regional experts; and conferences and campaigns focusing on these issues.

European Union (EU)

URL <http://europa.eu.int>

Established in 1954; location: Brussels, Belgium

Members: Austria, Belgium, Denmark, Finland, Germany, Greece, Ireland, Italy, Luxembourg, Netherlands, Portugal, Spain, Sweden, UK; the new members joining in May 2004: Cyprus, Czech Republic, Estonia, Hungary, Latvia, Lithuania, Malta, Poland, Slovakia and Slovenia

Description: EU member states have set up common institutions to which they delegate some of their sovereignty so that decisions on specific matters of joint interest can be made democratically at the European level. The five EU institutions with specific roles are the European Parliament, the Council of the European Union, the European Commission (executive body), the Court of Justice and the Court of Auditors.

Most of the cooperation between EU countries initially focused on trade and the economy. Today it also deals with many other subjects, such as citizens' rights; ensuring freedom, security and justice; regional development and environmental protection; and common foreign, security and defence policies.

Fight against Terrorism—The European Union's Broad Response

A chronological overview of the EU's action on all fronts in the international campaign to eradicate terrorism is available at URL <http://europa.eu.int/news/110901/>.

Council of the European Union

An overview of the Common Foreign and Security Policy (CFSP) in the Council is available at URL <http://ue.eu.int/Pesc/default.asp?lang=en>.

Council Directive 2001/97/EC gave the appropriate tools to the member states to fight the financing of terrorism more effectively, and started the process of EU lists and measures to be taken against those individuals, organizations or entities listed. It amended Council Directive 91/308/EC on prevention of the use of the financial system for the purpose of money laundering and gives a much wider definition of money laundering.

European Commission

The site of the *Directorate-General for External Relations* provides an overview of the CFSP in the Commission, available at URL <http://europa.eu.int/comm/external_relations/cfsp/intro/index.htm>. The site on *Conflict Prevention and Civilian Crisis Management,* at URL <http://europa.eu.int/comm/external_relations/cpcm/cp.htm>, focuses on the adopted proposal to implement the ban on conflict diamonds within a Community Certification Scheme for the international trade in rough diamonds. The scheme also aims to prevent conflict diamonds from discrediting the legitimate market for rough diamonds, which makes an important economic contribution, not least to certain developing countries in Africa. See also URL <http://europa.eu.int/comm/external_relations/cpcm/cp/ip02_1205.htm>.

This *Directorate-General for Justice and Home Affairs* deals *inter alia* with the fight against organized transnational crime, terrorism and judicial cooperation in general, and crime prevention, including combating the financing of terrorist groups, money laundering, economic crime ('white-collar crime') and cyber crime. See the summary of legislation at URL <http://europa.eu.int/scadplus/leg/en/s22004.htm>.

The legal and political background of the fight against terrorism is also covered in a comprehensive site on *Criminal Matters—Judicial Cooperation*, including issues such as political declarations, EU legislation, main proposals and Community acts, conventions and resolutions, and relevant background documents. See URL <http://europa.eu.int/comm/justice_home/doc_centre/criminal/terrorism/doc_criminal_terrorism_en.htm>.

The *Directorate-General EuropeAid* of the Commission established a new partnership with the private sector for the development of relevant policies. See URL <http://europa.eu.int/comm/development/body/theme/private_en.htm>.

Of particular interest is the Commission's *Green Paper—Promoting a European Framework for Corporate Social Responsibility* (July 2001), available at URL <http://europa.eu.int/comm/employment_social/soc-dial/csr/greenpaper_en.pdf>.

The Stability Pact for South Eastern Europe

The Stability Pact, initiated by the EU in 1999 and subsequently placed under the auspices of the Organization for Security and Co-operation in Europe (OSCE), represents the first serious attempt by the international community to replace the previous, reactive crisis intervention policy with a comprehensive, long-term conflict prevention strategy. The Stability Pact promotes a cross-country initiative to develop a regional power market, by coordinating international efforts to promote economic reconstruction and supporting private-sector activities in regional infrastructure projects. See URL <http://www.stabilitypact.org>.

Europol (European Police Office)

URL <http://www.europol.eu.int>
Established in 1992; location: The Hague, the Netherlands

Description: As the European Union's law enforcement organization, Europol's mandate is to contribute to improving the effectiveness of cooperation between the EU member states in preventing and combating organized crime and in supporting their actions against terrorism, counterfeiting and money laundering as well as financial crime and cyber crime.

Counter Terrorism Unit activities

Europol has combined its counter-terrorism activities in the *Counter Terrorism Program (CTP)* and the *Counter Proliferation Program (CPP)*, and has developed supporting programmes such as the *Networking Program* and the *Preparedness Program*. See URL <http://www.europol.eu.int/index.asp?page=publ_terrorism>.

The Fight against Money Laundering

In order to adjust the fight against money laundering at the highest level possible within the framework of a completed EU integrated market, Europol opened an Analytic Work File (AWF) for suspicious transactions. The main objective of the AWF is to gather suspicious transactions handled by the police or justice authorities of the member states. It aims to identify the potential links between suspicious transactions.

Europol also provides member states' law enforcement authorities with significant operational and analytical support via the Europol Liaison Officers (ELOs) and the analysts.

Financial Action Task Force on Money Laundering (FATF)

See under Organisation for Economic Co-operation and Development.

Foreign Policy Centre (FPC)

URL <http://fpc.org.uk>
Established in 1998; location: London, UK

Description: The FPC *Risk and Security Programme* research project tackles the need for better analysis of the various risks related to corporate exposure at home and abroad. It focuses on the nature of risks, their increasing complexity and the need for new solutions, as well as on the clarification of responsibilities given the growing number of actors affected.

Foreign Policy Research Institute (FPRI)

URL <http://www.fpri.org>

Established in 1995; location: Philadelphia, Pennsylvania, USA

Description: FPRI's *Center on Terrorism, Counter-Terrorism and Homeland Security* conducts studies on the goals, tactics and strategies of terrorism and the responses to it. Research includes the use of advanced computer technology scenarios to make projections on future terrorist actions, as well as the development of improved systems for protecting vital institutions and interests, focusing on the technology transfer of security assessment information from state actors to private-sector organizations. See URL <http://www.fpri.org/research/terrorism/>.

Forskningsstiftelsen Fafo (Fafo Institute for Applied Social Science)

URL <http://www.fafo.no>

Established in 1982; location: Oslo, Norway

Description: The Fafo research foundation ran the *Programme for International Co-operation and Conflict Resolution (PICCR)* in 1998–2003 (PICCR is now within the New Security Programme). The project on *The Economies of Conflict—Private Sector Activities and Armed Conflict* examines the impact of private-sector activities in the instigation and maintenance of armed conflicts—often sustained by economic activities of combatants with access to global markets. Global financial and commodity markets are used by combatants to transform control over natural resources into war fighting capacity to obtain financial resources, weapons and other materiel needed to sustain war. The aim of the project is to find answers to questions such as: how do certain private-sector activities help sustain armed conflict and what can be done about it? A series of PICCR reports and policy briefs is available on the Fafo website; e.g., on *Commerce or Crime: Regulating Economies of Conflict; Security, Development and Economies of Conflict: Problems and Responses; Globalising Transparency; Illicit Finance and Global Conflict; Dirty Diamonds;* and *Fuelling Conflict.* See URL <http://www.fafo.no/nsp/ecocon.htm>.

Fund for Peace (FfP)

URL <http://www.fundforpeace.org>

Established in 1957; location: Washington, DC, USA

Description: FfP is dedicated to the prevention and alleviation of the conditions that cause war. While the primary focus is on conflict prevention and resolution, of special interest for the role of business in conflict is its programme *The Human Rights and Business Roundtable*, launched in 1997. It was the first forum designed for multinational businesses and human rights organizations to discuss issues of common concern and to find common ground on issues that divide them. The Roundtable has evolved into an active partnership engaged in work on the problems and opportunities of economic globalization. It also develops strategic approaches for problem solving and for a better understanding of the role that each community plays in the foreign policy arena. See URL <http://www.fundforpeace.org/programs/hrbrt/hrbrt.php>.

Geneva Center for Security Policy (GCSP)

URL <http://www.gcsp.ch>

Established in 1995; location: Geneva, Switzerland

Description: Created under the framework of the Swiss participation in the NATO Partnership for Peace (PFP), the GCSP has three core missions: to provide expert training in international security policy; to conduct research in international security studies; and to foster cooperative networking with countries, institutions and experts. The GCSP forum on *Critical Infrastructure and Continuity of Services in an Increasingly Interdependent World* (Oct. 2003) addressed the coordination of planning and security measures in the protection of critical infrastructures across international borders, and between governments and the private sector. See URL <http://www.gcsp.ch/e/meetings/Recent/index.htm>.

George C. Marshall European Center for Security Studies

URL <http://www.marshallcenter.org>

Established in 1993; location: Garmisch-Partenkirchen, Germany

Description: The Conference Center of the Marshall Center serves as an international forum for defence contacts to share ideas on European security and to focus on methods to promote regional cooperation by incorporating the principles of democracy and the conditions for a market economy. The Conference Center assists Partnership for Peace nations in their efforts to establish national security structures. The annual conference programme focuses on a variety of security and economic concerns; e.g., on the *Economic War on Terrorism: Money Laundering and Financing Terrorism* (July 2003) and *Information Assurance and Cyber Terrorism* (Mar. 2004), with the aim of discussing security threats to critical national infrastructures, the role of the public and private sectors in managing the risks of such threats, and the case for a public–private partnership in protecting infrastructure.

Global Reporting Initiative (GRI)

URL <http://www.globalreporting.org>

Established in 2002; location: Amsterdam, the Netherlands

Description: The mission of GRI is to develop and disseminate globally applicable *Sustainability Reporting Guidelines*. These guidelines can be used voluntarily by organizations for reporting on the economic, environmental and social dimensions of their activities and services. GRI incorporates the active participation of representatives from various organizations such as those in business, accountancy, investment, the environment and labour. It is also an official collaborating centre of the United Nations Environment Programme (UNEP) and works with the UN Global Compact (GC). The GRI website includes a list of countries and sectors which use the guidelines. See URL <http://www.globalreporting.org/guidelines/companies.asp>.

Global Witness

URL <http://www.oneworld.org/globalwitness>

Established in 1993; location: London, UK

Description: Global Witness is an investigative organization. Its work is dedicated to exposing the link between natural resource exploitation and human rights abuses, particularly where resources such as timber, diamonds and oil are used to fund and perpetuate conflict and corruption. It publishes reports and lobbies policy makers to change current corporate and government practices that result in unregulated exploitation of resources, with an often devastating impact on people and national and regional stability. Global Witness has set a precedent with its work in Angola, which identified the conflict as one driven by motives of control and profit from resources (especially diamonds), rather than a true conflict of ideologies. Its website contains information organized by the industries or countries where it campaigns.

Group of Seven/Eight industrialized nations (G7/G8)

URL: There are several national websites, e.g., URL<http://www.g8.utoronto.ca> (G8 Information Centre, with links to other G7/G8-related sites)
Established in 1975 as the G7, and as the G8 in 1997

Members of the G8: Canada, France, Germany, Italy, Japan, Russia, UK, USA, and the European Union (as participant)

Description: The G7/G8 Summits bring together the leaders of these member states. The first Summit, held in Rambouillet, France, with six state participants, was held because of the concerns over the economic problems that faced the world in the 1970s. The process has evolved from a forum dealing essentially with macro-economic issues to an annual meeting with a broad-based agenda that addresses a wide range of international economic, political and social issues.

Building International Political Will and Capacity to Combat Terrorism—
A G8 Action Plan, 2003

URL <http://www.mofa.go.jp/policy/economy/summit/2003>
Since 11 September 2001 the G8 member states and other countries have successfully strengthened their own counter-terrorism measures, tackling three main areas of counter-terrorism activity: denying terrorists the means to commit terrorist acts (financing, false documents and weapons); denying terrorists a safe haven and ensuring that they are prosecuted and/or extradited; and overcoming vulnerability to terrorism. The G8 is further committed to supporting the UN Security Council's Counter-Terrorism Committee, and to work with the Financial Action Task Force on Money Laundering and international financial institutions to address terrorist financing. In June 2003 it established the Counter-Terrorism Action Group (CTAG).

Fighting Corruption and Improving Transparency—A G8 Action Plan, 2003

URL <http://www.g8.fr/evian/english/navigation/2003_g8_summit/summit_documents/fighting_corruption_and_improving_transparency_-_a_g8_action_plan.html>
At the June 2003 Summit in Evian, France, the G8 emphasized its determination to fight corruption and the mismanagement of public resources in both revenue raising and expenditures.

Fostering Growth and Promoting a Responsible Market Economy—
A G8 Declaration, 2003

URL <http://www.g7.utoronto.ca/summit/2003evian/growth_en.html>
The G8 acknowledges that, to support growth, it is vital that economies have sound legal systems, effective regulation and transparent corporate governance practices. It

welcomes voluntary initiatives that promote corporate social and environmental responsibility, such as the OECD Guidelines for Multinational Enterprises and the UN Global Compact principles.

Harvard School of Public Health

URL <http://www.hsph.harvard.edu>
Established in 1922; location: Boston, Massachusetts, USA

Description: The Harvard School of Public Health *Program on Humanitarian Policy and Conflict Research* has created the interdisciplinary *Economics and Conflict Research Portal*. This portal provides information and research on the role of economics in conflicts. It shows the importance of assessing how economic policies and players affect, and are affected by, conflict situations. The objectives of this portal are to build bridges between policy makers, civil society, corporations, journalists and academics; to share information; and to encourage dialogue between these actors and international corporations working in conflict zones. See URL <http://www.hsph.harvard.edu/hpcr/index.htm> and URL <http://www.preventconflict.org/portal/economics/login.php>.

Human Rights Watch (HRW)

URL <http://www.hrw.org>
Established in 1978 as Helsinki Watch, since 1988 the HRW; location: New York, N.Y., USA

Description: HRW is a large human rights organization which focuses on conducting fact-finding investigations into human rights abuses worldwide and on publishing those findings in books and reports every year, generating extensive media coverage. Of special interest is its website on *Corporations and Human Rights*, which provides commentaries, press releases, publications and reports on the issue of transnational corporations and human rights. See URL <http://www.hrw.org/corporations>.

See also HRW's *World Report 2003,* in particular the section on Business, Trade and Development, at URL <http://www.hrw.org/wr2k3/issues5.html>.

Initiative on Conflict Resolution and Ethnicity (INCORE)

URL <http://www.incore.ulst.ac.uk>
Established in 1993; location: Londonderry, Northern Ireland

Description: INCORE was set up by the University of Ulster and the United Nations University to undertake research and policy work that is useful to the resolution of ethnic, political and religious conflicts. Currently, INCORE's research focuses mainly on post-conflict issues, issues of governance and diversity, and methodology for research on violent societies. INCORE also produces an Internet-based Conflict Data Service providing current and historical information on all major conflicts and information on conflict-resolution institutions throughout the world. Particularly useful is the INCORE *Thematic Guide to Sources on Business and Conflict*, which provides substantive information on the relationship between economics, politics and sociology, and the specific role of businesses in conflict societies. See URL <http://www.incore.ulst.ac.uk/cds/themes/business.html>.

Institute for Multi-Track Diplomacy (IMTD)

URL <http://www.imtd.org>

Established in 1992; location: Arlington, Virginia, USA

Description: IMTD aims at promoting a systematic approach to peace-building and facilitating the transformation of deep-rooted social conflict. Since 1995 it has been exploring the connection between business and peace-building and has highlighted their 'natural' partnership. Research and development of a series of case studies highlight the role that business has played in resolving intractable conflicts world-wide, illustrated by practical examples of conflict areas (Cyprus, South Africa, Israel–Palestine, Northern Ireland and Asia) in which business leaders have used their skills and influence to transform their communities into more stable and peaceful environments. IMTD's *International Business Council (IBC)* was created to function in an advisory and participatory capacity, working with IMTD to explore and enhance the role of business in peace-building. See URL <http://www.imtd.org/initiatives-internationalbusiness.htm>.

Institute of Defence and Strategic Studies (IDSS)

URL <http://www.idss.edu.sg>

Established in 1996; location: Singapore

Description: IDSS, an institute of the Nanyang Technological University, focuses its research on issues relating to the security and stability of the Asia–Pacific region and their implications for Singapore and other countries in the region. IDSS routinely organizes conferences and workshops on issues of peace and security in the region: e.g., *After Bali: The Threat of Terrorism in Southeast Asia* (Jan. 2003), *The New Security Environment After 9/11* (Oct. 2002), *New Dimensions of Terrorism* (Mar. 2002) and *Providing Cyber Security in a Global Age* (Mar. 2002). See URL <http://www.idss.edu.sg/network_02.htm>.

Inter-American Development Bank (IDB) Group

URL <http://www.iadb.org>

Established in 1959; location: Washington, DC, USA

Members: Argentina, Austria, Bahamas, Barbados, Belgium, Belize, Bolivia, Brazil, Canada, Chile, Colombia, Costa Rica, Croatia, Denmark, Dominican Republic, Ecuador, El Salvador, Finland, France, Germany, Guatemala, Guyana, Haiti, Honduras, Israel, Italy, Jamaica, Japan, Mexico, Netherlands, Nicaragua, Norway, Panama, Paraguay, Peru, Portugal, Slovenia, Spain, Suriname, Sweden, Switzerland, Trinidad and Tobago, UK, Uruguay, USA, Venezuela

Description: IDB Group is the main source of multilateral financing for economic, social and institutional development in Latin America and the Caribbean through lending to public institutions and funding private projects, typically for development of infrastructure and capital markets. IDB Group consists of three institutions: the Inter-American Development Bank (IDB), the Inter-American Investment Corporation (IIC) and the Multilateral Investment Fund (MIF). As governments increasingly look to the private sector for finance, multilateral lending agencies such as IDB play a catalytic role. Currently, up to 10 per cent of IDB's non-emergency outstanding loans and guarantees may be made directly to private businesses without government guarantees. See URL <http://www.iadb.org/exr/topics/private.htm>.

International Alert (IA)

URL <http://www.international-alert.org>
Established in 1985; location: London, UK

Description: IA is an international NGO focusing on the generation of the conditions and processes conducive to the cessation of war and the generation of sustainable peace. One of its Policy Units deals specifically with the role of business in conflict societies, providing background information, case studies, tools for businesses and publications. In this unit the *Business and Conflict Programme,* founded in 1999, focuses on the peace-building practices, principles and policies of extractive transnational corporations and local businesses in partnership with multilateral agencies, governments and civil society. A key part of the programme is geared at influencing global policy on business and conflict at the corporate headquarters, governmental and multilateral levels. Of particular interest are a comprehensive report *The Business of Peace: The Private Sector as a Partner in Conflict Prevention and Resolution* (J. Nelson, 2000); and the policy report *Transnational Corporations in Conflict Prone Zones: Public Policy Responses and a Framework for Action* (J. Banfield, V. Haufler and D. Lilly, 2003), which surveys what key institutions are doing to promote conflict-sensitive business in conflict-prone zones. See URL <http://www.international-alert.org/policy/business.htm>.

The AI *Security and Peacebuilding Programme* seeks to promote security policies that support sustainable peace by addressing the factors that can destabilize tense situations and contribute to the outbreak, duration and intensity of violent conflicts. The focus is on the impact of the proliferation of light weapons and the activities of mercenaries and private military and security companies in zones of violent conflict. See URL <http://www.international-alert.org/policy/security.htm>.

The IA *Conflict Risk and Impact Assessment* (CRIA) project builds on the work begun at the UN Global Compact Dialogue on Companies in Zones of Conflict. See URL <http://www.international-alert.org/policy/business/pnr/conflict_risk_impact. htm>.

International Committee of the Red Cross (ICRC)

URL <http://www.icrc.org>
Established in 1863; location: Geneva, Switzerland

Description: ICRC conducts specialized research on the role of business in conflict areas and the relationship of transnational corporations and humanitarian organizations. Of particular interest is *Private Sector Relations,* through which the ICRC seeks to establish strategic partnerships that are mutually beneficial. The objective is to enhance the private sector's capacity to help victims of war and to promote humanitarian principles among companies operating in war-prone areas. As a result of geological and commercial interests, some companies find themselves increasingly involved in conflict-prone situations. The ICRC is establishing a dialogue at the headquarters and field levels with the aim of promoting fundamental humanitarian principles which are relevant to companies in such settings. See URL <http://www.icrc.org/web/eng/siteeng0.nsf/iwpList2/ICRC_Activities:Private_sector_relations>.

International Confederation of Free Trade Unions (ICFTU)

URL <http://www.icftu.org>
Established in 1949; location: Brussels, Belgium

Description: The ICFTU has 233 affiliated organizations in 152 countries. One of the most pressing tasks facing the international trade union movement is to address the power and influence of multinational enterprises (MNEs) as part of a trade union response to globalization.: the combination of the growth of foreign direct investment, technological changes, international financial markets, and a wide range of deregulation and privatization measures have made it possible for MNEs to dominate the global economy. The report *Trade Unions and Armed Conflicts: Using the Weapons of Dialogue and Solidarity* (Nov. 2003) explores the question of what trade unions can do in cases of armed conflict, whether a conventional war between two countries, a civil war or acts of terrorism.

International Crisis Group (ICG)

URL <http://www.crisisweb.org>
Established in 1995; location: Brussels, Belgium

Description: ICG is a multinational organization whose objective is to prevent and resolve deadly conflict. It has a field-based approach, with teams of political analysts working within or close to countries risking an outbreak, escalation or recurrence of violent conflict. ICG produces regular analytical reports containing practical recommendations targeted at key international decision makers. In the aftermath of the attacks of 11 September 2001, ICG launched a new project designed both to bring together ICG's work in existing programme areas (notably in Algeria, the Balkans, Central Asia, Colombia, Indonesia and Sudan) and to establish a new geographical focus on the Middle East and West Asia. ICG President Gareth Evans has in several speeches dealt with the business–security relationship, e.g., *War, Terrorism and Security Breakdown: the Current Risk Environment for Business* (RIIA Political Risk 2003 Conference, London) and *World Tensions and Their Impact on Business: The Costs of Neglect* (Presentation to ICC 34th World Congress, 2002, Denver, Colorado).

International Institute for Strategic Studies (IISS)

URL <http://www.iiss.org>
Established in 1958; location: London, UK

Description: The IISS's aim is to provide a primary source of accurate, objective information on international strategic issues. Its work is grounded in an appreciation of the political, economic and social problems that cause instability, as well as the factors that can lead to international cooperation. IISS runs programmes related to security and business. The *Living with Risk Project (Risk Analysis)* aims to develop a better understanding of the concept of risk analysis and the ways in which it can be applied to high-level decision making. It also addresses the issue of public perception of risk within the context of emergency situations. The research programme on *The Strategic Implications of the 'New Terrorism'* examines the origins of, and the threat of further, mass-casualty terrorist attacks as well as the consequences of efforts to guard against, deter and counteract future attacks. The programme on *Conflict Reso-*

lution, Peace Operations and Humanitarian Intervention focuses on questions related to the role of international financial institutions, such as the World Bank and the IMF, in post-conflict reconstruction and the multiple challenges posed by international efforts to administer war-torn territories.

International Labour Organization (ILO)

URL <http://www.ilo.org>

Established in 1919; location: Geneva, Switzerland

Description: ILO provides a *Business and Social Initiatives Database (BASI)* on business and social initiatives, including comprehensive information on private-sector initiatives which address labour and social conditions in the workplace and in the community. The database features corporate policies, reports and codes of conduct, with information on specific companies, countries, regions, business sectors, and labour and employment issues. See URL <http://oracle02.ilo.org/dyn/basi/vpisearch. first>.

International Monetary Fund (IMF)

URL <http://www.imf.org>

Established in 1945; location: Washington, DC, USA

Members: 184 countries (see URL <http://www.imf.org/external/np/sec/memdir/ members.htm>)

Description: IMF is an international financial institution established to promote international monetary cooperation; to support exchange stability in order to foster economic growth and high levels of employment; and to provide temporary financial assistance to countries to help ease balance-of-payments adjustment.

The IMF and the Fight Against Money Laundering and the Financing of Terrorism

IMF concluded in April 2001 that money laundering poses a threat to financial system integrity and may undermine the sound functioning of financial systems, good governance and the fight against corruption. It is contributing to the FATF's efforts, and supported them by adding FATF's *Forty Recommendations* and *Eight Special Recommendations on Terrorist Financing* to the list of associated standards and codes useful to the operational work of the Fund. It has also substantially increased technical assistance to member countries for strengthening financial, regulatory and supervisory frameworks to prevent money laundering and terrorism financing. See URL <http://www.imf.org/external/np/exr/facts/aml.htm>.

See also *Anti-Money Laundering and Combating the Financing of Terrorism (AML/CFT): Progress Reports* at URL <http://www.imf.org/external/np/aml/eng/ index.htm>.

International Money Laundering Information Network (IMoLIN)

URL <http://www.imolin.org>

Established in 1996; location: Vienna, Austria

Description: IMoLIN is Internet-based and has been developed in cooperation with leading anti-money laundering organizations. The network aims at the establishment of a common website through which information can be shared by national and international anti-money laundering agencies. The website provides information on national money laundering laws and regulations and contacts for inter-country assistance.

Interpol (International Criminal Police Organization)

URL <http://www.interpol.int>
Established in 1923; location: Lyon, France

Members: 181 member countries (see URL <http://www.interpol.int/Public/ICPO/Members/default.asp>)

Description: Interpol is the largest international police organization worldwide, set up to facilitate cross-border criminal police cooperation. Its priority activities concern public safety and terrorism, criminal organizations, drug-related crimes, financial and high-technology crime, trafficking in human beings and fugitive investigation support. Interpol's action against the financing of terrorism is directed by the *Public Safety and Terrorism Sub-Directorate (PST)* which deals with matters relating to terrorism, firearms and explosives, attacks and threats against civil aviation, maritime piracy and weapons of mass destruction. Interpol is also engaged in efforts against money laundering and corruption and provides a website on *Funds Derived from Criminal Activities*, at URL <http://www.interpol.int/Public/FinancialCrime/Money Laundering/default.asp>.

See also *Interpol's Resolutions on Terrorism,* at URL <http://www.interpol.int/Public/Terrorism/resolutions.asp>.

London School of Economics and Political Science (LSE)

URL <http://www.lse.ac.uk>
Established in 1895; location: London, UK

Description: LSE established the *Centre for the Study of Global Governance (CsGG)* in 1992. It maintains a research project on *Oil and Conflict* with particular reference to corporate responsibility as it applies to multinational oil companies. See URL <http://www.lse.ac.uk/Depts/global/OtherProjects.htm>.

Netherlands Institute for Southern Africa (NIZA)

URL <http://www.niza.nl>
Established in 1997; location: Amsterdam, the Netherlands

Description: NIZA was founded out of the merger of three organizations with a record of support for the anti-apartheid struggle dating back to the 1960s. Part of NIZA's Economic Programme is the *Transactions Campaign* against the conflict-sustaining illegal trade in diamonds and other raw materials. This campaign works for an effective system of monitoring the raw materials trade from conflict areas such as Angola, the Democratic Republic of the Congo and Sierra Leone.

North Atlantic Treaty Organization (NATO)

URL <http://www.nato.int>

Established in 1949; location: Brussels, Belgium

Members: Belgium, Canada, Czech Republic, Denmark, France, Germany, Greece, Hungary, Iceland, Italy, Luxembourg, Netherlands, Norway, Poland, Portugal, Spain, Turkey, UK, USA; the new members joining in March 2004: Bulgaria, Estonia, Latvia, Lithuania, Romania, Slovakia and Slovenia

Description: NATO is an alliance of 19 states from North America and Europe committed to fulfilling the goals of the 1949 North Atlantic Treaty. The *Partnership for Peace (PFP)*, initiated in 1994, is the basis for practical security cooperation between NATO and individual PFP partner countries. Activities of the programme include enhancing peacekeeping abilities and capabilities through joint defence planning and budgeting, military exercises and civil emergency operations. NATO also pursues efforts to better protect against and otherwise prepare for a possible disruption of NATO and national critical infrastructure assets, including information and communications systems. The *NATO Forum on Business and Security* (Feb. 2004) brought together government and business leaders, intelligence analysts and scientists to discuss common threats, and to examine together how to defeat them. See URL <http://www.nato-forum.com>.

Organisation for Economic Co-operation and Development (OECD)

URL <http://www.oecd.org>

Established in 1961; location: Paris, France

Members: Australia, Austria, Belgium, Canada, Czech Republic, Denmark, Finland, France, Germany, Greece, Hungary, Iceland, Ireland, Italy, Japan, Korea (South), Luxembourg, Mexico, Netherlands, New Zealand, Norway, Poland, Portugal, Slovakia, Spain, Sweden, Switzerland, Turkey, UK, USA

Description: OECD membership includes 30 countries; it also has relationships with 70 other countries, NGOs and civil society. The organization is committed to democratic government and the market economy and is best known for its statistical publications. The OECD plays a prominent role in fostering good governance in the public service and in corporate activity. It is engaged in various issues related to business and security, such as economics, money laundering and corruption, with special emphasis on guidelines for multinational enterprises, fighting bribery and corporate governance principles.

Business and Industry Advisory Committee (BIAC)

URL <http://www.biac.org>

Since 1962, BIAC has brought together the advice and counsel of the business communities of OECD member countries. The private sector supports the efforts of BIAC to combine analytical thinking and business experience in order to formulate an integrated set of public policy recommendations.

Principles of Corporate Governance

The OECD Principles, endorsed in 1999, and their implementation are the central areas of corporate affairs activities in the OECD member and non-member economies since the integrity of corporations, financial institutions and markets is particularly central to the health of economies and their stability. See URL <http://www. oecd.org/dataoecd/47/50/4347646.pdf>. See also the OECD–World Bank *Corporate Governance Roundtables* at URL <http://www.oecd.org/document/9/0,2340,en_ 2649_34813_2048457_1_1_1_1,00.html>.

Guidelines for Multinational Enterprises

The OECD Guidelines are recommendations from governments for multinational enterprises operating in or from adhering countries. They provide voluntary principles and standards for responsible business conduct in a variety of areas.

Fighting Bribery and Corruption

The OECD has assumed a leading role in preventing international bribery and corruption. Its Anti-Corruption Division serves as the focal point within the OECD Secretariat to support the work of the OECD in the fight against bribery and corruption in international business transactions through the implementation of the OECD Anti-Bribery Convention. See URL <http://www.oecd.org/topic/0,2686,en_2649_34855_ 1_1_1_1_37447,00.html>.

See also *Roundtable on Corporate Responsibility: Enhancing the Role of Business in the Fight against Corruption,* URL <http://www.oecd.org/document/47/0,2340, en_2649_34855_2512687_1_1_1_34855,00.html>; *Anti-corruption Instruments and the OECD Guidelines for Multinational Companies*, URL <http://www.oecd.org/ dataoecd/0/33/2638728.pdf>; and *Business Approaches to Combating Corrupt Practices*, URL <http://www.oecd.org/dataoecd/63/57/2638716.pdf>.

AnCorR Web (Anti-Corruption Ring Online)

AnCorR is a comprehensive worldwide information resource on corruption and bribery, with collections on a variety of topics related to corruption. The online service provides governments, businesses and civil society with the information they need to understand and implement effective policies and practices in the area of anti-corruption by offering references to books, journals, papers and reports as well as a large number of other resources. See URL <http://www1.oecd.org/daf/nocorruption web>.

Financial Action Task Force on Money Laundering (FATF)

URL <http://www.fatf-gafi.org>
Established in 1989; location: at the OECD, Paris
The FATF was established as an intergovernmental body at the 1989 G7 Summit in Paris with the objective of developing a coordinated international response to the mounting concerns over money laundering and implementing measures designed to counter the use of the financial system by criminals. The FATF issued its Forty Recommendations in 1990 (revised in 1996 and 2003), which provide the basic framework for anti-money laundering efforts as the principal standard in this field. In October 2001, following the terrorist attacks in the United States in September, the FATF expanded its mission and issued the Eight Special Recommendations on Terrorist Financing. The objective of these measures is to deny terrorists and their supporters access to the international financial system. For the recommendations see URL <http://www.fatf-gafi.org/index.htm>.

Egmont Group of Financial Intelligence Units

A number of countries have created specialized government agencies for dealing with the problem of money laundering. These entities are commonly referred to as financial intelligence units (FIUs) and serve as the focal point for national anti-money laundering programmes because they provide a possibility for rapidly exchanging information between financial institutions and law enforcement and prosecutorial authorities. In 1995 a number of FIUs began working together in an informal organization known as the Egmont Group. See URL <http://www1.oecd.org/fatf/Ctry-orgpages/org-egmont_en.htm>.

Development Assistance Committee (DAC)

The *Network on Conflict, Peace and Development Co-operation* brings critical issues affecting the structural stability and fragility of states to the attention of the DAC, other OECD bodies, and policy makers in the foreign affairs, trade, commerce and defence communities. The publication *A Development Co-operation Lens on Terrorism Prevention: Key Entry Points for Action* (2003) emphasizes the role of the private sector in helping partner governments to establish transparent mechanisms for encouraging domestic and international corporate responsibility. *The DAC Guidelines: Helping Prevent Violent Conflict* (2001) analyse the role of business in conflict situations and conclude that the private sector needs to be guided to guard against side effects of its investments which may have negative impacts on the local and national structural stability, may unwittingly play into the hands of extremists or may finance terrorists. See URL <http://www.oecd.org/dataoecd/15/54/1886146.pdf>.

Futures Project on Risk Management—Policies in Selected OECD Countries

The OECD International Futures Programme (IFP) launched the *Project on Risk Management Policies* as a follow-up to the Futures Project on Emerging Systemic Risks (2000–2002). This led to the publication in 2003 of *Emerging Risks in the 21st Century: An Agenda for Action*, a cross-sectoral analysis of risk management and novel risks in the 21st century. Five large risk clusters—natural disasters, technological accidents, infectious diseases, food safety and terrorism—are analysed and their implications for economy and society explored. Another focus is on the increasing vulnerability of major systems. The publication also identifies the challenges of assessing, preparing for and responding to conventional and newly emerging hazards of this kind and provides recommendations for governments and the private sector. See also the report *Security in Maritime Transport: Risk Factors and Economic Impact* (2003), which explores the risks posed to the international merchant maritime transport system by terrorist organizations; and *The Economic Consequences of Terrorism* (Working Paper no. 334, 2002). See URL <http://www.oecd.org/dataoecd/19/61/18521672.pdf> and URL <http://www.oecdwash.org/DATA/DOCS/eco-wkp-2002-20.pdf>.

Organization for Security and Co-operation in Europe (OSCE)

URL <http://www.osce.org>

Established in 1973 (as the Conference on Security and Co-operation in Europe, called the OSCE in 1995); location: Vienna, Austria

Members: Albania, Andorra, Armenia, Austria, Azerbaijan, Belarus, Belgium, Bosnia and Herzegovina, Bulgaria, Canada, Croatia, Cyprus, Czech Republic, Denmark, Estonia, Finland, Former Yugoslav Republic of Macedonia (FYROM), France, Georgia, Germany, Greece, Holy See, Hungary, Iceland, Ireland, Italy, Kazakhstan, Kyrgyzstan, Latvia, Liechtenstein, Lithuania, Luxembourg, Malta, Moldova, Monaco, Netherlands, Norway, Poland, Portugal, Romania, Russia, San Marino, Serbia and Montenegro, Slovakia, Slovenia, Spain, Sweden, Switzerland, Tajikistan, Turkey, Turkmenistan, Ukraine, UK, USA, Uzbekistan

Description: OSCE is the world's largest regional security organization, with 55 participating states. It is active in early warning, conflict prevention, crisis management and post-conflict rehabilitation. Its approach to security is comprehensive and cooperative, embracing a wide range of security-related issues, including arms control, preventive diplomacy, confidence- and security-building measures, human rights, democratization, election monitoring, and economic and environmental security. At the Ministerial Council Meeting in Bucharest (2001), participating states agreed in Decision no. 1 to adopt *The Bucharest Plan of Action for Combating Terrorism*. At the Porto Ministerial Meeting (2002) the OSCE made further commitments to joint action on preventing and combating terrorism in Decision no. 1 on *Implementing the OSCE Commitments and Activities on Combating Terrorism* and Decision no. 2 on *OSCE Strategy to Address Threats to Security and Stability in the Twenty-First Century*. OSCE also promotes cooperation and coordination with the United Nations Office on Drugs and Crime (UNODC) to support participating states' efforts to strengthen their ability to prevent and suppress terrorist financing.

Other OSCE projects and related documentation

The *Booklet on Best Practices in Combating Corruption* (2003) is a reference document on implementing anti-corruption measures. It provides examples of best practices in addressing corruption in OSCE countries. See URL <http://www.osce.org/osceprojects/show_project.php?id=414>.

The aims of the *National Workshops on Combating Money Laundering and Suppressing the Financing of Terrorism* (from Sep. 2002) are to raise awareness on technical and legislative aspects of money laundering and issues related to the financing of terrorism; to familiarize participants with legal and administrative tools to combat money laundering/financing of terrorism; and to identify needs for further legislative development relevant to combating money laundering/financing of terrorism. See URL <http://www.osce.org/osceprojects/show_project.php?id=240>.

Peres Center for Peace

URL <http://www.peres-center.org>

Established in 1996; location: Tel Aviv, Israel

Description: The Peres Center for Peace has established a project on *Business and Economic Relations* which is designed to promote peace between Israel and its Arab neighbours. It is based on the premise that economic stability and prosperity are key factors in developing sustainable peace in the region. Within this framework the Peres Center is working with business people from Jordan, Israel and the Palestinian Authority to develop integrated initiatives for the mutual benefit of all parties. The emphasis lies on creating realistic, strong ties between the principal economic players in society which are in a position to make genuine business changes, thus facilitating a shift in the regional macro-economic situation.

Royal Institute of International Affairs (RIIA)

URL <http://www.riia.org>
Established in 1920; location: London, UK

Description: RIIA, also known as Chatham House, launched the *New Security Issues Programme (NSIP)* in September 2002, with the objective of producing policy-oriented research and analysis of issues important for the new security agenda. The NSIP highlights issues which have not featured significantly on the security agenda, but which have implications for it. It also aims to develop links to government, business and NGOs in order to stimulate debate on issues that require the participation of a wider audience.

Social Science Research Council (SSRC)

URL <http://www.ssrc.org>
Established in 1923; location: Washington, DC, USA

Description: Within its *Program on Global Security and Cooperation (GSC)* SSRC promotes the production, integration and dissemination of new knowledge needed to understand and meet the security challenges of the 21st century.

Swiss Peace Foundation (Swisspeace)

URL <http://www.swisspeace.ch>
Established in 1988; location: Berne, Switzerland

Description: Swisspeace is an action-oriented peace research institute with a focus on the analysis of the causes of wars and violent conflicts. It develops tools for early recognition of tensions and formulates conflict-mitigation strategies. It is widening the scope of its engagement in civil peace-building to the private sector and is establishing the *Business and Peace Project* to investigate the complex relationship between violent conflicts and the economy. The focus will be on the negative consequences of business activities and their mitigation and on the potential of corporations as active partners in peace-building efforts. The relationship between fossil fuel wealth and violent conflicts was discussed at the annual conference for 2003 on *Adding Fuel to the Fire: The Role of Petroleum in Violent Conflicts*.

Terrorism Research Center (TRC)

URL <http://www.terrorism.com>
Established in 1996; location: Washington, DC, USA

Description: TRC is dedicated to the research of terrorism, information warfare and security, critical infrastructure protection, homeland security and other issues related to low-intensity political violence. TRC has a comprehensive online portal for its terrorism knowledge base; online forums on infrastructure protection, counter-terrorism, emerging threats, and cyber terrorism and information warfare; and information on terrorist profiles and terrorist attacks.

Transparency International (TI)

URL <http://www.transparency.org>
Established in 1993; location: Berlin, Germany

Description: TI is a global coalition of civil society, business and governments. It is devoted to combating corruption, focusing on prevention and reforms. TI works at the national and international levels to curb corruption. In the international arena, TI raises awareness of the damaging effects of corruption, advocates policy reform, works towards the implementation of multilateral conventions and monitors compliance by governments, corporations and banks. At the national level, the TI objective is to increase levels of accountability and transparency, monitor the performance of key institutions and press for necessary reforms. TI's *National Integrity Systems* are the sum of institutions and practices within a given country that address aspects of maintaining the honesty and integrity of government and private-sector institutions. TI's *Business Principles for Countering Bribery* provide a practical tool which companies can use as a reference for good practice. See URL<http://www.transparency. org/activities/nat_integ_systems/nis_index.html> and URL<http://www.transparency. org/building_coalitions/private_sector/business_principles.html>.

See also *Global Corruption Report 2003,* at URL <http://www.globalcorruption report.org>.

United Kingdom Department for International Development (DFID)

URL <http://www.dfid.gov.uk>
Established in 1997; location: London, UK

Description: DFID's main focus is on humanitarian crises and sustainable development. It also deals with issues relevant to business and conflict. These efforts are conducted within the *Conflict and Humanitarian Affairs Department (CHAD)*, which provides advice and support *inter alia* in conflict prevention and resolution, emergency response preparedness, contingency planning arrangements, and disaster and vulnerability initiatives. CHAD also aims to support security sector reform and post-conflict peace-building.

United Kingdom Ministry of Defence (MOD)

URL <http://www.mod.uk>
Established in 1971; location: London, UK

Description: The British MOD has established the *Joint Doctrine and Concepts Centre (JDCC)* as a part of its central policy area. The JDCC website contains the results of its research and analysis on strategic trends. See URL <http://www. mod.uk/jdcc>. The site also presents the JDCC's view of how the world might develop over the next 30 years and the effects on the UK's security. With regard to the defence and security implications of future business, JDCC states: 'Transnational companies will further increase in size but are unlikely to seek to exercise this power geopolitically. However, cooperation between companies and state governments on intelligence and information may increase in response to mutual threats such as terrorism and organized crime'. See URL <http://www.jdcc-strategictrends.org>.

United Nations (UN)

URL <http://www.un.org>
Established in 1945; location: New York, N.Y., USA
Members: 191 member states (see URL <http://www.un.org/Overview/unmember. html>)
Description: The UN objectives are to maintain international peace and security; to develop friendly relations among nations; and to cooperate in solving international economic, social, cultural and humanitarian problems and in promoting respect for human rights and fundamental freedoms. The aim of the six principal organs of the United Nations—the General Assembly, the Security Council, the Economic and Social Council, the Trusteeship Council, the International Court of Justice and the Secretariat—is to fulfil these objectives.

United Nations Action against Terrorism

URL <http://www.un.org/terrorism>
This comprehensive website contains information on all the essential UN activities related to the fight against terrorism.
Declarations: URL <http://www.un.org/terrorism/declarations.htm>.
UN General Assembly resolutions: URL <http://www.un.org/terrorism/ga.htm>, in particular the International Convention for the Suppression of the Financing of Terrorism (A/RES/54/109, 25 Feb. 2000).
UN Security Council resolutions: URL <http://www.un.org/terrorism/sc.htm#reso>.
UN treaty collection, Conventions on Terrorism: URL <http://untreaty.un.org/English/Terrorism.asp>.

United Nations and Business

URL <http://www.un.org/partners/business/index.asp>
This comprehensive UN website covers many aspects of the UN's relationships with business. Its main purpose is to provide information on partnerships and alliances between the UN and the private sector and foundations in furtherance of the UN Millennium Development Goals (2000). It also provides guidelines for doing business with the UN and links to websites of UN offices, agencies, funds and programmes which provide information about partnerships with the private sector.

United Nations Business Council (BCUN)

URL <http://www.unausa.org/newindex.asp?place=http://www.unausa.org/programs/bcun/bcun.asp>
BCUN is a catalyst for action, understanding and innovative business opportunities between member companies and the United Nations. Through a network of partnerships in economic development, health, education and technology, BCUN advances the common interest of the UN and business in a more prosperous and peaceful world.

United Nations Conference on Trade and Development (UNCTAD)

URL <http://www.unctad.org>
This website contains information on UNCTAD's purpose and members, press releases, further links, and discussion papers on issues pertaining to business and development.

United Nations Counter Terrorism Committee (CTC)

URL <http://www.un.org/Docs/sc/committees/1373>
On 28 September 2001, acting under Chapter VII of the United Nations Charter (on threats to international peace and security), the Security Council adopted *Resolution 1373*, reaffirming its unequivocal condemnation of the 11 September 2001 terrorist attacks in the United States, and expressing its determination to prevent all such acts. Resolution 1373 also established the Counter-Terrorism Committee (CTC), made up of all 15 members of the Security Council with a mandate to monitor the implementation of Resolution 1373 by all states and to increase the capability of states to fight terrorism.

United Nations Development Programme (UNDP)

URL <http://www.undp.org>
UNDP has various partnerships with the business sector. In 2003 it initiated the *Partnerships for Private Sector Development (PPSD)* project to help build the groundwork for an Afghan private sector, acknowledging that the development of the private sector is the key driver to long-term economic recovery and has the potential to contribute to reconstruction and national security by creating employment beyond the control of warlords or the drug trade.

United Nations Follow-Up Process to the International Conference on Financing for Development

URL <http://www.un.org/esa/ffd>
In this process the Monterrey Conference, held in Monterrey, N.L., Mexico, in March 2002, marked the first quadripartite exchange of views between governments, civil society, the business community and institutional stakeholders on global economic issues. The focus of this independent forum for private-sector engagement is on how to improve the process of risk sharing between public- and private-sector organizations in ways that provide developing countries better access to bond markets. International bond markets are the primary focus, since they are currently the most important source of long-term private-sector funding for developing countries. See URL <http://www.un.org/esa/ffd/ffdprivatesector.htm>.

United Nations Fund for International Partnerships (UNFIP)

URL <http://www.un.org/unfip>
UNFIP offers another platform for partnerships between the UN and the private sector, including information on partnership programmes. UNFIP promotes new partnersips and alliances with companies and foundations in furtherance of the Millennium Development Goals (2000).

United Nations Interregional Crime and Justice Research Institute (UNICRI)

Within the scope of the *Terrorism Prevention Unit*, UNICRI and the Max Planck Institute for Foreign and International Criminal Law will launch the *Journal on Terrorism and Organized Crime (JTOC)* onb the issues of terrorism and organized crime from political, social, legal and strategic points of view. See URL <http://www.unicri.it/call_for_papers.htm>.

UNICRI has several projects related to business and security, *inter alia* the *Global Programme against Corruption* and *International Terrorism* and on *Security of Maritime Transport.* See URL <http://www.unicri.it/on-going_projects.htm>.

Its pipeline projects, designed and awaiting funding, include *Comparative Analysis of the Anti-terrorism Measures adopted by EU Member Candidates.* See URL <http://www.unicri.it/pipeline_projects.htm>.

United Nations Global Compact (GC)

URL <http://www.unglobalcompact.org>

In an address to the World Economic Forum on 31 January 1999, UN Secretary-General Kofi Annan challenged business leaders to join an international initiative— the Global Compact. As an agreement between the UN and the international private sector, GC brings together companies, UN agencies, labour and civil society. It is a network-based initiative based on the five core UN agencies: the UN Office of the High Commissioner for Human Rights (UNHCR), the UN Environment Programme (UNEP), the International Labour Organization (ILO), the UN Development Programme (UNDP) and the UN Industrial Development Organization (UNIDO). The general aim is to encourage transnational corporations to operate in a socially responsible manner. GC is based on *Nine Principles* which the international business community is asked to practise or consider. As a regulatory instrument the GC does not police, enforce or measure the behaviour or actions of companies, but relies on public accountability, transparency and the enlightened self-interest of companies to promote joint and substantive action in pursuing the principles. See URL <http://www.undp.bg/globalcompact/en/the_9_principles.php>.

The GC website includes information on business associations, roles and responsibilities of corporations and networks; see URL <http://www.unglobalcompact.org/Portal>.

The GC policy dialogue on *The Role of the Private Sector in Zones of Conflict* provides a dynamic forum where representatives from companies, NGOs and trade unions identify key issues and concrete actions pertaining to the role of the private sector in conflict areas. See also *Global Impact Business Guide for Conflict Impact Assessment and Risk Management* at URL <http://www.union-network.org/UNIsite/In_Depth/Interna_Relations/World_Bank/TOOLBOXFinal06_27.pdf> and *Recommendations of the Transparency Working Group to Address Problems in Zones of Conflict* at URL <http://www.union-network.org/UNIsite/In_Depth/Interna_Relations/World_Bank/Transpfinalrev.pdf>.

United Nations Industrial Development Organization (UNIDO)

URL <http://www.unido.org>

Working with the private sector has become one of the highest priorities of UNIDO. It has launched the *Business Partnership Programme*, in which the business community plays an active role in supporting multilateral institutions. See URL <http://www.unido.org/doc/4364>.

See also the report *Why UNIDO Business Partnerships are Important,* at URL <http://www.unido.org/en/doc/12686>. UNIDO was added to the Global Compact group in the spring of 2003, reflecting a desire to cater for the needs of small and medium enterprises.

United Nations Office for the Coordination of Humanitarian Affairs (OCHA)

URL <http://www.reliefweb.int/ocha_ol/>
The OCHA has a website on the role of the private sector in the protection of civilians, including the practices of global corporations. Through expanding trade and investment, private-sector actors have exercised a growing influence on global policy, including policy in many conflict zones. Given the challenges to the international community in this respect, partnerships are increasingly necessary. With almost 96 per cent of the private sector engaged in the manufacturing of civilian goods and services, the private sector has a vested interest in peace-building and economic stability and in complementing, rather than exacerbating, humanitarian efforts. See URL <http://www.reliefweb.int/ocha_ol/civilians/private_sector/index.html>.

United Nations Office on Drugs and Crime (UNODC)

URL <http://www.unodc.org>
The Vienna-based *United Nations Terrorism Prevention Branch* of the UNODC conducts research on terrorism trends and assists countries in upgrading their capacities to investigate and to prevent terrorist acts. UNODC's *Global Programme against Terrorism* is an integral part of the UN'scollective action against terrorism. It works closely with the Counter-Terrorism Committee of the Security Council, providing technical assistance to member states and promoting international cooperation against terrorism. See URL <http://www.unodc.org/unodc/en/terrorism.html>.

Conventions Against Terrorism

URL <http://www.unodc.org/unodc/terrorism_conventions.html>
The need for private-sector cooperation is emphasized in the *Vienna Declaration on Crime and Justice: Meeting the Challenges of the Twenty-first Century* and in the *Plasn of Action,* available at URL <http://www.unodc.org/unodc/en/crime_cicp_resolutions.html> and URL <http://www.unodc.org/pdf/crime/terrorism/res56/261e.pdf>. The role of the private sector as protagonist in the response to the problem of drugs is stressed in various UN Drug Control Programme (UNDCP) reports.

The *Global Programme against Corruption (GPAC)* was launched in 1999 in collaboration with UNICRI, to assist member states in their efforts to build integrity to curb and prevent corruption by increasing the risks and costs of abusing power for private gain. The GPAC targets countries with vulnerable developing or transitional economies by promoting anti-corruption measures in the public sphere, in the private sector and in high-level financial and political circles. The *United Nations Convention against Corruption* was adopted by the General Assembly at a high-level political conference (Mexico, Dec. 2003). See URL <http://www.unodc.org/unodc/en/crime_convention_corruption.html>. The GPAC and the Convention against Transnational Organized Crime and its Protocols are available at URL <http://www.unodc.org/

unodc/en/organized_crime.html> and URL <http://www.unodc.org/unodc/en/crime_cicp_convention.html>.

United States Chamber of Commerce

URL <http://www.uschamber.org>
Established in 1912; location: Washington, DC, USA

Description: The United States Chamber of Commerce *Center for Corporate Citizenship (CCC)* is a business service organization whose objective is to enable and facilitate corporate civic and humanitarian initiatives, particularly in terms of civic engagement, economic development, economic security, and disaster management and economic recovery. The core competencies of the CCC are the facilitation of public–private partnerships and the coordination of crisis response networks, including initiatives on information sharing, economic and community safety, and critical infrastructure protection. See URL <http://www.uschamber.org/CCC/default.htm>.

Watson Institute for International Studies

URL <http://www.watsoninstitute.org>
Established in 1986; location: Providence, Rhode Island, USA

Description: The Watson Institute programme on *Global Security* examines threats to regional and global security; aims to bridge the gap between theory and policy; and analyses the transformation of war, and the prevention and management of violent conflict and post-conflict reconstruction. One of the projects within this programme, *Targeting Terrorist Finances,* investigates the ability of terrorist organizations to use the global financial system to support their activities. Various issues related to tackling the financial aspects of the war on terrorism are raised such as the sources of terrorist funds and how networks for terrorist financing operate and can be regulated. See URL <http://www.watsoninstitute.org/program_detail.cfm?id=4>.

World Bank Group

URL <http://www.worldbank.org>
Established in 1944; location: Washington, DC, USA

Members: 184 member countries (see Internet site)

Description: The mission of the World Bank Group—consisting of the International Bank for Reconstruction and Development (IBRD), the International Development Association (IDA), the International Finance Corporation (IFC), the Multilateral Investment Guarantee Agency (MIGA) and the International Centre for Settlement of Investment Disputes (ICSID)—is to fight poverty and improve the living standards of low- and middle-income countries by providing loans, policy advice, technical assistance and knowledge-sharing services. The Group has many projects related to business, security and peacekeeping: e.g., conflict prevention and post-conflict reconstruction, natural disaster management, social protection and risk management, vulnerability assessment and monitoring, infrastructure services for private-sector development, corporate governance and a global partnership for development. The Group has made strategic policy changes that are relevant for the role of business in development and conflict prevention, including: the increased institutionalization of its relationships with the private sector; a strengthened commitment to address corruption; and a more proactive role in post-conflict reconstruction and reconciliation activities. The World Bank's archives provide relevant information pertaining to the role of business in conflict.

Conflict Prevention and Reconstruction Unit (CPR)

The CPR Unit is concerned with the evolving role of the Group's involvement in conflict-torn areas. The *Conflict Prevention and Reconstruction Network (CPR Network)*, set up in 1998, reflects a new operational policy on partnership in work with conflict-affected countries. The unit has also developed the *Conflict Analysis Framework (CAF)* to enhance conflict sensitivity and the conflict-prevention potential of World Bank assistance. Through the *Post-Conflict Fund (PCF)*, established in 1997, the Group aims at assisting countries to make the transition to peace and economic growth.

Business and the Private Sector

The World Bank Group is engaged with the private sector through its *International Finance Corporation (IFC)*, *Multilateral Investment Guarantee Agency (MIGA)*, and key initiatives at the World Bank itself.

Corporate Social Responsibility and Sustainable Competitiveness

Within this programme, launched at the World Economic Forum in Davos in January 2000, many meetings have been organized related to the role of the private sector: *Successful Public–Private Partnerships: Perspectives of the Private Sector* (Apr., 2002); *Is There a Role for Business in Building Peace and Democracy?* (Sep. 2003); and *Redefining the Role of Business Leadership in Relation to Poverty and Development* (Sep. 2003). See URL <http://www.worldbank.org/wbi/corpgov/csr/events. html>.

Additional publications and research

The report *Natural Resources and Violent Conflict: Options and Action* argues that revenues from natural resources have financed wars in low-income countries, prolonging hostilities and making them harder to resolve. The report found that doubling the income per capita in low-income countries roughly halved the risk of civil war. The Group's research on the root causes of conflict finds that economic dependence on natural resources of the developing countries is strongly associated with the risk level for violent conflict.

Transition from War to Peace contains guidelines for the Group's involvement in economic measures throughout the development process in conflict societies. It stresses the need to create an enabling environment for the private sector and for public–private partnership in reconstruction.

Appendix 2
Private-sector organizations and institutions, active or interested in the field of security

Isabel Frommelt

African Business Round Table (ABR)

URL <http://www.abrnet.org>
Established in 1990; location: Johannesburg, South Africa

Description: ABR was set up by the African Development Bank (ADB) to strengthen the African private sector and to promote intra-African trade and investment. As a member of the NEPAD Business Group, ABR is dedicated to fostering sustainable economic growth and social development in Africa by helping to create a conducive business environment for responsible private-sector investment.

AVINA Foundation

URL <http://www.avina.net>
Established in 1994; location: Hurden, Switzerland

Description: The AVINA Foundation works in partnership with civil society and business leaders in their initiatives for sustainable development in Ibero-America. It was founded in the context of a deteriorating economic, social and environmental crisis in Latin America and has established more than 20 offices and service centres there. AVINA fosters activities that promote relations between civil society and private-sector leaders.

Business Council Europe Africa Mediterranean (BCEAM)

URL <http://www.bceam.org>
Established in 1973; location: Brussels, Belgium

Description: BCEAM was founded to support the crucial role of the private sector in economic development. Its objective is to be the principal private-sector interlocutor for the EU institutions and African countries on matters affecting the interests of the EU private sector in Africa. It groups all EU employers' associations in the private sector which specialize in developing economic relationships with African countries (representing a total of 1500 companies in the EU and over 3 million employees). BCEAM assists and advises those operating in Africa or cooperating with the private sector in their plans to attract potential investors. It covers the complete range of commerce and industry, including the agriculture, mining, transport, banking and service sectors.

Business for Africa

URL <http://www.africaplc.com>

Description: Business for Africa has a comprehensive website with information and links to business organizations and initiatives. The website is administered by *africaplc*, a multimedia business information publisher which markets, produces and distributes research, surveys, location studies and the quarterly journal *Africa investor (Ai)* (see URL <http://www.africa-investor.com/index.html>). It provides around 14 000 international investors with relevant business information from the continent of Africa. The website is also the platform for the NEPAD Business Group, which comprises over 1000 international companies operating in Africa. The site on *Partnership Opportunities* offers a forum to engage organizations to build a better Africa, providing information on partnership initiatives, opportunities, case studies and links to supporting organizations. See URL <http://www.africaplc.com/partnership_opportunities.php>.

Business Executives for National Security (BENS)

URL <http://www.bens.org>
Established in 1982; location: Washington, DC, USA

Description: The main objective of BENS is to enhance national (US) security, by bridging the gap between business and government and bringing the experience and expertise of the private sector to practical solutions for national security challenges. Its focus lies on two central security problems: to develop new tools to combat new security threats that cannot be deterred or negotiated away, and to find resources to reshape and rebuild the military forces for the 21st century. Within the framework of the programme on *New Tools, New Teams for New Threats*, BENS addresses issues such as *Tracking Terrorists' Financial Assets, Preparing Our Communities for Terrorism, Improving Intelligence Capabilities*. It also has projects on *Securing Ports* and *Defending Against Cyber Attacks*. The report on *Partnership or Alliance? The Future of Private–Public Cooperation on Information Security* (Z. Selden, 1999) discusses the appropriate relationship between the private sector and government in securing the national information infrastructure. See URL <http://www.bens.org/pubs_1199.html>.

Business Humanitarian Forum (BHF)

URL <http://www.bhforum.ch>
Established in 1999; location: Geneva, Switzerland

Description: BHF was founded for the purpose of bringing business and humanitarian organizations together in the interest of mutual understanding and cooperation, especially in areas of conflict. Its aim is to promote dialogue and to support and widen the exchange of information and experience between the business and humanitarian communities working closely with the private sector. BHF deals with such questions as why businesses cooperate with humanitarian organizations; the potential obstacles to cooperation; the key factors for successful cooperation; business assistance in time of crisis; and business contributions in post-disaster periods. See the brochure *Building Mutual Support between Humanitarian Organizations and the Business Community* at URL <http://www.bhforum.ch/en/documentation/index.cfm>.

BHF USA was set up in 2002 as the first national BHF affiliate organization; it cooperates with the UNDP Bureau of Crisis Prevention and Recovery in developing private-sector projects, especially in post-conflict countries such as Afghanistan.

Business for Social Responsibility (BSR)

URL<http://www.bsr.org>

Established in 1992; location: San Francisco, California, USA

Description: BSR began as an association of 50 companies dedicated to helping businesses to be both commercially successful and socially responsible. It helps companies of all sizes and sectors to achieve business objectives and efficiencies in ways that respect ethical values, people, communities and the environment. Among the most important business ethics issues faced by companies, BSR lists conflicts of interest, financial and accounting integrity, corruption and bribery. It aims to equip its members with the expertise to design and implement successful, responsible business policies, including the better management of risks. BSR is part of a growing global network of business membership organizations that focus on corporate social responsibility. The *BSR Forum* section of the website provides a forum for business leaders to participate and interact across this global network of programmes and partners. See URL <http://www.bsr.org/BSRForum/index.cfm>.

Business in the Community (BITC)

URL<http://www.bitc.org.uk>

Established in 1982; location: London, UK

Description: BITC was set up against a backdrop of high levels of unemployment and urban rioting. It is a movement of over 700 member companies in the UK (listed on the website) committed to continually improving their positive impact on society. The main objectives of BITC are: to develop responsible business practice; to translate company policy into local action; and to provide a platform for dialogue for collaborative action. BITC's website provides information for companies on measuring and reporting responsible business practice (the *Corporate Impact Reporting Initiative*). See URL <http://www.bitc.org.uk/resources/issues/reporting/index.html>.

Business Partners for Development (BPD)

URL <http://www.bpd-naturalresources.org>

Established in 1998

Description: BPD, a programme of the World Bank which was operative in 1998–2002, was a project-based initiative set up to study, support and promote strategic examples of partnerships involving business, civil society and government working together for the development of communities around the world. BPD demonstrated that such tri-sector partnerships could provide long-term benefits to the business sector and at the same time meet the social objectives of civil society and the state by stabilizing social and financial environments. BPD's core hypotheses were the following: business partnerships for development provide win-win benefits to all three parties; partnerships can be much more widely used throughout the world; and partnerships can be scaled up to national and regional levels. Guidelines and systems were developed in a project on *Natural Resources Cluster* (oil, gas and mining companies) for dealing with community issues and mitigating risk by optimizing development impact on host communities through tri-sector partnerships. See URL <http://www.bpd-naturalresources.org>.

See also the report *Putting Partnering to Work* (2002) at URL <http://www.bpdweb.org/products.htm>.

Caux Round Table (CRT)

URL<http://www.cauxroundtable.org>
Established in 1986; location: Secretariats in Europe, Japan, Mexico and the USA
Description: CRT is an international network of business leaders working to promote a moral capitalism. It advocates the implementation of the *CRT Principles for Business* aiming at: applying fundamental ethical norms to business decision making; raising the level of awareness of business leaders; and informing elite opinion about new opportunities to attack global poverty. Resources on its website range from principles for business and for governments, self-assessment and improvement processes, a guide to corporate social responsibility, and business ethics codes to anti-corruption measures. Of particular interest is the report *Dirty Money and National Security* (Sep. 2003), available at URL <http://www.cauxroundtable.org/Reports.html>.

Center for Ethical Business Cultures (CEBC)

URL <http://www.cebcglobal.org>
Established in 1978; location: Minneapolis, Minnesota, USA
Description: CEBC assists leaders in creating ethical and profitable business cultures at the enterprise, community and global levels.

Centre for Innovation in Corporate Responsibility (CICR)

URL <http://www.cicr.net>
Established in 1998; location: Ottawa, Canada
Description: CICR is a membership organization for small, medium and large Canadian companies. Its mission is to lead and assist businesses in redefining and realizing responsible international business practice. Its aim is to work in partnership with businesses active in or with developing countries to enhance business performance through sound corporate citizenship and responsible international business practices. CICR's virtual resource centre (knowledge brokering) is a comprehensive site for further topic-related research such as on codes of conduct, dialogues and discussion forums, community building, corruption, human rights at the workplace and technology transfer. CICR's concept of an integrated 'triple bottom line' of corporate responsibility represents an approach to understand and bringing together the three business environmental, social and economic 'bottom lines'. In this approach none of the three interrelated spheres of activities should be ignored or undervalued since they all can affect a company's ability to compete in a turbulent operating environment.

Centre for Tomorrow's Company

URL <http://www.tomorrowscompany.com/>
Established in 1996; location: London, UK

Description: The Centre for Tomorrow's Company is a think-tank aiming to research and stimulate the development of a new agenda for business. It is dedicated to creating a future for business which makes equal sense to staff, shareholders and society. A new programme, *Business and Society—Closing the Gap*, to start in late 2004, will deal with the need for corporations to understand and respond to society's needs in a way that works for all stakeholders. The programme aims at promoting dialogue and debate on the role of business in local and global society and on the implications for business vision, values and governance. A programme outline is available at URL <http://www.tomorrowscompany.com/Business and Society.doc>.

Collaborative for Development Action (CDA)

URL <http://www.cdainc.com>
Established in 1985; location: Cambridge, Massachusetts, USA

Description: CDA is a consulting firm working with humanitarian assistance programs and organizations. It focuses on economic and social development in Asia, Africa, Latin America, and Eastern and Central Europe and spearheads efforts that focus on the role of third-party actors in conflict or post-conflict contexts. Of special interest to researchers of business and conflict is the *Corporate Engagement Project (CEP)*. Its aim is to provide managers with a better perspective on which aspects of their operational decisions have direct or indirect impacts on the social environment. It provides advice *inter alia* on identifying operational options that have positive impacts on relationships among groups; on promoting overall social and political stability; and on designing management tools that will lower insurance, security, reputational and opportunity costs and contribute to establishing a positive legacy for companies. See URL<http://www.cdainc.com/projects.php>.

Committee for Economic Development (CED)

URL <http://www.ced.org>
Established in 1942; location: Washington, DC, USA

Description: CED is an organization of business and education leaders dedicated to policy research on major economic and social issues and the implementation of its recommendations by the public and private sectors. It is a resource for the business community's own policy-oriented activities. CED's efforts include *inter alia* recommending that US-based enterprises strive to maintain the same high standards of corporate engagement in all countries in which they operate, making no distinction between operations in the USA and abroad.

Corporate Social Responsibility (CSR) Europe

URL <http://www.csreurope.org>
Established in 1996; location: Brussels, Belgium

Description: CSR Europe is a business-driven membership network (see URL <http://www.csreurope.org/membership/default.aspx>) with the mission of helping companies achieve profitability while advancing sustainable growth and human progress by embedding corporate social responsibility in their business practice. It promotes a broader stakeholder dialogue between businesses, European policy makers, governments, investors, civil society and academics. Set up by former European Commission President Jacques Delors, CSR Europe is considered the major European authority on corporate social responsibility. As a decentralized and rapidly growing network, CSR collaborates with 16 business organizations in 14 European countries, and extending to organizations in Central and Eastern Europe. These national partner organizations (NPOs) promote corporate social responsibility at the national, regional and local level, reaching a total of over 1000 companies in Europe.

Council for Ethics in Economics (CEE)

URL <http://www.businessethics.org>
Established in 1982; location: Columbus, Ohio, USA

Description: CEE gathers leaders in business, higher education, religion and other professions working together to strengthen the ethics of business and economic life. It identifies and responds to emerging issues that are important for the pursuit of business ethics, and it helps to resolve these issues locally, nationally and internationally. CEE has a special concern for the worldwide consequences of the policies and practices of multinational companies.

European Business Ethics Network (EBEN)

URL <http://www.eben.org>
Established in 1987; location: Oslo, Norway

Description: EBEN is an international network dedicated to the promotion of business ethics in European private industry, public sector, voluntary organizations and academia. Its main goal is to promote ethical awareness in business decision making through the dissemination of information about initiatives, good practice, research and networking, including access to business ethics tools such as dilemma training and assessment of values in organizations.

European Sustainable and Responsible Investment Forum (Eurosif)

URL <http://www.eurosif.info>
Established in 2001; location: Paris, France

Description: Eurosif is a pan-European stakeholder network for promoting and developing sustainable and responsible investment. It was created as an initiative of five European Social Investment Funds (SIFs) from France, German-speaking countries, Italy, Netherlands and the UK, with support from the European Commission. Eurosif promotes transparency, disclosure and active share ownership, with regard to corporate practice and governance.

Global Business Dialogue on Electronic Commerce (GBDe)

URL<http://www.gbde.org>
Established in 1999; location: Williston, Vermont, USA

Description: GBDe is a worldwide CEO-led business initiative, established to assist in the creation of a policy framework for the development of a global online economy. It is a leading private-sector voice on e-commerce policy, demonstrating the willingness of the private sector to engage seriously in the policy development process. GBDe has demonstrated the ability of business to achieve consensus on complex and controversial aspects of e-commerce and has developed common positions in a number of key areas.

Global Corporate Governance Forum (GCGF)

URL <http://www.gcgf.org>
Established in 1999; location: Washington, DC, USA

Description: GCGF provides a convening venue for leading actors in corporate governance. The theme of public–private sector partnership was established through the *Private Sector Advisory Group (PSAG)*, which was set up jointly by the OECD and the World Bank Group. Through the PSAG, GCGF brings the experience and credibility of the international private sector to bear upon the problems and challenges facing corporate governance in developing countries. It also strengthens the engagement of private-sector counterparts in developing countries, which are key players in improving corporate governance. See URL <http://www.gcgf.org/partners/psag.htm>.

Global Profile

URL<http://www.globalprofile.co.uk>
Established in 2000; location: London, UK

Description: Global Profile dates back to the publication of a newsletter in 2000, which led to a series of lectures and articles. It is now an independent website which seeks to raise awareness on a variety of asymmetric challenges and threats to business and governments. It aims to implement a process of innovation and adaptability and to formulate effective new strategies of response. A key underlying idea is the increasing impact of conflicts on the business world and Western economies, causing serious consequences for commercial interests and economic viability, including international security and personal safety. Global Profile focuses on two themes: *market threats* (providing information on various types of asymmetric threats to business, such as anti-corporate activism, network warfare and cyber terrorism), and *business agility* (providing insight into the organizational and mindset traits for operating in a fast-changing, high-risk environment).

Global Public Affairs Institute (GPAI)

URL<http://www.gpai.org/>
Established in 1988; location: New York, N.Y., USA

Description: GPAI was founded by a group of executives with the belief that there was a need for a supplementary service to help public affairs and communications executives in multinational companies carry out their missions more effectively in international markets. GPAI programmes cover the strategic advisory and implementation activities of public relations, crisis management, employee communications and investor relations.

Information Assurance Advisory Council (IAAC)

URL <http://www.iaac.org.uk>
Established in 2000; location: Cambridge, UK

Description: IAAC provides policy recommendations on information assurance in the UK and Europe. Since 2000 it has provided a forum for policy dialogue between the private sector, government and academia. In 2002 it launched three initiatives to promote trust in the British information society, involving cross-sectoral interest groups from the public and private sectors: the *Public Policy Initiative on Protecting the Digital Society* (including a policy agenda for trust building), *Corporate Governance* (including corporate governance guidelines), and *Information Sharing.* See also URL <http://www.iaac.org.uk/initiatives/initindex.htm>.

The IAAC working group on *Risks and Dependencies* concentrates on enhancing risk assessment methodologies, with particular reference to their application in large-scale, complex infrastructures. The working group on *Threat Assessment* concentrates on issues surrounding the assessment and prediction of cyber-threats and on the collection, analysis and dissemination of attack and incident information. These working groups produce studies, roadmaps and exercise methodologies to stimulate new policies and initiatives in the public and private sectors. See URL <http://www.iaac.org.uk/Wgs/top_wg.htm>.

International Business Leaders Forum (IBLF)

URL <http://www.pwblf.org>
Established in 1990; location: London, UK

Description: IBLF was set up to promote responsible business practices and to achieve social, economic and environmentally sustainable development, especially by assisting new and emerging market economies. Its activities range from advocating that business should embrace a broader set of roles and responsibilities and brokering and participating in partnerships for practical action, to capacity building so that business, government and civil society can work in partnership. Its programmes include the *Business and Corruption Programme*, which aims to promote practical ways in which companies can tackle bribery and corruption and promote good corporate governance. In the *Business and Peace Programme*, a part of its Human Rights Programme, IBLF works with leading international companies. This programme aims to promote the role that business can play in contributing to long-term peace in conflict-prone areas, and to help companies to develop and implement suitable policies and practices. IBLF's website includes a broad selection of key organizations within the Corporate Social Responsibility (CSR) Forum for ethical business practices in new and emerging societies. Of particular interest is IBLF's *Conflict and Security Resource Centre,* with information on the issue of business in conflict and country case studies. See URL <http://www.pwblf.org/csr/csrwebassist.nsf/content/a1a2a 3a4a5.html>.

International Chamber of Commerce (ICC)

URL<http://www.iccwbo.org>
Established in 1919; location: Paris, France

Description: ICC represents world business in the global economy as a force for economic growth, job creation and prosperity. It has worldwide direct access to national governments through its national committees. Its activities cover a broad spectrum: arbitration and dispute resolution; making the case for open trade and the market economy system; business self-regulation; fighting corruption; and combating commercial crime. The ICC *Commission on Business in Society* aims to define the role of business in the context of globalization and changing societal expectations, including corporate responsibility issues and corporate governance. See URL <http://www.iccwbo.org/home/menu_business_society.asp>.

The priorities of ICC's *Anti-Corruption Commission* include: encouraging self-regulation by business in confronting issues of extortion and bribery; mobilizing the influence of international organizations to fight corruption; and the development of a work programme on money laundering. See URL <http://www.iccwbo.org/home/menu_extortion_bribery.asp>.

The publication *Fighting Corruption: A Corporate Practices Manual,* launched at an Anti-Corruption conference in April 2003, is available at URL <http://www.iccwbo.org/home/news_archives/2003/stories/anti-corruption.asp>.

Internet Security Alliance (ISA)

URL <http://www.isalliance.org>
Established in 2001; location: Arlington, Virginia, USA

Description: ISA was created to provide a forum for information sharing and thought leadership on information security issues. Another objective is to collaborate in developing and implementing information security solutions. The alliance of software engineering and electronic industry serves as an information source with regard to threats, best security practices and risk management strategies. Other activities include: the provision of early warning of emerging security threats; the provision of in-depth reports on vulnerabilities and threats; the facilitation of executive-to-executive communications about solutions to threats; and emerging trends and research leading to identification and resolution of root causes to problems.

Investor Responsibility Research Center (IRRC)

URL <http://www.irrc.com>
Established in 1972; location: Washington, DC, USA

Description: IRRC provides investor and corporate responsibility research and services and is committed to supporting good corporate governance. One of its services is the *Global Security Risk Monitor*—a global security risk profile and assessment product to assist fund managers, shareholders and corporate governance advocates in evaluating portfolios in the areas of terrorism and proliferation. It features profiles of companies whose operations in six countries designated by the US Government as state sponsors of terrorism or ties to proliferation-related concerns pose potential material risks to investors. It also features several country overviews (on North Korea, Libya, Sudan, Iran, Iraq and Syria) with security background information and analyses by economic sectors such as energy, finance, manufacturing, metals/mining and telecommunications. See URL <http://www.irrc.com/prod_serv/products_global_security.htm>.

Management Advisory Services and Publications (MASP)

URL<http://www.masp.com>

Established in 1972; location: Wellesley Hills, Massachusetts, USA

Description: MASP provides consulting services, management training, journals in IT security, internal control, and business contingency planning for executives, CIOs, auditors, security and disaster recovery professionals. Its *Contingency and Recovery Institute (CPR-I)* offers research and consulting in the fields of enterprise contingency, business continuity and resumption planning. See URL <http://www.masp.com/cpri/index.html>. MASP also organizes conferences and symposia on these issues.

National Association of Corporate Directors (NACD)

URL <http://www.nacdonline.org>

Established in 1977; location: Washington DC, USA

Description: NACD is a consulting organization and a membership association for boards and directors of US business corporations. It promotes: high professional standards for board and director conduct and performance; a forum for interaction among directors; guidance to boards in realizing their full potential; communication with the media, investors, corporations and business leaders; assertion of the policy interests of boards in selected legal and governmental arenas; and cooperation with international organizations on matters of corporate governance. NACD also organizes seminars and publishes reports. The *Report of the NACD Blue Ribbon Commission on Risk Oversight: Board Lessons for Turbulent Times* (2002) deals with topics such as uncertain economic environments, information theft, terrorism, and physical threats and technological vulnerability. It also analyses the increasing number of risks which corporations face today.

National Business Initiative (NBI)

URL<http://www.nbi.org.za>

Established in 1995; location: Johannesburg, South Africa

Description: NBI is an organization with more than 170 members (see the website). Its focus is the collective contribution of the private sector to socio-economic development in South Africa, acting in partnership with the South African Government to build a stable democracy in which a market economy functions to the benefit of all citizens. Two of its main achievements are: the establishment of the *Business Against Crime* business organization, which works closely with the government departments involved in combating crime; and the establishment of the *Public Private Partnerships (PPP) Centre*. See URL <http://www.pppcentre.com>. The NBI has also launched the quarterly newsletter *Partnerships*, available on its website.

Net Impact

URL <http://www.net-impact.org>

Established in 1993; location: San Francisco, California, USA

Description: Net Impact is a network of emerging business leaders committed to using the power of business to create a better world. Originally founded as Students for Responsible Business, Net Impact has developed into a network of 8500 business leaders offering programmes to help members broaden their business education, refine their leadership skills and pursue their professional goals. Its purpose is to help corporations to bear the responsibility that comes with the influential position that business leaders hold in society.

New Partnership for Africa's Development (NEPAD) Business Group

URL<http://www.nepadbusinessgroup.net>

Description: The NEPAD Business Group was established to help realize NEPAD's objectives by providing business knowledge and expertise. It comprises leading business organizations which have a broad constituency—both within and outside Africa—and are committed to helping the continent realize its full economic potential. It also acts as a medium between NEPAD and private companies which support its aims. The NEPAD Business Group shares information on trade and investment opportunities in Africa and encourages private-sector involvement in projects on sustainable development.

Novartis Foundation for Sustainable Development (NFSD)

URL <http://www.foundation.novartis.com>

Established in the 1960s; location: Basel, Switzerland

Description: NFSD's vision is that the commitment to disadvantaged people is one way in which a multinational company can meet its global social responsibility as a 'corporate citizen'. It has organized several symposia, e.g., on *Human Rights and the Private Sector* (2003) and *Development, Governance and the Private Sector* (2002) tackling the responsibilities of multinational companies. It also publishes articles in the field of business ethics and globalization, debating the obligations of multinational companies, their impact on the socio-economic development of their host countries and the 'corruption trap'. NFSD argues that it is a matter of corporate self-interest to behave in a socially and environmentally acceptable way, not only to avoid damaging companies' reputation but also to enhance the image of their goods and services. Worth special mention are a conference report and an article by Klaus Leisinger: *The Responsibility of Private Enterprises in the North–South Conflict* (1989) and *Multinationals and the Third World: Sell Solutions, Not Just Products* (*New York Times,* 21 Feb. 1988). See URL <http://www.foundation.novartis.com/business_ethics_globalization.htm>.

Security Management Online

URL <http://www.securitymanagement.com>

Established in 1972; location: Alexandria, Virginia, USA

Description: Security Management Online offers a central website where security professionals can exchange ideas, find solutions to daily problems, learn about new products and network with peers. The site has a library of current and archival information and a roundtable discussion forum, organized by industry and topics. *Security Management*, a journal published by the American Society for Industrial Security (ASIS), will organize a conference on International Security Management in April 2004 to tackle complex issues facing the international business community, such as terrorism, risk management, transportation security and business continuity. It will offer a forum for industry and security practitioners to share, network and solve problems.

Wolfsberg Group

URL <http://www.wolfsberg-principles.com>
Established in 2000; location: Basel, Switzerland
  Description: The Wolfsberg Group is an association of 12 global banks (listed on website), which aim to develop financial services industry standards, and related products for policies on 'know your customer', anti-money laundering and counter-terrorist financing. It subsequently published the *Wolfsberg Anti-Money Laundering Principles for Private Banking* (Oct. 2000, revised in May 2002); the *Statement on the Suppression of the Financing of Terrorism* (Jan. 2002); the *Wolfsberg Anti-Money Laundering Principles for Correspondent Banking* (Nov. 2002); and the *Statement on Monitoring Screening and Searching* (Sep. 2003). In its *Statement on the Suppression of the Financing of Terrorism* the Group emphasizes the role of financial institutions in assisting governments and their agencies through prevention, detection, information sharing and prompt response to governmental enquiries. It also supports the FATF Special Recommendations on Terrorist Financing. See URL <http://www.wolfsberg-principles.com/monitoring.html>.

World Business Awards in Support of the Millennium Development Goals

URL <http://www.iccwbo.org/awards/>
Established in 2000; location: International Chamber of Commerce, Paris, France
  Description: Through the World Business Awards, the International Chamber of Commerce (ICC), the United Nations Development Programme (UNDP) and the International Business Leaders Forum (IBLF) recognize the significant contribution of business enterprises, including those working in partnership with other stakeholders, in pursuit of the development targets to be achieved by 2015. The focus is on large-scale, well-known, existing partnerships, but the awards also recognize the less well-known, smaller-scale partnerships that exist in various parts of the world and have made a significant contribution. The spirit of the awards lies in the pursuit of innovative and productive approaches to sustainable development seen through the prism of the goals agreed by governments in the United Nations Millennium Declaration (2000). Nominations have been solicited for a new World Business Award honouring business efforts to achieve the Millennium Development Goals for the reduction of extreme poverty throughout the world by 2015. The third award is to be presented at the ICC World Congress in June 2004, following an award for Environmental Achievement (2000) and for Sustainable Development (2002). These awards are the first worldwide awards to recognize the significant role that business can play in the implementation of global development goals.

World Business Council for Sustainable Development (WBCSD)

URL <http://www.wbcsd.ch>

Established in 1991; location: Geneva, Switzerland

Description: WBCSD is a coalition of 165 international companies (covering 30 countries and 20 major industrial sectors), united by a commitment to sustainable development via the three pillars of economic growth, ecological balance and social progress. Its activities reflect the belief that the pursuit of sustainable development is good for business and that business is good for sustainable development. It also promotes the role of eco-efficiency, innovation and corporate social responsibility. A discussion paper *Running the Risk: The Sustainable Development and Risk Connection* (Nov. 2003) challenges traditional thinking on global risk: it argues that in order to deal with complex risks corporations require risk-management strategies embedded in the centre of their decision-making processes and gives key recommendations for chief executive officers. See URL <http://www.wbcsd.org/plugins/DocSearch/details.asp?type=DocDet&DocId=MjkzMg>.

World Economic Forum (WEF)

URL <http://www.weforum.org>

Established in 1987 (in 1970–87 called the Davos Symposium); location: Geneva, Switzerland

Description: The WEF is committed to improving the state of the world by developing initiatives to provide a collaborative framework for world leaders. It addresses global issues and facilitates dialogue between corporate, political, intellectual and other leaders on matters of global, regional, corporate and industry importance. Many of the debates at the WEF relate to the business–security linkage. In 2003, meetings were convened on *Successful Public–Private Partnerships (PPPs)* which have been identified as a key strategy for progress; *What Is the Role of Business in Areas in Turmoil?,* focusing on issues for companies operating in countries troubled by war or low-intensity conflicts, such as how they can best develop their business activities and at the same time contribute to regional development and preserve the security of the community; and *Private Sector Engagement in Iraq's Reconstruction*, which analysed the generation of profit while at the same time managing risks and building trust. Another important topic dealt with at Davos is *Corporate Citizenship*, defined as the manner in which a company manages its economic, social and environmental relationships, and the way in which it engages with its stakeholders. Within the framework of the *Global Corporate Citizenship Initiative (GCCI) Forum*, members aim to increase businesses' awareness, engagement, and support for corporate citizenship as a business strategy with long-term benefits for corporations and society. Further topics in recent WEF sessions and workshops—setting the 2004 agenda—illustrate the efforts to build bridges between the public and private sectors, especially in the light of terrorism and new risks.

World Monitors Inc. (WMI)

URL <http://www.worldmonitors.com>

Location: New York, N.Y., USA

Description: WMI is a consulting group that provides expertise for multinational companies, NGOs and multilateral organizations around the world which seek to align their business practices with human rights standards.

The *International Peace Forum (IPF)*, today a division of WMI, is founded on the conviction that companies have a social responsibility to the communities in which they do business, and that sensitivity to the issues surrounding conflict must be an element of long-term business strategy. IPF focuses on conflict prevention and works with corporations concerned with these issues to create responsible and effective peace-building initiatives in areas of actual or potential conflict. IPF also analyses the impact of investment in areas of conflict, and how the presence of local and foreign business can contribute to peace.

Appendix 3
Select bibliography

Isabel Frommelt

Books

Akintoye, A., Beck, M. and Hardcastle, C., *Public–Private Partnerships: Managing Risks and Opportunities* (Blackwell Science Ltd: Oxford, 2003).

Alexander, D. A. and Alexander, Y., *Terrorism and Business: The Impact of September 2001* (Transnational Publishers Inc.: Ardsley, 2002).

Banfield, J., Haufler, V. and Lilly, D., *Transnational Corporations in Conflict Prone Zones: Public Policy Responses and a Framework for Action* (Business and Conflict Programme, International Alert: London, 2003).

Birks, P. (ed.), *Laundering and Tracing* (Oxford University Press: Oxford, 1995).

Bray, J., 'Tackling the sources of conflict: what can companies do?', ed. R. Briggs, *The Unlikely Counter-Terrorists* (Foreign Policy Centre: London, 2002), pp. 78–89.

Briggs, R. (ed.), *Doing Business in a Dangerous World: Corporate Personnel Security in Emerging Markets* (Foreign Policy Centre: London, July 2003).

Briggs, R. (ed.), *The Unlikely Counter-Terrorists* (Foreign Policy Centre: London, 2002).

Bruce, G. and Whatford, N., 'Overcoming the threat: public–private partnership', ed. R. Briggs, *The Unlikely Counter-Terrorists* (Foreign Policy Centre: London, 2002), pp. 59–70.

Byrnes, F. C. and Kutnick, D. *Securing Business Information: Strategies to Protect the Enterprise and Its Network* (Addison-Wesley: London, 2002).

Cameron, D., *Global Network Security: Threats and Countermeasures* (Computer Technology Research Corporation: Charleston, N.C., 2000).

Coker, C., International Institute for Strategic Studies, *Globalisation and Insecurity in the Twenty-first Century: NATO and the Management of Risk*, Adelphi Paper 345 (Oxford University Press: Oxford, 2002).

David Hume Institute, *Money Laundering* (Edinburgh University Press: Edinburgh, 1993).

Gilmore, W. C. (ed.), *International Efforts to Combat Money Laundering* (Grotius Publications: Cambridge, 1992).

Haufler, V., *Public Role for the Private Sector: Industry Self-Regulation in a Global Economy* (Carnegie Endowment for International Peace: Washington, DC, 2001).

Hutchinson, B. and Warren, M., *Information Warfare, Corporate Attack and Defence in a Digital World* (Butterworth-Heinemann: Oxford, 2001).

Intriago, C. A., *International Money Laundering* (Eurostudy: London, 1991).

Lukasik, S. J., Goodman, S. E. and Longhurst, D. W., International Institute for Strategic Studies (IISS), *Protecting Critical Infrastructure Against Cyber-Attack*, Adelphi Paper 359 (Oxford University Press: Oxford, 2003).

Montana, P. J. and Roukis, G. S., (eds.) *Managing Terrorism: Strategies for the Corporate Executive* (Quorum Books: Westport, Conn., 1983).

Nelson, J., *The Business of Peace: The Private Sector as a Partner in Conflict Prevention and Resolution* (International Alert, Council on Economic Priorities and Business Leaders Forum: London, 2000).

Poole-Robb, S. and Bailey, A., *Risky Business: Corruption, Fraud, Terrorism and Other Threats to Global Business* (Kogan Page: London, 2002).

Quinley, K. M. and Schmidt, D. L., *Business at Risk: How to Assess, Mitigate and Respond to Terrorist Threats* (National Underwriter Company: Cincinnati, Ohio, 2002).

Tesner, S., *The United Nations and Business: A Partnership Recovered* (St Martin's Press: New York, 2000).

Wenger, A. and Möckli, D., *Conflict Prevention: The Untapped Potential of the Business Sector* (Lynne Rienner: London, 2003).

Articles, reports and working papers

Addison, T., Chowdhury, A. R. and Murshed, S. M., 'By how much does conflict reduce financial development?', Discussion Paper 48/2002 (United Nations University World Institute for Development Economics Research (UNU/WIDER): Helsinki, 2002).

Anderson, M. B. and Zandvliet, L., 'Corporate options for breaking cycles of conflict', Issue papers for the Collaborative for Development Action, 2001, URL <http://fletcher.tufts.edu/humansecurity/con2/ws2/anderson.pdf>.

Aninat, E., Hardy, D. and Johnston, R. B., 'Combating money laundering and the financing of terrorism', *Finance and Development*, vol. 39, no. 3 (2002), pp. 44–47.

Armstrong Whiting, M. and Cavanagh, T. E., *Corporate Security Management: Organization and Spending Since 9/11*, Conference Board Research Report no. R-133-03-RR (Conference Board: New York, 2003).

Baker, S. H., 'Triad in crisis: the important relationship of humanitarian, intervention and reconstruction organisations, the international business community, and societies in conflict', INCORE Occasional Paper, Londonderry, 2002.

Behrendt, S. and Khanna, P., 'Risky business: geopolitics and the global corporation', *Strategy & Business*, Issue 32 (fall 2003), pp. 69–75.

Bennett, J., 'Business in zones of conflict: the role of the multinational in promoting regional stability' (International Peace Forum: New York, 2001).

Bennett J., 'Multinational corporations, social responsibility and conflict', *Journal of International Affairs*, vol. 55, no. 2 (spring 2002), pp. 393–410.

Blasis, J. P. de, 'Business Continuity Planning reviewed after September 11, 2001', *Contact MBA: The Newsletter of the University of Geneva MBA Alumni Association*, vol. 13 (Oct. 2002), pp. 1–3.

Briggs, R., 'Corporate Security After September 11th', *Globalthinking* (Foreign Policy Centre, London), issue 7 (spring 2002), pp. 12–13.

Brisard, J.-C. (JCB Consulting), 'Terrorism financing: roots and trends of Saudi terrorism financing', Report prepared for the President of the Security Council United Nations, 19 Dec. 2002, New York, URL <http://www.nationalreview.com/document/document-un122002.pdf>.

Cilliers, J., 'Business and war', *African Security Review*, vol. 10, no. 3 (2001), pp. 117–19.

Collier, P., *et al.*, *Breaking the Conflict Trap: Civil War and Development Policy*, World Bank Policy Research Report (World Bank: New York, 2003).

Davies, R., 'Business: why do private companies have a role in conflict prevention?', Wilton Park Conference on Humanitarian Principles and Non-State Actors, 9 Feb. 2000, URL <http://www.iblf.org/csr/csrwebassist.nsf/content/f1d2b3l4.html>.

Dependability Development Support Initiative (DDSI), 'Roadmap: Public–Private Partnerships', Nov. 2002, Project no. IST-2000-29202, URL <http://www.ddsi.org/Documents/final%20docs/DDSI_D3_PPP_Roadmap_f.pdf>.

Evans, G. and Sahnoun, M. (Co-Chairs), 'The Responsibility to Protect: Report of the International Commission on Intervention and State Sovereignty (ICISS)' (International Development Research Center: Ottawa, 2001), URL <http://www.dfait-maeci.gc.ca/iciss-ciise/report-en.asp>.

George C. Marshall European Center for Security Studies, Report of the Conference on Organized Crime: The National Security Dimension, 29 Aug.–2 Sep. 1999, Garmisch-Partenkirchen, URL <http://www.marshallcenter.org/site-graphic/lang-en/page-conf-reports-1/static/xdocs/conf/static/conf-report_3.pdf>.

Global Witness, 'A rough trade: the role of companies and governments in the Angolan conflict' (Global Witness: London, Dec. 1998), URL <http://www.globalwitness.org/reports/download.php/00103.pdf>.

Gossen, R. and Mendes, E. (Co-Chairs), 'Global Compact Business Guide to Conflict Impact Assessment and Risk Management' (University of Ottawa: for, 2002), URL <http://www.union-network.org/uniindep.nsf/f8dff9d20fb56a28c1256bf9002e1d31/c550f48211dccaacc1256c31002013c5/$FILE/BusinessGuide.pdf>.

Greenberg, M. R., Wechsler, W. F. and Wolosky, L. S. (eds), 'Terrorist Financing: Report of an Independent Task Force' (Council of Foreign Relations: New York, 2002).

Janning, J. and Algieri, F., 'Security in Times of Terror: Policy Options for Germany and Europe', Findings of the Task Force on The Future of Security for the conference on The New Transatlantic Strategic Framework, Miami, Fla., 14–16 Feb. 2003, URL <http://www.cap.uni-muenchen.de/download/2003/2003_Miami_JJ.pdf>.

Hayes, K., 'Business as peacemaker: breaking the cycle of poverty & conflict' (Ashridge Business School: Berkhansted, Hertfordshire, 2001).

Latter, R., *The Terrorist Threat to Business*, Wilton Park Papers 62, Report based on the Wilton Park Conference on Terrorism and Business in the 1990s: Threats and Responses, 27–31 July 1992 (HMO: London, Sep. 1992).

Lenain, P., Bonturi, M. and Koen, V., 'The Economic Consequences of Terrorism', OECD Economics Department Working Paper no. 334 (Organisation for Economic Co-operation and Development (OECD): Paris, 2002).

Looney, R. E., *Strategic Insight: Economic Costs to the United States Stemming From the 9/11 Attacks* (Center for Contemporary Conflict: Monterey, Calif., 5 Aug. 2002).

Lunde, L., Taylor, M. and Huser, A., 'Commerce or Crime? Regulating Economies of Conflict', Fafo-report 424 (Forskningsstiftelsen Fafo, Institute for Applied Social Science: Oslo, 2003).

Mousseau, M., 'Market civilization and its clash with terror', *International Security*, vol. 27, no. 3 (winter 2002/2003), pp. 5–29.

Pauwels, N., 'Conflict Commodities: Addressing the Role of Natural Resources in Conflict', Briefing Paper no. 27 (International Security Information Service (ISIS) Europe: Brussels, Mar. 2003).

Pieth, M., 'International standards against money laundering', *Keisatsugaku ronshu* [Journal of police science] (Tokyo), vol. 51, no. 2 (Apr. 1998), pp. 37ff.

Pieth, M., 'The prevention of money laundering: a comparative analysis', *European Journal of Crime, Criminal Law and Criminal Justice*, vol. 6, no. 2 (1998), pp. 159–68.

Ragazzi, M., 'The role of the World Bank in conflict-afflicted areas', 2001, URL <http://wbln0018.worldbank.org/Networks/ESSD/icdb.nsf/D4856F112E805 DF4852566C9007C27A6/F40AAD96853192E985256C7500797CBE/$FILE/ WBRoleinCAA.pdf>.

Rattray, G. J., 'The cyberterrorism threat', eds J. M. Smith and W. C. Thomas, *The Terrorism Threat and U.S. Government Response: Operational and Organizational Factors* (US Air Force Institute for National Security Studies: Colorado Springs, Colo., 2001), pp. 79–118.

Ross, L. M., 'Oil, drugs and diamonds: how do natural resources vary in their impact on civil war?' (International Peace Academy: New York, 2002).

Sarewitz, D., Pielke, R. and Keykhah, M., 'Vulnerability and risk: some thoughts from a political and policy perspective', *Risk Analysis*, vol. 23, no. 4 (Aug. 2003), pp. 805–10.

Savir, U., 'Peace by piece', *World Link*, Jan./Feb. 1999.

Sherman, J., 'Options for promoting corporate responsibility in conflict zones: perspectives from the private sector', IPA Meeting Report (International Peace Academy: New York, Apr. 2002).

Switzer, J., 'Conflicting interests', >*elements* (Environment Council), 2002, pp. 10–12, URL <http://www.iisd.org/pdf/2002/envsec_conflicting_interests.pdf>

Tanzi, V., 'Money laundering and the international financial system', IMF Working Paper 96/55 (International Monetary Fund: Washington, DC, 1996).

Taylor, M. and Huser, A., 'Security, development and economies of conflict: problems and responses', Fafo AIS Policy Brief, Prepared for the Expert Consultations on Economics of Conflict and Development in Oslo, Nov. 2003.

Ward, C. A., 'The role of the United Nations Security Council in combating international terrorism', Paper presented at the Oxford Conference on The Changing Face of International Co-operation in Criminal Matters in the 21st Century, Christ Church, Oxford, 27–30 Aug. 2002.

Winer, J. M., *Illicit Finance and Global Conflict*, Fafo-Report 380 (Forskningsstiftelsen Fafo, Institute for Applied Social Science: Oslo, 2002).

About the authors

Said Adejumobi (Nigeria) teaches political science at Lagos State University. He has written extensively in the areas of governance, conflict and security studies. He has won several academic awards and fellowships in those areas of research, including the Norwegian Nobel Institute Fellowship, Oslo, Norway (2000); a Social Science Research Council (SSRC) Post-Doctoral Fellowship, New York (2002); an Institute of African Studies Post-Doctoral Fellowship, New York (2001); a Post-Doctoral Fellowship, Institute of African Studies, Columbia University, New York (2001); and Laureate, MacArthur Foundation Research and Writing Grants Competition, Global Security and Cooperation Program (2003).

Saad Alfarargi (Egypt) is Head of the Permanent Delegation and Permanent Observer of the League of Arab States to the United Nations in Geneva, to UN specialized agencies and to other international organizations in Switzerland. From 1995 to 1997 he was the Assistant Administrator and Regional Director of the Regional Bureau for Arab States in the United Nations Development Programme (UNDP), New York. From 1990 to 1995 he served as the Personal Representative of the President of Egypt to the Group of Fifteen (G-15) and as Adviser to the Prime Minister of Egypt.

Alyson J. K. Bailes (United Kingdom) is Director of SIPRI. She has served in the British Diplomatic Service, most recently as British Ambassador to Finland. She spent several periods on detachment outside the service, including two academic sabbaticals, a two-year period with the British Ministry of Defence and assignments to the European Union and the Western European Union. She has published extensively in international journals on politico-military affairs, European integration and Central European affairs as well as on Chinese foreign policy. Her most recent SIPRI publication is *Relics of Cold War: Europe's Challenge, Ukraine's Experience* (with O. Melnyk and I. Anthony), SIPRI Policy Paper no. 6 (2003).

Christine Batruch (Canada) is Vice-President for Corporate Responsibility at Lundin Petroleum AB, Geneva, Switzerland. A lawyer by training, she has worked in the non-profit, academic and business sectors. In the early 1990s she participated in the establishment of a number of non-profit and educational institutions in Ukraine, as part of the Soros network of foundations. She later became assistant professor of environmental law at the International Academy of the Environment, Geneva, and member of an advisory group at the United Nations Economic Commission for Europe (UNECE). She joined Lundin Oil, now Lundin Petroleum, in 1999.

Georges S. Baur (Liechtenstein) is the Deputy Head of the Liechtenstein Mission to the European Union in Brussels. He has been the editor of the legal journal *Jus & News* since 1997. From 2000 until the spring of 2003 he was Adviser to the Government of the Principality of Liechtenstein on issues of financial services. Among his recent publications are 'Fight against corruption according to Liechtenstein law', in *La Corruzione: Profile Storici, Attuali, Europei e Sovranazionali* [Corruption: old and current European and suprantional profiles] (CEDAM, 2003); and 'Wirtschaft und Recht: eine Hassliebe' [Economy and law: love–hate relationship], in *Management & Law* (eds H. Siegwart and J. Mahari, Helbing & Lichtenhahn, 2003).

Erik Belfrage (Sweden) is Senior Vice-President of Skandinaviska Enskilda Banken (SEB), and Adviser to the Chairman of SEB and to the Chairman of Investor AB. He also serves as Chairman of the Boards of the Swedish Institute of International Affairs, Stockholm, and the ICC–Commercial Crime Services, London; and as the Vice-Chairman of the International Chamber of Commerce Finance Committee. He is a member of the boards of several business organizations and of the Trilateral Commission, and has previously served in the Swedish Diplomatic Service.

Evan Berlack (United States) is Counsel in the Global Projects Department at Baker Botts LLP in Washington, DC. Prior to joining Baker Botts in 2001, he worked as a partner on International Trade and Transaction at Arent Fox Kintner Plotkin & Kahn, PLLC in Washington, DC. He has served as Co-chair of the Practising Law Institute's annual programme on Coping with US Export Controls, and has co-edited the annual volumes published under that name.

Thomas Biersteker (United States) is Director of and Henry R. Luce Professor of Transnational Organizations for the Watson Institute of International Studies at Brown University. Prior to that, he was an Associate Professor (1985–88) and Professor (1988–92) at the School of International Relations of the University of Southern California. His most recent publications include *The Rebordering of North America? Integration and Exclusion in a New Security Context*, co-edited with P. Andreas (Routledge, 2003) and *The Emergence of Private Authority in Global Governance*, co-edited with R. Hall (Cambridge University Press, 2002).

Crispin Black (United Kingdom) is Director of Janusian, the security risk management subsidiary of the Risk Advisory Group. As a lieutenant colonel, he left the British Army in 2002, after having served in the Cabinet Office Assessments Staff, preparing briefings for the Prime Minister and long-term strategic analysis for the Joint Intelligence Committee.

Phyllis O. Bonanno (United States) is President and CEO of International Trade Solutions, Inc. Previously, she served as the President and CEO of Columbia University (1997–2000), as Corporate Vice-President for international trade at Warnaco, Inc. (1986–97), and as the first Director of the US Trade Representative's Office of Private Sector Liaison in the Executive Office of Presidents Jimmy Carter and Ronald Reagan (1977–86). She is also on the boards of the Center for International Private Enterprise and the Canadian American Business Council, Washington, DC.

Andrew Bone (United Kingdom) is Head of Public Affairs and an official spokesperson for the De Beers Group. He has worked for the De Beers Group for 20 years, including six years (1986–92) buying diamonds in the Democratic Republic of the Congo. He oversees the Group's policies on corporate responsibility and sustainable development issues, regularly liaising with governments, the United Nations, diamond industry leaders and representatives of civil society. He has participated in the development of the Kimberley Process since the first meeting, in May 2000. He is also a visiting lecturer at the Westminster Business School in London.

Olivia Bosch (United States/United Kingdom) is a Senior Research Fellow in the New Security Issues Programme at the Royal Institute of International Affairs, London. Before her current position, she was a Visiting Fellow at the International Institute for Strategic Studies (IISS), preceded by a Senior Fellowship for a joint project on the new millennium and critical infrastructure protection organized by the IISS and the Center for Global Security Research (CGSR) of Lawrence Livermore National Laboratory. She has also served as a Director of the Council for Arms Control in London and as an UNSCOM inspector in Iraq (1996).

Niall Burgess (Ireland) is the head of the Early Warning, Conflict Prevention and Terrorism Task Force in the European Union Policy Unit. From 1997 to 1999 he was Head of the Human Rights and Humanitarian Affairs Unit of the Irish Mission to the United Nations in Geneva.

Gilles Carbonnier (Switzerland) is the economic adviser of the International Committee of the Red Cross (ICRC) and heads the Private Sector Relations Team at the ICRC's Directorate General. He is responsible for the overall development of relations between the ICRC and the business community, and provides economic advice on humanitarian action. He has field experience in Ethiopia, Iraq, Sri Lanka and several Latin American countries. He holds a Ph.D. in economics and has published articles on the interaction between war and the economy, including the role of private companies. Before joining the ICRC, he was involved in development cooperation programmes and international trade negotiations under the General Agreement on Tariffs and Trade (GATT)/World Trade Organization (WTO).

Isabel Frommelt (Liechtenstein) is a Research Assistant at SIPRI, conducting research on business and security issues. On a mandate of the Liechtenstein Government and in partnership with the Liechtenstein-Institut she recently organized the conference on Business and Security, After 11 September 2001. Previously, she was a Research Officer at the Swiss State Secretariat for Economic Affairs (SECO) in the Foreign Trade Department, responsible *inter alia* for elaborating third country economic and political profiles. In 2001–2003 she was at the Institute for Social Planning and Social Management (ISS) in Bern. In 2001, during the 56th UN General Assembly, she completed a six-month traineeship at the Liechtenstein Mission in New York, focusing on terrorism, humanitarian and conflict prevention.

István Gyarmati (Hungary) is Chairman of the Board of the Centre for Euro-Atlantic Integration and Democracy in Budapest and Co-Chairman of the International Security Advisory Board for Southeastern Europe of the Geneva-based Centre for the Democratic Control of Armed Forces (DCAF). He has been a Foreign Service Officer since 1974. His recent positions include Senior Vice-President for Policy and Programs of the EastWest Institute (2000–2003), Chief Advisor to the Foreign Minister on Security Policy and Chairman of the Organisation for the Prohibition of Chemical Weapons (1999–2000), Chairman of the Missile Technology Control Regime (1998–99) and Hungarian Under-secretary of Defence (1996–99).

Urho Ilmonen (Finland) is Director of Corporate Relations and Chief Security Officer of Nokia Corporation. His current role includes chairmanship of the International Chamber of Commerce (ICC) commission for intellectual property rights and chairmanship of the European Information and Communications Technology (EICTA) Commission for Legal and Consumer Policy Issues. Previously, he worked as Vice-President Legal of the Group Council for Nokia Mobile Phones of Nokia Corporation.

Patrick Lenain (France) is Counsellor to the Organisation for Economic Co-operation and Development (OECD) Chief Economist. Prior to that position, he served as the International Monetary Fund (IMF) Senior Representative in Kiev (1997–98); Chargé de Mission, Treasury Department, Paris; and the Principal Administrator of the European Commission in Brussels. His recent publications include 'Is the euro area converging or diverging?: implications for policy co-ordination', co-authored with A. de Serres, in *The World Economy* (Blackwell, 2002) and *The Economic Consequences of Terrorism*, co-authored with M. Bonturi and V. Koen (OECD Economics Department Working Paper no. 334, 2002).

John Maresca (United States) is President of the Business Humanitarian Forum, an international non-profit organization based in Geneva, Switzerland, which brings business support to humanitarian work and facilitates private-sector investment in post-conflict and developing regions. Previously, he served as the US Ambassador to several multilateral organizations and negotiations, and as a conflict mediator in the Caucasus and Mediterranean regions. He negotiated a number of international agreements, including the 1975 Helsinki Final Act and the 1990 Charter of Paris for a New Europe, and was sent as Special Envoy to open US relations with the newly independent states of the former Soviet Union. He served as an Assistant Secretary of Defense and was Chief of staff for two Secretary Generals of NATO. He has published books, chapters and articles on issues of international relations, conflict prevention, economic development and corporate responsibility.

Jan Metzger (Switzerland) is a Senior Researcher/Risk Network Coordinator for the Center for Security Studies at the Swiss Federal Institute of Technology in Switzerland. From 1999 to 2000 he was a Senior Consultant in the Government consulting division of Arthur Andersen and between 1994–98 he was a Research Assistant at the Institute for Political Science, University of St Gallen, Switzerland. His most recent publications include 'Nationwide risk analysis as an issue of security policy research and practice: the Comprehensive Risk Analysis and Management Network (CRN)' in *Future Trends in Security Policy 2001* (ed. G. E. Gustenau, 2002); and 'Der Bevölkerungsschutz in der Schweiz' [Civil protection in Switzerland], in 'Stichwort 20: Katastrophen- und Zivilschutz' [Catastrophes and civil protection], *GAI: ökologische Perspektiven in Natur-, Geistes- und Wirtschaftswissenschaften* [Ecological perspectives in science, humanities and economics], vol. 11, no. 1 (2002).

Claes Norgren (Sweden) is Director General of the Swedish Competition Authority and Director General of the Swedish Competition Authority. He served as the President of the Financial Task Force on Money Laundering (FATF) in 2003–2004. His previous positions include Chairman of the Basel Committee Task Force on New Capital Requirements (1999–2002), Chairman of the Banking Advisory Committee at the European Commission (1997–2002), and Director General of the Swedish Financial Supervisory Authority (1993–2002).

Kevin Rosner (United States/France) is a Fellow at the University of Reading, Centre for Euro-Asian Studies, UK, and an Associate Researcher with the Institut de Relations Internationales et Stratégiques (IRIS), Paris, in addition to consulting regularly with the NATO Science and Security Related Civil Technology Programme and the NATO Economic Directorate at NATO Headquarters. He specializes in oil, gas and hydrocarbons in the Russia, the Commonwealth of Independent States, and Central and Eastern Europe. He is the author of 'Pipeline security in insecure times', (2003) and co-editor of *Our Fragile World: Challenges and Opportunities for Sustainable Development* (EOLSS Publishers, 2003).

David Spence (United Kingdom) is a Political Counsellor of the European Commission. He is responsible for the Common Foreign Security Policy (CFSP) and disarmament issues at the European Commission's delegation to the United Nations and other international organizations in Geneva. He joined the European Commission in 1990, and has held positions as the Secretary of the Task Force on German Unification; the Head of Training in the Commission's Directorate-General for External Relations; and the Commission's Representative in the Council's CFSP Counter-Terrorism Working Group; and in the Group of Eight (G8) Working Group on Terrorism. He has published widely on European affairs and is the editor of *The European Commission* (Harper, 3rd edn, 2004).

Daniel Tarschys (Sweden) is Professor of Political Science and Public Administration at Stockholm University. In 2000 he served as the Personal Representative of the Swedish Prime Minister in the Convention which drafted the 2000 EU Charter of Fundamental Rights. In 1994–99 he was Secretary-General of the Council of Europe and he has previously served as Secretary of State in the Swedish Prime Minister's Office, Chairman of the Board of the Stockholm International Peace Research Institute (SIPRI) and Chairman of the Board of the Swedish Agency for Research Cooperation (SAREC).

Vadim Volkov (Russia) is Chair of the Sociology Department at the High School of Economics, St Petersburg Branch, and Associate Professor of Sociology at the Department of Political Science and Sociology of the European University in St Petersburg (EUSP). In 1999–2001 he was Social Science Research Council/MacArthur Foundation Post-doctoral Fellow in the International Peace and Security Program. He is the author of *Violent Entrepreneurs: The Use of Force in the Making of Russian Capitalism* (Cornell University Press, 2002) and of 'The political economy of protection rackets in the past and the present', *Social Research* (2000); 'Between society and the state: private security and rule-enforcement in Russia', *Politics and Society* (2000); and 'Violent entrepreneurship in post-Communist Russia', *Europe–Asia Studies* (1999). His research interests include economic sociology, problems of the state and violence, public and private security, comparative mafia studies, and politics in a cultural context.

Index

Abacha, Sani 244
Abkhazia 112
accrual accounting 38
Adams, James 50
Afghanistan:
  al-Qaeda in 6, 28
  terrorist links 93
  UN and 69
  war in 6, 7, 60, 87, 112, 221, 229, 243
Africa:
  AIDS in 13–14
  arms trade in 246
  business in 245–50, 252
  conflicts and poverty 248
  economic development 252
  mercenaries in 246, 247
  natural resources 163
  poverty 248, 251–52
  security in 251–52
  small arms 245, 246
  terrorism and 242–53
African Development Bank (ADB) 261–62
African Business Round Table (ABR) 296
Aid and Trade 262
AIDS (acquired immune deficiency
  syndrome) 13–14
air marshals 90
airlines 31
Ake, Claude 249
Akhmadov, Sais-Magomed 116
Al-Barakat Group 70, 72–73
Algeria 220
Amnesty International (AI) 158, 262
Amsterdam Treaty (1997) 89
Angola 247
  diamonds 129, 133, 136
  UNITA 129, 130, 132, 134, 138, 244
Annan, Kofi 22, 134, 137
anti-money laundering (AML) 63, 64, 65
Argentina 179
ArmorGroup 247
arms exports 4, 38
Artemis, Operation 85
Asian Development Bank (ADB) 263
Aum Shinrikyo 48
Australia 10, 66, 77

Australia Group 79, 80, 82
aviation industry 31, 52, 90, 186, 221, 224:
  security 6, 11, 90, 224
AVINA Foundation 296

Babangida, General Ibrahim 249
Balkans, Western 93, 94
banking 37:
  security and 102
  terrorism and 102–10
Baraev, Movsar 117
Basaev, Shamil 112, 116
Basque separatists 33, 47, 220
Berne Declaration (Erklärung von Bern, EvB)
  263
Bildt, Carl 160
Bioethics Convention (1997) 39–40
biotechnology 167–68
Blair, Tony 179
Blumenstyk, Goldie 256
Bonn International Centre for Conversion
  (BICC) 263–64
Bonn–Berlin Working Group on Travel and
  Aviation-Related Bans 70
border control 52, 225–27, 230
Bosnia and Herzegovina 95, 96
Brazil 256
British American Security Information
  Council (BASIC) 264
Brookings Institution 264–65
Bush, President George W. 47, 52, 74, 173,
  221
business:
  conflict and 162–66
  criminal activity, differentiating from
    122–23
  defence and 1–2, 3
  government and 7–8, 15
  post-war reconstruction 168
  role of 3–4, 121, 124
  scandals 15
  security and 2:
    cost of 9
  terrorism and 15, 245–50
  see also companies; financial industry
Business and Human Rights Resource Centre
  265

Business for Africa 297
business continuity plans (BCPs) 187, 192–93, 194, 195
Business Council Europe Africa Mediterranean (BCEAM) 296
Business Executives for National Security (BENS) 297
Business for Social Responsibility (BSR) 298
Business Humanitarian Reform (BHF) 297–98
Business in the Community (BITC) 298
Business Partners for Development (BPD) 298–99

Canada 13
Carnegie Endowment for International Peace 265
Caux Round Table (CRT) 299
Center for Contemporary Conflict (CCC) 266
Center for Defense Information (CDI) 266
Center for Ethical Business Cultures (CEBC) 299
Center for Global Development (CGD) 266
Center for Security Studies (Forschungsstelle für Sicherheitspolitik, FSK) 266–67
Center for Strategic and International Studies (CSIS) 267–68
Center for the Study of Global Governance (CSGG) 268
Center on International Cooperation (CIC) 268
Central Europe Pipeline Management Agency (CEPMA) 214
Central European Pipeline System (CEPS) 214–15
Centre for Defence and International Security Studies (CDISS) 268
Centre for Innovation in Corporate Responsibility (CICR) 299
Centre for Tomorrow's Company 300
charities: terrorists and 55, 66, 74
Charta 77 42
Chevron 249
China 78, 81, 256
citizenship 235–36
civil liberties 59, 73, 75, 251
Civil Liberties Organisation 249
Clarke, Richard 188
climate change 3, 22
Clinton, President Bill 28

COCOM (Coordinating Committee on Multilateral Export Controls) 78
cold war 2, 27 see also post-cold war era
Collaborative for Development Action (CDA) 300
Colombia 210
Committee for Economic Development (CED) 300–1
Commonwealth Association for Corporate Governance (CACG) 268–69
Commonwealth of Independent States (CIS) 174
companies:
    humanitarian law and 164–65
    ICRC and 166–69
    military 245, 246, 247–48
    natural resource 247
    oil 248–49
    security and 125
    security services 31
    'virtual' 195
Computer Emergency Response Teams (CERTs) 35, 192–93
computerised systems 13
computers 72, 187:
    hackers 187, 190
    incidents 189–91
    see also cyber terrorism
conflict:
    arms trade and 4
    business and 4, 16, 123, 162–64
    illusions about 27–28
    post-cold war 27–28
    war economies 163–64
conflict diamonds 129–47:
    concept of 129
    definition 132
Conflict Prevention and Post-Conflict Reconstruction Network (CPR) 269
Congo, Democratic Republic of 85, 96, 134, 136
Convention for the Elimination of Mercenarism in Africa 248
Convention for the Prevention of Torture and Inhuman or Degrading Treatment (1987) 39
Convention for the Protection of Human Rights and Fundamental Freedoms (1950) 39
Corporate Social Responsibility (CSR) Europe 300–1
corporations:
    security and 33, 34–36, 222

terrorism and 33, 34
corruption 75, 102, 163
Corsica 33
Council for Ethics in Economics (CEE) 301
Council of Europe (CoE) 39–42, 269–70
crime, organized 28, 30, 32, 93, 102, 104, 238
critical energy system infrastructure (CESI)
  210–16
critical information infrastructure protection
  (CIIP) 198, 199, 200
critical infrastructure 188
critical infrastructure protection (CIP):
  as biological phenomenon 207
  CIIP and 198, 199, 200
  conceptual perspective 200–1
  definition 197–200
  operational perspective 197–200

  preoccupation with 13
  recommendations on 207–9
  term unfortunate 207
criticality 201–7
Cuba 49
cyber security 193–95
cyber terrorism 187–96:
  definition 187–88
'cyber warfare' 190–91
Cyprus 94
Czech Republic 215

De Beers 129, 130–31, 132, 133, 134
De La Rue 133
defence: business and 1–2, 3
defence industry 4
Delors, Jacques 43, 85
democracy:
  dialogue on 240
  preferences for 42
  promotion of 40
  WMD and 237
Denmark 13
Deutsche Bank 72
developing world: climate change and 22
Diamond High Council 133
drug trafficking 49–50, 93

'eco-terrorist' movement 5
Ekine, Sokari 249
electricity failures 13, 210
electricity provision 193
Elf 249
emergency response plans 185

energy systems, protection of 210–16
Enron Corporation 15, 37
Ethics Resource Center (ERC) 270–71
Ethos Institute of Companies and Social
  Responsibility 271
EU (European Union) 18, 272–74:
  Action Plan to combat terrorism 88–95
  Action Plan to combat WMD proliferation
    10
  anti-terrorism clause 92–93
  anti-terrorist measures 21, 88, 92–93, 96,
    97–101
  Balkans and 94, 95, 96
  Barcelona Process 94, 238
  borders 90
  CFSP 85, 95
  Charter of Fundamental Rights 43
  civil rights and 99
  coherence 98, 99
  Commission 99, 135
  Common Commercial Policy 99
  Common Security and Defence Policy 212
  Constitution 43, 101
  COPS 97
  COREPER 97
  Council 96
  development aid 94
  Directive on Money Laundering (2001) 92
  Economic and Monetary Union 101
  energy and 212
  enlargement of 43, 84, 94
  ESDP 84, 95, 97, 98, 211
  European Arrest Warrant 89, 90
  European Convention, 2002–2003 84, 86
  foreign policy 84, 85, 98, 99
  future challenges 95–99
  intelligence 97
  internal security 89–91
  Iraq and 86, 96, 97
  Justice and Home Affairs 86
  Kosovo and 95
  national sovereignty 85
  non-proliferation clause 93
  Police Mission 95
  Schengen Convention 90
  security 85, 211–13
  Security Strategy 86, 98
  strategic export controls 77, 81
  terrorist attack and 86, 87–95, 100
  terrorist finance and 91–92
  terrorist lists 68–69
  third countries, assisting 92–95

threat assessments 97
  as trading partner 92, 93
  UN and 91
  values and 43–44
  WMD and 98
EU–US dialogue 18
European Bank for Reconstruction and
  Development (EBRD) 271
European Business Ethics Network (EBEN)
  301
European Centre for Development Policy
  Management (ECDPM) 271
European Communities 43, 85
European Corporate Governance Institute
  (ECGI) 272
European Court of Human Rights 39
European Economic Area (EEA) 106
European Multilateral Mutual Legal
  Assistance (1959) 105
European Peacebuilding Liaison Office
  (EPLO) 272
European Platform for Conflict Prevention
  and Transformation 272
European Sustainable and Responsible
  Investment Forum (Eurosif) 301
Europol (European Police Office) 89, 274
Executive Outcome 246, 247
extractive industries 161, 162
Extractive Industries Transparency Initiative
  (EITI) 162

failed states 6, 28
Falkland Islands 179
Fatal Transactions 130, 131
Financial Action Task Force on Money
  Laundering (FATF) 34, 47, 56–57, 58,
  62–63, 67, 289:
  Eight Special Recommendations on
    Terrorist Financing 52–54, 63, 91
  Forty Recommendations on Money
    Laundering 53
financial industry 35, 49, 50:
  reactions, speeding 105
  regulating 55, 66
  re-regulation 59, 74
  reporting 66
  see also banking
financial institutions:
  international 53–54
  private 72–73
  see also under names of
Foreign Policy Center (FPC) 274

Foreign Policy Research Institute (FPRI) 275
Forskningsstiftelsen Fafo (Fafo Institute for
  Applied Social Science) 275
Fortuyn, Pim 39
Fowler, Robert 130
France 96, 220, 225
Fund for Peace (FfP) 275
FYROM (Former Yugoslav Republic of
  Macedonia) see Macedonia

G7 (Group of Seven) 138, 277:
  Dubai meeting 8, 56
G8 (Group of Eight) 18, 277–78:
  Action Plan on Capacity Building (2003)
    61
  Counter-Terrorism Action Group (CTAG)
    54, 61
Garang, John 148
gas 212
Gehr, Walter 64
Geiger, Gebhard 209
Gelaev, Ruslan 112
Geneva Center for Security Policy (GCSP)
  276
Geneva Conventions 248
George C. Marshall European Center for
  Security Studies 276
Georgia 112
Germany 33, 66, 201–2, 206, 214, 225
Global Business Dialogue on Electronic
  Commerce (GBDe) 301–2
Global Corporate Governance Forum
  (GCGF) 302
global issues networks 138
Global Profile 302
Global Public Affairs Institute (GPAI) 302
Global Reporting Initiative (GRI) 276
Global Witness 129–30, 132, 133, 137,
  276–77
globalization:
  CESI and 212
  crime and 104
  financial exchanges and 34
  the local and 195
  protests against 5
  security and 16, 20
  terrorism and 48, 49, 242
governance, just 236–37
Greater Nile Petroleum Operating Company
  153, 154
Greenstock, Sir Jeremy 60–61
Guinea 245

Gulf region 215
Gulf War (1991) 3

Haimes, Yacov 208
Hall, Tony 131
Harvard School of Public Health 278
hawalas 57, 66
Helsinki Final Act (1975) 42
Helsinki Human Rights Committee 42
Helsinki Watch 42
HIV (human immunodeficiency virus) 13
Hoffman, Bruce 51
Hong Kong 66, 175, 176
human rights 19, 39, 40, 70, 125–27:
    Council of Europe and 39, 40, 41, 42
Human Rights Watch (HRW) 42, 130, 278
humanitarian law 164–65
humanitarian organizations 161–69
humanitarian problems 121, 122, 123–24, 128

IAEA (International Atomic Energy Agency)
    80
immigration, illegal 238
India 51, 58, 80, 81, 256
individual citizen 18–20
Indonesia 66, 93
information: private-public sectors and 17
Information Assurance Advisory Council
    (IAAC) 303
information systems:
    breaching 184
    protecting 194
Initiative on Conflict Resolution and
    Ethnicity (INCORE) 278
Institute of Defence and Strategic Studies
    (IDSS) 279
Institute for Multi-Track Diplomacy (IMTD)
    279
insurance 8, 223–25, 230:
    premiums 223
    terrorism and 15, 21, 90
Inter-American Development Bank (IDB)
    Group 279–80
Interlaken Process 70, 71
International Alert (IA) 280
International Business Leaders Forum (IBLF)
    303
International Chamber of Commerce (ICC)
    304
International Committee of the Red Cross
    (ICRC) 162, 164, 166–69, 280

International Confederation of Free Trade
    Unions (ICFTU) 281
International Convention for the Suppression
    of the Financing of Terrorism 53, 60, 72
International Court 164–65
International Crisis Group (ICG) 281
International Institute for Strategic Studies
    (IISS) 281–82
International Labour Organization (ILO) 282
International Monetary Fund (IMF) 53–54,
    63, 106, 163, 282
International Money Laundering Information
    Network (IMoLIN) 282–83
International Organization for Migration 93
Internet 188, 190, 194, 198
Internet Security Alliance (ISA) 304
Interpol (International Criminal Police
    Organization) 283
investment 123, 127
Investor Responsibility Research Center
    (IRRC) 304–5
Ionescu, Paul 211
IRA (Irish Republican Army) 47
Iran 9, 49
Iran–Iraq War 3, 79
Iraq 6, 49, 64, 81:
    debt 10
    US operational costs 10–11, 229
    war in 7, 10, 21, 86, 178, 185, 229, 243
        aftermath of 21, 176, 178
    WMD and 9, 10
Islam 29
Israel 30, 81, 111
IT (information technology):
    globalization 199
    large companies and 195
    protection 91, 196
    spread of 194–95, 196
    terrorism, data on 35
    vulnerabilities 194–95
Italy 13, 33

Japan 48, 77

Kahn and Wiener 209
Khartoum Peace Agreement (1997) 149–50,
    151
Kimberley Process 132, 133–39, 140–47, 163
Korea, North 9, 49, 64
Kosovo 95, 168

Laden, Osama bin 28, 69, 107, 112
Latin America 33
law:
    international, developments in 103–4
    international, soft 104
    rule of 41
League of Arab States 235–41
Liberia 245
Libya 49
Liechtenstein 102–10
Liscouski, Robert P. 197
Lloyds Bank 72
London School of Economics and Political
    Science (LSE) 283
Lundin 150–60
Luzhkov, Yuri 116

Maastricht Treaty (1992) 43, 96, 101
Macedonia 95, 96
Management Advisory Services and
    Publications (MASP) 305
Mandela, President Nelson 131
Masterman, J. C. 177
media 188, 189, 191
Mexico 256
military assets: values of 38
Military Professional Resources Incorporated
    247
military spending 227–30
Missile Technology Control Regime (MTCR)
    79, 80
Mogae, President Festus 131
money laundering 7, 34, 50, 56, 102:
    measures against 35, 63, 104
Morocco 89
Mozambique 246
Mubarak, President Hosni 149
mujahedin 112
Murzabekov, Ruslan 116
Musah, Abdel-Fatau 246
Mutual Legal Assistance Treaty (2002) 105

National Association of Corporate Directors
    (NACD) 305
National Business Initiative (NBI) 305
NATO (North Atlantic Treaty Organization)
    284:
    enlargement 215
    private sector and 2–3
    terrorism and 28, 47, 96
Net Impact 306

Netherlands 39, 166
Netherlands Institute for Southern Africa
    (NIZA) 283
New Partnership for Africa's Development
    (NEPAD) Business Group 306
NGOs (non-governmental organizations) 158
Nigeria 244, 248–49
Nokia 183–86
North–South relations 237, 238, 239–40
Northern Ireland 33
Norway 39, 166
Novartis Foundation for Sustainable
    Development (NFSD) 306
NPT (Non-Proliferation Treaty, 1968) 80
Nuclear Suppliers Group (NSG) 79, 80

O'Brien, Kevin 247
oil:
    Arab, importance of 237
    conflict and 148–60
    producing countries 20–21
    supply 2–3
    terrorism and 212
oil executives: attempt at capture 210
Okuntimo, Major Paul 249
OPEC (Organization of the Petroleum
    Exporting Countries) 112
Oppenheimer, Nicky 130
Organisation for Economic Co-operation and
    Development (OECD) 18, 38, 63, 284–86
Organization for Security and Co-operation in
    Europe (OSCE) 42, 287

Pakistan 66, 81, 93, 250
Palestine 33
pariah states see rogue states
Partnership Africa Canada (PAC) 131, 137
peace dividend 229–30
Peres Center for Peace 287
Perl, Raphael 243
Philippines 93
Portugal 40
post-cold war era 27–28
pre-emptive strikes 29
private sector:
    new role of 30–31
    public sector and 1–5, 15–16, 17, 27–36
    security and 1, 4, 6, 15, 27–36:
        spending on 219, 222–23
    terrorists' finances and 7
Proliferation Security Initiative (PSI, 2003)
    10

public sector:
  private sector and 1–5, 15–16, 17, 27–36:
    anti-competitive effects 17–18
  security and 1, 15, 27–36
public–private sector interaction 1–24, 27–36
  dialogue 32
  Western 20–21

al-Qaeda 243:
  Afghanistan and 6, 221
  fanaticism 33
  finances 55, 74
  intelligence on 178
  measures against 54, 55, 69, 107
  members in custody 54
  war on 47

Ralfe, Gary 130
re-nationalization 17
Red Army Faction 47
resource companies 124–25, 126–27
Rice, Susan 243, 252
Ridge, Tom 197
Rischard, Jean-François 138, 139
rogue states 6, 9, 81, 100, 250
Royal Institute of International Affairs (RIIA)
  288
Rumsfeld, Donald 12
Russia 58, 78:
  Chechnya 51, 111, 112
  Dubrovka Theatrical Centre 113, 117
  gas 212
  strategic export controls and 79, 81
  terrorism and 111–18

Saddam Hussein, President 9, 178, 179
Sanchez, Ilich Ramirez ('Carlos the Jackel')
  112, 149
Saro Wiwa, Ken 249
SARS (severe acute respiratory syndrome)
  14, 175
Saudi Arabia 66, 74
Schick, Professor Allen 37
security:
  business and 1–2
  costly 222, 231
  economy and 1
  finance and 30
  legal aspects 32
  need for 184
  privatization 30, 32
  'soft' 3

spending on 219, 222–23, 227–30, 231
West and 21–23
see also following entries
security companies 30, 31, 32, 167, 173–82,
  222, 223
Security Management Online 306–7
security problems:
  causes 21–22
  West 21–23
sex trade 93
Shell 249
shipping costs 226
Sierra Leone 131–32, 133, 136, 245, 246, 247
Social Science Research Council (SSRC) 288
Solana, Javier 86, 210
Somalia 246
Soros, George 49
South Africa 14, 58, 132, 136, 245–46
Spain 40, 220
Sri Lanka 116
states: vulnerability of 29
Stockholm Process on Implementing
  Targeted Sanctions 62, 71
Strasser, Valentine 247
strategic export controls 2, 7:
  limitations of 79–80
  national regulations 81–82
  private sector and 76–83
  WMD and 78
Sudan:
  conflict in 148–50
  EU and 150
  Lundin in 150–60
  radical groups in 28
  terrorism and 49
Sudapet 150
suicide bombing 112, 189
survival planning 175–76
Sweden 13, 158–59:
  National Council on Medical Ethics 39
Swiss Peace Foundation (Swisspeace) 288
Switzerland 66, 207, 214
Syria 49, 93

Taliban 55, 69
technology: terrorism and 48–49
terrorism:
  aid and 250
  asymmetric warfare 113–15, 118
  causes of 21–22
  confidence and 220, 221
  confidence gained 111

countering 51–58
definition 50–51, 52, 235, 238, 243–44, 245
drugs and 58, 116
economic dimension 220–31, 243–45
international response to 47–58
media and 33, 117
new environment for 48–50
as new threat 48–51
non-proliferation and 81–82
political 51
political dimension 243–45
pre-emptive strikes 29
'privatization' of 242
social resources 115–17
state 249
state-sponsored 49, 112–13
war on 6, 8–9, 28, 47, 48, 221, 243, 250, 251
Terrorism Emergency Response Team (TERT) 35
Terrorism Research Center (TRC) 288–89
terrorist attack, 9/11:
business and 6
cost of 33–34, 221
deaths 1, 219
effects of 5–8, 28, 33, 47, 73, 183–84, 219, 220
Islam and 29
new features 220, 242
US Government's response 6, 28, 221
terrorists:
finances:
assets, freezing 55, 66, 71, 92
blocking 7, 35, 47, 52–58
changing 56
criminalizing 64
definitions 71
legal issues 67–73
goal of 205–6
information exchange 57
intelligence on 67, 68, 177–81
listing 62, 65, 67–70, 74
religion 29
WMD and 13, 21, 28, 29, 49
Thailand 256
Thompson, Niobe 246
threats 20, 183:
new 27, 28–30, 48–51
Transparency International (TI) 289
transportation 31
Turkey 89

Union of Soviet Socialist Republics 112, 178–79
United Kingdom:
electricity failure 13, 210
IRA bombings 220
Joint Intelligence Committee 177–78, 179, 180
Lockerbie bombing 220
Ministry of Defence (MOD) 289–90
strategic export controls 76–77
terrorism and 96:
finances frozen 66
Turnbull Report 194
United Kingdom Department for International Development (DFIC) 289
United Nations (UN) 290–94:
Charter 60
Commission on Human Rights 157–58
Counter-Terrorism Committee (CTC) 7, 21, 59, 60–63, 64, 65, 73, 107
Development Programme 122
diamonds and 137–38
General Assembly Resolution 54/109 51
mercenaries and 248
Millennium Declaration 22
Monitoring Group 54–55
reform 240
report on terrorist financing 56
1267 Sanctions Committee 59, 62, 69, 70, 73
Security Council, terrorist financing and 60
Security Council Resolution 1173 129, 130
Security Council Resolution 1176 129
Security Council Resolution 1267 66, 69
Security Council Resolution 1333 69
Security Council Resolution 1368 60, 87
Security Council Resolution 1373 60–61, 64, 88, 92, 107
Security Council Resolution 1377 60, 61, 65
Security Council Resolution 1390 69
Security Council Resolution 1455 54
selectivity 236–37
terrorism and 47, 51, 59–75
Universal Declaration of Human Rights (1948) 41–42
United States of America:
air travel 186, 207, 219, 221, 224
anthrax attack 6–7, 219
ballistic missile defence programme 12

border control 225–26
business disciplines 15
BW defence 12
cargo inspection 226
CIA 50
Congress 8, 11, 221, 228
Consumer Access to a Responsible
  Accounting of Trade Act (2000) 131
Container Security Initiative (2002) 11,
  226
Custom–Trade Partnership Against
  Terrorism 11
defence industry 12
Defense Emergency Reserve Fund 250
diamonds and 134, 136
education 255–56
electricity failures 13, 210
embassies bombed 74, 244
Europe, cooperation with 28–29
Export Administration Regulations 76
FBI 54
genetically modified crops 14
Homeland Security Department 197, 221,
  226, 228
Homeland Security programme 6, 11:
  spending on 9, 228, 250
immigration controls 255–56
intelligence system 178
military spending 11, 12–13, 229, 250
New York World Trade Center 1, 27, 48,
  203, 220, 242
Oklahoma City bombing 48, 220
Patriot Act (2001) 67, 75, 255
Pentagon 27, 221, 242
Presidential Decision Directive 63 (1998)
  206
President's Commission on Critical
  Infrastructure Protection (PCCIP) 198,
  202, 203
recession 221
Seattle Port 227
security, spending on 222
State Department 50, 132
strategic export controls 76–77, 81
support for terrorists 112
taxes 11
Terrorism Risk Insurance Act (2002) 225
Terrorist Exclusion List 251
terrorist financing and 52
terrorist list 68, 69
trade budget 11
visa rules 11

Visa Waiver Program 11
  see also terrorist attack, 9/11
United States Chamber of Commerce 294

values 37–44
Vanaik, Achin 244
Venice Commission 40
Vivendi Universal 15

Ward, Curtis 64, 65
Wassenaar Arrangement 78–79
Watson Institute for International Studies 63,
  294
welfare state 42
WMD (weapons of mass destruction):
  proliferation 22, 81
  proliferation control 6, 9, 16
Wolfensohn, James 124
Wolfsberg Group 63, 307
World Bank 18, 53–54, 63, 163, 251, 294–95
World Business Awards in Support of the
  Millennium Goals 307
World Business Council for Sustainable
  Development (WBCSD) 308
World Diamond Council 133, 134, 136–37
World Economic Forum (WEF) 17, 134, 308
World Health Organization (WHO) 22
World Monitors Inc. (WMI) 309
World Trade Organization (WTO) 18, 256:
  Cancun summit 8
World War II 2, 177
WorldCom Incorporated 15
WTO (Warsaw Treaty Organization) 4

Zimmermann, Doron 206